RIFT AND REVOLUTION

RIFT AND REVOLUTION

THE CENTRAL AMERICAN IMBROGLIO

HOWARD J. WIARDA, editor

American Enterprise Institute for Public Policy Research
Washington and London

Library of Congress Cataloging in Publication Data
Main entry under title:

Rift and revolution.

(AEI studies ; 394)
Includes bibliographical references and index.
1. Central America—Politics and government—
1979-   —Addresses, essays, lectures. 2. Central
America—Foreign relations—1979-   —Addresses,
essays, lectures. 3. Revolutions—Central America—
Addresses, essays, lectures. I. Wiarda, Howard J.,
1939-   . II. Series.
F1439.5.R53 1983   972.8'052   83-21476
ISBN 0-8447-3539-6
ISBN 0-8447-3538-8 (pbk.)

AEI Studies 394

1 3 5 7 9 10 8 6 4 2

Printed in the United States of America

Contents

LIST OF TABLES AND FIGURES

Foreword

Central America and U.S. policy in that region have become major public policy issues in the United States. With this book and other publications of the American Enterprise Institute, we have joined the discussion. This is a study that explores the background of the Central American crisis from the points of view of both the domestic causes of the crisis and the international dimensions of it. It is a major study, the result of a long-term and continuing research undertaking.

For some time AEI has had a strong research and policy interest in Latin America. We have previously published studies of Mexico, the Caribbean, Brazil, Cuba, Puerto Rico, the transfer of nuclear technology to Latin America, trade patterns, U.S. foreign policy toward the region, and other topics. AEI resident scholars and fellows, both former and present, not only have written some of the best studies of the area but also have been strongly involved in influencing the policy process. Many of our analysts have gone directly into the government or have been consulted by the government in various ways.

In this book Howard Wiarda, director of our Center for Hemispheric Studies, has brought together some of the foremost scholars in Latin American studies. All have had extensive, direct research experience in Central America; almost all the scholars here represented have testified before the National Bi-Partisan (Kissinger) Commission on Central America. They are serious scholars and writers, and they have produced a careful, balanced book. The book is public policy oriented, it is grounded on solid, empirical research, and its authors present judicious conclusions and recommendations.

There is a considerable background to this book. It has emerged from a series of conferences, seminars, and panel discussions held at AEI over the past several years. These have been lively and thought-provoking discussions addressing a variety of issues from diverse points of view. Some of the initial findings and statements were first published by the authors in article form and in a special issue of the *AEI Foreign Policy and Defense Review*, "The Crisis in Central America (vol. four, no. two, 1982)," with Howard J. Wiarda serving as guest editor.

This book and the research undergirding it were funded jointly by AEI and a major foundation grant as part of our long-time and ongoing interest in U.S.–Latin American relations. For good or ill, we believe Latin American studies will be a "growth industry" for the foreseeable future. That is, as demonstrated in this book, the problems of Central America are profound, they will not go away quickly or easily, and they will continue to have important implications for the United States and for U.S. policy. We intend to continue our research and publications in this area, which has become increasingly significant to the United States both as a domestic and as a foreign policy issue.

WILLIAM J. BAROODY
President
American Enterprise Institute

Preface

It is only after we have committed ourselves, and then found ourselves trapped in a perplexing morass with no way out, that we begin to understand those third-world societies in which American power and prestige have recently been engaged. Such was the case in Vietnam, it was the case in Iran, and it is now the case in Central America. All of these wrenching events spawned a hindsight literature that, after the fact, enabled us much better to understand these areas than before. We often only weakly comprehend the societies and internal dynamics of third-world, non- or partially western nations; and by the time the serious books and scholarly analyses come out which enable us to discern clearly the nations in which we are committed, it is often too late. We are by then heavily involved in such murky situations that they defy all American notions of rational and ethical political behavior, unable or unwilling either to commit sufficient resources to see the policy through or to withdraw with a degree of honor and self-respect.

This book seeks to provide that necessary background and analysis. The contributions are by long-time experts in the field who have done extensive field work in Central America, who see the longer and larger historical picture, and who bring to their analyses reasoned and careful scholarly assessments. Some of the nation's foremost Central America scholars, historians, and political scientists are here represented. The book thus stands in contrast with the many "instant analyses" of Central America by "instant experts" to which we have, unfortunately, become accustomed and which prevail far too often in policy-making discussions. The perspectives provided here are probing, analytical, carefully researched, interpretive, and informed by a sense of history. For the problems in Central America are deep-rooted and historical; they did not begin, as we sometimes seem to think, with the Nicaraguan Revolution in 1979 or the rape and murder of the four religious women in El Salvador in 1980. With the exception of Ambassador Jeane J. Kirkpatrick's important statement, all the chapters here included were written expressly for this volume.

While longer on description and analysis, this book is purposely rather shorter on prescription. As with other AEI volumes on such major and current public policy issues as nuclear strategy and national security,[1] we felt it was necessary first to clear the air and to provide sound background and analysis, and only later to offer recommendations which, in the fast-changing Central American context, would in any case surely be outdated by the time the book appeared. We saw our role in this volume as providing essential historical and sociological interpretation and not so much policy prescriptions. Several of the contributions in this volume, particularly those by the Valentas and Ambassador Kirkpatrick, do offer policy prescriptions; astute readers who probe between the lines will find more; and in other of our publications,[2] strong and forceful policy recommendations have been set forth. But for the purposes of this volume we have determined first to fill a severe information and understanding gap with regard to Central America by offering a collection of stimulating readings, and to reserve detailed policy prescriptions for other forums where they can, in any case, be more effective.[3]

In the course of undertaking this study and preparing this book many debts have been incurred. William J. Baroody, Jr., president of AEI, has been exceedingly generous in his support and encouragement of this project. My research assistant Janine T. Perfit and our secretary Pamela Robertson assisted with this book in ways too numerous to mention. Thanks are due above all to the larger AEI "family" and staff, who help make this one of the premier think tanks in the country and a marvelous place to study, dialogue, write, watch the Washington world go by, and participate in that public policy process.

HOWARD J. WIARDA

Notes

1. Robert J. Pranger, ed., *Détente and Defense* (Washington, D.C.: American Enterprise Institute, 1976); Pranger and Roger P. Labrie, eds., *Nuclear Strategy and National Security* (Washington, D.C.: American Enterprise Institute, 1977).

2. Howard J. Wiarda, "The United States and Latin America: Change and Continuity," Paper presented at a University of Pittsburgh Conference on "Stability/Instability in the Caribbean Basin," Pittsburgh, October 1982, forthcoming in a volume edited by Alan Adelman and Reid Reading (University of Pittsburgh Press); Wiarda, "Conceptual and Political Dimensions of the Crisis in U.S.–Latin American Relations: Toward a New Policy Formulation," Paper

presented at the AEI Public Policy Week Forum on "The Crisis in Central America," Washington, D.C., December 6–10, 1982, and forthcoming in an AEI volume on *The Crisis in Latin America and in U.S.–Latin American Relations;* and Wiarda, "Changing Realities and U.S. Policy in the Caribbean Basin: An Overview," Paper prepared for the Atlantic Council's project on "Western Interests and U.S. Policy Options in the Caribbean Basin," and forthcoming in an edited volume with the same title (Washington, D.C., Atlantic Council).

3. Howard J. Wiarda, "The United States and Latin America in the Aftermath of the Falklands/Malvinas Crisis," *Latin America and the United States after the Falklands/Malvinas Crisis: Hearings before the Subcommittee on Inter-American Affairs of the Committee on Foreign Affairs, House of Representatives, 97th Congress, 2nd Session, July 20 and August 5, 1982* (Washington, D.C., 1982), pp. 22–42, 77–82; Wiarda, "Pluralism in Nicaragua," in *Papers Presented at a Conference on Nicaragua* (Washington, D.C.: Department of State, 1982); Wiarda, "United States Policy and the Certification for El Salvador," Statement prepared for the Committee on Foreign Relations, United States Senate, Washington, D.C., February 2, 1983; Wiarda, ed., "The Crisis in Central America," Special issue of the *AEI Foreign Policy and Defense Review,* vol. 4, no. 2 (1982); and Wiarda, *In Search of Policy: The United States and Latin America* (Washington, D.C.: American Enterprise Institute, 1984).

Contributors

THOMAS P. ANDERSON is professor of history and politics at Eastern Connecticut State University. He has previously taught at Loyola University, Wheeling College, and Yale University. Among his books are *Matanza: El Salvador's Communist Revolt of 1932; Human Rights in El Salvador; The War of the Dispossessed: Honduras and El Salvador, 1969;* and *Politics in Central America: Guatemala, El Salvador, Honduras and Nicaragua.*

ROLAND H. EBEL is associate professor of political science at Tulane University. He has conducted studies at both the national and the local levels in Guatemala, El Salvador, and Colombia. His publications include *Political Modernization in Three Guatemalan Indian Communities; Perspectives on the Energy Crisis;* "The Political Process in San Salvador"; "Four Towns in Colombia"; "Governing the City State: The Politics of the Small Latin American Countries"; "The Theory of the Post Agricultural Society"; and "Instability in Central America."

ERNEST EVANS is an assistant professor in the politics department at the Catholic University of America. He teaches courses in Latin American politics and in international relations. He is the author of *Calling a Truce to Terror: The American Response to International Terrorism* and of a number of articles on revolutionary movements.

MARK FALCOFF is resident fellow at the Center for Hemispheric Studies, American Enterprise Institute. He has taught at the Universities of Illinois, Oregon, and California (Los Angeles) and was a national fellow at the Hoover Institution, Stanford University, 1979–1980. His books include (with Ronald H. Dolkart) *Prologue to Perón: Argentina in Depression and War, 1930–43* and (with Frederick B. Pike) *The Spanish Civil War, 1936–39: American Hemisphere Perspectives.*

THOMAS L. KARNES is professor of history at Arizona State University. He taught previously at Stanford and Tulane universities. His books include *Failure of Union: Central America 1924–1960; William Gilpin,*

Western Nationalist; Latin American Policy of the United States; and *Tropical Enterprise: The Standard Fruit and Steamship Company in Latin America.*

JEANE J. KIRKPATRICK was appointed U.S. Permanent Representative to the United Nations in January 1981 and also serves as a member of the president's cabinet. Prior to her U.N. appointment, Ambassador Kirkpatrick was Leavey University Professor at Georgetown University in Washington, D.C., and resident scholar at the American Enterprise Institute for Public Policy Research.

Ambassador Kirkpatrick has written five books, one monograph, and numerous articles on American political issues and American foreign policy, including *The Reagan Phenomenon—and Other Speeches on Foreign Policy; Dictatorships and Double Standards: Rationalism and Reason in Politics; The New Presidential Elite; Political Woman; Leader and Vanguard in Mass Society: A Study of Peronist Argentina;* and *Dismantling the Parties: Reflections on Party Reform and Party Decomposition.*

Ambassador Kirkpatrick has participated in Democratic party politics as vice chairman, Coalition for a Democratic Majority, and as a member of the Democratic National Convention's National Commission on Party Structure and Presidential Nomination (the Winograd Commission) 1975–1978. During the 1980 presidential campaign, she was a member of President Reagan's foreign policy advisory group.

RONALD H. MCDONALD is professor of political science at the Maxwell School, Syracuse University. He has traveled extensively in Latin America and has published frequently items on the politics of Central America, particularly that of El Salvador. He is author of *Party Systems and Elections in Latin America* and has published research in the *Journal of Politics,* the *American Journal of Political Science, Inter-American Economic Affairs, Western Political Quarterly, Current History,* and others. In 1980 he was Fulbright Lecturer at the University of the Republic, Montevideo, Uruguay, and was formerly chairman of the Department of Political Science at Syracuse University.

EUSEBIO MUJAL-LEÓN is assistant professor of government at Georgetown University. He has written extensively on Spanish and Portuguese politics in a number of books and in such journals as *Foreign Policy, Problems of Communism, Studies in Comparative Communism,* and *West European Politics.* His book *Communism and Political Change in Spain* has recently been published by Indiana University Press. He is currently on leave at the Center of International Studies at Princeton University preparing a manuscript on Soviet–Latin American relations.

JIRI VALENTA is professor of national security affairs and coordinator of Soviet and East European Studies at the Naval Postgraduate School, Monterey, California. He is now a fellow at the Woodrow Wilson International Center for Scholars, Washington, D.C. The best known of his many publications is *Soviet Intervention in Czechoslovakia, 1968: Anatomy of a Decision.* Dr. Valenta has also written many studies on Soviet-Cuban involvement in the third world.

VIRGINIA VALENTA received a Bachelor of Arts degree from Mount S. Scholastica College in Atchison, Kansas, and a Master of Arts from the Department of Romance Languages at the University of Missouri. She also studied at the University of Mexico, Mexico City, and the University of Madrid, Spain. Mrs. Valenta has analyzed Soviet and Cuban policies in Latin America and is coauthor of articles on Soviet-Cuban involvement in the third world.

HOWARD J. WIARDA is a research scholar and director of the Center for Hemispheric Studies at the American Enterprise Institute. Before joining AEI, he was a visiting scholar at the Center for International Affairs at Harvard University and a visiting professor at M.I.T. He is professor of political science and adjunct professor of Comparative Labor Relations at the University of Massachusetts in Amherst.

Professor Wiarda is former editor of *Polity* and has served as the director of the Center for Latin American Studies at the University of Massachusetts.

He has published extensively on Latin America, southern Europe, the third world, and U.S. foreign policy. His most recent books include *Politics and Social Change in Latin America; The Dominican Republic: Caribbean Crucible; The State, Organized Labor, and the Changing Industrial Relations Systems of Southern Europe; Corporatism and National Development in Latin America; The Brazilian Catholic Labor Movement; Latin American Politics and Development; The Continuing Struggle for Democracy in Latin America;* and *Corporatism and Development: The Portuguese Experience.*

EDWARD J. WILLIAMS is professor of political science at the University of Arizona, Tucson. During the last decade Professor Williams has served as a Rockefeller Foundation International Studies Fellow, a Fulbright-Hays Senior Lecturer at El Colegio de México, and a visiting research professor with the Strategic Studies Institute of the U.S. War College. He has written five books and numerous articles on Latin American and Mexican politics and foreign policy. His contribution to this volume reflects research initiated in 1980 and continuing in both the United States and Mexico.

GARY W. WYNIA is professor of political science at the University of Minnesota. He was a foreign policy fellow at the Brookings Institution in 1968–1969. His publications include *Politics and Planners: Economic Development Policy in Central America; Argentina in the Postwar Era: Politics and Economic Policy in a Divided Society; The Politics of Latin American Development;* "Workers and Wages: Incomes Policy in Argentina"; and "The United States and Argentina: Starting Over."

PART ONE
Introduction

1

The Origins of the Crisis in Central America

HOWARD J. WIARDA

The Debate over Central America

The debate over Central America and U.S. policy there has been arduous and divisive. It is an important debate that has often taken place at the level of presidential politics and was a major issue in the 1980 campaign. Mr. Reagan's advisers were convinced that Jimmy Carter had "lost" Nicaragua to communism and that they could and would do better in El Salvador. The issue was the subject of intensive transition-team study[1] and was one of the major foreign policy agenda items of the administration inaugurated in January 1981. It remains to this day one of the most critical and controversial of our foreign policy issues.

The debate over Central America has raised important issues that go beyond that geographic area. Our involvement in Central America is also caught up in the lingering memories of Vietnam, over whether a "new Vietnam" was in the making there or, alternatively, whether we could by now overcome our "Vietnam complexes" and reassert our power as a major nation. Central America is additionally, "close to home" in a way that Iran and Vietnam were not, and the flow of refugees from the area as well as questions concerning oil supplies, the drug traffic, immigration policy, and social and human rights concerns make it as much a domestic issue as a foreign policy one. The Central America debate has, finally, raised a host of questions about the role and fairness of the media in covering these events, the foreign policy-making capacity of the United States, and its ability to deal with a major crisis on our very doorstep, even whether our campuses are poised on the verge of another upheaval like that in 1970.

3

While the debate over Central America and U.S. Central America policy has been long and hot, it has not always or consistently been infused with light. A variety of reasons may be suggested for this, not all of which will sit comfortably with us. Among these:

• We do not understand Latin America very well. This lack of comprehension and empathy lies at the root of our troubles throughout the area. Our knowledge is shrouded in myths and stereotypes. These include myths and stereotypes concerning virtually all groups: church, military, oligarchy, peasants, etc. As James Reston once wrote apropos of this point, "The United States will do anything for Latin America except read about it."[2]

• Not only do we not understand Latin America very well, but we do not *wish* to understand it better. Our attitudes toward the area are condescending and patronizing. We are always seeking to "teach" something to Latin America. The area is denigrated as "backward," "underdeveloped," at best "developing." We look at it from the point of view of cultural superiority and we refer to the nations especially of Central America as "banana republics." We do not deem them important or worthy of serious attention; we treat them as wayward children. We place little value on their institutions, and we assume that our preferred solutions are the way to resolve their problems. Our ethnocentrism is pervasive: The assumption is that "we know best," and we are uncomfortable with the idea that "they know best."[3]

• We use the wrong models or analytical frameworks to interpret the area. These include the "democracy-versus-dictatorship" model, the "developing nations" model, the "liberation" model, the "struggle for democracy" model, and others. For example, the democracy-versus-dictatorship model ignores the numerous halfway houses that Latin America has a genius for improvising; the "developmentalist" model generally ignores the distinct character of the Latin American development process; the "liberation" model ignores the conservative character of many Latin American peasant and worker movements; the "struggle for democracy" model assumes that democracy U.S.-style is really what Latin America wants. While there are elements of truth in all these models, none of them is adequate in itself for understanding Central America, and they are frequently wrong, misleading, and productive of erroneous policy prescriptions.[4]

• The debate has too often been dominated not by long-term Central America experts but by a number of "instant experts" whose knowledge of the area is short-term and superficial. These include policy makers, some congressmen and their staffs, journalists, and scholars whose expertise lies elsewhere. Without much background in the area or knowledge of its history, their analyses are often glib but ill informed. There is real expertise in this country on Central America, but because of a variety of factors that expertise is seldom reflected in the Washington area debate over policy.[5]

• The debate is heavily partisan and politicized. Both the Congress and the White House begin planning reelection strategy so far in advance that there is no between-elections respite. In such a charged political atmosphere, a reasoned, coherent, nonpartisan discussion of policy cannot be expected.

• The Central America debate is hence often a reflection of a U.S. *domestic* political debate and frequently has little to do with Central America itself. Both the American administration and its foes use the Central America debate to score political points. And the debate itself is cast in U.S. terms of reference (an independent judiciary, a professional and apolitical military, regular elections, etc.) that have only limited relevance to Central America. The dynamics of Central America's own political processes are often lost in a debate that more often than not has to do with U.S. domestic politics rather than that of Central America.

No book can entirely avoid these pitfalls, and we have not completely succeeded here. But we have tried in this volume to tap some of the national expertise on Central America and to present it in a coherent and organized manner. Additionally, to overcome the "instant expert" phenomenon, we have for the most part tapped historians and political scientists with long backgrounds and research experience in the area. Our contributors tend to emphasize that Central America's problems did not begin in 1979 or 1980 but have deep historical roots. They understand the history, sociology, economics, and politics of these countries as few of the "instant experts" do. Moreover, they are not so intensely bound up in the partisan debate that they cannot step aside for a moment and provide an unbiased view. This is not to say that all our authors have no axes to grind, but they do at least begin to approach an understanding of the complexities of the area without such gross distortions and prejudices that frequently mark the Central America debate.

The analyses and perspectives provided here tend to emphasize the long-term nature of the current Central American crisis. The problems of the area are viewed as structural and systemic, with deep historical roots. Because they are deep and systemic, no panaceas or "quick fixes" will serve to resolve them. Let us delve more deeply into the origins of the present crisis.

Sources of Misunderstanding about Central America

American understandings of Central America, we have said, are shrouded in myths and stereotypes: mustachioed comical men on horseback who gallop in and out of the presidential palace with frequent regularity, rich and oppressive oligarchies, "banana republics," a countryside teeming with restless peasants now often dressed in green fatigues and carrying carbines rather than the older "sleepy" sombreros, rapacious multinational corporations in cahoots with the Central Intelligence Agency, rebel priests whom we suspect may also now be carrying carbines, a small or nonexistent middle class, etc. These images shape not only popular beliefs about the area but also, at times, discussion at the policy level.

A good starting point in increasing our understanding of the area is to recognize its considerable diversity.[6] There are of course commonalities of language, culture, politics, religion, sociology, and underdevelopment throughout the area. But the differences are at least as striking. Costa Rica is very different from Nicaragua by all sorts of measures, and so is El Salvador from Honduras. Guatemala, with its large indigenous population, is different from all the rest. And whatever commonalities exist in these countries almost certainly do not apply in Panama or Belize, let alone Mexico.

Costa Rica's and Panama's per capita incomes are nearly twice that of Guatemala and three times those of El Salvador, Honduras, or Nicaragua. Guatemala has a large native Indian population; but as one goes farther south from the center of Mayan civilization there, the percentage of "Indianness" declines, and Costa Rica prides itself on its "Europeanness." Furthermore, Costa Rica has a sizable middle class that serves as a basis for its moderate, democratic, and middle-of-the-road politics; in the other countries the middle class is smaller, and there are few discernible trends toward "happy," liberal, bourgeois democracy. Levels of literacy and other social indicators similarly show wide variations.

A second approach toward increasing our comprehension of Central America is to attack some of the prevailing myths about the area, at the same time providing greater background information on how the politics and social life of the area function and are organized. Some of the main features that need highlighting:[7]

1. *The city-state size of the Central American countries.* The countries of the region are more like city-states rather than larger nation-states. They consist, for the most part, of a single enclave city and capital, and an outlying countryside—not much different in size and organization from a good-sized American county and its county seat.[8]

Distances between them, or their capitals, are very short—about twenty minutes by air. Their borders are often more ambiguous than they appear on maps, and there is considerable flow of goods and peoples across these unclear boundaries. What happens in one country therefore, because of the close proximity, also affects its neighbors. That is not to provide some simplistic "domino theory," but it is to say that the political and economic transformations in one country inevitably have an effect on the others.

Not only is a recognition of the small size and blurred boundaries of these countries important in understanding their interrelations, but politics in a city-state is also qualitatively different from politics in a nation-state. Virtually everyone knows everyone else who matters—or is interrelated. Hence politics tends to be more personalistic, family-based, cliquish, clannish, almost "tribal." Beneath the ideological and party differences that so much dominate outside discussions (largely because we do not know or understand these other levels) is a politics that is even more basic: family and extended family rivalries, clan alliances, clean and dirty business deals stretching back in time, etc., that are even more fundamental (and often hidden from view) than are the events that occur in front of the curtain (for the Americans and other outsiders to see).

2. *The nonformal character of institutions.* In such small-sized, intimate, and personalistic polities, the larger-sized and more impersonal institutions associated with bigger nation-states, such as mass political parties, pluralistic interest groups, and independent legislatures, are not always viewed as necessary, desirable, or possible. Families, clan groups, and informal patronage networks may be more important than the formal institutions. U.S. efforts to develop the formal mechanisms and agencies of a modern polity may not be wanted or useful in that context. The nonformal character of the polity makes it very difficult to understand for outsiders, who are used to and expect the institutional paraphernalia of the more developed countries to operate in the same way in Central America (and often does in fact operate in Costa Rica).

3. *The fear of disorder.* Central Americans prefer democracy, but they are not altogether convinced it works well or always in such divided, turbulent societies as their own. Given their troubled histories, the fragile nature of political institutions, and what they refer to as an all-encompassing *falta de civilización*, the great fear in Central America has been of breakdown into chaos and anarchy. Such breakdowns are feared not only politically but even more fundamentally in the social and economic spheres, threatening to tip the society over

that narrow precipice separating a meager but survivable existence from a headlong tumble into the abyss.[9]

Nationwide upheaval threatens further to undermine the often thin veneer of Western civilization on which society is based and to precipitate an even more brutal form of "jungle" politics. To Central Americans of all classes, from the highest to the lowest (whose existence is most precarious and may be even more strongly opposed to disorder than the elites), the stakes in preventing such complete breakdowns are high. That helps explain what to North Americans seems to be the sometimes excessive use of force and repression in these societies; it also explains why, to the consternation of their American mentors, the El Salvadorans voted so strongly for the tough, disciplined, man-on-horseback symbol of authority Roberto D'Aubisson in 1982, and not for the more centrist-pragmatic-reformist candidates.

4. *The need for strength and authority.* If Western civilization is but weakly and sometimes superficially institutionalized in Central America, then strong leadership and strong government must sometimes be employed to defend it. "Above all there is order," said Bolívar, the George Washington of Latin America; it is a sentiment his successors in the area have consistently echoed. Hence while strong support for democracy is expressed in survey interviews, those same surveys reveal equally widespread support for strong, almost viceregal presidential leadership and a tolerance for government by decree-law that Americans would find abhorrent.[10] Countless politicians throughout the area have made speeches (though usually not when North Americans are listening) arguing that they need authority for their cattle and therefore they will need authority for their people as well—and without their audience blanching.

But authority and discipline, while desired and legitimate, must be exercised with restraint and fairness. To employ the Thomistic thinking that still shapes so much of the political philosophy of Central America, authority cannot degenerate into tyranny; it must be exercised justly and for the common good. A viciously rapacious or indiscriminately violent regime, such as that of Trujillo or the latter Batista, or one that gravitates from mild authoritarianism to brutal totalitarianism and a level of corruption that goes beyond the pale, such as the latter Somoza, cannot be tolerated. Such brutality and rapaciousness help justify, again in traditional Catholic terms in this strongly Catholic area, a "right to rebellion" against an "unjust ruler," a right that in Central America is traditionally as strong as the equally Catholic precept of an "obligation to obedience."[11]

5. *The accommodation of new power contenders.* Most of Central America has only sporadically been democratic, but that does not mean it has been entirely and unalterably opposed to change. In fact the changes in the past half-century have been enormous, but they have not always come under democratic means or auspices, nor have they been through the institutional paraphernalia which our own society prefers. The fact that there are other routes to modernization besides the U.S. one or, alternatively, the Soviet one is difficult for Americans to grasp; and it has led to a whole list of misinterpretations about Central America, in the press and elsewhere, concerning such institutions as the "oligarchy," its presumed "resistance to change," etc.[12]

Now it is true that there are rigidities and resistance to change built into Central American society probably to a greater degree than in our own. Within its own terms and institutional arrangements, however, Central American society has—until recently (the reasons for the changes and their implications will be explained in the next section)—been more accommodative, malleable, and flexible than we usually think.

As Central America has gradually modernized since roughly the 1930s, new social groups—the middle class, new business entrepreneurs, some workers' and peasants' organizations, bureaucrats and technicians—have risen to prominence. According to the rules of the Latin American political "game,"[13] these new sociopolitical forces are to be accommodated within "the system" if (1) they have demonstrated, by means of strikes, violence, force of arms, or electoral mobilization, a sufficient power capability to make their continued exclusion inappropriate and unrealistic; and (2) they agree not to try to eliminate entirely the older historical groups (the Church, the armed forces, and the traditional elites).

Under these conditions a variety of new groups and classes *have*, over the longer term, been admitted to "the system." The "effective nation" in Central America now constitutes 30–40 percent of the population (if measured by the percentage voting, participating in a modern money economy, or by other criteria), whereas fifty years ago it only constituted 5–10 percent. These are major changes, even revolutionary changes if looked at cumulatively, and not unlike the processes occurring in other modernizing nations.

But note too that these changes have occurred under military regimes as well as under civilian regimes, in authoritarian contexts as well as in democratic ones. Moreover (and a point that is elaborated below), the means used to achieve change have also varied enormously, coming through both democratic elections and coups, dem-

9

onstrations, *pronunciamientos,* cabinet shuffles and reshuffles, populist challenges, alterations of elites, and various forms of structured violence.[14] The point is that while change in Central America has not always or consistently come through U.S.-preferred solutions (democratic elections and the like), the changes on Central America's terms and through its own institutional arrangements have been considerable nonetheless. How these indigenous channels for change were cut off or eliminated in some countries in recent years, thus precipitating the present troubles throughout the area, is taken up in the next section.

6. *Elections as peripheral.* Elections in Central America, with Costa Rica being the major exception, have not always been central to the main arenas of politics. These latter include, as we have seen, clan and family rivalries, military factions maneuvering for power usually in alliance with civilian groups, competitive patronage networks and opportunities, and the like. In this setting elections are viewed as tentative and carry only indefinite legitimacy.[15] Like an opinion poll, they show the current balance of domestic power; but they do not always provide a definitive "right to rule" for a given period. Elections should thus be viewed not as ends in themselves conveying final legitimacy on some leader or party but as part of an ongoing process implying further, virtually continuous negotiations.

The results of elections may be challenged or overturned, depending on changed circumstances. This also implies that the whole political process in Central America tends to be almost infinitely malleable and that elections, political parties, campaigning, etc., must be looked at in a light different from the U.S. understanding of these institutions. That is a terribly difficult point for Americans to understand, but it is crucial if we are to come to grips realistically with Central America. Elections are one route to power, but other legitimized means are also available.

7. *The need for ad hoc-ism.* Latin America, it may be argued, has long demonstrated a positive genius for ad hoc, improvised solutions to its wrenching political problems. These often appear to be illogical, irrational, even "comic opera" to a U.S. or Western European audience; but we argue here they may be quite logical, rational, and sensible in Central America. Such ad hoc-ism also flies in the face often of our nice, neat distinctions between military and civilian regimes or between dictatorship and democracy.

In fact, most Central American regimes consist of such "strange bedfellow" and "halfway house" solutions as mixed juntas consisting of civilians *and* soldiers, coalitions (however temporary) of the major power contenders and even classes, regimes that came to power through extraconstitutional means but that later tried to legitimize themselves through elections often of a plebiscitary or ratificatory sort, and often shifting-sand combinations of these. Such solutions are not always soul-satisfying in a moral sense, nor do they conform to the ideological neatness that we prefer in our political discourse. But they may be quite functional and viable in the Central American situation, deserving of our serious study and maybe even tolerance rather than the knee-jerk condemnations and snide superiority with which North Americans too often view their Latin American neighbors.

   8. *A love-hate relationship with the United States.* The United States is widely admired throughout Central America for its democracy, strong economy, and technology, to say nothing of its rock, Coke, and jeans. At the same time, it is widely disliked and distrusted for its interventionism, overbearingness, and insensitivity to the region's needs. There are both love and hate aspects to the U.S.–Central American relationship.

   Most prudent Central American leaders come to recognize realistically the immense power of the United States in their area, and their immense dependency on it, and to adjust accordingly. The United States is not only the major military presence throughout the region, but it is also the dominant trading partner, the major market for Central America's products, and virtually its only source of investment capital, foreign assistance, loans, and technology. In addition, a point not well understood by most Americans, the U.S. embassy in all these countries operates as one of the most important actors in internal, domestic political affairs, along with the army and the economic elites—and not necessarily in that order. In other words, the United States is not only the most important external power operating throughout Central America but the American embassy in San Salvador, Guatemala City, or wherever, operating in its proconsular capacity, is also a major domestic force if not *the* major domestic force.[16]

   The realistic Central American president recognizes the considerable presence of the United States in his part of the world and makes his accommodation—unless he is willing to try to flout the United States à la Fidel Castro, with all the possibilities for disaster à la Nicaragua such a stance invites. He recognizes and seeks to channel the immense manipulative power of the United States while also learning that as against the U.S. "shark," the Central American "sardines" also have considerable maneuverability.[17]

   Hence the complexities and nuance of U.S.–Central American

11

relations. While the United States has great power, there are also severe constraints on the use of such power. And while the Central Americans expect the United States to lead and be a catalyst (a "locomotive," to use the current metaphor) for development, that role must be exercised with understanding and restraint if it is to be effective. And while the "dependency relations" thus described operate chiefly to the advantage of the United States, the Central American countries also have, under skilled leadership, considerable capacity to manipulate the United States to their own advantage.

These are some of the major aspects of what we can appropriately call the *system* of Central American politics. It is complex, labyrinthine, often Byzantine—but every bit as *systemic* as are other political systems. The trouble for most Americans is that we weakly comprehend the internal dynamics of the Central American nations, only some of the major dimensions of which have been hinted at here. This lack of comprehension, understanding, and empathy toward Central America is as much true of high government officials as of the general public, as true of Democrats as of Republicans. We are heavily engaged, again, in a part of the world that we do not and have not wished to understand.

The analysis offered in the preceding pages depicts Central America as having *systems* of government and politics quite different in many respects from our own but perhaps almost as complex. As these are *systems* of society and politics, so too the crises through which these countries are now going are *systemic* crises. That is, they are not ephemeral, superficial, and therefore easy of resolution but long term, deep-rooted, structural, and therefore difficult of resolution, probably requiring a generation or more. Let us then turn to an examination of the long-term causes of the present systemic crisis in Central America.

The Origins of the Crisis in Central America

One could, it is sometimes suggested, trace the roots of the difficulties in Central America back to the Spanish colonial period—even to the structures of the pre-Columbian Indian civilizations—and there is some validity in that claim.[18] We have argued here, however, that the Central American systems have not been entirely unviable and unresponsive historically, on their own terms, accommodating to at least some change. Moreover, our concern in this volume is chiefly the "modern" period in Central American history, corresponding with the acceleration of the change process since the 1930s. Let us examine these medium-term and systemic changes after that time in an effort to understand the imbroglio in which we now find ourselves.

The period since the 1930s in Central America has been one of accelerated social change. As economic and social modernization proceeded, a variety of new social and political groups began to emerge, challenging or, most often, seeking a place for themselves in the older system of hierarchy and elites. The rising groups included a new business-commercial-import-export sector sometimes distinct from but often interconnected with the older landed elite, an emerging and aspiring middle class that included both civilians and military officers, more militant and mobilized student groups, and a nascent trade union movement.[19]

These changes were managed not entirely unsatisfactorily in most of the countries from the 1930s on into the 1960s. In Nicaragua the elder Somoza ruled as an authoritarian, but it was a generally mild authoritarianism, and he also opened the gates to middle-class and mestizo civilians and *militares* and provided for considerable modernization of his country. Costa Rica had a democratic revolution in 1948 that ushered in stable, progressive middle-class rule. In Honduras there was also gradual progress under both civilian and military rule. In El Salvador a nationalistic and developmentalist military came to power in 1958 that in some areas supplanted the proverbial "fourteen families" and in others ruled alongside them. Guatemala was the most turbulent: dictatorship in the 1930s that also stimulated some modernization, a revolutionary period from 1944 to 1954, followed by U.S.-abetted reaction and considerable turbulence and guerrilla struggle in the 1960s. Nevertheless, Guatemala also registered some important economic and social changes during this period.[20]

Indeed, throughout the area impressive economic gains were made in the 1950s, the 1960s, and on into the 1970s. We know of the postwar Japanese, West German, and maybe even Brazilian "miracles," but to think that Central America's growth was also, almost, at a "miracle" rate comes as something of a surprise. But in fact the growth rates in Central America all through that period were in the range of 5 to 7 percent per year—considerably greater than in the United States. The economic quickening led to even more accelerated social and political change.[21]

But if the political systems of the area were not altogether unresponsive and their economies were booming, wherein lie the roots of their present troubles? The causes are complex; let us try to sort them out.

The first cause might be termed "political cloture" or "political sclerosis." In Nicaragua the more moderate form of authoritarianism of Anastasio Somoza, Sr., gave way to a more brutal and intolerable form by his second son. Additionally, the level of graft reached unacceptable proportions after the 1972 earthquake. And whereas in the past graft, nepotism, and the benefits of modernization had been shared fairly broadly and among a number of families, by the mid- to late 1970s the Somozas had become excessively greedy, monopolizing the opportunities for enrichment for themselves and preventing others from gaining a share. Eventually, all groups in Nicaragua had reason to oppose the Somoza regime.

In El Salvador the progressive and nationalist military regimes that had governed during the 1960s were replaced in the 1970s by brutal and repressive regimes that closed off the opportunities for change. In Guatemala too, a more or less centrist regime was replaced in the 1970s by a brutally repressive one. Honduras too went through a period of greater repression though as usual it was more tempered there than that of its neighbors; and even happily democratic Costa Rica was plagued in the late 1970s by an incompetent administration that exacerbated its growing economic difficulties. Clearly, political blockage was greater in some countries than in others, but it is significant that those countries where cloture was strongest were at the same time the countries whose internal difficulties are presently of most concern to the United States.

A second factor is accelerated social change in an institutional context incapable of handling such changes.[22] Continued modernization in Central America had set loose forces that the political system was not able to manage. Modernization, therefore, rather than leading to stability as our assistance programs had assumed, helped lead instead to increased frustration, fragmentation, and eventual breakdown.

The problem has several dimensions worthy of attention. First, the social mobilization now occurring began to include peasant and Indian elements for the first time, thus raising the possibility of a broadly based mass challenge as contrasted with the more limited changes of the past. Second, it proved far easier for the traditional accommodative mechanisms by which the Central American nations had habitually dealt with change to cope with the moderate, limited, and "in-the-family" aspirations of the new entrepreneurial elites and middle classes of the 1930s–1950s than the far larger and more systemic mass challenges of the 1960s and 1970s. Third, the United States, ironically, was one of the major causes of the instability we would later seek to prevent. Through our Agency for International Development, Peace Corps, literacy, road-building, and other programs, we helped raise popular expectations to potentially revolutionary proportions. At the same time, a number of the reforms we helped finance in the name of development—U.S.-style political parties, trade unions, farmers' cooperatives, and the like—had the practical effect of destroying many traditional institutions (patronage, clan, family networks), without really institutionalizing viable modern ones, thus leaving an institutional vacuum and eventually precipitating the fragmentation and societal unraveling we had sought to prevent.

A third major cause of the instability in Central America is the distribution of income.[23] We have said, and the economic statistics support this interpretation, that the Central American economies "boomed" from the 1950s through the early 1970s. Some of this new wealth did "trickle down" to help benefit the new middle and urban working classes that we now find in all the cities of the area. But the new wealth generated in the boom years was terribly unevenly distributed. The same statistics that document the boom also indicate that the distribution of income throughout the region actually became more uneven. The gaps between the wealthy and the middle classes *and* the poor widened rather than closed. Widespread, growing graft, corruption, and the ostentatious display of wealth on the part of new-rich military officers and civilians built further envy and resentments.

In Nicaragua, for example, the level of graft accompanying most major business transactions rose from a more or less tolerable and "normal" 5–10 percent to an intolerable 25–30 percent, thus precipitating disaffection with the regime even on the part of the business community. In El Salvador, Guatemala, and, to a somewhat lesser degree, Honduras, military corruption and rake-offs similarly became intolerably high—and all this in a time of rising, even revolutionary expectations on the part of the lower classes. These rising gaps between rich and poor, or the perception of same, especially in a time of higher expectations, helped provide a context in which revolutionary appeals might flourish.

A fourth major cause precipitating upheaval was the growing economic crisis of the 1970s and continuing into the 1980s. There were two major oil "shocks," in 1973 and then again in 1979. North Americans likewise experienced the traumas associated with such skyrocketing oil prices but not nearly to the degree Central America did. Central America has *no* oil of its own, has no available substitutes such as coal, must import *all* of its petroleum, and is therefore much more vulnerable than we. It now costs many more bags of sugar to buy one barrel of oil than it did in 1972; the same applies to coffee, bananas, cacao, and other Central American products.

Beginning in the mid-1970s, furthermore, the prices for these primary products went through some tremendous fluctuations which further devastated the economies of the area. The price trend was generally down, at least as compared with the cost of manufactured goods which Central America must import. There were times when sugar was given away free in American grocery stores. Consumer drinking habits also began to shift away from coffee and sugared drinks and toward decaffeinated or nonsugared beverages. That trend was good from the point of view of our collective and individual figures and blood pressures, but it was ruinous for the economies of Central America.

The world depression that deepened in 1979 and worsened thereafter was, one is tempted to say, the final straw.[24] We have seen how devastating the recession was in the United States; but in Central America, with its weak institutions and inadequate social programs, the effects were even more wrenching. Unemployment reached 25–30 percent; underemployment went even higher. And since all these countries are so heavily dependent on the United States, when our economic locomotive faltered, the small "sidecars" following suffered enormously. One need not go much further than this worldwide economic depression of recent years to explain the destabilization of Central America.

The economic crisis of the late 1970s and early 1980s had a profound debilitating effect not just on the general economic situation and the living standards of the people but also on the political system and the entire model of politics to which Central America had become accustomed. The accommodative model which we have described earlier as working not entirely intolerably on into the 1960s was based on one big assumption: an ever-expanding economic pie. So long as the pie keeps expanding, there are always new pieces to hand out to the rising, aspiring groups—without the traditional wielders of power having to be deprived of their share. The political "game" can thus take evolutionary rather than revolutionary directions.

But once the pie becomes stagnant or even contracts—as occurred in two or three countries of the area—the politics of accommodation and gradual absorption can no longer work. There are no new pieces to hand out to the new groups. In a context of contraction, some groups must go without or be deprived. Politics becomes a zero-sum game in which for every one who gains, someone else must lose. It is difficult, well-nigh impossible, to be a political leader in these circumstances, and democratic politics becomes almost impossible. Competition for the fewer pieces left is likely to degenerate into violence, civil strife, perhaps revolution, civil war, or national breakdown. In our own society we have seen the effects of economic stagnation in producing rising social tension, social fragmentation, even violence. We should not be surprised, therefore, when in Latin America even worse conditions produce considerably greater strife than the United States has experienced. This is the essential problem in Central America: Not only has the economic downturn been disadvantageous for many groups and individuals, but it has also undermined the entire *system* and *model* of accommodative politics on which the nations of the area have historically been based.

The *systemic* nature of the problem makes clear it is not one that will quickly or easily go away. And it reinforces also the view that it was a long time in building. It did not spring up just with the killing of the nuns in El Salvador in 1980. That was, without minimizing the tragedy and horror in that event, only a single incidence of what is in fact a far deeper and larger crisis. The long-term roots of the Central American crisis are what lie at the heart of all the analyses in this book. The fact that the problem has been building and fermenting for at least twenty to thirty years implies it will likely take at least that long to be resolved or to resolve itself.

A fifth major cause of the Central American crisis has to do with the changed international context in which the area's politics takes place. There are conflicting currents here, and not all of them can be addressed, let alone resolved, in a brief introduction. Our authors, also, approach these issues from diverse perspectives.

Clearly one major factor is the declining U.S. influence through-out the area since the mid-1960s.[25] There is now less U.S. aid, less U.S. investment, fewer U.S. businessmen, less military assistance (until, most recently, the rather special U.S. involvement in El Salvador and with regard to Nicaragua), a lessened U.S. *presence* in virtually all areas. This is not to say that the United States no longer has influence in the region; it does and it is major. But it is to say that the U.S. presence overall is less than it was, creating in some countries a vacuum of leadership. U.S. National Security Council adviser Norman Bailey once wrote an article in which he likened the U.S. role in the area to that of a caudillo (strong leadership coupled with benevolence).[26] Today, both the strong leadership and the benevolence have been lessened.

A second factor is the increasing assertiveness, independence, and nationalism of the Latin American states. Such independence is obviously more difficult for the small, weak, dependent states of Central America than it is for Argentina or Brazil. Still, the sentiment is strong throughout the area to reduce somewhat their dependence on the United States and to diversify their international relations. Such sentiment is particularly strong among the younger generation of Central American leaders, who are both more nationalistic and more on the left than their elders, and it is strong among both civilian and military elites. Prudent Central American presidents, of course, recognize they must make their accommodations with the United States and that they need its capital, technology, and markets. But it is nonetheless the case that the United States is not so popular in Central America as it once was, and in a host of areas this change makes it considerably more difficult for U.S. policy to function effectively.

Finally, there is the rising presence of the Soviet Union and Cuba in Central America. The increasing role of these two outside actors is described and documented in Jiri and Virginia Valenta's paper in this volume and need not be repeated here. The point is that—Alexander Haig's unfortunately overblown language about the East-West struggle's being decided in El Salvador to the contrary—there *are* a rising Soviet and Cuban influence and presence in Central America which have major destabilizing implications for the Central American countries and for U.S. foreign policy.

In the public arena, there is a great deal of discussion about this matter, much of it mistaken and/or focused on tangential issues. Two thickets in this underbrush, especially, need clearing. First, I know of no responsible student of or policy maker on Central America, within or without the U.S. government, who does not believe the basic causes of the problems in Central America are socioeconomic and political. No one really believes, despite frequent assertions to the contrary, that the Soviet Union is the prime cause of the upheavals there. Rather what the Soviets and Cubans have the capacity to do is to exploit, exacerbate, and take advantage of the instability that already exists. It is not so much instability per se in Central America that primarily concerns the United States; rather it is the Soviets' and Cubans' rising ability to meddle in a U.S. sphere of influence, to foment even greater instability than already exists in an area considered vital to us, and to use the internal, long-term, and systemic crisis in Central America to cause difficulties for the United States while also serving their own interests.

The second thicket requiring clearing has to do with U.S. attitudes toward socialist regimes. It is obvious that the United States would prefer to have states throughout the area in accord with its own economic and political model. But it can live with socialist regimes and has done so in numerous instances—Burnham in Guyana; Manley in Jamaica; Betancourt, Leoni, and Pérez in Venezuela; Jorge Blanco in the Dominican Republic; José Figueras, Daniel Oduber, and Luis Alberto Monge in Costa Rica. The rub comes when a socialist regime jettisons its independence and allies itself with the Soviet Union, à la Cuba. It is not socialism per se to which the U.S. government necessarily is opposed but only a form of socialism that becomes monolithically Marxist-Leninist and aligns itself internationally with the Soviet Union. That is a posture that no U.S. government, of whatever party, has felt it could afford to countenance.

These would seem to be among the major causes of the Central American imbroglio as discussed in the various contributions to this book. The discussion makes clear that the web of causation is much more complex than what is portrayed in the media and at the popular level, and that the interrelations between the indigenous and the external causes of the unrest there is not either-or but complicated and closely intertwined. Indeed, the discussion serves to indicate how uninformed and simplistic the debate often is, our frequent lack of understanding of the complexities of the area, and how the popular discussion is often beside the point. This book is aimed at filling some of these vast gaps in our knowledge.

The Book: A Look Ahead

Part two, on the domestic dimensions of the crisis, begins with an essay by Thomas Karnes. Karnes, professor of history at Arizona State University, focuses on Central America's past: its historical legacy of violence and instability and the failure to establish a confederated union among polities that by themselves may be too small to be viable either economically or politically. His essay is followed by a careful exploration by Professor Gary Wynia of the Department of Political Science at the University of Minnesota of the economic and political causes of rebellion in Central America, and particularly of the complex interrelations between these economic and political variables.

In an especially interesting contribution, Professor Roland Ebel of Tulane University analyzes the development and decline of the Central American "city-states." Professor Ebel shows why and how politics in a city-state-sized nation, where everyone who counts knows everyone else or is interrelated, is different from that in a larger nation-state, and how the city-state *systems* of Central America began in recent decades to unravel. In his stimulating contribution, Professor Thomas Anderson of Eastern Connecticut State University, one of the country's leading experts on Central America, points to persistent poverty and intense competition for limited resources as lying at the heart of the Central American revolution. Professor Anderson's essay contains brief summaries of each of the countries of the area and is especially good in its dissection of the particular role of the middle classes in Central America, their relations with the armed forces, and the dismal litany of Central America's recent developments.

Professor Ronald H. McDonald of the Maxwell School at Syracuse

19

University has contributed a major chapter to the volume dealing with civil-military relations in Central America. Professor McDonald shows not only how and why the patterns of Central American civil-military relations are quite different from those in less praetorian societies but also how these relations have changed in recent years, precipitating greater social and political fragmentation. In the next essay Professor Ernest Evans of Catholic University and an expert on terrorism traces the evolution of newer strategies by revolutionary movements in Central America and why, in Nicaragua and El Salvador, these newer strategies have been more successful than those followed by a series of aborted guerrilla movements in the 1960s.

Part three, of the study turns to the international dimensions of the Central American crisis. Jiri Valenta and Virginia Valenta begin this section with a detailed discussion of the increased Cuban and Soviet presence in Central America. They demonstrate convincingly that the causes of instability in Central America are not just indigenous but are also externally induced; they also offer detailed prescriptions for American foreign policy in dealing with this changed balance of power in the Caribbean. In the following essay Professor Eusebio Mujal-León of Georgetown University's Government Department focuses on the emerging European presence in Central America and the degree to which, for them, Central America has become a major foreign policy issue or, alternatively, an instrument for domestic political considerations.

One of the major actors in the Central American discussion has been Mexico. In his chapter Professor Edward J. Williams of the University of Arizona places Mexico's Central America policy in the context of that country's overall foreign policy and relates it also to the modernization of the Mexican military. The Central American revolutionary caldron, he concludes, has led to a new vibrancy in Mexican foreign policy.

In the chapter by U.S. Ambassador to the United Nations Jeane J. Kirkpatrick, an intriguing perspective on Central America is offered, one which had—and continues to have—important implications for U.S. foreign policy in the region. Ambassador Kirkpatrick's essay was written at the height of the 1980 election campaign; because of its importance as a policy statement, we determined to republish it here in its original form. The chapter includes a dissection and critique of the Carter administration's Latin American policy, a prescription for new directions, and a set of theoretical and background comments especially valuable for this book on the general problems of legitimacy, order, violence, authority, and change in Central America.

Finally, in one of the more provocative essays in the book, Mark

Falcoff of AEI examines Central America as a reflection of U.S. domestic politics. Frequently, he argues, what passes for a debate over Central America is really a U.S. domestic quarrel having more to do with executive-congressional relations, partisan posturing, the jockeying for power of rival think tanks and interest groups, and the electoral possibilities of those in and out of power than it does with Central America itself.

It is a solid and interesting collection; hopefully it will help rectify that lack of understanding and comprehension about Latin America that, we have repeatedly argued, lies at the heart of our difficulties there.

Notes

1. Jeane J. Kirkpatrick, "Dictatorships and Double Standards," *Commentary*, vol. 70 (November 1979), pp. 34–45; Constantine Menges, "Central America and Its Enemies," *Commentary*, vol. 72 (August 1981), pp. 32–38; Roger Fontaine, Cleto Di Giovanni, Jr., and Alexander Kruger, "Castro's Specter," *The Washington Quarterly*, vol. 3 (Autumn 1980), pp. 28–39; and The Committee of Santa Fe, Lewis Tambs, ed., *A New Inter-American Policy for the Eighties* (Washington, D.C.: Council for Inter-American Security, 1980).
2. These points are elaborated in Howard J. Wiarda, "The United States and Latin America in the Aftermath of the Falklands/Malvinas Crisis," Testimony prepared for the Subcommittee on Inter-American Affairs, Committee on Foreign Affairs, U.S. House of Representatives, July 20, 1982, and published in *Latin America and the United States after the Falklands/Malvinas Crisis: Hearings before the Subcommittee on Inter-American Affairs, Committee on Foreign Affairs* (Washington, D.C., 1982).
3. For a more detailed discussion see the author's edited volume, *Politics and Social Change in Latin America: The Distinct Tradition*, 2nd rev. ed. (Amherst: University of Massachusetts Press, 1982); also his "The Ethnocentrism of the Social Sciences: Implications for Research and Policy," *The Review of Politics*, vol. 43 (April 1981), pp. 163–97.
4. See Howard J. Wiarda, ed., *The Continuing Struggle for Democracy in Latin America* (Boulder, Colo.: Westview Press, 1979); and Wiarda, "Can Democracy Be Exported? The Quest for Democracy in United States–Latin America Policy," Paper prepared for the Inter-American Dialogue on United States–Latin American Relations in the 1980s, sponsored by the Latin America Program of the Woodrow Wilson International Center for Scholars, Washington, D.C., and forthcoming in a volume edited by Kevin Middlebrook and Carlos Rico.
5. For a longer analysis see Howard J. Wiarda, "Power and Policy-Making in Washington in the Latin America Area: Impressions and Reflections," Paper presented at the Center for International Affairs, Harvard University, April 20, 1982.

6. See the paper prepared by the author entitled "Changing Realities and U.S. Policy in the Caribbean Basin: An Overview" for the Atlantic Council's Study Project on *Western Interests and U.S. Policy Options in the Caribbean Basin* (January 1983), and forthcoming in a volume with the same title.

7. The materials presented here were developed in a preliminary way in Howard J. Wiarda, "The Central American Crisis: A Framework for Understanding," *AEI Foreign Policy and Defense Review*, vol. 4, no. 2 (1982), pp. 2–7. The entire issue of that journal is devoted to Central America.

8. See the essay by Roland H. Ebel in this volume.

9. See the essay by Jeane J. Kirkpatrick in this volume.

10. Glen Dealy, *The Public Man: An Interpretation of Latin American and Other Catholic Countries* (Amherst: University of Massachusetts Press, 1977).

11. Howard J. Wiarda, "Democracy and Human Rights in Latin America: Toward a New Conceptualization," *Orbis*, vol. 22 (Spring 1978), pp. 43–66; also published in *Human Rights and U.S. Human Rights Policy* (Washington, D.C.: American Enterprise Institute, 1982).

12. A complete discussion is in Howard J. Wiarda, *Corporatism and National Development in Latin America* (Boulder, Colo.: Westview Press, 1981).

13. The discussion follows the classic statement of Charles W. Anderson, *Politics and Economic Change in Latin America: The Governing of Restless Nations* (New York: Van Nostrand, 1967).

14. James L. Payne, "The Politics of Structured Violence," *Journal of Politics*, vol. 27 (May 1965), pp. 362–74; also Howard J. Wiarda, *Critical Elections and Critical Coups: State, Society and the Military in the Processes of Latin American Development* (Athens: Center for International Studies, Ohio University, 1978).

15. The discussion follows that of Anderson, *Politics and Economic Change in Latin America*, especially chapter 4.

16. Howard J. Wiarda, *Dictatorship, Development, and Disintegration: Politics and Social Change in the Dominican Republic* (Ann Arbor, Mich.: Xerox University Microfilms Monograph Series, 1975).

17. The metaphor derives from Juan José Arévalo, *The Shark and the Sardines* (New York: L. Stuart, 1961).

18. See the essays collected in Wiarda, *Politics and Social Change in Latin America*.

19. A good overview is Kalman H. Silvert, *The Conflict Society: Reaction and Revolution in Latin America* (New York: American Universities Field Staff, 1966).

20. A country-by-country analysis may be found in Howard J. Wiarda and Harvey F. Kline, *Latin American Politics and Development* (Boston, Mass.: Houghton Mifflin, 1979).

21. Gary W. Wynia, *Politics and Planners: Economic Development Policy in Central America* (Madison: University of Wisconsin Press, 1972).

22. The best general statement is Samuel P. Huntington, *Political Order in Changing Societies* (New Haven, Conn.: Yale University Press, 1968).

23. See the essay by Gary W. Wynia in this volume.

24. Richard E. Feinberg with Robert Kennedy, "Western Interests and U.S. Policy Options in the Caribbean Basin: The Policy Paper" (Washington, D.C.:

The Atlantic Council, 1983).

25. This and other new realities of U.S.–Latin American relations are dealt with in Howard J. Wiarda, "Conceptual and Political Dimensions of the Crisis in U.S.–Latin American Relations: Toward a New Policy Formulation," Paper presented at the AEI Public Policy Week Forum on "The Crisis in Latin America," Washington, D.C., December 6–10, 1982, and in *The Crisis in Latin America and in U.S.–Latin American Relations: Strategic, Economic, and Political Dimensions* (Washington, D.C.: American Enterprise Institute, 1984).

26. Norman Bailey, "The United States as Caudillo," in Hugh M. Hamill, Jr., ed., *Dictatorship in Spanish America* (New York: Knopf, 1965).

PART TWO

Domestic Dimensions of the Crisis

2

The Historical Legacy and the Failure of Union

THOMAS L. KARNES

Most stories of Latin America begin with Christopher Columbus, and Central America's narrative is no exception. Although other explorers entered the Caribbean shortly after his 1492 voyage, Columbus made the most substantial investigation of Central American waters when in 1502 he coasted from the Bay Islands in the Gulf of Honduras to the Isthmus of Panama. The subsequent conquest did not come directly from Spain, however, but from the neighboring colonies of Mexico and Panama. Hernán Cortés and his lieutenants extended the subjugation of Aztec and Maya into Honduras, Guatemala, and El Salvador, eventually bumping into Spanish forces moving up from Panama, seeking the supposed wealth of Costa Rica and Nicaragua. This portion of the conquest ended about 1545 with the defeat of the lesser Indian tribes. The more highly developed Mayas, centered in Guatemala but found throughout much of the region, were too numerous and too stubborn to be eliminated by the military. Instead, Church and state combined to impose a process of both segregation and assimilation to reduce the Indian and complete the conquest.

The Development of a Concept of Self-Government

The settlement pattern also aped that of the rest of Latin America. Where land and free labor afforded, a system of haciendas developed, with agricultural exports to the mother country providing the major sources of income. In some sections, such as much of Costa Rica, where the Indian laborer was in shorter supply, small farms became more common, although large estates were not unknown.

Since the conquest came from several directions and a variety of sponsors, early government proved confused and diffused. As agents

27

from Mexico, Darién, and Santo Domingo argued jurisdiction—even fought over it—stability came to reside in the councils of the towns and villages, especially those more distant from the centers of power. In time Spanish authority asserted itself, the chief agency being an *audiencia,* created in 1543 for the lands ranging from the present Mexican states of Chiapas and Yucatán to Panama.

After some shuffling, Spain in 1570 settled upon Guatemala City as the seat of the *audiencia* and gave it control over lands from Costa Rica northward to and including Chiapas.[1] This government, popularly known as the "Kingdom of Guatemala," also included a captain general with many of the trappings of a viceroy. Technically the *audiencia* fell under the viceroy at Mexico City, but that tie significantly weakened as a consequence of the crown policy of permitting direct communication between Guatemala and Spain under many circumstances. Distance and discouraging travel conditions played their part as well, and localism thrived.

On paper Central Americans had little self-government, and had any organizational charts existed in Spain, they would have shown long, undotted lines bringing political, economic, and even religious centralism from the metropolis to the Central Americans. But in fact Spain's rulers always had greater concerns, and Central America contributed little to the mother country. The vast majority of Creole farmers and Indians toiled their lives away with little knowledge of viceroys or the world power struggles that engrossed Spain. The elite—officials, merchants, and planters—were not unaffected by progress; they read books and sent their children to Europe for school. Prosperity and even the Enlightenment in time reached the "Kingdom," and life could be good for some of the squires, but their self-interest and Spanish policies brought little comfort to the majority of Central Americans for two and one-half centuries. As decades passed some of the Creole elite did well enough to raise their expectations and feel inhibited by Spain's mercantilism.

Spain's adjustment to the Napoleonic invasion and occupation of 1808, which set aside King Ferdinand VII, catalyzed the many Creole complaints and brought demands for independence from all over Latin America. Central Americans played their part, too, but waged no war against Spanish troops. Instead, Central American independence rode piggyback on the shoulders of the Mexican viceroyalty. In that region conservative forces forestalled revolution by some chicanery and some cooperation with loyalists, the result being an empire under Agustín de Iturbide, who called himself Emperor Agustín I. The Central Americans, who had made few serious noises for freedom, were stirred by Iturbide's actions and frightened by Mexican troops dispatched by Iturbide to persuade doubters to join him. There were many doubters, but they wisely said little in the presence of the "invasion."

Such leadership as Central America enjoyed came from a Spanish general, Gabino Gainza, acting captain general of Central America. Gainza at first urged the several towns' *cabildos* (councils) to stand aloof from the Mexican empire, but by 1821 he had changed his mind and thrown his influence on the side of Iturbide. A slight majority of Central American towns and villages voted to accept annexation to Mexico, but dissent remained significant. Especially in El Salvador did Mexican troops need force to bring locals into line with Iturbide's brief government, as the Salvadoran provincial assembly pathetically annexed itself to the United States. (No response ever came from Washington.) Fighting broke out elsewhere in Central America over the issue of joining Mexico, but soon Iturbide ran out of troops to send south, for he had to defend himself at home. After a year few folks were still impressed by his pretensions and costly government, and he failed to pay the army. For this foolishness his former supporters turned on him and forced his "abdication" in March 1823.

Almost immediately the Central Americans sent delegates from each town to Guatemala City to determine a new course of action. Representing districts that were themselves scarcely yet organized, these men nevertheless declared their independence from Mexico and "any other power," elected a chief executive to govern the provinces provisionally, and drafted a constitution—all while trying to keep the provinces solvent. For the moment this government called itself the United Provinces of Central America, changed to the Federal Republic of Central America when the constitution was promulgated in 1824.

The delegates agreed readily enough to establish a new republic but instantly faced the same issue then bedeviling almost all of Latin America—that of the relationship between the new national government and the old local governments. The division was often philosophical, sometimes geographical, but always colored by attitudes toward the former mother country. Generally those people who still felt some yearning for Spain and thought of themselves as conservative favored a unitary or centralist form of government with considerable authority retained in Guatemala City as under the old *audiencia*. Not surprisingly much of this sentiment resided in the province of Guatemala, but supporters could be found in every province in varying strength.

Their opponents, traditional liberals in their attacks upon Church power and Spanish ties, usually adopted a federalist hat. In Central America this meant that the national government would be weaker,

29

local autonomy would be preserved to some unspecified extent, and substantial degrees of paranoia toward Guatemala would be exhibited.[2] These feelings were especially strong in the province of El Salvador and its capital, San Salvador. Classifications and labels shifted frequently, but the differences were real and often very bitter. Some feel for this can be found in the slang terms used by one group for the other; conservatives called the enemies "Fiebres," and the liberals referred to their opposition as "Serviles"—clear enough vilification without translation in either case.

Yet the intensity of this division must not mislead the student; party discipline did not exist, and single issues could change parties in midstream. Economic interests vied with political philosophy in garnering votes, some of the specific questions being—what would replace the old Spanish commercial monopolies, what would bring about free trade (which Great Britain sought and espoused, but closed down in wartime), what was to be done about the new English mercantile firms threatening to become as powerful as the old Spanish houses of trade? Would the Church still retain its position as chief landlord, banker, educator, healer of the body? Would the old families still dominate society? Each of these questions threatened to engulf Central America, but none could surpass localism in its capacity to rive the entire region.

Perhaps a stronger central government, such as most conservatives wanted, would have saved Central America from disunion between 1824 and 1838, but as a major historian once wrote of a subsequent attempt at a federal government, Central America was united with spit.[3] It is tempting to compare the Federal Republic of 1824 with the United States under the Articles of Confederation, and we of the wiser twentieth century can see why neither of them worked. Yet between 1778 and 1789 the Yankee version accomplished several significant and permanent measures and retained (or developed) enough cohesion to transform that government—admittedly through major surgery—into a powerful and lasting republic.

Perhaps the Central Americans were not so frightened by the prospect of disunion as their northern brethren had been a generation before, and perhaps the Central American Federation fell apart before its leaders realized what was happening. Its history is brief enough; a Central American republic existed from 1824 only until 1838. A score of other attempts to reconstruct this nation were conceived in the following century. None lasted more than three years, most never left the drawing board, yet reunion became a Central American shibboleth, a slogan, a political plank still proffered today. What can be learned from the first attempt?

THOMAS L. KARNES

The suitability of that first constitution has generated much debate in Central America and elsewhere among scholars and politicians, and that dead horse has probably been flogged enough.[4] If the document failed the people, why did they not change it? It should be considered that the Central Americans did not stay together because they lacked the will to overcome their vigorous and stubborn form of parochialism. History had taught them the security of the village. In the words of the Argentine writer and president Domingo Sarmiento, the Central Americans made a sovereign state out of every village. That could be satisfaction enough in a world dominated by giant powers with whom Central Americans could never compete, some of whom were already at the doorstep.

The specific steps in disunion can be chronicled from the early failure to select a federal district. The constitution made provision for a capital in a central location, but the rivalries among the provinces for obtaining the site overwhelmed the delegates, and funds were never forthcoming, nor seriously discussed. Perhaps the Central Americans lacked the political savvy for the ultimate compromise of a capital for a university or a prison, in the Yankee fashion. Perhaps they felt or feared too deeply to compromise.

Instead the capital remained in Guatemala City for the first decade, then pressure forced its temporary move to Sonsonate and finally to San Salvador between 1834 and 1838. Both Guatemala City and San Salvador were also provincial capitals, and in neither instance did federal officials extricate themselves from local matters and the often powerful local officials.

A second danger lay in the lack of authority given to the "Executive Power," or president. In subsequent years Latin Americans have strengthened the presidency at the expense of the congress and the courts, believing that down that road more order could be found. But in 1824 the Central Americans had more experience with despotism of the Bourbon variety and made congress supreme over an ineffectual president. The oddity is that the conservatives favored this arrangement, and in normal times they would not have, but the strength of their faction lay in Guatemala, which by numbers, constitution, and tradition could dominate the powerful branch of the congress—and the entire federation—if the president were a figurehead from another province.

The first man to hold that impaired position was a Salvadoran liberal, Manuel José Arce, who nosed out Central America's leading intellectual, José Cecilio del Valle, a Honduran moderate of considerable political experience, as demonstrated by his refusal to accept the vice presidency.

31

Arce and the congress initiated a nineteenth-century liberal program. They struck down slavery and titles of nobility along with some of the necessities of life, the most important being regular revenues. Understandably the new government abolished many old Spanish taxes, but their void was not filled and the nation lacked income to build a badly needed infrastructure or even pay off old war debts. A loan from the ubiquitous London banking firm of Barclay, Herring, Richardson and Company carried such onerous terms (probably because Central America had to bid against the rest of Latin America for the money) and netted so little that it left the Central American physical problems unchanged. Most of the provinces, or states as they now began to call themselves, suffered even more than the republic from the scarcity of funds, and congressmen from outlying states found themselves borrowing from Guatemala in order to live while awaiting their back salaries from home. At times Guatemala was the only state providing revenue for the national government, a condition that obviously could not long continue.

The reforms proved politically expensive, and some moderate liberals moved slowly over to the conservative side, the leader being President Arce himself. His liberal friends turned on him; Salvadoran partisans declaimed against his lack of help in providing a bishopric for that state; Guatemalans accused him of fraud and human rights violations. In retaliation the federal government built an army that threatened the very existence of Guatemala as a state, and even the Guatemalan chief of state faced brief imprisonment on Arce's charges.

Under varying guises civil war broke out from northern Guatemala to Costa Rica. This fitful conflict lasted about three years and brought more anarchy than victory. But a new leader emerged, bearing the banner of the Federal Republic, a cause already seriously threatened. This man, Francisco Morazán, Honduran liberal and successful military commander, has filled a historiographical vacuum as the badly needed hero of Central American federalism.

By 1829 Morazán had defeated the remaining conservative military forces and assumed a military dictatorship over much of Central America. No longer was the issue one of states' rights, but rather one of liberal versus conservative, with each group using whatever government best met its needs. Morazán now set out to destroy *servilismo*, attacking the party in each of the five states, first by weakening the Church. He announced religious freedom, disestablished the Church, attacked its special courts hanging over from Spanish times, exiled an archbishop for political reasons, and forced members of the three most active religious orders to leave the republic. Then he created two state universities—in Nicaragua and El Salvador—and helped introduce Anglo-Saxon legal codes, educational methods, immigrants, and merchants.

A vindictive victor and an inexperienced administrator, Morazán nevertheless became the heart of Central Americanism, then and now, more than any other person. Born in Honduras, ruler of the Federal Republic from capitals in both Guatemala and El Salvador, he attacked states' rights in every region of the nation and was put to death in Costa Rica. He was elected president in 1830 and reelected in 1834 after losing to José Cecilio del Valle, who died shortly after election.

Morazán's reelection made the conservatives restive as they anticipated even more radical reforms. He lost Guatemalan followers of both political persuasions when he moved the capital to San Salvador, while Costa Ricans, always the most inclined toward separatism, and enjoying new-found prosperity from coffee exports, did everything possible to ignore his regime. States took advantage of the attacks on the federal government to commence collecting and retaining the federal customs duties paid in each state, and in the confusion many merchants discovered they could often get away with paying no tariff at all.

The most bitter anti-Morazán feeling centered in Guatemala, where the reforms had been sweeping, and personalism critically divisive among liberal leaders. Minor uprisings increased, but the coup de grâce for Morazán's government could scarcely have been anticipated. Cholera had swept from Europe to America, perhaps as early as 1833; by 1836 it afflicted Central America, Guatemala first, leading to the logical presumption of many that the epidemic had been carried by English merchants trafficking in goods from next-door Belize.[5] Incidence of the disease among the Indians seemed disproportionately high, and they blamed the English for the disease and even charged that it had been spread deliberately by the British consul Frederick Chatfield. Both factions employed every anticholera measure they knew, but accomplished little until the virus had run its course.[6]

The individual obtaining greatest advantage from the epidemic, however, had come but recently onto the political scene. An uneducated Guatemalan mestizo, José Rafael Carrera, had served as drummer in the Guatemalan army fighting Morazán back in 1828, had married advantageously, and had reached the position of company grade officer when the cholera arrived. He left that army to join a mob of Indians seeking his leadership against the government. Untrained Indians and mestizos alike rallied to Carrera, who had already developed a reputation for bravery bordering on the fanatic. He whipped his untrained followers into a capable, if ferocious army which took Guatemala City and soon engaged Morazán's federal forces in a war that embraced all of northern Central America.

Amid the chaos of the war and Morazán's constant absence from the capital as he battled Carrera, the Federal Republic of Central America died. The liberal-versus-conservative struggle and the Morazán-versus-Carrera war continued into 1840, but no ideological point remained. Morazán finally was driven into exile in Peru, returned in 1842 to attempt the overthrow of the Costa Rican government, was captured and put to death by firing squad. Carrera grew and matured as president and dictator, using and occasionally being used by the white conservatives of Guatemala, until his death in 1865.

But what of the Federal Republic? In 1838 the Costa Rican assembly voted secession on the grounds that the republic did not exist. Only in El Salvador did remnants of the federation still express themselves. But by 1841 they, too, were under fire as Carrera drove Morazán out of the state and into asylum. Of course, there were persons who still felt that federalism provided the proper government for the Central Americans; that ideal never dies. But the participation of Guatemala and Costa Rica was essential, and it was not forthcoming. No election was even held to replace Morazán when his second term ended. The archaeologist-cum-diplomat John Lloyd Stephens, dispatched by President Martin Van Buren to renegotiate a trade treaty, reported back to Washington that he could find no federal government at all.[7]

Aftermath of the Failed Central American Republic

The federation had failed badly, yet successors to it have been attempted more than a score of times. What went wrong with it, and why do Central Americans keep trying to replace it?

Every study of the first Central American union has seen fit to rip the flesh and bones apart seeking the poisons that killed that body and the degree of their toxicity. Central American writers have been inclined to blame the nature of the 1824 constitution or the bitter partisanship of the time. Historians from the United States have complicated the question of causation by citing the absence of democracy at any level in Central America, lack of political experience, British interference, weak American support, and so on, using any combination the author wishes. But thought should also be given to the possibility that no central government collapsed, because no central government existed. The failure was of a dream, not of a nation. Perhaps the Central Americans never wanted any form of strong central government at all but limited their hopes to an alliance of villages that in time of emergency would spring up like minutemen to repel the foreign invader.[8]

This last interpretation helped to explain the strange creation known as the Pact of Chinandega. In the same months of 1842 that Morazán, back in Central America from exile, strove to overthrow the Costa Rican government, representatives of Honduras, El Salvador, and Nicaragua met in Chinandega, Nicaragua, to draft a new constitution for a Central American republic. It met no success, but that is not significant; what matters is that during a period of civil war in almost every state, with strong opposition from Guatemala and Costa Rica, with Morazán struggling to reestablish his brand of federalism—with all of these reasons for not trying a new government at that time—three states nevertheless tried, and naively expected all five to participate. Can it be believed that the leadership of the three middle states (all then in liberal hands, as opposed to the conservatives ruling Costa Rica and Guatemala that season) thought that they could make a few changes in the old constitution of 1824 and come up with a better government capable of withstanding the same problems?[9]

The Chinandega constitution proclaimed that the individual states were free and sovereign in all things not especially reserved to the federal government, such as making treaties with other nations. All of the usual appurtenances were included—congress, executive, justices—we need not linger long, for the government lasted only a few months. Too much rivalry among the current caudillos guaranteed failure, irrespective of the design of the government.

In addition to its impossible timing, the 1842 Pact of Chinandega should be remembered for its pioneering role; in the next twenty years three or more states took formal steps to unite into some form of federal nation seven more times. Not one proved successful. Usually the participants were Honduras, El Salvador, and Nicaragua, with normally isolationist Costa Rica and Carrera-dominated Guatemala rarely sharing in the plans. At best, these groups amounted to little more than brief military alliances or commercial treaties. The agreements were also tinged with irony, for a major purpose was to reduce the degree of meddling that each state indulged in, though it was that very meddling that prevented the creation of the nation that they sought.

Even when Frederick Chatfield's unique form of British policy in Central America threatened to cull one of the states from the others, cooperation came hard. Serious resistance to British policy, in fact, came first from the United States, which after the war with Mexico finally recognized that the British presence in the Caribbean might prove both lasting and dangerous. The immediate issue in the 1840s was the matter of right of way for the construction of a canal, but the relations of the two Anglo-Saxon nations were critically exacerbated by the efforts of their respective agents to extend hegemony over portions of the Caribbean at the same time. The British had in the nineteenth century gradually acquired: the Bay Islands off Honduras; a preposterous arrangement permitting control of the Miskito "Kingdom" on the coasts of Honduras and Nicaragua; near-protectorates of Guatemala and Costa Rica; a colony in British Honduras; and the Nicaraguan town of San Juan del Norte, at the strategic outlet of the San Juan River into the Caribbean, believed by many to be one terminus of the most likely route for a future canal. All of this empire had been built without objection from the United States—whether before or after the Monroe Doctrine's enunciation not seeming to matter.

One reason for Britain's success had been the activity of private merchants and the durability of the able Chatfield, who managed to stay on duty while American agents never reached their posts or functioned only briefly until ill health or death prevailed.[10] But by 1849 the United States broke out of its torpor; healthier diplomats negotiated treaties with Honduras (for a "transcontinental" railway) and Nicaragua for a road or canal route. The British and Americans pursued collision courses now, designed to meet in the strategic Gulf of Fonseca, where the Americans purchased—but Chatfield occupied—the Honduran island known as Tigre. This comic opera diplomacy came to a halt when the British government agreed with President Zachary Taylor to hold treaty negotiations to cool off the two powers.

The resulting Clayton-Bulwer Treaty, unsatisfactory to Americans in its vagueness, did not drive the British out of the Caribbean, nor even entirely halt their expansion. But in retrospect, the Americans made clear that the sea would in time be American, even if for the next few decades any canal attempt would be a joint endeavor of the two nations. The treaty probably forestalled a third Anglo-Saxon war and saved Central America from further carving by the powers.

Yet in disunion lay Central America's continued weakness, as tempting to individuals as to great states manifesting their destinies. In the middle of the nineteenth century, private filibuster and private corporation briefly threatened Central American sovereignty more than the Anglo-Saxon governments did. Greed for California gold triggered these activities. Cornelius Vanderbilt, owner of the profitable Hudson River steamboat fleet, decided to compete with the Panama Railroad for the transisthmian traffic to and from California. His ships steamed up the Río San Juan to Lake Nicaragua, where passengers and freight transferred to mule or carriage for the brief overland trip to the Pacific Coast and a rendezvous with another steamer and California.

When local politics and international business threatened his franchise, Vanderbilt joined Nicaraguan liberals to recruit a known quantity, William Walker from Tennessee, to overthrow the conservative administration of Nicaragua. Walker proved more filibuster than the various conspirators planned on and soon took over the government and made himself president of Nicaragua from 1854 to 1857. Aiming for greater things, Walker allied himself with some of Vanderbilt's partners and campaigned to restore the Central American Federation under his own rule. He failed—ultimately he was killed by Hondurans—in part because people did not double-cross the Commodore, but in part because he brought deep Central American principles into operation.

Walker's early successes, his victory over some Honduran conservatives, and his execution of some Central American leaders convinced even liberals that the "Gran Patria" was endangered by the "grey-eyed man of destiny." Patriots from Costa Rica, El Salvador, Honduras, and even faraway Guatemala united to help Nicaraguans drive the Yankee from their soil. Attention should be called to the name of this war. In Central American annals the struggle against William Walker and his American sponsors is called the National War, a title never borne by any other conflict in the history of that region; it has been memorialized in flags, stamps, ceremonies, and heroes, from generals to a Costa Rican lad who gave his life burning a Walker ammunition dump. Walker ruined the lovely old city of Granada, legalized slavery once again, sought to import British and Americans through easy land grants, and turned Central American brother against brother more than usual. But the Central Americans most remembered that the liberals who had supported the old cause of unity for three decades had also brought the mad foreigner to the land and he had nearly destroyed it.

Political Strong Men

For the decade after Walker's death in 1860 reaction restrained Central America. Guatemala had set the pattern under the administration of Rafael Carrera, who enjoyed conservative support throughout his administration from 1838 to 1865. After Walker's death Carrera bolstered himself by helping place friendly presidents in the neighboring states. But by the 1880s modernism began to sweep Central America. Some of this came from the dramatic expansion of coffee as an export crop. Very small business before midcentury, the commodity became the chief export item for both Costa Rica and Guatemala by the 1870s and soon assumed major significance in Nicaragua and El Salvador. Highly prized on the world market for its quality, Central American coffee revolutionized the region. It demanded a stable working force, good transportation from *finca* to coastal port, better harbors, financing, foreign markets, political encouragement. These items were stock in trade for the liberal dictators who rode the coffee carts onto the stage in the 1870s and 1880s, capitalizing on their close ties with foreign investors. The first of these new liberals, Justo Rufino Barrios, became president of Guatemala in 1873 and attacked the clergy and old aristocratic families with equal vigor, disestablishing the Church and seizing its property, providing for religious freedom, and planning vast economic and educational changes. Guatemala could not afford all of his plans, nor would Central America accept his scheme of restoring the old federation by force. His dreams died with him in battle against the Salvadorans in 1885.

His counterpart, General Tomás Guardia, governed Costa Rica between 1870 and 1882. Guardia went so far as to limit some of his own powers by means of a new council of state. He also brought Henry Meiggs and Minor Keith to Costa Rica, giving them vast landholdings in exchange for construction of a railway from the capital at San José to Puerto Limón on the Caribbean. A stupendous task, it was completed too late to stimulate the coffee industry much, but it became the basis of the banana commerce at the end of the century.[11]

In Nicaragua liberalism held less philosophical significance but was almost purely regional. It returned to power in 1893 in the person of José Santos Zelaya, who in progressive, but cruel fashion, dominated his land until 1909. With major or minor figures each of the Central American republics endured some form of liberal strong man in the last third of the century, and many of their marks are still to be seen.

The liberal, progressive Central American dictator permanently crippled the Church, which was never again to exert the control of Carrera's day. The new dictator also expanded the old Central American custom of interfering in one another's affairs to the point that by the 1880s the procedures were almost standardized. Strong man contended or allied with strong man for survival and prestige. Continuation in office (*continuismo*) was a sign of success often rewarded by greater investment from abroad—from London, Amsterdam, and later New York. Success brought success; investment strengthened the dictator, and strong dictators got more foreign investment. Finally these profits helped remodel the armies of the liberal dictator. Not modern by any means, they nevertheless moved far beyond the personal mobs of the generation before and approached the status of national military forces. Governments institutionalized the draft, put the army to work on civic projects, and turned the troops into local police when other agencies failed. The army also learned political lessons and became a force never again to be ignored.

Growing U.S. Hegemony

Amid all this change the Central Americans began to pay the price for their location, the most strategic in the world, certainly before the days of intercontinental missiles. From the time of Balboa, explorers recognized the need for a highway—or better—a waterway across the Isthmus of Panama at some spot, and only the lack of technology and medical knowledge delayed construction. The Spaniards built a road in colonial times to transport goods and the silver of Peru. Private interests completed a Panama railroad in 1855 and effectively ended operation of Vanderbilt's Accessory Transit Company across Nicaragua. Then Viscount Ferdinand de Lesseps, fresh from his triumph at Suez, became interested in the Panama question. Assisted by much national pride, and stimulated by a bought press and a great deal of fraud to cover inadequate surveying, his French Panama Canal Company began digging through Panama in 1883. By 1889, less than one-third finished, the company gave up, leaving in testimony to its failure 16,000 dead workers, some rusty and worthless equipment, and enough scandals to level a French government. [12] The investors sought to unload their holdings, but a major problem existed.

President U. S. Grant's Interoceanic Canal Commission had dispatched seven expeditions to Central America to investigate several possible canal routes. After very thorough labors the commission had, in 1876, recommended as most practical a course through Nicaragua, using the Río San Juan, Lake Nicaragua, and a canal—to be constructed—linking the lake to the Pacific, practically Vanderbilt's old highway. Furthermore, by treaty the United States held a nonexclusive right from Nicaragua to construct a canal, and given the unanimous vote of Grant's engineers, America could well ignore the French tender. But the French stockholders correctly assumed that the only means of avoiding total financial loss would be by persuading the U.S. government to change its preferred site to Panama and purchase the French franchise.

The Panama story needs no retelling here. New Panama Canal Company agents and money stepped in when Colombian greed pushed Theodore Roosevelt too far. A few hired Panamanians staged a rebellion in November 1903, and American naval forces prevented the Colombian government from putting down the uprising. Immediately the Panamanians declared their independence; Roosevelt promptly recognized the new state, and within two weeks the republic of Panama and the United States completed a treaty which granted the latter perpetual rights to a canal zone and the construction through it of an interoceanic canal. From the point of view of the Central Americans these events did little more than demonstrate the new power, if not yet hegemony, of the United States in the Caribbean.

Hegemony came soon enough. In 1904 the first American shovels scooped into Panama's mud. Just a few months later, the man chiefly responsible for this act, President Theodore Roosevelt, announced the most sweeping amendment to the Monroe Doctrine ever decreed. The Dominican Republic had defaulted on its foreign debt, and many of its European creditors clamored for diplomatic or military action by *some* nation to accomplish repayment. Because of the new canal project Roosevelt exhibited more concern than usual about the prospect of force being exerted by foreign states to collect the debt. (The destructive behavior, supported by the Permanent Court of Justice at The Hague, of Germans toward a defaulted Venezuela just two years before, also disturbed Roosevelt.) To make clear his position he announced his policy in his Annual Message of December 1904. In what became known as the Roosevelt Corollary to the Monroe Doctrine, he concluded that

> Chronic wrongdoing . . . may . . . require intervention by some civilized nation, and in the Western Hemisphere the adherence of the United States to the Monroe Doctrine may force the United States, however reluctantly, in flagrant cases of such wrongdoing or impotence, to the exercise of an international police power. . . . We would interfere with them only in the last resort, and then only if it became evident that their inability or unwillingness to do justice at home and abroad had violated the rights of the United States or had invited foreign aggression to the detriment of the entire body of American nations.[13]

Never so clearly had any American statesman expressed his belief in the concept of a *mare nostrum* for the Caribbean and American hegemony of the whole region adjacent to the North American continent. What did it portend for Central America, some of whose states had often exhibited "their inability to do justice at home"? Roosevelt foresaw that issue, as well. To avert a general Central American war against Guatemala's President Manuel Estrada Cabrera, Roosevelt, seconded by Porfirio Díaz of Mexico, sent the *Marblehead* to Central America. Using the cruiser's good offices, delegates from all the Central American states plus Mexico and the United States agreed on an armistice and, more important, further discussions about methods to accomplish permanent peace in the region. These talks led to an ambitious conference in Washington in 1907, again under the aegis of Roosevelt and Díaz. Clearing the air, the ministers stipulated that none of the five states had outstanding claims against another and that each would grant full amnesty to all political prisoners.

After five weeks of discussions (typically much of the time was absorbed by talks of a new federation) the Central American states signed a treaty and six conventions, plus many other matters. In rare concurrence these were all ratified within eighteen months. The most important provided that all of their mutual disputes were subject to *compulsory* arbitration. To aid in this unusual procedure the Washington treaties created a Central American Court of Justice, called by the World Peace Foundation, "the most remarkable judicial organ in this world." The court's first term was set at ten years, and each nation would select one justice for the five-man court. Then recognizing the problems of preventing international disputes, the states compacted that Honduras, weak and centrally located, would be permanently neutral; that they would prohibit the use of their territories for staging revolts against one another; and that they would not grant diplomatic recognition to a Central American state coming into office as the consequence of rebellion. With a Platt Amendment containing Cuba, sovereignty in Panama, a receivership for the Dominican Republic, and complete peace machinery established for all of Central America, Roosevelt could hope that he had outlawed strife in the Caribbean. He had also turned the Caribbean into an American lake.

How long did peace last? The question is not a bad joke. Readers today might find it hard to understand the degree of confidence with which statesmen viewed the future of Central America in 1907. The Hague Court, Andrew Carnegie (who built a peace palace for the Central Americans), and the World Peace Foundation watched the experiment keenly, international jurists as well as statesmen of the time viewing Central America as a test tube offering clues for the world at large.

Reviews of the court would have to be classified as mixed initially. It handled one minor dispute well, and it spent months clarifying to itself and to litigants the limits to its jurisdiction in personal suits, but it could not survive a decision in conflict with policy from Washington.

Nicaragua, not yet the linchpin of American control over the Caribbean, became extremely restive in the last years of the José Santos Zelaya dictatorship. He had succeeded in antagonizing British and American investors, Nicaraguan conservatives, and most of the neighboring governments, whom he threatened to unite in *his* version of a Central American federation. His local opponents rebelled in 1909, rid themselves of Zelaya, then in the usual pattern split widely over his successor. The United States worked out an agreement among the factions which it was hoped would also settle the matter of the outstanding foreign debts. Several men held the presidency in the next few years, and one of them, Adolfo Díaz, asked for and received the aid of U.S. Marines to protect his position. By 1912 most of the civil wars had stopped, and under Washington's protection Díaz remained in office until 1917. This latest protectorate also cried for financial support, and this came about by tying in the old canal issue.

A treaty that would have created for Nicaragua a relationship similar to the one between the United States and the Dominican Republic failed of ratification in the U.S. Senate. A second treaty agreement that would have provided a "Platt Amendment" for Nicaragua also lost in the Senate; in both instances the measures had the enthusiastic championship of President William H. Taft, evidence, perhaps, that the White House had lost some of its mastery with the passing of TR. But a third try, which omitted the right of American intervention, swept through the Woodrow Wilson administration. Called the Bryan-Chamorro Treaty, the agreement went into effect in 1916 over the energetic objections of Costa Rica, Honduras, and El Salvador, all of whom sued in the Central American Court of Justice, contending that the treaty violated their rights. Specifically the treaty gave to the United States exclusive rights to lands necessary for the construction of a canal through Nicaragua; a ninety-nine-year lease on a site for a naval base in the Gulf of Fonseca; a ninety-nine-year lease on Nicaragua's Corn Islands in the Caribbean; a payment of $3 million by the United States to Nicaragua to help reduce the foreign debt. Costa Rica sued in the court on the grounds that its government had not been consulted on the canal issue, for any Nicaraguan waterway would automatically assume the use of the Río San Juan, which Nicaragua shared with Costa Rica. Honduras and El Salvador went to the court over the naval base issue, each of them arguing that any foreign base in the Gulf of Fonseca would threaten the security of all the states bordering on that body.

The court ruled against Nicaragua in each instance, but at the suggestion of the United States, Nicaragua denied the court's jurisdiction over treaties with outside powers, ignored the rulings, and gave notice of its intention to leave the court. The court died when its ten-year term ended in 1917.[14] Meanwhile, the Bryan-Chamorro Treaty faced trouble in Washington, where many senators sympathized with the view of the other Central American states or argued that the United States had created a government for the specific purpose of concluding this treaty. But Wilson sold the measure as the solution to Nicaraguan anarchy, and it gained ratification in 1916.[15]

The 1907 package of Central American treaties remained in effect until their modification by a similar group in 1923. How well had they worked? Their chief sponsor, the United States, had destroyed the court by pursuing its own ends. The action did not prove the court's lack of usefulness, nor did it destroy the other measures. Dana G. Munro, a historian who personally took part in many of the State Department's recommendations in those years, found that between 1911 and 1917 no Central American government had been overthrown by force. Whether this record resulted from the 1907 peace machinery or from the very active presence of the United States in Central America during those years would be hard to sort out, but nevertheless the achievement is noteworthy.

The Central Americans felt that the policies needed another chance and that they would succeed if they were accompanied by measures to create a new federal republic. Although the impetus came from El Salvador, prompting came from a new element in Central American history. Within Guatemala a Central American unionist party had gradually reached maturity and proposed that a fitting centennial celebration would be the reestablishment of the old federation. The proposal was set off from a score of others in major elements. This plan called not for a mere confederacy or other loose agreement, but for no less than the complete reconstruction of Central America. Old boundaries would be thrown out, and new districts created on somewhat functional lines, theoretically ending old rivalries and jealousies by modern gerrymandering. The scheme went nowhere. But among Central Americans dreams of confederation never disappear, and several statesmen suggested to Washington that times seemed propitious to meet again in Washington and perhaps remodel the 1907 treaties.

Enough turbulence had returned to Central America to make this suggestion completely palatable to the State Department, and in 1922 Secretary of State Charles Evans Hughes convoked a second Washington–Central American conference. This time the United States took an even more direct role; the former co-host, Mexico, was not invited; Secretary Hughes chaired the sessions; the old Court of Justice was not to be tried again; and additional topics could be added to the agenda only by unanimous consent. Clearly there would be no revival of the Bryan-Chamorro question. Hughes let the delegates wrangle for a few weeks over the matter of placing the confederation issue on the agenda—it was of little concern to the United States—until the Central Americans decided not to support it. Then they got down to serious business. The basis of any agreement would be another Washington peace treaty. A new, but much weaker court was approved, with its jurisdiction sharply reduced and its decisions not binding. Commissions of inquiry, sponsored by Hughes, were expected to accomplish the pacific settlement of disputes. A new concept was to be tried to reduce revolts; the five signatories agreed not to extend diplomatic recognition to a Central American government achieving office by force, a policy that the United States—a nonsignatory—agreed to adopt also for the Central American region.[16]

As in 1907 the Washington treaties worked well initially. For the first few years both meddling and warfare were reduced in Central America. But it is also true that during the period U.S. influence and presence were never more apparent. (U.S. forces continued to occupy Nicaragua, for example, from 1912 until 1933, except for about a year.) But again the treaties could not surmount a major issue. This one was not provoked by the United States but by the Central Americans themselves.

In 1931 during serious economic disorders, the government of El Salvador was set aside by General Maximiliano Hernández Martínez. Despite the viciousness with which he suppressed a peasant rebellion, Hernández Martínez was recognized by Costa Rica as well as other non–Central American states in the hemisphere. When it became clear that nonrecognition would have little effect on Hernández Martínez and that most of Central America would denounce the Washington agreement, the United States somewhat reluctantly followed suit, and the treaty died. Did any way remain for the United States to help bring peace and stability to Central America? A new grand plan was in the offing, but first the residue of the old one had to be removed.

To prevent revolution in Nicaragua, President Taft had dispatched the marines to Managua in 1912. Wilson reduced their number to little more than a legation guard but maintained their presence throughout his administration, helping to control elections. Assuming that cash would reduce some of Nicaragua's embarrassment, the Bryan-Chamorro Treaty was ratified by the United States in 1916. As we have seen, the treaty created enormous ill will and did little for Nicaragua's finances because most of the $3 million went to creditors. But Nicaragua remained more peaceful and even received modest American and other investments; in 1925 the marines went home. A sudden revolution brought 2,000 of them back again, to be followed by a special diplomatic mission in 1927 headed by Henry Stimson, President Calvin Coolidge's personal representative. Although Stimson got most parties to accept his proposals, one group led by Augusto César Sandino, refused and took to the bush to continue rebellion. Under the circumstances Washington felt it necessary to leave the marines, and so they stayed until the *guardia nacional,* a sort of national police force, was established enough to replace the marines. Their last departure was completed in January 1933. Within a year the president of Nicaragua and his nephew, the new strong man, Anastasio Somoza, arranged for Sandino's murder. What the rise of the Somoza dynasty might mean for the next fifty years no one could foresee, but the United States could honestly claim in 1933 that nowhere in Central America was it represented by military forces, and the new president broadcasting his program of the "Good Neighbor" could be inaugurated in March 1933 with clean decks.

The Good Neighbor Years

In December 1933 the Seventh International Conference of American States convened in Montevideo, Uruguay. Secretary of State Cordell Hull represented the United States and in an informal, low-key manner outlined the new policy of the Franklin D. Roosevelt administration toward Latin America. Promising programs of lower tariffs, reciprocal trade agreements, and investment aid, Hull greatly reduced tensions in the Caribbean by voting to accept with only slight demurral a convention that denounced the right of states "to intervene in the internal or external affairs of another." All of Latin America praised the vote, and nothing in decades was to improve relations between the United States and Central America more than this acquiescence on the part of the Roosevelt government. (The only uninvited Yankee presence in Central America was a customs collector in Nicaragua—and he departed when the final guaranteed loans were paid off in 1944.[17]) Roosevelt emphasized his determination to continue the non-intervention policy by personally attending the Buenos Aires conference of 1936, which condemned intervention in an even stronger convention.

How were these promises translated into action during the twelve years of the Good Neighbor? Cuba, Bolivia, Mexico, Haiti, the Dominican Republic, and Panama all produced critical problems which in an earlier day might have brought military response from the

United States; in each instance Roosevelt either avoided the threat of the use of force or eliminated an existing American presence by cutting old strings. In Central America no very serious matter arose to disturb the semi-wartime posture that the administration assumed before 1941. After Pearl Harbor the five Central American republics demonstrated the success of Roosevelt's new program by all declaring war upon the Axis nations immediately (Costa Rica's congress performing that action even before the United States did), and on January 1, 1942, they all signed the United Nations Declaration. They played minimal roles in World War II but made maximum efforts to expand their contribution of foods and other raw materials to the larger nations doing the fighting, and in its turn U.S. policy supported the continuation of regular trade patterns to reduce economic conflict that could lead to social distress. For example, badly needed as ships were for military purposes in Europe, the United States permitted the major fruit companies to lease their own ships back again from the government in order to keep Central American nations' economies reasonably stable.

Yet there were signs of internal distress in Central America as the war drew to a close. In Costa Rica old parties fell into disfavor, and new, more socially oriented groups took over under names such as Social Democrats, Democrats, and National Republicans. Communist and anti-Communist charges became popular when progressive labor code and social security systems were enacted in 1943. General strikes in El Salvador brought the resignation of the old despot General Hernández Martínez (1931–1944). In Honduras Tiburcio Carías Andino held on from 1932 to 1948, also resigning in the midst of demands for social reform and new contracts with the American banana companies, though little real change took place. Guatemala's Jorge Ubico y Castañeda (1931–1944) destroyed the Communist party early in his administration and built the economy with ruthless efficiency, but he too faced demands for reform, and a strike of students ended his career. Only in Nicaragua did change not appear to be on the horizon as Anastasio Somoza prepared to turn his dictatorship into a dynasty.

While these dictators held sway, the usual rhetoric for a federation stayed silent, but as they were swept out of office, the old dream reawakened. In 1945 the new presidents of Guatemala and El Salvador announced the complete merger of their two nations, a meaningless change that endured less than six months, even after the two asked for the adherence to their plan by the other three presidents as a 125th birthday celebration.

Radical influence in social reform expressed itself most clearly in Costa Rica and Guatemala in the postwar era. In usually quiet Costa Rica, fighting broke out as a consequence of the 1948 election. Otilio Ulate appeared to have won, but his victory was nullified by a congress dominated by his opponent, Rafael Angel Calderón Guardia, who drew support not only from the Communists but also from Nicaragua's ruler, Anastasio Somoza. Protecting Ulate was a junta managed by José Figueres Ferrer, who fought off the Nicaraguans, outlawed the Communist party, and turned the presidency over to Ulate. Subsequently Figueres was to serve as president in his own right and make a rather loud splash in Central American politics for the next three decades.

In Guatemala social reform moved further to the left than elsewhere in Central America. After the long Ubico dictatorship many classes of Guatemalans sought major change, and this was promised them by Dr. Juan José Arévalo, who took office in 1945. With nowhere else to go, labor had joined the Communist leadership in helping Arévalo get elected, but traditional groups resisted, and his administration was marked by a score of rebellions. The split became more marked when Arévalo touted a cabinet member, Jacobo Arbenz, for his successor. With government help Arbenz won easily and hastened the radicalization of the nation. Russian ties were greatly increased, labor unions spearheaded a drive on anti-Communists, threats were made to arm the unions at the expense of the army, and a sweeping program of agrarian reform was undertaken.

Fear of the growing presence of a Russian satellite in Central America caused the Dwight D. Eisenhower administration great concern, and when in 1954 Guatemala began to receive arms from Czechoslovakia, the American government determined to help unseat Arbenz.[18] The task proved easy. The archbishop had already called for Arbenz's overthrow, and the army had no loyalty for him. Through the Central Intelligence Agency the United States armed and organized the substantial opposition to Arbenz, Guatemalan exiles marched with little resistance upon the government, and Arbenz fled his country. Revolution in Guatemala was not dead but sidetracked and modified, and the old groups were back in control.

Perhaps more serious than another Central American barracks revolt was the termination of the policy of nonintervention, the Eisenhower action being the first exception to the Roosevelt promise made in 1933. Although a covert action, the role of the CIA was soon revealed by American writers. The action proved a jarring disillusionment for those Americans who thought the old days had ended. It also persuaded Latin Americans that the CIA could be behind every adverse action in their lives, from soccer losses to hurricanes.

Economic Troubles in the Region

Intervention may come and go, but economic solutions to Central America's political problem never quite disappear. Hardly had Arbenz left Guatemala before a United Nations agency, the Economic Commission for Latin America, began seeking new approaches to the perennial question. With assistance from the Organization of American States, ECLA suggested that Central America might learn from the European integration efforts after World War II. ECLA concluded that Central America's heavy reliance on exporting raw materials and agricultural products to the developed world was resulting in a worsening of the terms of trade—purchasing a tractor in 1960 cost twice as many bags of coffee as in 1950, for example—and compared with the developed world Central America was going backward. The solution, said ECLA, was to find greater markets for Central American industry by creating a market of the whole region. Given Central America's fondness for unification plans, a Central American common market received much enthusiasm.

The basic treaty was signed in Managua in 1960, and simple goals were immediately achieved. Within seven years, common tariffs on goods from outside Central America applied to 98 percent of the goods the region imported, and tariffs had been abolished on 95 percent of goods traded within Central America. Special legislation protected infant or "integrated" industries in each of the five states, and a Central American bank functioned as did a clearinghouse. By 1970 zone trade increased nine times. All weaknesses had not been eliminated, and a true common market had not been achieved, but Central America had a functioning customs union that was beginning to attack the tougher questions, when war broke out again.

This 1969 struggle, known as the Soccer War because it began while the states of Honduras and El Salvador vied bitterly and indecently with each other for a spot in the finals of the World Cup the next year, crippled the common market. The causes include an old boundary dispute, heavy migration of Salvadorans into Honduras, the misuse of these people as tools in a Honduran land reform program, internal policies, the soccer matches—the list can go on. The official war lasted four days, but casualties proved very heavy, and the common market nearly died with them. The peace treaty was not signed until 1980, and many issues remained unaddressed.[19]

Some benefits of the common market survive. Inter-American

Development Bank reports show that between 1961 and 1981 every Central American nation markedly reduced its imports from the United States and Western Europe and turned instead to the region and the rest of Latin America for goods at much better terms of trade; Central American exports followed the identical pattern.[20]

Political Instability

But by the late 1970s Central America's cup had overrun again. El Salvador had not yet recovered from its "victory" in the Honduran war when it suffered the trauma of a bitterly contested and fraudulent presidential election. More than 100,000 Salvadorans returned home from their lost lands in Honduras to join 2 million peasants without land who faced a stronger military-oligarchy combination than ever before. The oppressed turned to their only remaining weapon, guerrilla warfare. El Salvador has suffered from frightful civil strife ever since, with no sign of abatement; more than 10,000 persons were killed in 1981 alone, it is estimated.

The so-called Sandinista opposition to the Somoza regime in Nicaragua began achieving minor successes in the 1960s. When the Jimmy Carter administration attacked the civil rights record of that government and then in 1978 halted the sale of military equipment to Nicaragua, the Anastasio Somoza Debayle government could no longer resist. He resigned in 1979, and the Sandinistas took over. The price of 50,000 dead and $5 billion in damage did not include the vast adjustments and tensions that accompanied the initiation of a radical government into the Somoza fiefdom.

Guatemala, too, is governed by violence. This state of siege may be described as something less than civil war, but kidnapping, murder, and highly organized but often promiscuous assassination are commonplace. Perhaps 20,000 Guatemalans have been killed in this fashion in twenty years. Even the formerly segregated Indians have been brought into the conflict as targets of the left and the right.

Supported by the United States as an outpost of its hemispheric defense against communism, Honduras peacefully elected its first civilian president in eighteen years in 1981. It found itself increasingly caught up in the neighbors' troubles as exiles of all classes sought asylum in Honduras while planning their military return to the home country, decidedly not a new development in Central America.

As usual Costa Rica kept its composure while the rest of the region tried to destroy itself, but like the others Costa Rica had been badly crippled by the staggering inflation in energy costs during the 1970s, and in the next decade learned the piper's charges. International lending agencies viewed the nation as nearly bankrupt and insisted upon a chilling austerity before granting relief from the crushing debts burden. Additionally, the wars next door had their fallout, and Costa Rica suffered from its reputation as a hospitable nation when thousands of Nicaraguan, Guatemalan, and Salvadoran refugees entered the land without depositing their hatreds at the border.

It should be added that a new Central American republic was born; the former British colony called British Honduras became independent on September 21, 1981, with no pain except a fear of a Guatemalan *Anschluss*, against which contingency British troops still remained in Belize.

Central America has always been of concern to the United States, but never before the 1970s did the region so thoroughly and continually occupy a place in the attention of the American government and the American people. The situation threatened to divide the Americans, too, between those who would give vast military assistance to any anti-Communist government and those who were opposed to violators of the civil rights standards irrespective of politics.

To some observers Central America provides a view of the world under a microscope. If that is true, the world's immediate future never appeared more obscure. Back in 1821 some of the Central American villages voted to join Iturbide's Mexican empire "until the clouds of the day rolled by" and the people could better see where they were going. More than a century and a half later one does not have to be a pessimist to wonder when those clouds will begin to vanish. In the past Central American states have often fought one another bitterly, but never have the struggles *within* states been so hateful as today. No matter whom one blames for blood baths in Guatemala and El Salvador today, the ultimate fact is that Guatemalans are killing Guatemalans and Salvadorans are killing Salvadorans.

Only slight change has occurred in the major themes of these states. Personalism in the presidency has clearly declined, at least for the moment. But the economic conditions have improved little this century; vast numbers of Central Americans still reside on the doorstep of starvation, as they peer in at great wealth. Foreign nations are less overt in their intervention than before, but they are still potent. Costa Rica still tries to protect its sacred isolationism, while providing asylum for all, a juggling act supreme. Meanwhile, the centralizing, centripetal forces struggle to hold to an ideal that somehow has yet to lose itself entirely to the fragmenting, centrifugal provinces. How long can they continue to hold out against each other?

Notes

1. Only occasionally has Panama—as Spanish province or independent republic—been considered a part of Central America, and it has played only a small role in the internal affairs of the region. It will therefore not be treated in this chapter as one of the Central American nations.

2. Although some parallel with the U.S. federalist issue of the late eighteenth century is obvious, Central American "federalists" sought a government that might more properly be called a confederation.

3. Salvador Mendieta, *La nacionalidad y el Partido Unionista Centroamericana* (San José, C.R., 1905), p. 46.

4. One authority concludes that not the constitution but weak leadership's inability to enforce it allowed the states to separate; see Ralph Lee Woodward, Jr., *Central America: A Nation Divided* (New York: Oxford University Press, 1976), p. 93.

5. This narrative of early Central America is based on the accounts of Thomas L. Karnes, *The Failure of Union: Central America, 1824–1960* (Chapel Hill: University of North Carolina Press, 1961), chaps. 3 and 4, and Woodward, *Central America*, passim.

6. The fascinating career of Frederick Chatfield (in Central America from 1834 to 1852) is described in Mario Rodríguez, *A Palmerstonian Diplomat in Central America* (Tucson: University of Arizona Press, 1964).

7. Stephens's articles and the sketches made by his English companion Frederick Catherwood first publicized in modern times the glories of the Mayan civilization for the outside world. John Lloyd Stephens, *Incidents of Travel in Central America, Chiapas and Yucatan*, 2 vols. (New York: Harper Brothers, 1841).

8. Woodward, *Central America*, pp. 92–112; Dana G. Munro, *The Five Republics of Central America* (New York: Russell and Russell, 1918), pp. 24–32; Rodríguez, *Palmerstonian Diplomat*, pp. 151–56; Rodrigo Facio, *Trayectorio y crisis de la Federación Centroamericana* (San José, C.R.: Imprenta Nacional, 1949), pp. 59–85; Alejandro Marure, *Bosquejo histórico de las revoluciones de Centro-America* (Guatemala City: Tipografía de "El Progreso," 1877), pp. 125–91; Karnes, *Failure of Union*, pp. 90–95.

9. Again it is tempting to refer to the Founding Fathers, who met in 1786 at Annapolis, we have been told, "to take into consideration the trade of the United States." See Rodríguez, *Palmerstonian Diplomat*, p. 149, for the best available summary of the federal-state tax question.

10. Joseph B. Lockey describes this series of failures in "Diplomatic Futility," *Hispanic American Historical Review*, vol. 10 (August 1930), pp. 265–94.

11. The relationship of Central American development, foreign enterprise, and the philosophy of positivism is best analyzed in Woodward, *Central America*, pp. 151–75. Watt Stewart, *Keith and Costa Rica* (Albuquerque: University of

New Mexico Press, 1964), describes the building of the railroad from the central highlands to the Costa Rican coast.

12. For the diplomacy and construction of the canal the most thorough and readable account is David McCullough's, *The Path between the Seas* (New York: Simon and Schuster, 1977).

13. James D. Richardson, ed., *A Compilation of the Messages and Papers of the Presidents*, vol. 15 (Washington, D.C., 1918 ed.), pp. 6894–930.

14. Philip M. Brown, "American Diplomacy in Central America," *American Political Science Review*, vol. 6 (Supp., 1912), and Manley O. Hudson, "The Central American Court of Justice," *American Journal of International Law*, vol. 26 (October 1932), reflected some of the early enthusiasm for the court.

15. Unfortunately, while Washington considered the Bryan-Chamorro Treaty important enough to risk destruction of the Court of Justice, nothing came from the treaty. No Nicaraguan canal has yet been built; by mutual agreement the two governments terminated the treaty in 1971.

16. Dana G. Munro, *The U.S. and the Caribbean Republics, 1921–1933* (Princeton, N.J.: Princeton University Press, 1974), pp. 116–26.

17. Federico Gil, *Latin American–United States Relations* (New York: Harcourt Brace Jovanovich, 1971), p. 163.

18. Richard H. Immerman, *The CIA in Guatemala* (Austin: University of Texas Press, 1982), is the most recent and best-documented study of this episode. Immerman sees no conspiracy to save United Fruit but concludes that Eisenhower's fear of communism coincided with United's interests (pp. 123–27).

19. Thomas P. Anderson, *The War of the Dispossessed* (Lincoln: University of Nebraska Press, 1981), pp. 167–75.

20. *Annual Reports, 1981*. Inter-American Development Bank.

3

Setting the Stage for Rebellion: Economics and Politics in Central America's Past

GARY W. WYNIA

Explanations for the current political conflicts in Central America are plentiful, but selecting among them is no simple task. Can we say with confidence, for example, that poverty has been the primary cause of popular revolt? Or was political repression responsible? And what about the region's domination for over a century by the United States: Has resentment of American penetration finally caused entire nations to rise up against their oppressor? Each of these explanations is quite plausible, as are many others, yet none by itself is all that satisfying. To begin with, no matter how hard we search for a single cause of political rebellion, we always discover that there was more than one, whether the case under study is that of France, China, Cuba, or some other country. There is no reason to believe it is any simpler in Central America. Second is the fact that not all of the Central American nations have responded in the same way to what appears to be similar conditions. Obviously several things come to-gether, often in different ways, to structure a nation's politics.

If we are to sort out the forces at work in Central America, a little more homework is necessary. One of our assignments would have to include a closer look at the region's recent past, if only to comprehend the choices that were made and evaded by the people who have run things in these five countries. Economic deprivation, political repres-sion, and popular revolt are not new to Central America. Political elites, native and foreign technocrats, businessmen, labor leaders, party politicians, and military officers have been dealing with them in one way or another for several decades. Their record is not very im-pressive, but their efforts cannot be ignored if we are to understand today's events.

Not too long ago Central America became the laboratory for an ambitious experiment in economic development. Several policy innovations, most of them authored by teams from regional agencies and financially backed by the U.S. government, were tried in order to promote economic growth within the region. Today it is fashionable to dismiss the entire effort as ineffectual. Although national economies did grow, income disparities also increased, and the region's welfare remained tied to the sale of its agricultural goods in the international marketplace. Moreover, according to some observers, economic innovations designed to advance the region's development enriched foreigners who invested in the region more than did the Central Americans themselves. In the words of its critics, the experiment was "a phony one."[1] To a certain degree they are correct; there was no dramatic change, and most people were little affected by what was accomplished. But to dismiss it all so categorically ignores the fact that after 1950 much did change within Central America, some of it intended by those who designed its development programs, but much of it unplanned yet unavoidable given the forces at work.

It is worth taking a moment to review what actually happened, focusing primarily on the development efforts of Central American governments during the 1960s and how they contributed to social changes that complicated the lives of those who governed the five nations and the traditional elites who back them. The process of change was neither simple nor linear, following a direct progression from one intended innovation to another. Several forces were at work, some of them complementary and others not closely related at all.

The Central American Experiment

Central Americans did not follow suit when Mexico and several of the South American countries turned to import substitution industrialization in response to world depression in the 1930s. Instead, its leaders clung to the export of cash crops and traditional ways of doing things. Nor did they respond to inevitable social protests during hard times with innovative politics, such as the populism practiced in Brazil and Argentina or the reformism of President Lázaro Cárdenas in Mexico. Instead they dealt with social protest as harshly as they always had in order to preserve their privileges. A decade later their conservatism seemed vindicated, for after World War II, the region's economic fortunes improved again as the price of coffee trebled between 1945 and 1954.

Nevertheless dissatisfaction with the structure of the Central American economies and their external vulnerability grew, especially among a new generation of economists and businessmen returning from study abroad. Like their colleagues in South America two decades before, they argued that the export orientation of their economies was impeding their overall economic development. The export sector, producing for a world market, had little incentive to invest earnings in production for the domestic market. Such incentives did not develop because profit and productivity increases, improved management and labor skills, and other factors conducive to economic growth remained highly concentrated in the export sector. But little reform seemed possible at the time, given the distribution of economic and political power favoring the minority of commercial farmers who were content to import the manufactured goods they needed from abroad. For the most part they owned and operated large plantations that produced coffee, cotton, and sugar for export using the cheap labor of a poor rural population. The system worked quite well for Central American producers, and, understandably, they were not receptive to any innovations in economic strategy that might upset the economic order.[2]

At first it seemed that the region's landowning elites had little to fear. In no Central American country did import substitution industrialization appear to be even remotely feasible. In fact nothing seemed right for industrialization in the early 1950s. To begin with, the expansion of existing industry offered few good prospects. Characterized by excess capacity and inefficient production, it consisted primarily of the processing of agricultural products. Since these products were similar throughout the region, each country tended to support the same type of uncompetitive industries in protected national markets. Even more constraining was the small size of national markets. In the mid-1950s the average per capita income in the five countries was $255, ranging from a high of $353 in Costa Rica to a low of $198 in Honduras. Moreover, as a unit the region's 12 million people had even less purchasing power than the city of San Francisco. Clearly no significant industrialization could be achieved in separate national markets.[3]

Central America had two options: It could do nothing or it could try to overcome the small size of its national markets. In the past inertia would have guaranteed the selection of the first option, but this time the advocates of change were ready to offer a painless way of pursuing the second. They were prepared primarily because others had already done their homework for them.

The United Nations Economic Commission for Latin America had since its creation in 1949 busied itself with looking for ways to accelerate economic development in Latin America and to reduce the region's vulnerability to external economic forces. Among its proposals was the notion of increasing the size of markets through the use of regional economic integration, an idea popular in other parts of the world as well as Latin America after the war. Studies by ECLA concluded that though the potential combined market of the five countries would not permit the development of large industrial complexes or the producton of heavy machinery, it would be sufficient to sustain investment in the manufacturing of some intermediate and most consumer goods, including such things as petroleum derivatives, tires, fertilizers, insecticides, glass containers, copper wire, and light bulbs. And once these industries had established themselves, the commission argued, increased purchasing power would stimulate the growth of others.[4] The idea intrigued Central American leaders who were willing to consider new ways to promote economic growth as long as they did not upset or undermine the power of commercial agriculture and the rural elites to whom presidents were beholden for their political power.

Economic integration in Central America was designed, organized, and initially financed by the people of ECLA. When they completed their work, the U.S. government, as part of its foreign assistance efforts after 1958, stepped in with enough funds to finance the Central American Common Market Secretariat, start a regional development bank, and, with the help of the Inter-American Development Bank, aid the completion of projects in each country aimed at improving the region's infrastructure. And most important politically, at the beginning controversial and divisive issues were dropped from the integration agenda. Farm policy was ignored, as were labor issues; instead, the creation of a free trade area designed primarily to promote new investment in industry became the sole objective.

Formal integration began slowly, but once some trust had been established, its creation accelerated at a very rapid pace. It began in the early 1950s when several bilateral treaties aimed at increasing intraregional trade were signed. Each was of short duration but provided for the creation of free trade arrangements for specified products and the future inclusion of new products through negotiation. A second plateau was reached in 1958 with the signing of the Multilateral Free Trade and Economic Integration Treaty, which extended the existing trade agreements and committed its signers to the creation of a free trade area within ten years. But the most important advancement came two years later in 1960 with the signing of the General Treaty of Central American Economic Integration, by Guatemala, El Salvador, Honduras, and Nicaragua, with Costa Rica joining in 1962. Under the General Treaty all but a few specified items were to be

TABLE 3-1

CENTRAL AMERICA: SHARE OF MANUFACTURING IN GROSS DOMESTIC PRODUCT,
1960, 1970, 1980
(percent)

	1960	1970	1980
Costa Rica	14.2	18.6	22.2
El Salvador	14.5	18.3	15.7
Guatemala	12.9	15.8	16.7
Honduras	12.0	14.2	17.0
Nicaragua	15.6	23.0	24.3
Latin America (average)	21.7	24.6	25.8

SOURCE: Inter-American Development Bank, *Economic and Social Progress in Latin America: 1980–1981*, p. 26.

traded freely within a period of five years. It was trade per se, rather than the distribution of its benefits, that preoccupied the treaty's signers. Potentially controversial issues—such as what to do if new investments were concentrated in only one or two countries—were ignored for the moment to ease agreement on the market's creation; such issues would, however, plague the market a decade later when disparities in integration's benefits caused a rebellion by the disadvantaged Hondurans.[5]

Integration's initial effects on trade were impressive. The volume of intraregional trade increased substantially, with imports from within the region as a proportion of total imports rising from 6 percent in 1960 to 24 percent in 1970. Manufacturing also grew, its share of the gross domestic product rising by as much as 47 percent in Nicaragua and 30 percent in Costa Rica and El Salvador, compared with 13 percent in Latin America as a whole during the 1960s. (See table 3-1.) It is also estimated that integration added 150,000 new jobs, or about a 14 percent increase in the labor force between 1958 and 1972.[6]

North American firms supplied most of the investment, increasing their total in the region from $389 million in 1959 to $677 million by 1977. Corporations that had previously exported to Central America set up operations there to avoid the Central American Common Market's high external tariffs, acquiring the assets of local companies where possible or starting new operations where necessary. For the most part they were assembly operations, putting together materials that were brought from outside the region, such as cosmetics, pharmaceuticals, chemicals, and home products. By the mid-1970s an estimated 1,458 North American firms had made investments in the region, among them many of the companies listed in the Fortune 500.[7]

When viewed in aggregate terms for the region as a whole, the contributions of regional integration to Central American economic growth are impressive, though clearly integration was not the only thing that kept growth up during the 1960s. But the experiment was never as secure as its creators had claimed. Before long the issues that its founders had avoided began to haunt it, and gradually they tore it apart. Most prominent was the question of the inequitable distribution of foreign investments among the five countries. Not surprisingly, investments clustered where infrastructures were already strong and where labor was accessible, namely, everywhere but Honduras. The Hondurans fought back, however, first threatening to leave the market unless they were given special treatment, and then, in 1971, withdrawing from the CACM until some of their grievances were met. But they were not alone. Eventually everyone protested against one inequity or another, forcing continual renegotiation of agreements from 1971 onward that led to new restrictions on trade and the fixing of quotas on the export of textiles, footwear, and clothing. Other problems also arose, the most crucial being a war between Honduras and El Salvador in 1969 that disrupted diplomatic relations between the two nations for almost a decade. Although the 1970s ended with the shell of the CACM in place, few were optimistic about its future. Typical of the assessments made at the time was the annual CACM Secretariat report, which somberly concluded in 1980 that

> The experience of the past decade, to go back no further, clearly demonstrated that the almost complete coverage of the (free-trade) zone does not of itself constitute a condition to satisfy the interests and aspiration of all participants. To the foregoing must be added the fact that recent events in the region force us to believe that incompatibilities may appear between unrestricted free trade and the real capacities of the various countries to operate under a system of this kind.[8]

In other words, it was not working any more. Its dismal performance, though disappointing to its creators, should not have been much of a surprise, however. One only need recall that free trade had been tried because it seemed to offer such an easy and painless route to national development. Presidents were told that little would be required of them during its implementation; a new generation of technocrats would run it for them, foreigners would finance it, and the private sector would eagerly take advantage of it. No wonder they welcomed it after decades of holding the line against industrialization. But hidden beneath the excitement of free trade were the interests of five very separate nations who, though appearing at long last to have rediscovered the virtues of regional cooperation preached long ago by their founding fathers, were still rivals in a mismatched competition for investment and development.

As an observer of the effort concluded a decade after its creation:

> The avoidance of "high" costs that characterized the Central American integrative experience affected the gradual emergence of a larger political entity among the participants. Instead of learning to upgrade the common interest, the members learned to put in practice those measures whose economic consequences could be lessened by foreign assistance and that, consequently, demanded a minimum of sacrifices from them. Instead of the gradual transfer of expectations to a larger entity, each participant pursued the satisfaction of his individual interests by means of very uncooperative methods, such as retaliatory measures against its partners or the zealous protection of its national produce from regional competition.[9]

The Price of Change

Whatever their shortcomings, integration and industrialization left their marks on the region. The fundamental features of Central American life did not change significantly to be sure, but some things were different after 1970, and the region's elites spent much of their time trying to deal with them. Anyone familiar with Central America in the 1950s who returned two decades later would have seen the difference immediately. There were several hundred small industries, most of them foreign owned, many more native entrepreneurs, and a small but growing industrial work force. The region's demographics had also changed. In fact, the population had nearly doubled in three decades, and by 1980 almost 45 percent of the population lived in towns and cities compared with only 24 percent living in such areas in 1950. (See table 3-2.)

As might be expected, social structures changed more during this period than at any time since independence. The mechanization of agriculture forced thousands off the land, a middle class of sorts developed, many more people than before attended universities, and economic elites became a little more diverse in their interests and less united on economic issues. As one Central American observed,

TABLE 3-2
CENTRAL AMERICA: POPULATION GROWTH, 1960–1981

	Total (millions)		Annual Average Growth (percent)	
	1960	1981	1960–1970	1970–1981
Costa Rica	1.3	2.3	2.6	2.8
El Salvador	2.4	5.0	3.0	3.0
Guatemala	4.0	7.2	3.0	2.9
Honduras	1.9	3.8	3.1	3.2
Nicaragua	1.4	2.5	2.4	2.4

SOURCE: Inter-American Development Bank, *Economic and Social Progress in Latin America: 1980–1981*, p. 395.

a modest "jet set" made its debut in the area, and something of a capitalist "take-off" seemed to be in the making. Agricultural producers followed suit, and by the end of the 1960s, regional chambers of commerce and agricultural and industrial production organizations (e.g., sugar, cotton, coffee, etc.) became active. The region's governments faced a new phenomenon: that of national and regional pressure groups, which were to play an increasing role in years to come.[10]

If new entrepreneurial elites made the lives of Central American leaders more complicated, it was the growth of organized labor that made the lives of both government and business difficult. The composition of the labor force was altered by industrialization and urbanization. In the 1950s about 65 percent of the economically active population lived off agriculture, but by 1980 it had dropped to 50 percent (28 percent in Costa Rica). Moreover, the percentage of the work force employed in industry increased from about 10 percent in the 1950s to almost 20 percent by 1980. Employment in the service sector, not surprisingly, grew even more rapidly, employing 30 percent of the work force by 1980.[11] What to do with a larger and more demanding work force preoccupied the region's conservative entrepreneurs and governments during the 1970s.

Predictably they tried to deal with labor paternalistically using both carrot and stick to discourage unionization; governments, for example, built entertainment and sports facilities which they turned over to employers' organizations for use by their employees. At the same time, unions were seldom allowed to disrupt important economic activities or exercise much political influence. The contrast between the behavior of organized labor in Central America and that of its peers in Chile or Argentina was striking; in the latter it became a major fact of economic and political life, often restricted in its activities but never completely dominated, whereas in Central America it was still treated as a child who required close supervision by strict parents. Not until the 1970s did it begin to break the noose placed around its neck, but even then its conquests came slowly.

Perhaps most important politically was the emergence of a small but assertive middle class and with it a new generation of university graduates who had developed their own ideas about improving the quality of economic and political life in their countries. Most settled for personal enrichment in business, but many chose to assert themselves politically, first as student activists and later by forming Social and Christian Democratic parties pledged to the democratization of their autocratic political systems and to economic reform. Some actually asserted themselves as early as the 1940s when José Figueres and his Liberación Nacional party created a constitutional regime in Costa Rica that still survives, and President Juan José Arévalo and Jacobo Arbenz in Guatemala established a popularly elected reformist regime whose life was ended abruptly by Guatemalan conservatives aided by the Central Intelligence Agency in 1954.[12] But it was not until the 1970s that the democratic politicians laid down their most powerful challenges to autocratic government in El Salvador, Guatemala, and Nicaragua. And it was only after they had tried and been resisted by electoral fraud and the force of arms by those in power, that some among them chose to support the cause of armed rebellion.

It would seem that what has occurred in Central America during the past few years might have been predictable a decade ago. But when one looks back, one discovers that the forecasters were by no means certain that revolt and internal war awaited the region. Some came away from Central America in the 1960s impressed by how well it was progressing, claiming that traditional values were swiftly giving way to modern ones under the pressure of innovation and industrialization. Ahead lay more change and the gradual transformation of entire societies economically, socially, and perhaps even politically, they argued. Indeed, one need only read the optimistic forecasts made during the early 1960s by the people responsible for administering programs like those of the Alliance for Progress to be reminded of how hopeful they were. Regional integration was in place, development plans seemed manageable given the small size of each country, and commercial elites appeared quite responsive to innovation and expansion.

There were, at the same time, those who were less optimistic and who warned that modernization would not be so easy, first, because of elite opposition to the kinds of structural changes believed essential for the promotion of sustained economic development and, second, because rigid autocratic governments showed no sign of being able to adapt to the increased economic and political demands that were placed on them.[13] And, of course, there were still others who predicted that regardless of how well development programs worked and how adaptable political institutions were, political rebellion could not be prevented, since incremental modernization could in no way overcome the popular hostility to authorities who had exploited and repressed their people for generations.

To some extent each prediction proved to be correct, at least partly. The values of many Central Americans did begin to change swiftly, and if one looked only at Costa Rica, one could find a steady, though economically bumpy, trail leading to many of the predicted consequences of modernization. One need only turn to El Salvador or Guatemala, however, to discover how people from the middle and working classes grew in numbers and asserted themselves politically, only to be denied participation because of the threat their moderate projects posed to those in power. Then there is Nicaragua, where a revolution occurred not just because of the pains of modernization but also because of popular reactions to increased repression.

Still there is more to what happened in the region than any of these provocative but simple theses suggest. Many things occurred during the 1970s, and we are now only beginning to sort out their effects. Of particular interest are the relative importance of the economic shocks the region suffered and the political conflicts that increased in number and in intensity in Nicaragua, Guatemala, and El Salvador, and how they might have been related. One wonders, for example, if political conflict increased primarily because the economic pie did not grow as rapidly as planned, causing discontent leading to protest and conflict, or whether economic conditions were of only marginal importance to those people who had other things on their mind when they expressed themselves through violent protests in the late 1970s. A brief look at economic conditions during the past decade will help sort some of this out.

The Decade of Disappointment

The region's economies did not do so badly during the 1970s if one looks only at national product growth rates. (See table 3-3.) Costa Rica, Guatemala, and Honduras were close to the Latin American

TABLE 3-3
CENTRAL AMERICA: ANNUAL VARIATIONS IN GROSS DOMESTIC PRODUCT,
1961–1980

	1961–1970	1971–1975	1978–1980
Costa Rica	6.0	6.1	5.2
El Salvador	5.7	5.5	3.7
Guatemala	5.5	5.6	5.7
Honduras	5.2	2.1	6.0
Nicaragua	7.0	5.6	−1.3
Latin America (average)	6.7	6.6	5.2

SOURCE: Inter-American Development Bank, *Economic and Social Progress in Latin America: 1980–1981*, p. 7.

average annual growth rate, El Salvador a little below, and Nicaragua significantly below, especially after 1977, primarily because of its internal war. But such data tell only part of the story. Although their economies grew at good rates, they were punished severely by two blows that were struck by outside forces. The first was the initial petroleum price increase made by the Organization of Petroleum Exporting Countries in 1973. Among other things, it caused domestic prices, which had seldom risen more than 1 or 2 percent a year in the past, to rise by 15 and 16 percent throughout the region in 1974 and 1975. And with higher inflation came a decline in real wages. To be sure, the burst of inflation was nothing compared to what was experienced in Argentina and Brazil, but it was enough to reduce the confidence of native entrepreneurs and foreign investors unaccustomed to such changes in price levels. Inflation was brought down again in 1977 and 1978, but in 1979 a new crisis occurred, one that was more severe than that experienced in 1973. It came in two stages: The first was another sharp increase in petroleum prices, and the second a world recession that drastically reduced prices for Central America's coffee, cotton, and sugar exports and brought economic growth to a halt by 1981. By the end of the decade the fuel bills of each country had increased astronomically, from a high of 1,150 percent in Guatemala to a low of 650 percent in Costa Rica (see table 3-4), causing heavy borrowing abroad at just the time income from raw product exports was declining, making the debt burden increasingly harder to handle.

External conditions were not the only causes of the region's suffering. Not to be overlooked are some of the particular problems that arose within individual countries. The worst was the earthquake that

TABLE 3-4
CENTRAL AMERICA: VALUE OF PETROLEUM IMPORTS, 1973, 1976, 1980
(millions of U.S. dollars)

	1973	1976	1980
Costa Rica	31.5	73.9	206.3
El Salvador	16.1	64.6	142.6
Guatemala	33.2	132.0	380.4
Honduras	26.0	53.8	170.1
Nicaragua	23.6	69.4	173.6

SOURCE: Inter-American Development Bank, *Economic and Social Progress in Latin America: 1980–1981*, p. 34.

hit Nicaragua in 1972, almost totally destroying the capital, Managua, leaving thousands homeless. The Nicaraguan economy never entirely recovered. To make matters worse, President Somoza's mishandling of relief funds and reconstruction efforts deeply divided the country's business community and ended cooperation between the public and private sectors until Somoza was overthrown in 1979.

When the 1980s began, the Central American economies were in worse shape financially than at any other time since the 1930s. But that fact, though significant, does not by itself tell us much about why the region's politics went the way they did. To be sure, one could plausibly argue that the deterioration in wages during the middle of the decade, which was marginally more severe in El Salvador and Nicaragua than in Costa Rica and Honduras, became a cause of popular unrest. It is indeed possible that the disappointments of those in the middle and urban working class over their own lack of economic progress grew in the 1970s, causing them to feel deprived unfairly and therefore to become more rebellious than would have been the case had economic growth been faster and new opportunities for investment and increased income greater.[14] The fact that labor movements had grown in size during the 1970s and were more demonstrative no doubt contributed to an increase of social conflict and a rise in repression in response. Moreover, once set in motion, the action-reaction cycle escalated, with increases both in the size of protests and in the ferocity of official responses to them, especially in Nicaragua and El Salvador. Yet as persuasive as this "relative deprivation" argument is, one cannot help but doubt that such conditions and attitudes were sufficient to cause revolution, especially when we learn how dissimilar public reactions to similar deteriorating conditions were elsewhere, such as in Mexico, Venezuela, and other countries in Latin America.

Politics: The Missing Link

Economic crises, demographic pressures, and unsatisfied expectations are part of the environment in which political rebellions occur. But they do not always cause some people to take up arms against authorities. There was, after all, only one revolution of the Nicaraguan variety during the 1970s. Moreover, Costa Rica and Honduras have remained relatively calm, even though economic conditions there were not remarkably better than in neighboring countries. Obviously something more than economic forces were at work.

To begin with, it is worth noting that guerrilla organizations had been operating in the region before 1970 but only gained political importance near the end of the decade. Rather than ask if economic conditions, structural or current, provoked rebellions, it seems wiser to examine more closely those who rebelled.

The guerrilla forces did not arise in a political vacuum but in societies governed by military and civilian elites who from the outset were frightened by the social and political consequences of the "cost-free" economic modernization programs begun in the 1960s and the demographic changes that occurred simultaneously. Space does not permit a review of each nation's politics during the 1970s, but one need only look briefly at the Somoza regime or the military officers who governed in El Salvador and Guatemala in the mid-1970s to understand the nature of the political problem. What they feared most were challenges either to their authority or to the existing economic order. Governing their nations became increasingly difficult after 1970 as more and more claims were made upon authorities by a more diverse business community and by increasingly assertive opposition political parties. In addition, labor unions and peasant organizations, many of which were encouraged by Roman Catholic clergy working within local communities, began to make their presence felt during the 1970s. With the exception of Costa Rica, the region's conservative political leadership was not ready for the kind of open competitive politics that their opponents demanded, nor were they prepared to deal peacefully with the many conflicts that arose between employer and employee, landowner and tenant farmer, political party leaders and the corrupt judiciaries and interior ministries that harassed and repressed them. It was frustration with this kind of rigidity at the top, with a leadership frightened by issues of social justice and political participation, that led many once compliant people to seek redress through more direct action.

It would be naive, however, to think that frustration with the way political authority is exercised always causes people to turn immediately to the force of arms. It is no secret that most of the Central Americans who have sought some kind of political renovation during the past twenty years have tried to gain it primarily through peaceful means. Their parties were the Christian Democratic ones in El Salvador and Guatemala, the Social Democratic party in El Salvador, and the Conservative party in Nicaragua. They were joined by thousands of students and many in the Catholic clergy. At first they took seriously the promises of open politics made to them by those in power (often made in lip-service responses to pressures from the United States) and tried to secure their entrance using electoral means, only to be denied it through the government's rigging of elections, intimidation of voters, and annulments of results.

One can only speculate about how all of the pieces of the rebellion puzzle fitted together in Nicaragua or how they will fit together in El Salvador and Guatemala. One piece which merits closer study, but which has been lost in the rush to study the ideological character of the contesting forces and rebellion's economic causes, is the role of young people, many of them of middle-class origins, in the political protests that have led to violence. In our eagerness to understand rebellion as a conflict of the masses with elites, we often exaggerate the part played by the masses in the struggle. Being the most vulnerable to repression and intimidation by the military and police, they are sometimes the least able to take up arms against authorities. Insurrections may involve the masses, but seldom more than a few of them, at least at the outset of the struggle. Fidel Castro's 26th of July movement in Cuba is a case in point. It was not a mass movement but a small guerrilla army that, because of its skill and Batista's ineptness, defeated a much larger army, and earned the gratitude of the vast majority of the Cuban people, who could not, by themselves, defeat Batista. Something similar has been happening in Central America.

In a provocative article written in 1982 about the war in El Salvador Mexican social critic Gabriel Zaid stressed the need to understand the frustrations of the sons and daughters of the Salvadoran middle class as we try to account for the rebellion against the country's ruling class. As university graduates who believed themselves to be sensitive to their nation's problems and aware of their social and economic causes, some among them believed that they were much better prepared to govern in the new age than those then in power. When they demanded that the doors at the top be opened to them, they met only obstruction by entrenched authorities threatened by their youthful idealism. Many held firm to their democratic beliefs, hoping to achieve reform peacefully, while others gave up in frustration after having seen election victories taken from them arbitrarily. For the latter the violent destruction of the existing order became the only way of getting their chance to govern. It seems, as Zaid argued, that "student guerrillas go to the country in order to return to the city; to gain the experience, the credentials, the access to power that one must have to change things. . . ."[15] What gains them a following is not the purity of their ideology or the consistency of their platforms but their ability to take the initiative against repressive authorities who sooner or later force everyone to take sides, if only as a means of personal survival. If they succeed, as did the Sandinistas in Nicaragua, they remain belligerent, never forgiving those whom they had to fight to the death in order to secure their right to lead.

One should not make too much of Zaid's observations, for the characterization of the region's guerrillas as power-hungry rebels from the middle class hardly captures the many motives and life histories of those involved in the struggle. But it is a necessary reminder of the importance that aggressive leadership and personal ambition play in the expression of political protest. Even when reasons for revolt are abundant and justification is strong, the aggrieved seldom act unless some among them stand up to lead them. Only when leaders and followers come together, as they did in Nicaragua in 1979, after years of futility and defeat, does rebellion finally occur.

Conclusions

Of necessity we must simplify what we observe, creating some kind of intellectual order so that we can separate the real causes of events from the spurious ones. Nowhere do we try harder with less satisfaction than in the study of political revolutions. Understanding the Central American experience is no exception.

Many things began to change in Central America after World War II. But even when combined over time, the changes were hardly far sweeping. Instead, as in most of Latin America, economic change came incrementally, affecting some people a great deal while bypassing others entirely. Many North Americans invested in the region's economies; intraregional commerce grew; bankers, traders, and industrialists became more numerous; and new life was given to a small but growing urban working class. The result was not an industrial revolution but the addition of new institutions to what remained primary product export economies still ruled by those whose power came from their control over commercial agriculture. What did change were not economic structures but the number and diversity of interests within the modern sector, and the competing demands they made on traditional authorities.

Some political regimes are more able than others to cope with the multiplication of economic and class interests. The Costa Ricans, for example, handled it with little difficulty because they had already created a political process capable of mediating among those who competed for official favor. None of the region's other regimes were as prepared to make room at the top for the newcomers, preferring instead to rely on the paternalistic ways of the past. Perhaps the most rigid was Somoza's operation in Nicaragua. After decades of making Nicaragua safe for its national business community and building an alliance between public and private capital that seemed to assure the regime's survival for decades, a very selfish Somoza drove businessmen into the opposition by his handling of the 1972 earthquake, giving the forces that sought his defeat a boost that they needed. Each national experience has been different, but if the countries' rulers shared anything, it was their preference for combat over negotiation and co-optation when challenged by anyone, be they Christian Democrats or Marxists.

Perhaps rebellions would have occurred in Central America had there been no regional integration, no enclave industrialization, no increase in urban population, and no growth of the middle and working classes. Rural discontent has always been high, resentment of U.S. domination great, and political frustration on the rise. We shall never know, of course. Yet one cannot help but wonder if economic modernization did not play some small part in setting the stage for rebellions against political dictatorship and economic injustice.

Notes

1. See, for example, Tom Barry, Beth Wood, and Deb Preusch, *Dollars and Dictators: A Guide to Central America* (Albuquerque, N.Mex.: Resources Center, 1982), pp. 32–44; also North American Congress on Latin America, *Report on the Americas*, vol. 14, no. 2 (March–April 1980), pp. 8–18.

2. Roger Hansen, *Central America: Regional Integration and Economic Development* (Washington, D.C.: National Planning Association, 1967), p. 10.

3. Ibid., p. 15.

4. Ibid.

5. For a summary of the formative years, see *Comercio exterior de Mexico* (April 1982), pp. 141–46. Also see Royce Q. Shaw, *Central America: Regional Integration and National Political Development* (Boulder, Colo.: Westview Press, 1978), chaps. 1–2.

6. William R. Cline and Enrique Delgado, eds., *Economic Integration in Central America* (Washington, D.C.: Brookings Institution, 1978), p. 397.

7. Barry et al., *Dollars and Dictators*, pp. 34–40.

8. Quoted in *Comercio exterior de Mexico* (April 1982), p. 143.

9. Issac Cohen Orantes, *Regional Integration in Central America* (Lexington, Mass.: Lexington Books, 1972), p. 84.

10. Francisco Villagran Kramer, "Central America in Transition: From the 1960's to the 1980's," Wilson Center Working Paper No. 90, 1981, p. 4.

11. Ibid., p. 16.

12. For an excellent discussion of the Guatemalan case, see Stephen Schlesinger and Stephen Kinzer, *Bitter Fruit* (New York: Anchor Books, 1982).

13. See, for example, Gary W. Wynia, *Politics and Planners: Economic Development Policy in Central America* (Madison: University of Wisconsin Press, 1972).

14. For an intriguing argument in support of the "relative deprivation" explanation of rebellion in Central America, see John Booth, "Toward Explaining Regional Crisis in Central America: Socioeconomic and Political Roots of Rebellion." Unpublished paper, available only on request from author, c/o Department of Political Science, University of Texas at San Antonio, Texas.

15. Gabriel Zaid, "Enemy Colleagues," *Dissent* (Winter 1982), p. 22.

4

The Development and Decline of the Central American City-State

ROLAND H. EBEL

Introduction

The current instability in Central America can be explained in a variety of ways. In fact, a good deal of the difficulty the United States is having in evolving a coherent foreign policy toward the area is that our understanding of what is happening there is marked by so many contradictory theories. For many, the problems there stem simply from an area-wide attempt by historically suppressed classes to throw off oppression and redress decades of social and economic injustice, while others would argue that these very classes are the unwilling victims of revolutionary agitators. For some, the primary explanation is the intervention of outside Communist forces, while others would stress the interventionist role of international capitalism. Some would emphasize the collapse of the area's postwar economy, particularly a slowing down of the economic growth engendered by the Central American Common Market (CACM), while others would view that very growth as producing severe economic and social dislocations in these societies. Some interpreters blame the recalcitrance of entrenched, reactionary elites, while others would explain things in terms of the disintegration of those elites.[1]

The obvious fact of the matter is that all of these explanations are partly correct and cannot be treated in isolation. What has been happening in the isthmus is that a particular type of political system which came into being some fifty years ago, namely, the Central American city-state, now either is disintegrating or is under severe challenge by disaffected groups. Whether it will totally collapse, recover, or take some new form will be decided by the internal and external political forces operating in the various countries.

The Central American city-state that began to emerge in the isthmus during the 1920s had three essential characteristics. First of all, it was a dual society in which modern economic and political life came to be overwhelmingly concentrated in a single urban center—usually the capital city. Yet the rural areas, which contained the bulk of the nation's population and natural resources, became a reservoir of labor and materiel for the urban center. Second, these urban centers, which not only contained the more privileged segments of the population but also had the greatest potential for modernization and growth, were protected from the masses and mass demands by their armed forces. Third, these modernizing urban centers were linked to each other and to the international economic and political system through the multinational corporations and such regional organizations as the CACM, the Central American Defense Council, the Central American Nutrition Institute, and the Regional Organization for Central America and Panama.

This combination of a modernized urban core, protected by the military and receiving economic and technical inputs from external industrial countries, coexisting with an underdeveloped periphery of peasants and townsfolk, produced the paradoxical mixture of stability and instability that characterized Central American politics until the late 1970s. On the one hand, these nations were subject to a seemingly endless succession of strikes, demonstrations, coups, and threatened coups. On the other hand, these polities were quite resistant to real social and economic change and evidenced a marked continuity in domestic policy and international posture.

The reason for this was that the power structure of the Central American city-state was composed of a finely balanced set of forces and mechanisms which, while subject to periodic disruption, nevertheless had an amazing self-righting capacity. The primary stabilizing elements of the system were a set of corporatively organized upper-sector groups which not only monopolized domestic production but were also capable of considerable growth through the absorption of capital, technology, and management expertise from abroad. These organizations were protected by personalistic links with the military, with elements of the leadership of the aspiring middle classes, and, to an extent, with the rural masses through village officials and through paternalistic relationships with the peons on the farms (*fincas*) and plantations.

The destabilizing elements were the emerging trade unions in the cities and the politicization of the only partly integrated lower-middle-class elements such as schoolteachers, students, technical personnel, and clerical workers. These groups, while benefiting from the growth

71

of the urban center, nevertheless often had a precarious existence depending on tax revenues and general economic growth for their livelihood. Any downturn could lead to the postponement or reduction of their salaries or future opportunities and thus radicalize this sector. Furthermore, to accommodate the aspirations of the lower middle sectors, higher education was expanded, thus increasing the competition for middle-class jobs. Ultimately the stability of the entire system rested on maintaining low levels of politicization among the rural and urban masses and maintaining sufficient economic opportunities in the city to absorb the more ambitious members of these groups.

The Central American city-state, stimulated by the Alliance for Progress and the Central American Common Market, reached the apogee of its development in the 1960s. A series of factors, however, including the breakup of the CACM, changes in the internal economic systems of these nations, the dramatic rise in oil prices with the resulting worldwide recession, and the political mobilization of the urban and rural lower classes have worked together to undermine the viability of these political systems. Insurrection and dictatorship have been the inevitable result.

The Development of the Central American City-State

Historical Factors. In one sense the six countries of the isthmus have always been city-states. The Spanish colonization pattern, which was really an extension to the New World of the patterns adopted during the reconquest of Spain from the Moors, was to establish cities as defensive sites and administrative centers from which to exploit the population and resources of the countryside. The Spanish conquistador and his descendants were colonizers, not settlers; and as such, they planted cities instead of scattered rural settlements or farm towns.[2] Thus, throughout the colonial period Central America was formally composed of a hierarchically arranged series of towns governed by successive levels of Spanish officials with Guatemala City as its capital. In practice, the combination of distance, natural barriers, and regional rivalries tended to make each administrative unit semi-autonomous, centered in its regional capital. In fact, the current national boundaries of the Central American states are largely those of the old colonial provincial jurisdictions under the Kingdom of Guatemala.

After independence from Spain (1823) the newly created United Provinces became a tenuous confederation of regional urban centers wracked by intense regional rivalry and internecine quarrels. The urban elites were neither sufficiently united nor strong enough to protect themselves from the rural caudillos; thus, between 1839 (the year of the breakup of the United Provinces of Central America) and 1920 the individual nations of the isthmus were dominated by essentially rural interests. The traditional Central American city-state had ceased to exist.

The modern Central American city-state can be dated from about 1920 when three of the six countries of the region (Panama, Nicaragua, and Costa Rica) had achieved sufficient modernization to reach a 10 percent level of urbanization; and all but Honduras had reached that plateau by 1930. Between 1930 and 1970 urbanization in the five traditional Central American states doubled from 11.3 to 23 percent of the total population, with the largest surge coming in the 1950s.

The modern Central American city-state can be said to have emerged in three broad stages. The period between 1870 and 1920 saw the development of export agriculture, particularly coffee. Urbanization was low; export agriculture earned sufficient income to satisfy the small elite and began to finance the internal improvements of these countries. The masses lived by subsistence agriculture and cottage industry and were essentially unpoliticized. Thus, domination of the political system was left to the Liberal caudillos who, with their retinue, emerged out of the ever-changing partisan and personalistic rivalries of the planter class. Although the capital city had always been the cultural center of these nations, political power was more widely dispersed geographically among localized segments of that class.

Commercial agriculture, however, carried within itself the germ of urbanization. The production and exportation of coffee and bananas, while centered in the countryside and relying on a rural work force, also required an infrastructure of warehouses, railroads, docks, and countinghouses. Thus, concentrations of clerical, technical, and manual workers began to build up in the urban centers associated with export agriculture. This, in turn, generated a corps of secondary businesses and social organizations designed to service the industry and its workers.

Between 1920 and 1940, the capital cities began to achieve a political and economic "critical mass" that would make them the keystone of the political system over the ensuing half-century. With the development of telecommunications, motorized transport, and a more professional military and bureaucratic establishment, these growing capital cities became more effective centers of political and governmental control.

By 1940 nascent import substitution industrialization, coupled with the expansion of educational, governmental, and commercial activity, produced a middle class of lawyers, doctors, teachers, students, engineers, and clerical workers which would strike for power in Guatemala and El Salvador in 1944, Costa Rica in 1948, and Honduras in 1957. These same developments, delayed for three decades by the particular nature of its power structure, finally emerged in Nicaragua in the 1970s.

The rise of the middle classes to power in the 1940s and their embrace of "populist" political goals put the final touches on the Central American city-state and gave it its particular characteristics. Oriented toward greater political and economic participation for the middle classes (that is, universal suffrage, regular elections, and the right to organize political parties and interest groups), Central American populism stimulated the formation of a multitude of middle- and lower-sector political organizations dedicated to articulating the demands of their supporters and capable of winning elections. This had a dual effect. On the one hand, because these groups were able to win elections by mobilizing the urban vote and generating other forms of mass support such as strikes and demonstrations, political systems historically oriented simply to providing benefits for the elite were forced to distribute more benefits to the urban populace—particularly to the middle classes who dominated the more democratic aspects of the political process. On the other hand, because the economies of these nations were weak and their distributive capacity was thereby limited, other groups felt compelled to develop their "power capabilities"[3] to offset the electoral power of the middle-class groups: the agribusiness elite to protect its traditional privileges and the urban lower classes (and, in some cases, rural workers) to achieve benefits not readily conceded by their middle-class allies. The weapons of the elite included investment and production decisions, lockouts, and the financing of political parties and military adventures; strikes and demonstrations were the weapons of the urban working class. Ultimately, these tactics degenerated into assassination, at one end of the political spectrum, and insurrection, at the other. Thus was created the political system so aptly described by Charles Anderson: a concatenation of urban-based power contenders threatening to use their power capabilities to influence each other and the state.[4]

Geo-economic Factors. Although often overlooked as an important socioecological variable, one of the major factors determining the kind of economic, political, and social structures likely to develop in a country is its size. To be specific, the smaller the country, the more concentrated its population and politico-economic power structure are likely to be. Given the fact that the independent nations of Central

America are, on the average, the size of a New England state, it is only natural that the segment of the population engaged in "modern" pursuits would tend to congregate in a single place.[5] Given the small size of these nations and the limited amount of diversity that countries the size of Maine or Massachusetts could logically support, the capital cities became the center of modern economic, social, technological, and intellectual life. The buses, trains, manufacturing plants, banks, shopping centers, insurance companies, universities, newspapers, theaters, political party headquarters, and military academies were invariably located there. Any person of talent and ambition wishing to participate in the modern sector was forced to migrate to the capital city or, at least, to one of the lesser urban centers. Thus, the metropolitan area generally grew and prospered at the expense of the rural periphery, and as long as it could absorb the more articulate and socially mobile segments of the rural areas, for a time at least it served as a political safety valve for discontent.

The mini-state also tended to produce the mini-economy. The fact that the Central American city-states were small economies with small populations greatly limited the size of their internal markets. This, in turn, severely limited the number of economic enterprises of any size that could successfully compete within their national economies. Thus, from the outset of import substitution industrialization in the 1920s, manufacturing tended to be lodged in the hands of the one or two enterprises within a given industry which, because of an early start or its relative efficiency, could survive in a restricted market. After World War II, when transnational corporations began to operate in these markets, their technological superiority further concentrated both the location and the control of the modern business sector. The capital cities naturally became the command center of these mini-economies.

For a while the economic, social, and political concentration in a single city had a positive symbiotic result. As the modernization of one urban sector advanced—usually with international support—this stimulated the development of other sectors. As economic growth provided new employment opportunities for the technocratic middle class, schools and universities were stimulated to expand both enrollments and course offerings. These institutions provided both consumers and employees for business and industry. As long as the urban centers could provide educational, economic, and professional opportunities for the most ambitious segments of the rural population, the potential leaders of rural revolutionary movements could, in effect, be co-opted by the city.

This particular type of socioeconomic structure, however, had po-

75

tential liabilities as well. To begin with, the fact that modern business activities—whether growing and marketing bananas, importing machine tools, or manufacturing pharmaceuticals—were concentrated in a small number of firms resulted in the Central American nations' becoming economically dependent on the success of a limited number of modern economic enterprises. This "internal dependency" was only further aggravated, after the creation of the CACM, by a growing "external dependency" brought about by the entry of sophisticated multinational corporations into the manufacturing, marketing, and export agriculture sectors of these nations.[6]

A second problem associated with these urban-based mini-economies was the fact that they were overwhelmingly export oriented. Those enterprises that were concerned with supplying primary products to the world market were acutely subject to its instability, while manufacturing, almost always of the import substitution variety, was inherently inelastic and greatly affected by decisions made in the industrial and financial capitals of the world. Thus, the entire socioeconomic structure of the urban-industrial sector of the Central American city-state was extremely fragile, a fact that produced a nagging sense of insecurity throughout the social structure.

These economies were also involved in a paradox in that general economic growth (as measured in gross domestic product) was considerable, while per capita economic growth was very low.[7] This meant that while general economic activity was increasing, these economies were incapable of producing any sizable surpluses. This intensified the resistance of the urban elites and middle sectors to any change in the political or economic power of the rapidly growing popular sectors which were being socially and politically mobilized by the economic development and modernization of the urban center itself, since any such change carried with it the threat of a redistribution of income and social opportunity.

Finally, the demographic (or "demopolitical") situation of these societies has to be considered. Population growth averaged 2.8 percent per year between 1960 and 1981. During the 1950s and 1960s, however, the economies of the urban centers were growing sufficiently fast to provide employment for the more ambitious and able of the rural migrants to the cities. The cities—particularly the capital cities—also offered other opportunities for social mobility and general well-being: education, hospital care, and a money income (as opposed to systems of barter and payment in kind characteristic of much of the economic relationships in the countryside).[8]

The viability and stability of the Central American city-state rested, to a considerable degree, on a delicate balance between low levels of social and political mobilization in the countryside and the ability of the urban centers to function as a safety valve for discontent. Throughout the 1950s and 1960s these social systems managed to maintain a tenuous balance between mass mobilization and urban capacity for social and economic absorption. For one thing, the traditional parochialism of village life, reinforced by patterns of patronalism and *compadrazgo*,[9] had a depoliticizing effect by creating hierarchies of respect, obedience, and social control extending from the urban centers into the countryside through the various levels of the political parties, governmental structures, plantations and *fincas*, and religious organizations.[10] Further, rural migrants to the cities often perpetuated these kinds of relationships by entering into patronalistic or clientalistic relationships with their employers. Finally, lower-class mobilization was retarded by the fact that the urban work force was, initially at least, widely dispersed among relatively small enterprises.[11] Where the work force was concentrated, as in factories, warehouses, railroads, etc., unionization and politicization took place much earlier. Ultimately, the spur to industrialization by the Central American Common Market also accelerated the politicization of the urban working class; and the increased commercialization and mechanization of agriculture in the late 1960s and 1970s, similarly stimulated by the CACM, increased the flow of migrants to the city. Both developments undermined the precarious demopolitical balance of the Central American city-state.

The Politics of the Central American City-State

The social, economic, and geo-demographic factors that gave rise to the city-state also produced the particular type of political system that marked these societies.[12] Simply put, in the Central American city-state national politics was essentially city politics, or more precisely, the politics of the capital city. That is, almost all of the relevant national political forces were concentrated in the capital city and interacted there. Because the political system was centered in the economically growing area of the country and was substantially shielded from rural and urban lower-class demands, it manifested a form of "stable instability" which, while giving rise to a seemingly unending series of coups and threatened coups, never succeeded in altering the power structure or general policy orientations of the government. Each new regime, whatever its political or ideological cast, followed essentially the same policies and maintained the same distribution of benefits as its predecessors. The current crisis in Central America is due to the fact that the stabilizing elements in these systems of governance are breaking down and the city-state is no longer as effectively shielded from rural and urban lower-class demands. If we are to attempt to comprehend the nature of the breakdown and something of the future of these societies, it is necessary to understand how these polities were structured and how they worked.

Political Structure and Organization. As the Central American city-states began to take their modern form in the late 1930s and early 1940s and changed from narrowly based "oligarchic republics" into more politically competitive "populist republics," both the newly emergent middle classes and the oligarchy (in both its old and its new forms)[13] were forced to create new types of political organization through which to press their claims and engage in the political struggle. This led to a veritable explosion of interest groups and political parties during the period between 1945 and 1960.[14] Although this development gave these political systems a superficial appearance of pluralistic democracy, they behaved in a way at variance with their counterparts in the more mature industrial democracies in the West.

To begin with, with the possible exception of Costa Rica and Panama, the Central American political structures tended to be interest-group dominant. That is, such powerful interest groups as the military, the Church, growers' associations, chambers of commerce, and the multinational corporations were generally older, more long-lived, and more powerful than almost any of the nations' political parties. This was due to a number of factors. For one thing, Central American interest groups were organized around the enduring interests of the society, whereas political parties were usually built around personalistic leaders or vague and transient ideological or historical symbols. Furthermore, because of the disparity in their financial base, political parties could not dispense the continuing rewards to their members that interest groups, with their greater economic and fiscal resources, could provide. Finally, interest groups were not as subject to defeat as were political parties. That is, the importance to the society of the activities they were engaged in gave them an enduring functional status that was not based on the constant variability of electoral popularity. In the Central American city-state it was these major interest groups that oversaw the production and marketing processes and, thus, generated the revenue that was collected by the government. Because of this, most of the economic interest groups were allowed a good deal of autonomy in the areas of concern to them and, when a new public policy was required, exercised considerable influence in those areas. Routine public business in a given policy area was conducted by negotiation between the interest group and the government agency responsible for that area. If matters could not be solved through routine negotiations, they were carried to the ministerial level. Matters of continuing dispute were ventilated in the congress and through the press. The president of the republic, in consultation with the military, served as chief arbiter of disputes arising among the various interest groups and government agencies—particularly when a matter had to be raised to the ministerial level.

Because of their economic power, technical skill, and high level of organization, upper-sector interest groups tended to survive the vagaries of regime change in the Central American city-state. After all, coffee had to be grown, pharmaceuticals distributed, and textiles manufactured regardless of the specific regime in power. Thus, over the long run the well-organized upper-sector group was more important in decision making than the political parties.

A second behavioral difference between Central American and Western pluralism was that political parties tended to be alternative power structures rather than aggregative institutions. That is, they did not stand between the state and the various interests, thereby serving, as in the Western democratic model, to aggregate and compromise the particularistic demands of those groups. Rather, as Charles Anderson has suggested, they have traditionally served as vehicles through which the middle and lower middle sectors could compete with the traditional elites and their powerful organizations for social and economic as well as political power.[15] As such, they were, more often than not, gigantic patronage organizations. Although some parties had a more ideological cast (the Christian Democrats, for example) and some had a loose programmatic character (the parties of the so-called Democratic left), the majority were oriented toward gaining the spoils and prestige of office.

At the upper level the parties were primarily a vehicle for the social promotion of aspiring members of the professional middle class. This was achieved through the publicity afforded them by political activity and by placing their leaders in positions of political prominence. At their lower levels, Central American parties were clientelistic organizations that provided jobs, contracts, and contacts for their rank-and-file adherents. Access to a government job could completely change the economic and social status of a member of the provincial middle or lower middle class. To be appointed a district superintendent of roads, for example, meant not only a steady salary for the lifetime of the government but also opportunities to rent trucks or earth-moving equipment at nominal prices to friends and relatives, to sell surplus stocks of diesel fuel, and to improve one's property and

79

that of friends and relatives with the departmental equipment and manpower he controlled. By this activity the party stalwart was amassing political IOUs for the time he would be out of office and would need to gain a livelihood elsewhere. Furthermore, if one of his friends were rising in a competitive party, he might support that party in the next election, with the expectation of receiving some government position after the voting. Because of the constant shuffling of both leaders and followers between political parties, a peculiar pattern of mutual accommodation and tolerance developed during the height of the city-state system (1950–1970). Persons who were the "ins" one day knew that they could be the "outs" the next and would be compelled to operate their businesses or professions in the fairly restricted social setting of the capital city. As a consequence, a serious attempt was made not to allow political rivalries to overly disrupt social or economic relationships. Defeated politicians would normally continue to do business with their opponents and often join them in a new coalition of parties or factions for the next electoral campaign.

This pattern of mutual accommodation within an urban-centered political system was reinforced by the fact that in the capital city middle- and upper-sector political elites were a part of a gigantic "old boy network" which transcended the political parties—and often even the interest groups. This network was made up of military officers, businessmen, lawyers, journalists, etc. who were interconnected through marriage or *compadrazgo* and by business and social connections. Related to this was the phenomenon of multiple job holding whereby an individual worked in a variety of jobs and organizations in the course of a week, thereby bringing him into association with numerous elites in different fields.[16] This, in turn, gave rise to smaller networks of associates from various professions and social ranks (often called *panaliñas* or *camarillas*) who provided each other with business, financial, legal, political and general career assistance. These *panaliñas* (and alliances of *panaliñas*) often constituted the core of the urban-based political parties and party factions.[17] After the heat of an election or political battle these same support networks served to dampen hostilities and to reintegrate the combatants once more into the traditional patterns of business, professional, and social intercourse.

A third important difference in the behavior of Central American political structures stems historically from the fact that in the city-state lower-sector groups—whether in the form of organized interest groups, spontaneously emerging aggregations, or political parties— were systematically suppressed. As a result, political dissent (as opposed to mere political rivalry) tended to flow into guerrilla movements or other types of combat groups. In fact, dissent generally, whether emanating from the upper, lower, or middle sectors, often took the form of disruptive or violent behavior because of the lack of permanent, ideologically stable parties operating within a tradition of bargaining and compromise through which the society could react constructively to changing social and economic conditions. In other words, during this period the Central American city-state had evolved reasonably successful methods of resolving conflicts between individuals, factions, and sectors within broad class boundaries but was notably unsuccessful in mediating interclass disputes. Thus, one of the crucial elements that helped to maintain a tolerable level of stability in these volatile political systems was the political passivity of the rural masses. Although higher levels of education, social and political communication, and generally enhanced expectations served to politicize the members of the middle class who were associated with the universities, banks, business enterprises, newspapers, government agencies, and political parties concentrated in the capital cities, until the mid-1970s attempts to mobilize the campesinos to take action in support of radical social and political change were notably unsuccessful. This was due, in no small part, to the fact that the Central American campesinos were often themselves small farmers, artisans, or shopkeepers and feared economic change as much as the big businessmen. Other factors reinforcing these attitudes were the perceived security of the traditional paternalistic relationships between *peón* and *patrón* on the haciendas and the cultural parochialism and defensiveness of village life.[18]

In most cases these systems were presided over by the military—either directly or indirectly.[19] In the Central American city-state the primary function of the military was to protect the modernized, urban core from unmanageable economic and political demands of the rural and urban masses.[20] In carrying out this function, the military generally performed a dual role in the city-state. As a corporatively organized institutional interest group, the military operated within these systems as a power contender or, given its tendency toward interservice rivalry and excessive loyalty to a given graduating class,[21] as a set of power contenders. Yet, because of its traditional monopoly of force, other power contenders have viewed it as a potential ally in the struggle for power. Thus, the military has usually governed in coalition with other political groups. In fact, often various segments or factions of the armed forces functioned as spokesmen for different sectors of the economic elite and their middle-class supporters.

Finally, the Central American city-states were characterized by a particular pattern of international linkages. At the regional level the urban elites were linked together in an "alliance of capital cities" through the CACM and the CONDECA (Central American Defense Council). At the wider international level the United States, concerned about the threat of increased Soviet penetration in the Western Hemisphere following the Cuban Revolution, established a network of economic, social, and cultural programs in the area to stimulate economic and technological development through U.S. aid and private investment.

In summary, during the decades from 1945 to 1975 the political systems of the Central American city-states could be seen as composed of numerous "power contenders," that is, various interest groups, political parties, and guerrilla organizations pursuing class or sectoral interests on the one hand and personalistic rivalries and individual ambitions on the other through the use of their particular power potential—a strike, a demonstration, military force, negotiations, electoral support, etc.[22] These power contenders, whether organized as political parties, interest groups, guerrilla movements or armed forces, were interconnected by the complicated sociopolitical linkages which marked the Central American city-states: civil servants who were weekend guerrillas, soldiers who "moonlighted" as members of a right-wing death squad, populist politicians who provided legal services for business corporations, etc.[23] These power contenders, particularly the upper-sector interest groups, also enjoyed a semicorporative relationship to the state through their government-granted charters and by special access to certain government ministries and autonomous agencies.

The Central American city-state epitomized what Charles Anderson aptly identified in the 1960s as a "living museum" of political organizations—power contenders (such as the military, the Church, a guerrilla group, etc.) constantly shouldering their way into an influential position by means of a strike, a demonstration, or a threatened coup, but without any of them ever being eliminated from the system. Thus, the city-state gave the impression of always being in a state of political ferment, but when the dust settled from any given upheaval, the same elites retained their positions of power, the upper-sector groups continued to pursue their interests, and the political parties took on new names.

This state of affairs fully satisfied no one; yet to change it posed dilemmas for each of the major components in the system. Although they invariably came out on top, the continued political instability—particularly the demand by lower-sector groups for inclusion on an equal footing with the groups already participating in the system—created a climate of uncertainty for the upper sectors. Yet, to attempt to stabilize the system by expanding its electoral and competitive aspects or by permitting the legalization of large-scale trade unions and campesino organizations would only have meant greater power sharing with the middle and lower classes. A more authoritarian solution, however, would have meant the possibility of ceding greater economic influence to the military, the risk of heightened middle-class political agitation, and the loss of the legitimacy accorded their activities by an electorally based constitutional system. The middle classes wanted more meaningful political participation through a competitive party system but also feared the social and economic demands of lower-class populism, since to accede to these demands implied the shift of substantial portions of the national income and political power to groups outside of the urban center. Finally, the lower classes began to demand recognition for their worker and campesino organizations and for left-wing political parties. How to overcome the dilemmas of this system without precipitating either violent or thoroughgoing revolution was a problem each of the city-states faced. Each took a slightly different road in attempting to solve it.

Attempts to Stabilize the City-State. In general three broad strategies were used to maintain political stability in the Central American city-state: elite accommodation (Guatemala, El Salvador, and Nicaragua), lower-class co-optation (Honduras), and pluralistic bargaining (Costa Rica). Elite accommodation involved a threefold strategy: (1) the creation of a set of techniques to facilitate interelite bargaining, (2) permitting a certain degree of participation (if not actual influence) to the politicized middle classes, and (3) the virtual exclusion of lower-sector groups from any significant participation in the political system.

The limited party system of Guatemala. In Guatemala, elite accommodation was based upon a complex system of relationships between top military officers, economic notables, and political leaders through an officially "licensed" four-party system which allowed the middle classes to participate in the nominating process and in the ratification of the winning slate. The attempt was made to segregate political activity into two broad arenas—an official arena made up of the middle- and upper-class political organizations in the urban center and an unofficial arena containing the unlicensed, nonlegalized mass organizations. At the top of the official arena was a fragmented and highly competitive complex of top military officers, economic notables, and political leaders who competed for the control of the state and the resources it had the power to distribute. This political complex was divided into a number of loosely structured and constantly shifting "mafias"[24] organized around various economic sectors and political interests.

Until the mid-1970s, excessive competition within this elite was mitigated by a number of assumptions and tacit understandings concerning the way the polity was to function, namely, that (1) a limited number of traditional political parties acceptable to the military-civilian elite would be allowed to compete for office,[25] (2) the military would control the executive while civilians would be allowed to dominate congress, (3) within limits, the military would permit various factions to compete for power through the electoral process, and (4) public policy would be oriented toward defending private property, stimulating the growth of a capitalist economy, expanding employment opportunities for the middle classes, and providing a minimal level of social welfare benefits for selected segments of the urban and rural masses without seriously challenging the existing social structure.

The second level of the official arena was composed of the organized upper-sector interest groups and the administrative agencies of the state. It was these organizations and the interrelationships between them that kept the everyday business of the society going. By and large the major interest groups oversaw the production and marketing process and, thus, generated the revenue that was collected by the government and reallocated to the urban middle class as salaries and social benefits.

The third level of the official arena contained the political parties, which, though important in recruiting political leadership, once this leadership was in place, gave way to the economic and technical power of the upper-sector groups.

The bottom level or the unofficial arena of the Guatemalan political system has traditionally been made up of the nation's unorganized masses—Ladino campesinos, Indians, industrial workers, and the unemployed or underemployed urban population. Normally politically inert, these groups have been periodically mobilized by political power brokers who have parlayed electoral support for personal or group benefits.

It is this layer of the Guatemalan political system that has undergone the most rapid transformation. Since 1976, a large number of mass organizations have been allowed to form. Many urban trade unions have received legal or tacit recognition and have become more militant in industrial relations. The Catholic Church has also been very active in the countryside in organizing agricultural cooperatives, campesino unions, and study groups. These organizations have become linked to the radical sectors of the official arena through left-wing guerrilla groups and front organizations such as the Comité Guatemalteco de Unidad Patriótica (CGUP). The latter organizations are usually funded and led by dissident sectors of the middle classes motivated by a combination of political idealism and political romanticism. Often based in the universities but drawing scores of "weekend revolutionaries" from government offices, business firms, and the Church, this network came to constitute a "disloyal opposition" to the regime. It was combated by the government, both by official counter-insurgency techniques and by the clandestine "hit squads" of the right, funded and led by the political elite and often manned by off-duty members of the police and security forces.

Thus, political issues were increasingly fought out in the two arenas: the official arena, in which, until the coup of 1982, *relatively* peaceful competition was engaged in by the state-sanctioned political parties and interest groups; and the unofficial arena, in which these same political groups fought it out in violent combat through the guerrilla organizations and assassination squads of both the right and the left.

In summary, it can be argued that the emergence of the two arenas provided a certain degree of stability in Guatemalan politics for sixteen years. Over that period elections were held regularly and were reasonably (though by no means entirely) honest.[26] There was a peaceful turnover of power from one regime to the next, the legislative branch increased its role in the decision-making process, and the bureaucracy increased its effectiveness and its penetration of the countryside. But it is clear that this was a superficial and short-lived stability. As the so-called democratic process became more stabilized within the official arena, the unofficial arena became more active. In other words, there has been a "spillover effect." As the bottom layer of the official arena (political parties and political committees) became more politicized and better organized, yet effectively shut out from influence (if not participation) in the political process by the upper two levels, it operated increasingly in the unofficial arena. To combat this, the Laugerud and Lucas regimes moved to give some mass organizations and hitherto excluded political parties' official recognition. Feeling threatened by these moves, upper-sector groups—both political parties and interest groups—sought to decapitate the leadership of these organizations by assassination and terror. Generally, attempts to stabilize the official arena have tended to expand and ultimately destabilize the unofficial arena. Once the unofficial arena reaches a "critical mass" in terms of organization and numbers, full-scale insurrection is the inevitable result. Obviously, the coup of March 1982, which was intended to stabilize the official arena and pacify the unofficial one, failed on both counts.

Limited opposition in El Salvador. In El Salvador the city-state was slower in developing than it had been in Guatemala. This was due to the fact that the military and the traditional economic elites attempted to slow down the process of politicization because of their fear of the Communist-inspired populism that had exploded in the peasant uprising in 1931.[27] In fact, Salvadoran politics cannot be understood at all apart from an awareness of the fact that the elites' fear of radical populism was greater there than in any other Central American country. This caused the elites, the military, and broad segments of the middle classes to opt for what might be called a "developmentalist synthesis."

Although subject to fits and starts and oscillations in policy, the synthesis that emerged was built around three fundamental principles. First, economic development, particularly industrialization, was to be the primary social objective. This would be left in the hands of the already existing economic elites as long as they proved willing and able to bring it about. Second, a moderate program of social and political reform would be enacted to satisfy middle-class demands as long as the fundamental social structure remained undisturbed. Third, the country would be run by the traditional coalition of the military, the economic elites, and the middle-class technocrats, with the military having ultimate authority. Limited political opposition was to be allowed.[28]

To create a political structure capable of implementing these objectives, a hegemonic political party patterned after the Mexican PRI was created by the military. Originally established as the Partido Revolucionario de Unificación Democratica, it reemerged as the Partido de Conciliación Nacional (PCN) after a brief civilian interregnum in 1960.

The policies of the developmentalist synthesis did have a salutary effect on Salvadoran society, at least initially. The country, particularly the urban middle sectors and elites, enjoyed a rapidly growing economy at the height of the synthesis (1961–1972), though after that date the economy tapered off because of the disruption of the CACM brought about by the Soccer War (1969). Industrialization and the economic infrastructure were increased considerably, and social reform in such areas as minimum wages, taxes, and increased provision of education, potable water, housing and electricity helped the middle and lower classes in the capital city.[29] Population growth, however, tended to outstrip temporary gains in productivity and income, and

El Salvador's manufactured goods could not compete in price and quality outside Central America.

It was at the height of the developmentalist synthesis, reinforced by the reformist ideology of the Alliance for Progress, that the regime of Col. Julio Adalberto Rivera (1962–1967) undertook its experiment in controlled democratization. It secured passage of an electoral reform bill which established a proportional representation system for the National Assembly. This permitted the urban middle classes to create political parties which began to challenge the hegemony of the PCN coalition. An opposition party (PAR) won control of the capital city for the first time in 1961, and the Christian Democrats (PDC) controlled it from 1964 to 1974. Beginning in 1964 the PDC began to increase its congressional representation and by 1972 had become sufficiently strong to mount a major campaign for the presidency. In doing so it challenged the political foundation of the synthesis.

The developmentalist synthesis in El Salvador had been an attempt to design and build a society which would preserve the traditional hierarchic social structure while, at the same time, creating a modern industrial state. To do this required the preservation of a ruling elite while allowing the middle and working classes to develop. Participation by the urban middle sectors in elections and decision making at the municipal, congressional, and bureaucratic levels was seen as a way of obtaining their support and cooperation in the task of nation building. It was assumed, however, that the middle classes would accept *participation* and not seek to *supplant* the directing class or radically to disturb the traditional social structure by politicizing the campesino. In other words, the politicization of the middle class was to be permitted as long as it could be confined to the modernized urban core of the Salvadoran city-state.

The breakdown in the tacit political agreement underlying the developmentalist synthesis began in 1969 with the outbreak of the Soccer War between El Salvador and Honduras. The conflict generated such patriotic fervor that the PCN, contrary to expectations, overwhelmingly defeated the PDC in the 1970 elections for the National Assembly. As a result of this defeat, the Christian Democrats made the fateful decision to fight the presidential elections of 1972 in alliance with two left-wing parties: the Social Democratic party (MNR) and the Communist front party (UDN).[30] It also determined to break into the massive campesino support for the PCN. These moves convinced the elites that the Christian Democrats could not be trusted to maintain the political boundaries of the Salvadoran city-state, that their candidate, José Napoleón Duarte, would become another Pío Romero Bosque,[31] and that to allow them to win would once again raise the specter of peasant radicalism. The *matanza* of 1931 returned to haunt both the Salvadoran left and the right.

The PCN was also under pressure from its right wing. President Fidel Sánchez Hernández had called for a number of reform initiatives to ameliorate the agrarian problem. He had also refused to crack down on the activities of liberal priests, student radicals, or striking teachers. Thus, confronted with the first serious internal challenge since its founding, the PCN split into moderate (PCN) and hard-line (FUDI) parties.[32] The PCN became a party under siege from both the left and the right. It felt it had to block the democratic opposition in order to safeguard the developmentalist synthesis as it understood it. The fraudulent elections of March 1972 were the result of this determination.

However justified by short-range considerations, Duarte's willingness to lend support to the abortive coup that followed had disastrous consequences for El Salvador's political system. It led to the virtual destruction of the moderate left in El Salvador, to the exile of the most widely respected democratic leader in the country, and to the almost total undermining of electoral politics as a credible form of political opposition.

The collapse of the democratic experiment (built around limited competition between urban-based political parties) after the fraudulent elections of 1972 greatly undermined the Salvadoran city-state. With the party system destroyed as a viable mechanism for institutionalized political opposition under moderate, democratic leadership, its place was taken by a plethora of combat groups representing all sectors of the society. Common cause was now effected between guerrilla organizations based in the countryside and alienated sectors of the urban middle and lower middle classes—particularly the Church, the Catholic university (UCA), the trade unions, the MNR, and elements of the PDC. The Duarte presidency (December 1980–April 1982) and the 1982 elections can best be understood as a last-ditch attempt to save the city-state by shifting power away from both the oligarchy and the radicalized lower sectors into the hands of the original creators of the Salvadoran city-state: the urban middle class and the more moderate elements of the military, the bureaucracy, and the entrepreneurial elite. The failure of the Christian Democrats to win those elections has once again placed the task of protecting the Salvadoran city-state into the hands of the military, which, due to serious limitations in its combat effectiveness and financial support, has become increasingly dependent on assistance from the United States.

Elite co-optation in Nicaragua. The Nicaraguan city-state was created in the twentieth century by the Somoza dynasty. Until the 1930s the Nicaraguan polity was composed of two warring oligarchies and their rural allies centered in the rival preindustrial city-states of Granada and León. Over the next five decades the modern Nicaraguan city-state, centered in Managua,[33] went through essentially four stages from creation to dissolution: (1) a "personal consolidation" stage (1927–1936) during which Anastasio Somoza eliminated his political and military rivals and secured personal control over the state and large segments of the national economy; (2) an "elite consolidation" stage (1936–1967) during which business and middle-class groups became the junior partners of the regime; (3) a "militarization" stage (1967–1978) during which Anastasio, Jr. ("Tachito"), sought to suppress by force the rise of middle- and lower-class opposition; and (4) insurrection and collapse (1978–1979).

The Somoza regime began as a personalistic military dictatorship over a weak, preindustrial country. By the end of the 1940s Somoza realized that to manage his vast personal holdings and to develop the economy in which they functioned demanded a level of international support and domestic stability which could only be achieved through some form of accommodation with the old oligarchy and the potentially disruptive elements of the modernized sectors of the society centered in Managua. The political formula used to bring about this accommodation was composed of the following elements: an agreement giving a third of the congressional seats to the Conservative party, a banking system that guaranteed financing both to the various segments of the elite and to the Somoza interests, appropriate participation for the multinational corporations in the new industries spawned by the CACM, international financing by the United States Agency for International Development and the international banking system, and a set of special privileges for the National Guard, whose job it was to protect the urban elites and the Somoza clan against mass demands and to support U.S. security interests in the Caribbean. George Black describes the Somocista system well when he writes:

> From its earliest days, Somoza power had rested on the family's ability to achieve dominance within the ruling class and then reach mutually beneficial agreements—political pacts on one hand, commercial alliances on the other—with the remaining bourgeois sectors. Accepting these rules, the bourgeoisie . . . flourished. With their consolidation, their need for Somoza grew. Agribusiness, com-

merce and industry were allotted, with each group enjoying certain preserves, and the crude monopolistic control
they exercised over the mass of the Nicaraguan people produced an increasingly violent class conflict which a unified
bourgeoisie relied upon Somoza to suppress.[34]

Ironically, it was the relative success of the system which began to
undermine it. Inflows of capital to segments of the old elite engaged
in commercial agriculture gave them a financial base separate from the
Somozas,[35] and the growing middle class became restive under the
family dictatorship. The growth in the urban centers outside of Managua of a large, unemployed lower class, displaced by the concentration and mechanization of agriculture, created an army of alienated
youths prepared to attack the city-state centered in Managua from
which they were excluded.

The final dissolution of the Nicaraguan city-state came from
within it—stimulated by the political aftermath of the 1972 earthquake. The generalized corruption of the National Guard and the
"sweetheart" reconstruction contracts favoring the Somozas over the
rest of the entrepreneurial class were perceived as a violation of the
political formula that had governed intraelite relationships. The murder in 1978 of Conservative leader Pedro Joaquín Chamorro was the
trigger which moved the entrepreneurial middle class to join the Sandinistas in dismantling the Nicaraguan city-state.

Lower-class co-optation in Honduras. In a certain sense the city-state
never developed in Honduras. The direction of urban evolution in the
twentieth century there has been away from a single urban center
toward competing ones as the growth of the banana and shipping
industries shifted the center of commercial activity from Tegucigalpa
to the north coast cities of La Ceiba and San Pedro Sula.[36] This had the
effect of concentrating the newer entrepreneurial groups in the north
coast cities and the older mining and bureaucratic elites in Tegucigalpa.[37] The fact that the development of the newer commercial centers took place roughly simultaneously with the emergence of trade
union organizations in both Central America and the United States
predisposed these emerging elites, including the North American banana companies, to use more co-optative rather than totally repressive
measures in handling both rural demands and urban mass demands.

The pattern of political development that set Honduras apart was
the fact that three of the nation's major power contenders—the army,
the trade unions, and the campesino organizations—developed relatively late (1950–1965), and at roughly the same time, along with a

proliferation of business groups.[38] Coupled with this was a gradual decline in the strength and status of the traditional power contenders—the Liberal and National parties. Because these sectors all emerged together, a tenuous balance of power was created that forced them to respect each other's interests. In fact, the land tenure problems posed by Salvadoran migration into Honduras, which was a major factor in precipitating the Soccer War between the two countries, forged something of a military-campesino alliance during the early 1970s. The relationships of the upper- and lower-sector interest groups with the military governments after the war were managed in an essentially corporative manner in the sense that their demands were articulated "directly to the military governments and bureaucracies pertinent to their specific interests."[39]

As a consequence of the decentralized urban structure, the rivalry between the elites in these centers, and the openness of the military to forging political alliances with mass groups, the city-state only partially developed in Honduras. Neither the campesino organizations nor the lower-class urban groups were ever completely walled off from participation in the polity; the entrepreneurial elites and middle classes never became concentrated in a single urban political system; and the military never took on as its primary function and role the protection of the urban sectors.

One final bit of irony remains to be noted. Because of the lack of extreme political polarization in Honduras and the willingness of the military to turn formal power over to the civilians in 1981, the Reagan administration has come to view Honduras as a major ally in the fight against subversion in Central America. Rather large increases in military assistance in recent years have come close to creating a dual government in the country—civilian and military. It is entirely conceivable that the military, in its readiness to assist the U.S. combat the left in El Salvador and Nicaragua, could convert the country into something more nearly resembling the Central American city-state than it now is—with the army at its core.

Pluralistic bargaining in Costa Rica. Because of its thirty-five-year history of political stability and constitutional government, the viability of Costa Rica has generally been taken for granted by political analysts and policy makers concerned with Central America. Still, that nation has evolved a city-state system, which, though different in many respects from its neighbors, is nevertheless subject to many of the same stresses and strains. With the establishment of the social democratic synthesis[40] in 1948, political stability has been secured by providing relatively open access to decision making to all segments of the society. This has taken two primary forms: electoral participation for the rural and urban lower classes and extensive opportunities for social mobility for the urbanized middle class.

The dominant Partido de Liberación Nacional, though directed by middle-class politicians, has always had a strong campesino electoral base, and the multiparty opposition coalition (variously named Partido Unión Nacional, Unidad, etc.) usually had a considerable trade union following under the populist Partido Republicano or the Moscow-oriented Partido Vanguardia Popular. Furthermore, trade unions and campesino organizations have been allowed the freedom to organize and press their claims in the political process.

Social mobility for the middle classes has been achieved primarily through the expansion of the government bureaucracy, the autonomous institutions, the various nationalized industries, and through the subsidization of private business. In fact, government expenditures accounted for 60 percent of the gross national product of Costa Rica in 1982.[41]

Access to the system by all groups has been further reinforced by the absence of a national military establishment dedicated to walling off the modernized urban core from the mass of the population. The lack of a military budget has also freed up resources for investment in social welfare programs, education, and bureaucratic expansion, which has greatly expanded the urban professional middle class.

The Costa Rican city-state, thus, consists of a heavily urbanized population substantially subsidized by government revenues and highly organized into a multiplicity of interest groups capable of pressing their claims upon a democratically elected, politically responsive government. This system, which has stabilized the Costa Rican city-state for the past thirty-five years and given it the region's highest standard of living,[42] now threatens to undermine it. Although between 1960 and the mid-1970s Costa Rica had "an impressive record in terms of general economic performance,"[43] it has not been immune to the economic shocks that have buffeted the rest of the region: the rise in petroleum prices (currently requiring practically the entire coffee crop to pay for),[44] the decline in commodity prices, and the disruption of the CACM. These dislocations, which have drastically decelerated economic growth, ballooned the public debt, doubled the levels of unemployment, and dramatically increased inflation,[45] have had an unusually severe effect on an urbanized, salaried population so heavily dependent on government revenues and the success of a relatively few, highly vulnerable export crops and import substitution industries.

Costa Rica can probably no longer afford the kind of city-state it has created. The 450 percent devaluation of the peso, its 65 percent inflation rate, its public and private debt of $4 billion—one of the highest per capita in the world—are just some of the indexes which raise questions about its long-term viability. The increasing number of strikes, the emergence of terrorist organizations, and the recent creation of an antiterrorist squad are worrisome portents for the future. Because it is built on a very narrow resource base, the Costa Rican city-state can probably not survive without considerable inflows of funding from the international economy. Since it constitutes a peaceful, democratic island in an otherwise turbulent political sea, the United States has no alternative but to try to keep the Costa Rican city-state afloat.

The Results of Attempts at Political Stability. How effective were these attempts to stabilize the political systems of these Central American city-states? First, on the positive side, throughout the latter 1960s and early 1970s a certain level of stability within the traditionally active urban centers was achieved. Guatemala transferred power constitutionally and peacefully for four successive elections between 1966 and 1978. El Salvador watched the growth of a viable democratic opposition and was recognized for its successful political modernization until the debacle of the 1972 presidential elections.[46] Even in Nicaragua it appeared that insurgency had been defeated as late as 1977.[47]

Second, economic development and modernization appeared to be moving ahead at a very favorable rate. As can be seen from table 4–1, Central America did better than the rest of Latin America on most economic indexes. Furthermore, anyone returning to Guatemala City, San Salvador, or San José in the late 1970s after a twenty-year absence could not fail to be impressed by their growth and physical improvement.

Third, the stabilization of the Central American city-state enabled the process of economic integration under the CACM to develop substantially. Before 1964 intra-isthmian trade represented 18 percent of total exports. By 1972 it had grown to 25 percent. Conversely, both exports to and imports from the United States dropped by 2.2 and 6.7 percentage points, respectively.

On the negative side, the achieving of political stabilization by elite consolidation coupled with the political exclusion of the masses resulted in the increasing alienation and political mobilization of the

TABLE 4-1

ECONOMIC GROWTH IN CENTRAL AMERICA AND LATIN AMERICA, 1961–1978
(percent)

	Annual Variation in GDP	Growth of Manufacturing Value Added[a]	Value of Agricultural Exports[b]	Increase in Irrigated Land[c]
Central America	5.7	7.4	239.1	87.5
Rest of Latin America and Caribbean	4.8	5.4	209.1	42.5

a. For 1961–1968.
b. For 1970–1978.
c. For 1961–1976.

SOURCE: Inter-American Development Bank, *Economic and Social Progress in Latin America*, 1980–1981 Report, tables 1-2, 1-12, and 1-14, and *Statistical Abstract of Latin America*, vol. 20, table 402, as adapted in Roland H. Ebel, "The Coming of the Post-Agricultural Society: An Exercise in Economic and Political Futurism," *Inter-American Economic Affairs*, vol. 35, no. 4 (1982).

lower classes. On this point it is interesting to compare real working-class wages, as elaborated by John A. Booth, with degrees of insurrectionary activity. Table 4-2 shows that between 1963 and 1967, the apogee of the Central American city-state, real wages generally increased and after that they fell. In general, there is a close correspondence between the extent of the fall in wages and the degree of insurrectionary activity. In another area of mass mobilization—industrial strife—Booth shows that in Guatemala, El Salvador, and Costa Rica the number of industrial disputes declined as real wages increased, with quite remarkable increases in such disputes as real wages declined.[48]

A fifth result of these attempts to stabilize the city-state—also negative—was an increase in dependency. Whether one looks at the military, cultural, or economic spheres, these urban enclaves found it increasingly necessary to obtain resources and support from abroad in order to sustain a modern, affluent way of life. For example, the external public debt in the region grew fivefold between 1960 and 1970 and eightfold between 1970 and 1979.[49] Similarly, the ratio of external public debt to the value of exports of goods and services rose from 7 to 19 percent between 1970 and 1978.[50] Finally, U.S. military assistance to Central America jumped from $4.8 million in 1953–1961 to $88.8 million during the decade of the 1970s.[51] The Central American city-state obviously was unable to support itself.

TABLE 4-2
INSURRECTIONARY ACTIVITY AND WORKING-CLASS WAGES,
1963-1977
(percentage change)

Insurrectionary Activity (by country)[a]	Real Working-Class Wage Indexes	
	1963-1967	1967-1977
Nicaragua	+45.0	-40.0
El Salvador	+15.0	-17.0
Guatemala	b	-34.0
Honduras	b	- 8.0
Costa Rica	+10.0	+17.0

a. Countries are listed in descending order by degree of insurrectionary activity.
b. No data available.
SOURCE: For insurrectionary activity by country—author; for percentage change in real working-class wage indexes—adapted from Booth,"Toward Explaining Regional Crisis in Central America," table 3 and figure 1.

Finally, both the successes and failures enumerated previously created an increasing economic and political fragility in what at one period had been fairly tough and flexible political systems. For example, because these city-states were not self-sufficient, much less able on their own to support a large, modern, urban population, the economic well-being of the urban sector increasingly depended on international economic linkages both between the isthmian states and with the major industrial countries. Economic shocks like the Soccer War or the oil price rise of 1973 greatly disrupted these economies. The resulting rivalry and conflict between segments of the elite and/or their middle-class associates, as real national income declined, undermined the tenuous system of intraelite bargaining and accommodation on which the city-state rested. Severe political destabilization was the outcome.

The Breakdown of the Central American City-State

The tenuous stability of the Central American city-state throughout the 1950s and 1960s was based on three major elements: a system of mutual accommodation among middle- and upper-sector urban elites; low levels of mass mobilization—particularly rural mobilization; and a steady infusion into the modern urban sector of economic resources, technology, and political support from abroad. Each leg of this tripod of supports, while always fragile at best, underwent a crisis in the late 1960s or early 1970s and collapsed in a number of countries by the end of the decade.

The first crisis that undermined the stability of the Central American city-states, particularly in Guatemala, El Salvador, and Nicaragua, was brought about by the substantial economic growth achieved during the 1950s and 1960s.[52] This growth, while improving urban living standards substantially,[53] also created a much more diverse, multifaceted economy. Because of the importance of government policy to the functioning of a modern economy,[54] political rivalries between major interest groups (industrialists versus importers of industrial goods, domestic manufacturers versus multinational corporations, and traditional agricultural producers [coffee and bananas] versus the newer commercial agricultural enterprises [cotton, rubber, sugar, and beef]) for the control of the state increased considerably. As a result, the many new industrial and commercial sectors that emerged fractured what had been a competitive economic oligarchy into a number of downright hostile elites. The military, which had often mediated conflicts between these groups and protected them against mass demands, became increasingly divided and drawn into intraelite contests for economic advantage by opportunities for personal enrichment. These rivalries, exacerbated by direct participation of military commanders in both governmental and political party positions, resulted in the formation of numerous alliances or *panaliñas* made up of economic, military, and party elites, each of which represented a sector of the economy. Often these "mafias," as the assassinated Guatemalan political leader Manuel Colom Argüeta put it, had a paramilitary arm which was responsible for the numerous assassinations of political leaders in that country during the 1970s.

A second crisis—the rapid mobilization of mass organizations—also was largely the result of economic growth. Between 1961 and 1978 the Central American economies grew by 5.7 percent per year. Although agriculture grew at a slower pace than manufacturing,[55] most of the increase was in the area of export crops. This came about largely by the application of modern technology to larger and larger tracts of land—land which by usage and custom had been available to the campesino for subsistence farming. The problem of land seizure was compounded by the continued growth of population in the rural areas.

This combination of a growth of industrial employment and the squeeze on land for subsistence agriculture exercised a "pull-push" effect on the overpopulated rural areas. For a while, urban migration functioned as a safety valve for potential rural discontent and thus served to shield the city-state from excessive mass demands. The "oil shock" of 1973, however, had a catastrophic effect upon the urban lower classes. Industrial growth was almost halved, while inflation increased sixfold between 1972 and 1974.[56] The result was a drop in real wages which has been fairly steady ever since.[57] Trade union organization and militancy were a natural consequence of this situation, particularly since the downward trend in wages and standards of living among the urban working classes was accompanied by increases in literacy, organizational techniques, and modern communications media.[58] Urban migration, which at one point had been the city-state's safety valve, had by the decade of the 1970s, increased the sheer number of urban masses available for mobilization against that state.

Urban working-class militancy was matched in the countryside by the development of cooperatives, village improvement societies *(comités pro-mejoramiento)*, and religious study groups under the auspices of both Roman Catholic missionaries *(comunidades de base)* and Protestant missionaries.

The third crisis undermining the Central American city-state—the reduction of economic and political supports from abroad—was composed of a number of elements. The first blow was the Soccer War of 1969, which seriously disrupted intraregional trade and the industrial growth that had been generated by it. Second, the rise in oil prices launched a wave of double-digit inflation which persisted for most of the decade. Third, these difficulties were compounded by a drop in commodity prices, which made it difficult for the urban centers to earn the foreign exchange necessary to pay for the goods on which their living standards were based. Finally, with the exception of Honduras, former President Carter's human rights policy greatly reduced military assistance to the nations of Central America.[59]

With the many elements at work undermining the area's political systems, it is not surprising that the "recessive" Machiavellian forces of conflict and insurrection became "dominant" during the 1970s.[60] The Central American city-state was brought into being by revolution, and revolution will certainly reshape, if not destroy it. With the exception of Costa Rica, the failure of the middle-class populist revolutions of the 1940s and 1950s to establish the electoral process as the only legitimate means of achieving power and to open meaningful participation in their nations' political life to the urban and rural lower classes, created a city-state system that would last for a period of time but ensured that the revolutionary process would continue in other forms. By walling off the modern urban core from the countryside and from the urban lower classes as well, the middle-class populists not only failed to create an electoral base large enough to control the politics of the city-state democratically but also, in the process, created an alienated group that eventually would be large enough and strong enough to attack that state. Still, during the 1960s the urban industrial class was sufficiently optimistic about its future in the Central American city-state to keep it from making common cause with its rural counterparts (the bulk of whom were co-opted into accepting the traditional power structure by the security provided by the *peón-patrón* relationship anyway), thus dooming the guerrilla *foco* strategy to failure.[61] During the 1970s, however, the intraelite crisis and the collapse of the party system in El Salvador, Guatemala, and Nicaragua as a viable road to power pushed many sectors of the urban middle and working classes into making common cause with the revolutionary groups in the rural areas. This has had the effect of obscuring the line between the city and the countryside. Groups long excluded from effective participation in the Central American city-state are now seeking *national* political power and *national* political change with the assistance of urban-based political organizations.[62] Conversely, as belated attempts at land reform attest, the city has been forced to attempt to come to terms with the countryside.

The Future of the Central American City-State

What can be said about the future of the Central American city-state? Two broad possibilities present themselves. The first is the replacement of the city-state by the nation-state. This could come about in at least two ways: by the Nicaraguan model, which involves the attempt to create a nation-state by the defeat of the city-state; or by the Costa Rican model, which is based on the voluntary opening up of the city-state to the political participation of all sectors of the nation.

A second possibility is that the city-state will save itself by becoming a fully developed garrison state. The likelihood of this happening in countries like El Salvador or Guatemala depends on three factors: the loyalty of the military to the traditional city-state, the willingness of the United States to support and finance it, and whether the bulk of the middle class casts its lot with the insurrectionaries (as in Nicaragua) or with the elites (as in El Salvador).

U.S. policy seems to be oriented toward the second course—saving the city-state. In reaction against successful revolution in Nicaragua, its strategy in the region seems largely to be dedicated to strengthening the three legs of the tripod of supports which have traditionally undergirded it: encouraging elections (aimed at restoring some degree of consensus within the urban groups), the military defeat of guerrilla forces (aimed at depoliticizing the masses), and economic and military assistance (aimed at propping up the modern urban sectors and giving the military the capability to protect them). Whether this strategy will be successful or not will depend on the future of the world economy and the tenacity of the American government and the various contending groups. In the meantime, the price of sustaining the Central American city-state is the thousands of innocent lives lost and the millions of dollars of labor and resources destroyed by the violence.

Notes

1. Summaries of the first two positions appear in Robert A. Pastor, "Our Real Interests in Central America," *Atlantic Monthly* (July 1982). Regarding Communist subversion, see W. Scott Thompson's essay "Choosing to Win," in the symposium entitled "El Salvador: The Current Danger," *Foreign Policy* (Summer 1981), pp. 79–83. For views on the role of international capitalism and economic and social dislocation, see Susanne Jonas, "Fifty Years of Revolution and Intervention in Central America," and James F. Petras and Morris H. Morley, "Economic Expansion and U.S. Policy in Central America," both in *Contemporary Marxism* (Summer 1981). Regarding economic decline, see John A. Booth, "Toward Explaining Regional Crisis in Central America: The Socioeconomic and Political Roots of Rebellion," Paper delivered at the 44th International Congress of Americanists, Manchester, England, September 5–10, 1982. The theory concerning elite fragmentation is presented in Viron P. Vaky, "Hemispheric Relations: 'Everything Is Part of Everything Else,' " *Foreign Affairs*, no. 3 (1980), pp. 619–21. Elite recalcitrance is an idea mentioned in Ralph Lee Woodward, Jr., *Central America: A Nation Divided* (New York: Oxford University Press, 1976), pp. 255–56.
2. Richard Morse, "The Heritage of Latin America," in Howard J. Wiarda, ed., *Politics and Social Change in Latin America: The Distinct Tradition* (Amherst: University of Massachusetts Press, 1974).
3. Charles W. Anderson, *Politics and Economic Change in Latin America: The Governing of Restless Nations* (Princeton, N.J.: D. Van Nostrand, 1967), pp. 97–101.
4. Ibid., pp. 89–97.
5. For a more detailed exposition of this point see the author's "Governing the City-State: Notes on the Politics of the Small Latin American Countries," *Journal of Interamerican Studies and World Affairs* (August 1972), pp. 325–28.
6. Banana cultivation and marketing had traditionally been controlled by transnational corporations. Cotton and other tropical fruits, nuts, and oils became increasingly dominated by foreign investors after 1960.
7. Between 1960 and 1980 average GDP increased by a total of 173.7 percent for the six Central American nations, while per capita GDP increased by an average of only 61.8 percent. Inter-American Development Bank, *Eco-*

nomic and Social Progress in Latin America, 1980–1981 Report, Statistical Appendix, table 3.

8. For a discussion of the ameliorating effects of these urban processes, particularly at the time it was written, see Irving Louis Horowitz, "Electoral Politics, Urbanization and Social Development in Latin America," in Glenn H. Beyer, ed., *The Urban Explosion in Latin America* (Ithaca, N.Y.: Cornell University Press, 1967).

9. *Compadrazgo* is the term used to denote the system of godparentage which established links of obligation and loyalty between individuals of different generations. Patronalism refers to the patron-client relationship that often existed between employers and employees, between managers and subordinates, or between officials or professionals of different rank or status.

10. For a description of these systems in rural Guatemala see the author's "Political Modernization and Community Decision-Making Process in Guatemala: The Case of Ostuncalco," *Annals of the Southeast Conference on Latin American Studies*, March 1970.

11. Bryan Roberts, *Organizing Strangers: Poor Families in Guatemala City* (Austin: University of Texas Press, 1973), pp. 29–31. See also his discussion of the informality of lower-class politics in chapters 7 and 8.

12. Although broadly similar in many respects, the political system of Costa Rica, because of its democratic development, manifests a number of significant differences from the rest of Central America.

13. The old oligarchy would have been composed largely of the owners of agricultural plantations and major commercial establishments. The new oligarchy embraces people in industry, the import business, and nontraditional agricultural exports. In many cases the members of the old oligarchy invested their money in the newer forms of industry and commercial agriculture.

14. For a discussion of the growth of these organizations in Guatemala see Richard N. Adams, *Crucifixion by Power: Essays on Guatemalan National Social Structure, 1944–1966* (Austin: University of Texas Press, 1970), chap. 6; Ronald Schneider, *Communism in Guatemala: 1944–1954* (New York: Praeger, 1958); and Roger Plant, *Guatemala: Unnatural Disaster* (London: Latin American Bureau, 1978). For Honduras see James A. Morris and Steve C. Ropp, "Corporatism and Dependent Development: A Honduran Case Study," *Latin American Research Review*, vol. 12, no. 2 (1977). For Costa Rica see Oscar Arias Sánchez, *Grupos de Preción en Costa Rica* (San José: Editorial Costa Rica, 1971).

15. Charles W. Anderson, "Central American Political Parties: A Functional Approach," *Western Political Quarterly* (March 1962).

16. A young lawyer in San Salvador, for example, might have worked for a government agency in the morning, a law firm in the afternoon, and helped his wife operate a commercial college at night. Weekends might be spent overseeing a small *finca* or writing a story as a stringer for an American news magazine. Many of these business and professional opportunities would have been obtained through the assistance of a *compadre* or associate in the urban "old boy network."

17. See Thomas P. Anderson, *Politics in Central America: Guatemala, El Salvador, Honduras and Nicaragua* (New York: Praeger, 1982), p. 54.

18. This was particularly true in Guatemalan Indian communities, where the self-contained village was looked upon as a barrier against the encroachment and penetration of Ladino culture and politico-economic control.

19. A number of patterns of military rule can be identified: (1) direct military rule as under Gen. Omar Torrijos in Panama (1968–1978), Col. Enrique Peralta Azúrdia (1963–1966), and Gen. Efrain Ríos Montt (1982–1983) in Guatemala; (2) direct rule with civilian support—Gen. Torrijos (1978–1982), the Guardia Nacional under the Somozas in Nicaragua (1934–1974) and Gen. Oswaldo López Arellano and successors in Honduras (1972–1980); (3) indirect rule under civilian-military coalitions obtaining power through elections as in Guatemala (1970–1982) and El Salvador (1948–1979); (4) indirect rule under civil-military coalitions brought to power by a coup as in El Salvador (1979–1982); and (5) indirect rule through control of the security apparatus and other powerful cabinet positions as in El Salvador (since February 1982) and Honduras (since November 1981).

20. Generally, the small, skilled sector of the urban working class benefited in limited fashion from the wage structure, educational opportunities, and social welfare programs in the capital city; the mass of occasional and unorganized workers were largely excluded from its benefits.

21. Military school graduating classes, known as *tandas*, retain intense loyalties and function within the military as intraservice *panaliñas*. Leonel Gomez and Bruce Cameron, "El Salvador: The Current Danger," *Foreign Policy* (Summer 1981), pp. 75–76.

22. C. Anderson, *Politics and Economic Change*, pp. 89–97.

23. The author remembers on one occasion being taken on a tour of the city hall in Guatemala City by a high-level functionary. As we made our way from office to office, my host often said, "You know the secretary I just introduced you to? She's with the FAR . . . (or) he's with the EGP . . ." etc.

24. The term was used by a former Guatemala City mayor and party leader to describe the military-elite coalitions in Guatemala just before his assassination: "Colom Argueta's Last Interview," *Latin America Political Report*, April 6, 1979.

25. The parties were: the postrevolutionary (1954) Catholic left (DCG), the old populist revolutionary political tradition (PR), a civilian antipopulist, anti-Communist party (MNR), and PID, a military developmentalist party from the Peralta era (1963–1966).

26. The elections of 1966 and 1970 were generally considered to be honest; the election of 1974 was an outright fraud, though the outcome, if not the actual count, in 1978 was accurate. The election of 1982 was perceived to be fraudulent and led to a coup. See Kenneth F. Johnson, "The 1966 and 1970 Elections in Guatemala: A Comparative Analysis," *World Affairs* (Summer 1971), pp. 34–35, and *Facts on File* (1978), p. 190.

27. Thomas P. Anderson, *Matanza: El Salvador's Communist Revolt of 1932* (Lincoln: University of Nebraska Press, 1971).

28. Alastair White, *El Salvador* (New York: Praeger, 1973), chap. 7.

29. Roland H. Ebel, "The Decision-Making Process in San Salvador," *Latin American Urban Research*, vol. 1 (Beverly Hills, Calif.: Sage Publications, 1970).

30. James Dunkerley, *The Long War: Dictatorship and Revolution in El Salvador* (London: Junction Books, 1982), p. 169.

31. Pio Romero Bosque was the democratically elected populist president whose administration (1927–1931) opened the floodgates of rural political mobilization that culminated in the *matanza* of 1931.

32. FUDI stands for Frente Unido Democrático Independiente. Its leader is also alleged to have founded the right-wing guerrilla organization ORDEN: T. Anderson, *Politics in Central America*, p. 68.

33. Woodward, *Central America*, p. 136.

34. George Black, *Triumph of the People: The Sandinista Revolution in Nicaragua* (London: Zed Press, 1981), pp. 62–63. For a discussion of Nicaragua as Somoza's "private state," see Thomas W. Walker, ed., *Nicaragua in Revolution* (New York: Praeger, 1982), pp. 15–19.

35. Philip Wheaton and Yvonne Dilling, *Nicaragua: A People's Revolution* (Washington, D.C.: EPICA Task Force, 1980), p. 4.

36. Woodward, *Central America*, p. 204.

37. The centralization and growth of the Honduran state after the 1950s partially offset the decline of Tegucigalpa due to commercial shifts.

38. Morris and Ropp, "Corporatism and Dependent Development," pp. 42–44.

39. Ibid., p. 45.

40. Roland H. Ebel, "Thomism and Machiavellianism in Central American Political Development," Paper delivered at the 44th Congress of Americanists, Manchester, England, September 5–10, 1982, pp. 22–24, 39–40.

41. John A. Booth, "Representative Constitutional Democracy in Costa Rica: Adaptation to Crisis in the Turbulent 1980s," Paper presented at the Rocky Mountain Council for Latin American Studies, Glendale, Arizona, February 25–27, 1982, p. 21.

42. Costa Rica leads the region in the percentage of revenue spent on education, in life expectancy, and in literacy. It ranks second to Nicaragua in infant mortality and second to Panama in per capita GDP. Inter-American Development Bank, *Economic and Social Progress in Latin America*, 1980–1981 Report, pp. 215, 246, 254, 284, 314, 325.

43. Inter-American Development Bank, *Economic and Social Progress in Latin America*, 1982 Report, p. 229.

44. *Mesoamerica* (February 1982), p. 4. This may moderate somewhat because of the recent lowering of OPEC oil prices. It is expected, however, that the favorable terms of the San José Agreement, whereby Mexico and Venezuela provide concessionary aid to the oil-importing countries in the Caribbean, will also be tightened. *Latin America Weekly Report*, April 22, 1983, p. 6.

45. Economic growth had declined from 8.9 percent per year in 1977 to -3.6 percent in 1981; the ratio of disbursed public debt to GDP rose from 26 percent in 1976 to 155 percent in 1981. Inter-American Development Bank, *Economic and Social Progress in Latin America*, 1982 Report, p. 230.

46. For this point of view see Ronald H. McDonald, "Electoral Behavior and Political Development in El Salvador," *The Journal of Politics* (May 1969),

pp. 397–419; Woodward, *Central America*, p. 241; and Ebel, "The Decision-Making Process in San Salvador."

47. William M. LeoGrande, "The Revolution in Nicaragua: Another Cuba?" *Foreign Affairs* (Fall 1979), pp. 31–32.

48. Booth, "Toward Explaining Regional Crisis in Central America," figure 2.

49. Inter-American Development Bank, *Economic and Social Progress in Latin America*, 1980–1981 Report, table 58.

50. See unnumbered statistical table, "Ratio of External Public Debt," taken from the World Bank's *World Development Report*, August 1980, as presented in Petras and Morley, "Economic Expansion," p. 74. Interest payments rose from $6 million in 1960 to $32 million in 1970 to $404 million in 1979: Inter-American Development Bank, *Economic and Social Progress in Latin America*, 1980–1981 Report, table 60.

51. See unnumbered statistical table, "U.S. Economic and Military Assistance to Central America, 1953–1959," taken from USAID, Statistics and Research Division, Office of Program and Information Analysis Services, *U.S. Overseas Loans and Grants and Assistance from International Organizations*, July 1, 1945–September 30, 1976, and July 1, 1945–September 30, 1979, as presented in Petras and Morley, "Economic Expansion," p. 78.

52. Some of the problems and crises discussed are now appearing in Honduras and Costa Rica.

53. For example, per capita consumption in Central America increased by 53.6 percent between 1960 and 1978. See Roland H. Ebel, "The Coming of the Post-Agricultural Society: An Exercise in Economic and Political Futurism," *Inter-American Economic Affairs*, vol. 35, no. 4 (1982), table 9.

54. Government policy affects a modern economy in such areas as subsidies, public credit, interest rates, exchange rates, taxes, and duties. See C. Anderson, *Politics and Economic Change*, pp. 54–61.

55. Agriculture grew at 4.7 percent per year, and manufacturing at 7.8 percent per year.

56. Growth of manufacturing value added fell from a yearly average of 9.0 percent between 1961 and 1970 to 5.2 percent per year for the period of 1971–1975; see Ebel, "Post-Agricultural Society," table 2.

57. Booth, "Toward Explaining Regional Crisis," tables 2 and 3.

58. Pastor, "Our Real Interests in Central America," p. 29.

59. U.S. military assistance decreased from $11 million in 1976 to $161,000 in 1979. Costa Rica received $5 million in 1977 but nothing in the previous decade or in 1978; see Booth, "Toward Explaining Regional Crisis," table 7.

60. Richard Morse, "Toward a Theory of Spanish American Government," in Wiarda, *Politics and Social Change in Latin America*. For an application of Morse's terminology to Central America, see Ebel, "Thomism and Machiavellianism."

61. The leading tenet of *foquismo* "as expressed by its leading propagandist Régis Debray was that the insertion of a small nucleus (*foco*) of revolutionary fighters into the countryside would act as a spark for mass rebellion." Dunkerley, *The Long War*, p. 89.

62. The organizational links between the Salvadoran FMLN (and its five guerrilla organizations) and the Revolutionary Democratic Front (FDR) and its forty-three trade union, campesino, teacher, student, and middle-class groups are an example. A similar organization exists in Guatemala: The Unidad Revolucionaria Nacional Guatemalteca, with its four main guerrilla groups, is linked with the Comité Guatemalteco de Unidad Patriótica and its various political groups.

5

The Roots of Revolution in Central America

THOMAS P. ANDERSON

Is is undoubtedly true that Central America is becoming the focus of world attention. Evidence is everywhere, from the portly Russians in Managua's Intercontinental Hotel to the lanky North American trainers with the Salvadoran army. Yasir Arafat and Colonel Khadafy, the Argentines and the Israelis, have all managed to influence events in the region. But outside interference is only fanning the flames of fires which burn on the fuel of local grievances. It is the contention of this paper that internal conditions for revolution exist in Central America and that the roots of the revolution lie in the increasingly bitter competition between political groups and social classes for the scarce resources of the region. The struggle is a complex one, and the conditions in no two countries are identical; yet there are parallels which must be emphasized as well as differences which must be pointed out. Therefore, after a general look at the situation of Central America, each of the countries of the region will be examined separately.

To the casual traveler, a large part of Central America must seem a paradise in the tropics. At higher elevations the climate is salubrious. Fruits and grains seem to spring out of the well-watered ground with only the most incidental care. The old scourges of malaria and yellow fever are almost things of the past. The traveler is tempted to believe that it would be paradise indeed were it not for the bloody-mindedness of some of the people who live there. Even the persistent poverty which is seen on every hand seems somehow a mistake—the result of crooked, incompetent, or slothful politicians. A more efficient and honest administration, a better distribution of wealth, a more equitable tax program, ought to be able to solve the problems and sweep Central America into a golden future.

Such a view fails to take into account the precarious economic situation in which the region finds itself. Although much of the population crowds itself into the five capital cities, the basis of wealth is still the land and its products. In El Salvador, despite decades of attempts at agricultural diversification, coffee remains king. Likewise, in Honduras, the banana is still central to the country's survival, though coffee, sugar, and other crops are also of great importance. Guatemala, Nicaragua, and Costa Rica are more agriculturally diversified, but there too the essential basis of wealth is the land. Unfortunately for Central America, there is not a major product raised there that cannot be grown, and often more cheaply grown, elsewhere in the world. In coffee, so vital to the fortunes of the region, there has been a world glut for years.

Because of the generally gloomy outlook for agricultural prices, many planners have seen the solution in industrialization. But the region lacks both the raw materials of industrial expansion and a trained, literate work force. So far, only light industry, aimed at satisfying the demands of the burgeoning urban population, has emerged.

The failure to develop new sources of income is reflected in the gross national product and the per capita share of that product. Guatemala's GNP grew 3.98 percent in 1980, but because of the swelling population this translated into only a 0.97 percent rise in per capita income. For El Salvador, the figures were even worse—a decrease of 8.69 percent in GNP and of 15.71 percent in per capita income, representing the effects of the civil war as well as the state of coffee prices. Costa Rica and Honduras experienced only very modest rises in individual income, of 1.25 and 1.17 percent, respectively. Only Nicaragua showed a solid gain in personal income, with a 7.95 percent rise, but this was merely a bouncing back from the civil war year of 1979 when personal income fell 24.63 percent.[1]

One major factor in the economic picture is the pressure of population increases. In his thoughtful study *Scarcity and Survival in Central America,* William Durham holds that the major problem is one of distribution and access to the land rather than population concentration.[2] To a certain extent this is doubtless true, but it is likewise true that without the pressure of population the conflicts which arise from the maldistribution of land and wealth would not have reached the acute stage in which we find them today. Nicaragua's annual population growth rate in the period 1975–1980 averaged a fantastic 4.56 percent. El Salvador had a growth rate of 3.71 percent, and Honduras was just behind it with 3.61 percent. Guatemala's growth rate of 3.07 percent and Costa Rica's 2.71 percent were less spectacular population increases but still were sufficient to put an increasing burden on already shaky economies.[3] As these populations burgeon, the problem of wealth distribution intensifies. This problem did not begin yesterday, nor will it be solved tomorrow.

The central factor has always been the distribution of the land. Chester Bowles once said that: "Many years of observation in the developing nations . . . have convinced me that in these vital areas the most important economic and political question is: who owns the land?"[4] David Browning, a British geographer, points out that to the Indians the land was a goddess. No one, of course, could own a goddess. One had only the right, after performing certain rituals, to till a little of her flesh in accordance with the customs of the tribe.[5] Interviewing Guatemalan Indian refugees in Chiapas, Mexico, who were fleeing from the Ríos Montt government's persecution, the present writer heard these same sentiments expressed by a modern Indian from Chahul in the Quiché department.

The Spaniards did not look at things that way. They could and did own the land, raping it as they raped the Indian women. But until the late nineteenth century a kind of compromise had been worked out, whereby the great estates, worked by tenant farmers called *colonos*, occupied perhaps the best lands, but other lands were set aside for the villages, and especially for those villages which remained predominantly Indian. The great liberal reforms of the 1870s changed all that and greatly accentuated the competition for the land. The liberal reformers saw the world through the eyes of Adam Smith and Jeremy Bentham. They were determined to "rationalize" the landholding patterns, and to do this they took away the lands of the Church, an institution they considered irrational and backward, and also the lands of as many of the villages as they could, so that individual entrepreneurs could farm them efficiently and rationally. In some countries the process was a slow one. In Guatemala it is being completed only today under the guise of the government's antiguerrilla campaign. In 1932 this process of individual entrepreneurs' taking over the land was encroaching upon the Pipil Indians of El Salvador's Izalco region. This persuaded them to join with the Communist party in the largest peasant revolt ever to hit Central America. Following the failure of their revolt, some ten to twenty thousand of them were brutally massacred.[6]

This breakdown of communal landholding had a number of results. It greatly expanded the hacienda system. It turned over much of the land previously used to feed the people to the production of cash crops for the world market, thus creating local food shortages and driving up food prices. Further, from a psychological point of view, it resulted in a feeling of competition and confrontation, what Kenneth Johnson, speaking of nearby Mexico, has called a war of all against all, a "zero sum game."[7]

The move toward individual ownership and the acquisition of individual wealth had been based on the rationalist philosophy of nineteenth-century liberalism. Yet, from the point of view of the land-hungry small farmer, the system did not seem rational at all. Land was left as pasture for cattle, for export, or for the tables of the affluent, land which could have been sown to maize and fed hundreds of peasants. Some crops, such as bananas, left vast reserves of land lying fallow, because this cash crop so quickly exhausts the soil. In the 1960s, El Salvador experienced this with cotton, which left behind a land drained of nutrients and poisoned with pesticides. There were other paradoxes. Vast stretches of Central America were committed to a product which contained absolutely no nutritional value at all: coffee. The government economists could, of course, point out that these cash crops brought in the foreign exchange needed to support the infrastructure of a modern state, but such statements meant little to a man who would never own a car, benefit from modern medicine, or have access to clean water. Anger and resentment grew in the twentieth century, and sometimes boiled over, as in El Salvador's 1932 revolt. Occasionally, a populist government, such as that of Guatemala, would attempt to solidify itself in power by creating a land reform scheme, but such attempts were bitterly resented by the landowners and generally turned back.

If agriculture was at an impasse, couldn't Central America modernize and diversify through industrialization? The development model caught on after World War II. Washington provided the advice, and such great banking institutions as the World Bank, the Inter-American Development Bank, and the Export-Import Bank provided the funds. As there was a lack of basic industrial resources, light industry, tailored to the world market and the needs of local consumers, would be the key. Such industrialization proceeded most rapidly in Costa Rica, where a literate and technically sophisticated labor force was at hand, but it also made great apparent strides in Guatemala and El Salvador. This last-mentioned country even became a kind of model for such developmental schemes in the 1960s. David R. Raynolds, in his book *Rapid Development in Small Economies,* focused on El Salvador and declared that, in 1967, its economy had reached that fabled "take-off point," after which the economy is presumably going to set a straight course for easy street.[8]

Such optimism left a number of things out of account. One problem lay with product substitution. A plastics factory would be started, and whole native handicraft industries, employing many times the number in the factory, would be put out of business. A soft drink bottling plant would go into operation, and the nutritious native juices sold by street corner vendors would no longer be in demand. Alastair White clearly noted this process in regard to El Salvador, where many handicraft specializations have completely disappeared.[9]

108

Another problem, which has been noted in third-world countries by the Brazilian scholar Josue de Castro is that the payment of relatively high industrial wages to a relative few tends to drive up prices for the unemployable many. Lastly, the lure of the capital cities was vastly increased, and many of the increasingly landless people of the interiors migrated to the capital, only to be disappointed and to swell the ranks of the slum dwellers. This population growth accentuated the "city-state" nature of these countries.

Urbanization and industrialization are associated in the popular mind of North America with the rise of a middle class, and the tendency is to associate such a class with the virtues of hard work, individualism, and democracy. A strong and numerous middle class has come to exist in all the major cities of Central America, and it is hard working, just as most Central Americans are. It is individualistic even to a fault, but it has never, except in Costa Rica, which must be an exception to so many things that can be said about Central America, produced a stable and democratic state.

In seeking to explain why this is so, one must note that the middle class developed late in Central America. An aristocratic landholder class was already in place, sure of itself and its position, and holding the keys to the economic and social prizes which could be won. The aspiring urban middle class therefore took its social betters as role models. The desire of the middle class is to achieve the status of landholder and gentleman. Industry and commerce are only a means to that end. The Melvilles, quoting the Guatemalan anthropologist Humberto Flores Alvarado, typify the middle sectors as being almost without class consciousness, mere power seekers engaged in aping the ruling class.[10] The problem with this is that the interests of the middle class and the old oligarchy do not really coincide very closely. In committing itself to those who demand a maintenance of the status quo, the middle class cuts itself off from the masses of the people and creates an antagonism against itself. The Salvadoran middle class has been warm in its response to the reactionary National Republican Alliance (Alianza Republicana Nacionalista, or ARENA), which is run by such representatives of the old landed wealth as Mario Redaelli.

This helps to explain the otherwise baffling distrust of the Sandinistas in revolutionary Nicaragua toward middle-class former allies such as Alfonso Robelo and Enrique Dreyfus. To the leaders of the masses, every middle-class politician is a potential reactionary only waiting for a chance to show his true colors. This attitude, which is patently unfair, deprives the revolution of much of its technical expertise and sharpens the notion of class struggle.

One particular part of the middle class which played a special role in creating the antagonisms of the present revolutionary situation is the officer corps. Not all officers are of middle-class origin, though many are, but they follow an upwardly mobile middle-class profession. They are for all practical purposes the military itself, since the enlisted men are peasants and laborers who were so unfortunate as to run into the press gangs. The officer class has become highly professionalized, especially in the period since World War II, because of the interest that the United States has shown in building up military competence in the region. Many have trained in Panama or at garrisons in the United States. This training has not been exclusively military by any means. The average Central American officer has had heavy doses of economics, business management, and engineering. This has created what the present writer has referred to elsewhere as the "myth of military omnicompetence." The officer feels himself superior to the mere civilian in his ability to administer government and even business. Like Gilbert and Sullivan's "modern major general," he knows a little about everything, except perhaps the art of leading men in battle.

Originally thought of as the guardians of the established order, the professional military men have slowly usurped many of the prerogatives of the oligarchy. They began to take over the governing functions of the state in Guatemala, El Salvador, and Nicaragua by the 1930s. This occurred later in Honduras, and only Costa Rica was able to throw off the danger of military rule by abolishing its army in 1948. Finally, in Nicaragua in 1979, the scourge of the military was ended when the people defeated the Guardia Nacional and dismantled it utterly. In Guatemala, and more recently in El Salvador and Honduras, the officers have gone beyond mere political control of the state and have become a new landed gentry and a rival to the established oligarchy. The opening of much new territory through the ambitious road building and development schemes of the Laugerud and Lucas governments in Guatemala provided the generals and colonels with many opportunities to seize land, much of it previously held by the Indian peasantry. If the peasants objected to such activities, they were simply massacred, as at Panzós in 1978. One result of this activity in Guatemala has been to drive the formerly passive Indians into the arms of the guerrillas. In a recent interview with the present writer, Maya leader Pablo Seto declared, "the indigenous people are the pillars of the revolution."

The acquisition of large holdings by the military in El Salvador was facilitated by the flight of much of the traditional landholding class because of the civil war and the bungled land reform program of the Duarte government. In Honduras the process has been more subtle and has progressed chiefly through the wealth accumulated by the officers in their various clandestine operations such as drug smuggling. These facts have become clear to the present writer through extensive interviews in El Salvador and Honduras.

The monopoly of political power and the growing concentration of economic power and landholding in the hands of the officer class have caused them to be identified by those seeking to change the social order as the supreme enemy of the revolutionary process. This in part accounts for the savage ferocity of the battles that rage through much of Central America. The officers believe that they must ruthlessly exterminate to survive; their enemies believe the officers must be totally uprooted and driven out, as happened in Nicaragua, if there is to be a redistribution of the scarce resources of these poverty-stricken lands.

For those in the aspiring middle class who remain civilians, participation in the political life of the nation must be through the party system. Yet participation in political parties can be a frustrating experience. Only in Costa Rica have the parties per se exercised real control over the past two decades. Even where traditional, long-term parties with deep roots existed, such as the Liberals and Nationals in Honduras or the Liberals and Conservatives in Nicaragua, they became mere vehicles for men whose real power was based on the control of the military machine. Somoza used the Liberal party as an adjunct to the National Guard in Nicaragua. Oswaldo López Arellano, the long-term Honduran strong man, manipulated the National party to his own ends, but his real power came from firm control of the military machine.

In El Salvador and Guatemala the currently active political parties tend to be of more recent origin, though El Salvador's Christian Democratic party (Partido Demócrato Cristiano, or PDC) and the Party of National Conciliation (Partido de Conciliación Nacional, or PCN) have existed for more than two decades, as has Guatemala's National Liberation Movement (Movimiento de Liberación Nacional, or MLN), which was founded to lend legitimacy to the takeover by Carlos Castillo Armas in 1954.

Throughout the region parties also tend to be personalist, as is true elsewhere in Latin America. The MLN is dominated by Mario Sandoval Alarcon; the National Authentic Center (Central Auténtico Nacional, or CAN), which broke from it, is the machine of Carlos Arana Osorio. In El Salvador, the two strongest parties, ARENA and the PDC, are controlled by the towering personalities of Roberto D'Aubuisson and José Napoleón Duarte, respectively. If a leader is successful and brings his party to power, then he can bestow favors upon his rank and file. Otherwise he and his followers must wander in the frustrating political wilderness.

Whenever a new leader comes to power in Central America, whether he be soldier or civilian, he always promises sweeping changes for the benefit of the people. There is a brief fiesta of semi-Marxist rhetoric, and then the government gets down to ruling for the benefit of those who brought it to power. For, as Eduardo Galeano has observed, "Power is like a violin—one picks it up with one's left hand and plays it with the right." [11] Over the years, most people have come to doubt that any leader coming to power through coup or election can resolve the struggle for resources and the land. Many have come to believe that only a drastic reordering of society can save Central America from economic and social disaster.

Those seeking change turned naturally to Marxism as the one philosophy which offered both a blueprint for change and a seemingly scientific certainty of attaining it. At first the Marxist movements of the region had little contact directly with Moscow. Men like Agustín Farabundo Martí learned their Marx while studying at the local university and then tried to adapt the teachings to the local condition. In Martí's case, this led to his launching of the doomed revolt of 1932 in El Salvador. University Marxists continued to abound during the 1940s and 1950s, but they accomplished little. The real function of the Communists in those decades was to be a boogie man for the governments. Repression was always launched against political foes with the excuse that the government was cracking down on communism. The ascendancy of Fidel Castro in Cuba served as an example for the local Marxists, though he could give them little direct aid.

The appeal of Marxism is, of course, global, but it fit in very nicely with the mind-set of the Central American intelligentsia. Catholicism had conditioned them to a religion of absolute values. The correct values had to be championed against error, through apologetics, and if necessary by stronger means. In colonial times stronger means had meant the Inquisition. In secular life, too, the values of the society were those of confrontation and dogmatism rather than compromise and conciliation. Political parties and movements were much less willing to tolerate differences with their opponents than North American groups were. The frustrations of the local intelligentsia also predisposed them to radical notions. A degree from the local university was often worthless without the right friends and connections within the ruling elite.

In 1960 a group of young and idealistic Guatemalan army officers, unhappy over the participation of the Ydígoras Fuentes government in the Bay of Pigs scheme, launched an abortive coup. Two survivors of that movement, Lieutenants Marco Antonio Yon Sosa and Luis Turcios Lima, then launched a Marxist guerrilla movement known from the date of their revolt: Movimiento Revolucionario del 13 de Noviembre (MR-13). Shortly after the Guatemalan revolt, various rebellious elements in Nicaragua came together as the Frente Sandinista de Liberación Nacional (FSLN), a Marxist-leaning movement dedicated to wresting control of the country from the iron grip of the Somoza family. These would be the twin prongs of the revolutionary movement in Central America. El Salvador was still paralyzed from the effects of 1932, Costa Rica was democratic and prosperous, and Honduras, as local wits had it, was too backward even to have a revolution. For many years, then, the parallel movements continued an unequal struggle. Almost all the early leaders died in the course of the guerrilla campaigns. None of the original Guatemalan leaders are left, and of the Sandinistas only tough Tomás Borge survived prison and torture to emerge as interior minister under the Marxist regime. It was not until after the sham of the 1972 elections in El Salvador that Salvador Cayetano Carpio and his Fuerzas Populares de Liberación (FPL) emerged as the first of El Salvador's many guerrilla movements, and it would not be until the 1980s that the Honduran guerrillas launched their campaign.

Almost all the early Marxist leaders made a singular tactical error. They failed to line up the masses of the peasantry on their side. Perhaps the problem was the background of the guerrilla leaders themselves; they tended to be educated either through the universities or the military academies and rather contemptuous of the peasants. Perhaps too, their doctrinaire ideology convinced them that they should rely on the urban workers, despite the example of the Chinese revolution. This is not to say that there were not efforts to organize the masses of the peasantry, but they tended to run afoul of cultural differences, and in Guatemala of linguistic differences as well. All this changed in the mid-1970s, and the radicalized peasantry was handed to the Marxist guerrilla movements on a platter; for it was not the Marxists but rather members of the Church who had raised the consciousness of the masses.

The metamorphosis of the Catholic Church from one of the most supine and decrepit of institutions into one of the most vibrant and dynamic is a startling event in the history of modern Latin America. It has had tremendous reverberations in the Central American region. The triumph of the liberals in the late nineteenth century, with their positivistic and anticlerical notions, marked the defeat and near destruction of the old Church. Shorn of its wealth and deprived of much of its moral authority, the Catholic Church sank into lassitude, content merely to survive, and taking pains not to offend the new liberal masters of the state and the economy. The revival of this institution in the middle of the twentieth century was due partly to internal factors, the better education of the clergy, and a renewed interest in the social teachings of the Church, and partly to external factors, in particular the arrival of large groups of North American missionaries who came after World War II. These missionaries were encouraged by their own government in order to further U.S. aims in the cold war and to stop the spread of communism by fostering a religion which was presumably the antithesis of Marxism. It did not work out that way, however, for the incoming missionaries, particularly the Jesuits, Capuchins, and Maryknollers, soon became identified with the progressive elements in the Central American Church.

The Second Vatican Council in the early 1960s had changed the orientation of the Catholic Church from sacramentalism to one which emphasized the role of the laity as the people of God. This encouraged those elements seeking change in the Latin American Church, and when the region's bishops met at Medellín, Colombia (1968), the role of the laity and the importance of temporal salvation through the elimination of hunger, poverty, and disease were stressed. The laity were to work through the *comunidades de basa* (basic communities) to raise their consciousness and comprehend the problems that existed around them, for, as the social encyclicals of the popes going back to Leo XIII had emphasized, it is almost impossible to preach the good news of salvation to those wallowing in misery and despair.[12] Thus the Church had reversed its role from that of the traditional handmaid of power to that of the precursor of social change.

Nowhere did this have a more profound effect than in Central America, whose people, especially in the peasant communities, have always been profoundly Catholic. (The men had never abandoned the practices of Catholicism to the women as they had done in Mexico and certain other parts of Latin America.) In response to the dynamic sermons of idealistic clergy, lay leaders emerged in the early 1970s ready to fill the gap in a region where there might be only one priest for approximately every twenty thousand believers. Church-led peasant movements began to emerge, such as the Salvadoran Christian Peasants Federation (Federación Cristiana de Campesinos Salvadoreños, or FECCAS) and the National Peasants Union (Unión Nacional de Campesinos, or UNC) in Honduras. In the Nicaraguan revolution lay leaders, priests, and nuns played a large part; in the Guatemalan struggle the priest-organized peasant movements met with severe repression.

Perhaps the transformation of the FECCAS in El Salvador is instructive. Organized by clergy and lay workers spreading the word of God, it soon became a militant force for the defense of peasant rights, though it lacked legal standing. This led to severe repression by the military government, whereupon the FECCAS joined with other peasant, labor, and intellectual groups to form the powerful Popular Revolutionary Bloc (Bloque Popular Revolucionario, or BPR) in the mid-1970s. The BPR tried the peaceful means of demonstration and petition, only to find itself answered in bullets. It turned to seizing embassies and government buildings. These more militant tactics only led to increased violence. Finally, under the leadership of Facundo Guardado y Guardado, in 1979 the BPR announced that it was Marxist-Leninist and joined forces with Salvador Cayetano Carpio's FPL, which became its armed element.[13] Eventually the BPR would become a major component of the Democratic Revolutionary Front (Frente Democrático Revolucionario), which currently functions as the rebel government in exile.

That a Church group could become part of a Marxist movement seems strange until the similarities between Marxism and certain aspects of the "theology of liberation," as the new humanistic doctrines of the Church are called, become clear. Liberation theology agrees with the Marxists on the essential point of man's alienation from his environment. Man must be restored to wholeness through a restitution into the hands of the poor and downtrodden of the means of production and the resources for production. César Montes, the Guatemalan guerrilla leader who replaced the fallen Luis Turcios Lima, pointing to Pope Paul VI's encyclical *Popularum Progressio* where the pope speaks of consciousness raising among the peasants, commented, "The Pope is more intelligent than the Guatemalan Right. Read this and you'll see how exactly he nails down the causes of violence."[14]

The Marxists, reinforced by a strong segment of opinion within the Church, thus proposed to take control of the scarce productive resources of the region—by force if necessary. The increasingly impotent oligarchy and the still powerful officer class would be driven out of their entrenched positions. Much of the middle class, which had shown itself incapable of effecting meaningful change through the systems of political parties, was also to be swept away, and a disciplined redistribution of resources was to take place in which the socialist state would have a leading role. The attempt to implement this scenario, and the resistance of the entrenched groups, backed by the United States, are basic factors in the convulsive struggle in progress in the early 1980s. But although there are similar factors at work among the Central American countries, there are many factors peculiar to each state, and these must also be taken into account.

Guatemala

The key moment in Guatemalan history is June 1954, when the regime of Jacobo Arbenz Guzmán was toppled by the Central Intelligence Agency using Colonel Carlos Castillo Armas as its vehicle. That the role of Castillo Armas was secondary, and that of the CIA primary, is all too clear from the extensive research of Schlesinger and Kinzer. As they point out: "The fragile political institutions created by the 1944 constitution did not have a chance to mature." [15] These institutions had been designed to create a moderate and progressive redistribution of the country's resources. Under President Juan José Arévalo (1945–1950), these changes had been more or less accepted both in Guatemala and abroad, but President Arbenz, though essentially a middle-class reformer, stepped up the pace of change and instituted a land reform (which seems quite modest when compared with the U.S.-backed reform in El Salvador in 1980) but which seemed quite drastic for his day. He had further failed to destroy the Communist party and even allowed a handful of its members in influential positions in his government. It was for all these sins that he was overthrown. This was a time when the Dulles brothers, closely connected with United Fruit, one of the victims of the land reform and anti-Communist to the point of paranoia, ran the foreign policy of the United States.

Guatemala throughout the twentieth century has followed a pattern of military rule. Arbenz himself was a soldier, and there had previously been only two civilian chief executives in the century, Arévalo and the infamous Manuel Estrada Cabrera, whose dictatorship began the period. But the systematic military rule imposed by Castillo Armas and his successors went beyond previous practice. Under the excuse of anticommunism, the country was militarized to a high degree. The eruption of actual Marxist guerrillas in November 1960 only served to accentuate a process already under way. Under this system, the president is the highest-ranking military figure and transmits his orders through the minister of defense and the chief of staff, who are second and third in command, respectively. The president also controls the police apparatus under the minister of the interior. The one exception to this system was the presidency of the civilian Julio César Méndez Montenegro (1966–1970). But it was not so much of an exception as it appeared, for Méndez Montenegro was

THOMAS P. ANDERSON

forced to sign a humiliating capitulation to the generals promising that he would not interfere with military appointments or disturb their conduct of the antiguerrilla campaign.[16] In the next three elections, to make sure that a civilian would not accidentally make it to the presidency, the army insisted that all candidates be military men. Rotating the office among the military elite avoided the problem of having a long-term strong man of the Somoza type who would tarnish Guatemala's image abroad. As Manuel Colom Argueta, the distinguished Guatemalan politician, observed shortly before his own assassination: "It is very comfortable to have a disposable president who can be traded in every four years for another 'democratically elected' one."[17]

Politically entrenched, the military consolidated its economic hold. The senior officers gained estates and other holdings, often with the cooperation of the oligarchy, which sought to ingratiate itself with the class which was displacing it. The very size of the military budget made the army a financial power and, through its welfare fund, a banker as well. Not even in Somoza's Nicaragua was the link between the military and the nation's economy so complex and complete.

The military, however, did not operate Guatemala alone. The shifting coalitions of political parties which backed the "official candidate"—that is, the one the military had picked to win—also played their part. These conservative parties were even allowed to maintain their own private armies and death squads to supplement the military's own death squads, which systematically exterminated all those who might cause trouble. Certain powerful clans, whose businesses oscillated between the legal and the illegal, also maintained a share of input into the governing process.

In such a society, official violence and terror were the inevitable results. Those who profited from the arrangement, who controlled the resources of Guatemala, fought desperately and savagely to make sure that their control was maintained. The enemy were "the Communists," who could be anyone from the genuine Communists who were in the guerrilla movements to middle-class politicians, such as Manuel Colom Argueta or Alberto Fuentes Mohr, both of whom were assassinated in 1979 by the death squads directly linked, it was generally believed, to the military. The bodies of people who had been tortured appeared regularly on the streets of the capital and on country roads. In July 1980, political killings occurred at the rate of twenty a day.[18] Urban violence against politicians, journalists, labor organizers, and educators was matched by rural violence against the peasants, especially those who dared to organize farm workers and those suspected of aiding the guerrilla movement. As time went on, this vio-

lence was directed more and more against the members of the indigenous community.

The Indian community represents over 40 percent of the Guatemalan people. They maintain their own native languages, mostly
Maya dialects, and their own religious and social organizations. Generally they live apart from the Spanish-speaking Ladinos (non-Indi-
ans). The Arbenz government had made halting attempts to improve
their precarious economic situation, but later governments tended to
ignore them, except at election time. The indigenous population
played very little part in the upheavals of the 1950s and the guerrilla
movements of the 1960s and early 1970s. The guerrillas tended to
concentrate their activities in such Ladino regions as Zacapa and Ja-
lapa, away from the Indian-speaking western highlands. The Indians
simply endured, suffering whatever fate was imposed upon them. As
Galeano observes, "The Indians' Holy Week ends without a resurrec-
tion . . . . They celebrate their own defeat." [19]

This began to change in the middle of the 1970s for two principal
reasons. First of all, the discovery of oil in western Guatemala encouraged the government to create access to that region. A highway, called
the Transversal, was run from the department of Izabal on the Atlantic coast through Alta Verapaz and El Quiché into Huehuetenango.
Other roads were also run, airports built, and a general penetration
achieved. As this was through the heart of Indian Guatemala, dislocation of the populace was the result. The now valuable lands were
snapped up by the soldiers. Dispossessed peasants ended up either
working for these new masters or were shunted off northward into the
Petén, where the government promised development but actually
dumped bewildered people into an area without access to the market.
The Indians protested. One result was their massacre. The most famous killings took place at Panzós on May 29, 1979, when Indians
from El Quiché marched into the town to protest against the seizure of
their lands and were slaughtered for their trouble.[20] This was followed
by other similar events. By that time, the Indians had begun to organize themselves, encouraged by Catholic clergy. They began to
bring their protests to the capital, occupying churches, government
offices, and embassies. This occasioned the Spanish embassy tragedy
of January 31, 1980. Over thirty persons were burned to death, including Indians and two prominent Guatemalan negotiators, after the
police stormed the building and an incendiary device held by one of
the Indians went off.[21] Thus, as they were pushed from their precarious hold upon the land, the Indians began to react.

Second, the guerrillas discovered the Indians. A new movement,
the Guerrilla Army of the Poor (Ejército Guerrillero de Pobres, or

EGP) sprang up in 1976 and began to create a new center of rebel strength in the western highlands. The guerrillas took the trouble to learn some of the more prominent Indian dialects and to win over members of the community. For reasons mentioned previously, this was the right moment and the seed fell upon good ground.

For many Indians, the decision to radicalize has been a tragic one. The government of Romeo Lucas came down hard on the people of the highlands, but after he was toppled in a lightning coup on March 23, 1982, by Efraín Ríos Montt, the lot of the Indian grew worse. General Ríos Montt produced certain cosmetic changes in Guatemala. The streets of the larger cities ceased to be cluttered with the unsightly remains of death squad victims. Guatemala was presenting a new image to the world. But in El Quiché and Huehuetenango, a war of extermination was going on against the indigenous people, presumably because they were tainted by communism but also, in part, as a way of seizing their lands. Soldiers were surrounding villages, setting them afire, and exterminating every living thing, human or animal, and even burning the crops and stores of grain. Pitiful hordes of refugees fled into Mexico. Numerous testimonies taken in Chiapas, Mexico, in August 1982 by the present writer, indicate that these massacres were being perpetrated by the regular army.

Thus the struggle for Guatemala's resources has entered into a new phase. The Indian population, which was always fair game for Ladinos to exploit and kill, is now to be reduced and culturally destroyed so that other sectors might better survive. Doubtless the current trend of events is repugnant to Washington, or at least to those in government who understand the situation, but Ríos Montt appears a bastion against communism, and the United States is caught up in a situation beyond its control.

El Salvador

All the nations of the region, even Costa Rica, have oligarchies which pass around among their members the wealth and power of the country, but no oligarchy ever was so entrenched as that of El Salvador. That there were fourteen families that controlled everything was a gross exaggeration, but that people would believe that *los catorce* existed suggested something about the nature of Salvadoran society.

Early in 1932 an event occurred which seriously curtailed the political power of the oligarchy. Urged on by Communist agitators, and increasingly deprived of their traditional lands by the coffee growers, the peasants, mostly Pipil Indians, of the western part of the country launched a massive uprising. It was put down by the military strong man who had just taken over by coup the previous December, Maximiliano Hernández Martínez, who then proceeded to have some ten thousand or more of the rebels shot. This calculated frightfulness made El Salvador very quiet for four decades. It also put the military firmly in the saddle politically. From that time on, until Duarte assumed the presidency of the junta in 1980, every chief of state was a soldier. A curious bargain was struck between the military and the oligarchy, giving one the reins of power, the other economic control. Political power and economic control must eventually coincide in any society, but for decades the bargain held despite a mutual distrust and dislike between the middle-class soldiers and the haughty oligarchs. This is not to say that no means of gaining wealth was open to the officer class. Graft and corruption held the officer corps together, and many managed to purchase modest estates by the end of their military and political careers.

This system worked as long as there was enough to go around for both the civil elite and the military elite and as long as the country was prosperous enough to stave off a resurgence of popular discontent. The first real cracks in the system began to appear after the disastrous war with Honduras in 1969. The aftermath of that event was that some hundred and thirty thousand Salvadorans who had been living and working in Honduras came tumbling home destitute and that the lucrative Honduran market for El Salvador's light industry was lost.[22] These things happened at a time of sharp natural increase in the population and created a host of unemployed, estimated to be a fifth of the work force, with another 40 percent only partly employed.

All this served to discredit the regime of General Sánchez Hernández, and it appeared as though the opposition coalition's candidate in the 1972 presidential race, José Napoleón Duarte, could beat the military candidate, General Molina. Massive fraud at the polls, however, saved the military regime, and General Molina was duly installed. A group of young army officers, not so much anxious for democracy as desirous to take advantage of the situation to get themselves ahead, then staged an abortive coup in which Duarte became involved. This led to his arrest, torture, and exile. After that, the ruling PCN never took any chances, all elections being well rigged in advance, including the presidential election of 1977, which brought to power General Carlos Humberto Romero.

The fraudulent elections of 1972 had caused many to despair of peaceful change. The Marxist firebrand Salvador Cayetano Carpio launched his guerrilla movement, and soon several other bands were in the field as well. These might have been contained, but another, more dangerous phenomenon also arose, the mass popular organizations. The BPR and the United Popular Action Front (Frente de Acción Popular Unidad, or FAPU) together represented perhaps as many as two hundred thousand Salvadorans. As described earlier, when peaceful protest led only to brutal repression, these groups joined forces with the guerrilla bands. By 1979, assassination and terrorism by both the government itself and those seeking to topple it were daily occurrences.

Two spectacular government massacres of demonstrators in May 1979 convinced many in the army itself that General Romero would have to go, and after consulting the Jesuit university, and probably the U.S. embassy, a coup was arranged for October 15, 1979. It went smoothly, but its aftermath was not peace. The ruling junta contained the social democrat Guillermo Manuel Ungo and Román Mayorga, rector of the Jesuit university, along with a conservative businessman and two colonels. Ungo and Mayorga attempted to reach a compromise with the armed leftist forces in the field and the popular organizations, but they were frustrated by the attitude of the army and security forces which continued to press for a military solution. As a result, Ungo and Mayorga left the junta in January 1980, and the Christian Democrats moved in; their leaders Antonio Morales Erlich and, eventually, José Napoleón Duarte were named to a new junta.

Duarte, a Notre Dame–trained engineer, eventually became president of the junta and great things were expected of him, especially in Washington where he was regarded as the one man who could salvage the situation, but it turned out that Duarte could do little. The military and security forces marched to a different drummer. They were controlled by Colonel José Guillermo García, who plainly did not take his orders from Duarte. In April 1980, a civil war began which seemed endless, the military flatly refusing to negotiate with the Marxist rebels. Duarte's ambitious land reform scheme, largely drafted in Washington and far more drastic than the one which got Arbenz in so much trouble in the 1950s, was constantly frustrated by the violence of the military, of the rebels, and of the right-wing death squads, which seemed to operate with impunity in government-controlled areas. The land reform's director, José Rodolfo Viera, and his two North American advisers were murdered in January 1981, dealing the program a blow from which it has never recovered. Bank nationalization in March 1980 failed to solve the deteriorating economic situation and the mass flight of capital.

The spring of 1982 thus found the military unable to dislodge the rebels from their mountain strongholds, the GNP declining at the rate of almost 10 percent per year, and the death squads still at their grisly work. Yet, until a couple of weeks before the March 28 elections, the U.S. embassy still expected Duarte's PDC to capture enough seats in the constituent assembly to be able to govern. Actually, considering the record upon which the PDC ran, it did well to get the largest number of seats of any of the six parties contesting the election. But, since all of the other parties were to the right of the PDC, a right coalition was formed under Roberto D'Aubuisson, who became president of the assembly.

This has created a realignment of the power structure. In the person of the charismatic rightist fanatic D'Aubuisson, the army found itself faced with a formidable rival for power. His ARENA party sought to turn back the clock in El Salvador and give the lion's share of the dwindling resources back to those who once possessed them. The end of the multisided upheaval in El Salvador is still not in sight.

Honduras

There are a number of clichés often used in discussing Honduras which do not stand up very well under close examination. According to these clichés, Honduras has never had the great inequality of landed wealth which is found in neighboring El Salvador. Further, Honduras has been a relatively democratic country, thanks to its long-standing two-party system. Also, Honduras tends to be a peaceful place not given to violent change. The first of these clichés runs up against the statistical facts. Using data from 1952, and the situation has if anything deteriorated since that date, Durham shows that 75 percent of Honduran farms were under ten hectares and accounted for only 16.1 percent of total farmland, while 38 percent of the farm-land was held by 0.8 percent of the farms, all over 200 hectares in size. Farms of more than 500 hectares, or roughly 1,200 acres, accounted for 28.2 percent of the arable land. Comparison of the land tenure profile, using 1965–1966 data for Honduras and 1971 data for El Salvador, actually shows the patterns to be quite similar and led Durham to conclude: "Although Honduras has more land and larger farms than El Salvador, the pattern of land distribution has made the land short-age problem of the small farmers there no less acute there than it is across the border." [23] Land reforms since then have been more cosmetic than real.

General Oswaldo López Arellano ruled Honduras from the time of his illegal seizure of power in October 1963 until his final ouster in March 1975, though he used a puppet civilian president in 1971 and

1972. He was followed by two other successive military dictators, the last of whom only bowed out with the election of a civilian in the fall of 1981. There has not been as much violence in Honduras as in Guatemala or El Salvador, to be sure, but there have been many violent episodes all the same, such as the brutal attacks upon Salvadoran immigrants by the government-backed death squad called the Mancha Brava, which precipitated the war of 1969. Nor can one forget the gruesome murders of peasants and priests in Olancho in 1975 by gangs of landholder vigilantes, or the turmoil and violence surrounding the Isletas commune in the late 1970s. All is not placid in Honduran society.

Still, certain institutions do challenge the government's monopoly of power through peaceful means. Unionism took a giant stride in 1954 with the strikers' victories against United and Standard Fruit companies, and two powerful labor confederations exist, each with a rural and urban component. The proudly autonomous National University also is a force to be reckoned with, as is the independent and often vociferous press. The late 1970s, however, saw increasing government encroachment against the prerogatives of all these institutions.

During the same period, the Salvadoran rebels began to use the southern mountains of Honduras as a relatively safe staging area for their campaigns. This caused the Honduran army to move into the region and begin cooperation against the rebels in league with its former enemy, the Salvadoran army. One result of that was the Rio Sumpul massacre, when hundreds of civilians, caught between the two armies as they tried to flee into Honduras, were indiscriminately massacred.

With the fall of Somoza in July 1979, a new problem faced Honduras, the influx of thousands of National Guards and other Somocistas, who set up camp along the Honduras-Nicaragua border and proceeded to raid into their homeland. The Honduran government has looked the other way and has, in fact, aided the Nicaraguan rightist rebels whenever possible, thus creating an explosive situation which might lead to war. This evidently would not displease the current military commander of Honduras, Colonel Gustavo Alvarez, who appears to be a strong man in the López Arellano tradition.[24]

Honduras is therefore a country very typical of the region in having profound dysfunctional tendencies likely to lead to all-out armed conflict. The seizure of the San Pedro Sula Chamber of Commerce by a dozen Cinchonero guerrillas in October 1982 might have been the first stroke of a civil war.

Nicaragua

Somoza's Nicaragua resembled the previously discussed states of Central America in having a high proportion of the wealth concentrated in the hands of a few. Indeed, perhaps a quarter of the total wealth of the country was in the hands of the Somoza family and its close associates. It differed, however, in certain important respects. First of all, it was a family enterprise, in a sense that even El Salvador under the "fourteen families" was not. Second, Nicaragua was penetrated by U.S. investment to a degree far beyond that of any other country of the region. Booth Fisheries, General Mills, Borden, and a host of other North American firms had operations there.[25] Third, a certain amount of apparent opposition was allowed, from the Conservative party, which sometimes contested elections against Somoza's Liberals; from the newspaper *La Prensa*, edited by the maverick journalist Pedro Joaquín Chamorro Cardenal; and from university intellectuals. As these opposition groups were ineffective, they were tolerated.

As long as they put up with the Somoza family's hogging the lion's share of the wealth, the upper middle class, whether Liberals or Conservatives, could make a good life for themselves. This class tended to be more urbane than that of any other Central American state and more North American in orientation and outlook. Indeed, one of the ironies of the region is that the two countries of Latin America which were most North Americanized, Cuba and Nicaragua, have had the most profound anti-Yankee revolutions. This is no coincidence—nationalist resentment against the United States lies at the heart of both revolutions. The Somozas, like Cuba's Batista, were regarded by their own people as a front for the North Americans, and the resentment against the last of the family, the West Point–trained Anastasio Somoza Debayle, could not help but spill over against his gringo protectors.

The last of the Somozas began to topple when his capital city did, on December 23, 1972, in the great earthquake. In the aftermath of the disaster, Somoza and his National Guard looted relief supplies and directed aid funds into their own pockets. The new archbishop of Managua, Miguel Obando y Bravo, promptly began a string of denunciations which would not stop until Somoza fell. A second nail was driven into the coffin of the regime in the murder of Pedro Joaquín Chamorro, evidently by thugs hired by someone close to Somoza, in January 1978. This frightened many middle-class individuals who had been accustomed to picking up the crumbs of profit left by the family while denouncing the Somozas from the safety of their private clubs.

A profound consensus began to form among all elements of society that Somoza must go. The family had taken too much of the nation's resources and had now become too oppressive.

The only group that proved capable of providing leadership for this consensus was the Sandinista movement. This Marxist guerrilla movement had never attained great popularity and, despite an occasional major victory, such as the seizure of the guests at U.S. Ambassador Turner Shelton's farewell party in December 1974, was not considered any threat to Somoza as late as the summer of 1977.[26] But by the fall of 1978, almost every group, from disgruntled business leaders to hungry peasants, had rallied behind them, much to the horror of the U.S. embassy. It was this broad coalition with the FSLN, much of it ideologically not in tune with the Sandinistas, which finally toppled the Somozas in July 1979.

This was seen in Nicaragua as a great national crusade against the Somozas and also against North American domination. Nicaraguans have long memories and recall that it was against the U.S. Marines that Sandino himself had fought, that Anastasio Somoza García had been put into power by those same marines, and that ambassadors from the beginning of the regime down to Turner Shelton had been so closely identified with the family as to seem their special envoys to the United States. This is not to say that good relations between the Sandinista government and the United States would have been impossible, but rather that any hectoring on the part of the United States was likely to be met with massive resistance rather than capitulation. Although the FSLN might suppress freedom of the press and freedom of political association at home, and though its economy might be a shambles, it would continue to be popular in Nicaragua as long as it was perceived as being hated in Washington. This was ensured by the profound nationalist roots of the Nicaraguan revolution.

Costa Rica

This country is considered by most observers to be so different from the rest of Central America that it is seldom brought into discussions of the region. As in the case of Honduras, there are many clichés about Costa Rica, and, as in the Honduran case, many of them are inaccurate. This is said to be a democratic nation of largely European yeoman farmers, a kind of Central American Switzerland with a high standard of living and extensive public services.

The democracy can trace its continuity back only to 1948, when the last army-backed regime was tossed out and the army abolished. This is well within the memory of those who today wield most of the

125

power in the country, though it is also true that in early times Costa Rica had more frequent democratic regimes than its neighbors. The actual ethnic composition of a country is hard to identify, but a stroll down the streets of San José would not show the casual observer a population much different from that which might be found in Tegucigalpa or Managua.

The most important question is that of the land, for the revolutions to the north of Costa Rica are mostly over control of this resource. In area, Costa Rica is not much larger than El Salvador. Traditionally the population has been much smaller than Salvador's, but there has been a spurt in the past decade so that some 2.2 million persons now occupy the national territory and this number is rapidly increasing. The landholding yeomanry which once existed has largely disappeared. After careful study, Mitchell A. Seligson concluded that "Development of export-oriented agrarian capitalist production has had a devastating effect on the peasant way of life." He notes that from 1963 to 1973 there was a growth of minifundia—that is, farms too small to sustain a family, thanks to persistent subdivision. At the same time, the growth of very large estates had been "nothing short of spectacular." Nor, writing in 1980, does he find any relief in sight.[27]

This process is not new; it began with the introduction of the coffee culture in the late nineteenth century and picked up with the banana industry and the rise of sugar cane planting in the twentieth century. The situation did not previously reach revolutionary potential, because of the existence of safety valves. There was light industry in San José where the displaced peasantry could work, jobs in agribusiness which paid fairly well, or fresh lands to clear, a chance to start all over. But the past decade has seen a crippling of the nation's economy. Now that export crops have displaced the yeomen, there is no market for those export crops. The light industry has also weakened, and the government, unable to sustain the admirable social services through taxation, has been forced to borrow so heavily that today it is virtually bankrupt.

Land reform is a solution suggested by the traditions of democracy and social justice ascribed to the country, but this would require compensation to the former owners, loans to the new owners, and the ability to sustain a period of agricultural dislocation. Seligson's conclusion is that it is unclear that the dwindling national resources would be able to handle these problems.[28] In the absence of a sweeping land reform, seizures of land by the peasantry have become all too common, and these have sometimes led to violence. A Marxist peasant organization called the United National Federation of Agricultural Workers and Campesinos (Federación Unitaria Nacional de los Trabajadores Agrícolas y de Campesinos, or FUNTAC) has come into existence and is raising the consciousness of the peasantry in the same manner as similar groups are doing in El Salvador and Guatemala. The Monge government faces a revolutionary example across the border and resource competition at home that could bring about profound changes in Costa Rican life.

Conclusion

The dismal litany of this chapter has been that resource competition and persistent poverty lie at the heart of the Central American revolution. If this is so, it would seem futile to consider supporting the status quo on the desperate hope that the old order can hang on until some miracle rearranges the world political scene and exorcises the specter of communism throughout the planet. The sailor in Edgar Allan Poe's tale survived the maelstrom not by fighting it, but by observing its tendencies and using them. The causes of the revolution must be understood and the course of the revolution guided to create a society in which most of the population share in the existing resources and in which new resources are developed. The picture painted in this chapter suggests that this will not be easy, and may indeed be impossible, but the alternative is a continuation of the dark and chaotic struggle which can only perpetuate human misery.

Notes

1. *This Week Central America and Panama,* August 30, 1982.
2. William H. Durham, *Scarcity and Survival in Central America: Ecological Origins of the Soccer War* (Stanford, Calif.: Stanford University Press, 1979), pp. 170–72.
3. *This Week Central America and Panama,* August 16, 1982.
4. Thomas Melville and Marjorie Melville, *Guatemala: The Politics of Land Ownership* (New York: Free Press, 1971), p. xi.
5. David Browning, *El Salvador: Landscape and Society* (London: Oxford University Press, 1971), p. 16.
6. Thomas P. Anderson, *Matanza: El Salvador's Communist Revolt of 1932* (Lincoln: University of Nebraska Press, 1971), p. 136.
7. Kenneth F. Johnson, *Mexican Democracy: A Critical View,* rev. ed. (New York: Praeger, 1978), pp. vi, 1–9.
8. David R. Raynolds, *Rapid Development in Small Economies: The Example of El Salvador* (New York: Praeger, 1967), pp. 94–99.

9. Alastair White, *El Salvador* (New York: Praeger, 1973), p. 143.

10. Melville and Melville, *Guatemala: Politics of Land Ownership*, pp. 2–3.

11. Eduardo H. Galeano, *Guatemala: Occupied Country* (New York: Monthly Review Press, 1969), p. 83.

12. Penny Lernoux, *Cry of the People: The Struggle for Human Rights in Latin America* (1980; reprint, New York: Penguin Books, 1982), pp. 11–12, 40–41.

13. Thomas P. Anderson, "El Salvador," *Yearbook on International Communist Affairs* (Stanford, Calif.: Hoover Institution Press, 1980), pp. 354–55.

14. Galeano, *Guatemala: Occupied Country*, pp. 34–35.

15. Stephen Schlesinger and Stephen Kinzer, *Bitter Fruit: The Untold Story of the American Coup in Guatemala* (Garden City, N.Y.: Doubleday, 1982), p. 254.

16. Melville and Melville, *Guatemala: Politics of Land Ownership*, pp. 193, 254.

17. *Latin America Political Report*, April 6, 1979.

18. *Latin America Regional Report*, July 11, 1980.

19. Galeano, *Guatemala: Occupied Country*, p. 30.

20. *Panzós Testimonio* (Guatemala: Centro de Investigación de Historia Social, 1979), pp. 27, 31.

21. *This Week Central America and Panama*, February 4, 1980.

22. Thomas P. Anderson, *The War of the Dispossessed: Honduras and El Salvador, 1969* (Lincoln: University of Nebraska Press, 1981), pp. 141–42.

23. Durham, *Scarcity and Survival*, pp. 111–13.

24. *Latin America Update*, September/October 1982.

25. "La Presencia Imperialista," *Cuadernos de Amanta 1.*, no. 1 (August 1979), p. 9.

26. Penny Lernoux, "The Somozas of Nicaragua," *The Nation*, July 23, 1978, pp. 72–77.

27. Mitchell A. Seligson, *Peasants of Costa Rica and the Development of Agrarian Capitalism* (Madison: University of Wisconsin Press, 1980), pp. 23, 146, 168.

28. Ibid., p. 165.

6

Civil-Military Relations in Central America: The Dilemmas of Political Institutionalization

RONALD H. MCDONALD

Since independence, the military has been a key variable in the political processes of the Central American republics. A good case can be made that the political role of the military has been unique for each of the five republics. Certainly the range of experiences over the past generation has been great, with Costa Rica having no formal military establishment and Nicaragua moving from a patrimonial state in which the military served at the favor of the Somoza family regime to a revolutionary state in which the military serves to defend the revolution. Even in the three remaining countries (Guatemala, El Salvador, and Honduras) the range of experiences with the military in politics has been considerable and varied. There is a common theme in all these cases, however, as the nature and context of military involvement in politics in the region has evolved over the years. That theme is the crisis of institutionalization in the region within the context of modernization, specifically the imbalances which have evolved between civil and military institutions.

Modernization and Civil-Military Relations

Economic development and other forms of modernization have proceeded in all five countries over the past generation, and with them have slowly evolved increased political awareness and social mobilization of the populations.[1] To maintain order and manage development, there has been a growing need for viable institutions.[2] The only realistic option in the region has been either stronger civil institutions or stronger military ones. In all the countries except Costa Rica, the struggle to develop stronger civil institutions has been frustrated by both domestic and foreign resistance. Military organizations have been encouraged by domestic elites, who value the stability possible with a strong military, by the United States, which has generally seen the military as a bastion against the intrusion of alien ideologies and revolutionary movements, and by the military officers themselves, who value the increased viability, capability, and prestige of their organizations. Military organizations have increasingly modernized their forces, professionalized their elites, increasing their bureaucratic and organizational capabilities, their technical skills, their leadership, and gradually institutionalized a sense of collegial identification and collegial interests.

Individual rivalries, hostilities, and animosities still divide military elites, as do generational and rank differences, but the sense of group action and group interests has increased. The rather old-fashioned type of regime based on a single dictator, an entrenched military tyrant, a family, or a small clique has increasingly become incapable of governing nations of growing complexity and heightened political awareness. The clash has been between military and civil elements, much as it has been for generations, but the context has changed. The more modern organizations have overwhelmed the more traditional, and for strategic reasons the military has had a distinct advantage over the civil organizations in responding to modernization and the opportunities created by it.[3]

Costa Rica, so far an exception to this tendency as a result of extraordinary leadership, a favorable environment, and good fortune, managed to institutionalize its civil processes and organizations relatively early, while simultaneously controlling possible threats to them from the military, ultimately abolishing the latter altogether. The old-fashioned patrimonial dictatorship of the Somoza family in Nicaragua built a military wholly dependent and subservient to its limited interests. With the degeneration of the family leadership and its increasingly outmoded style of government, the only politically viable alternative was revolution—literally the reconstituting of Nicaraguan society. No independent institutionalized military existed to provide a successor to the traditional regime.

In the remaining three countries (Guatemala, El Salvador, and Honduras) semi-institutionalized military organizations have dominated collectively as groups (rather than an individual strong man) their nations' politics for the past generation in the vacuum created by the failure of civil organizations and processes to institutionalize. The one-sided contest is now under attack by radical elements that want to change the systems, and the prospects for revolution in each of the three countries suggest struggles which are far greater in scope, loss of life, and general chaos than what has already been seen in Nicaragua.

With serious financial and economic problems confronting it, even Costa Rica is not immune to such a struggle, and its options are in some respects even more vexing. It must either maintain and strengthen its present civil institutional structures and processes, which under the circumstances (should they persist) may be difficult, or follow its neighbors in building a professional military organization, which in turn ultimately could threaten its own civil institutions. The alternative to these options for Costa Rica may be an emerging revolutionary confrontation as well.

Three Patterns of Change. Three general patterns of change can be identified for the military organizations in each of the countries, which help to explain both the evolution of civil-military relations and the divergencies which currently exist between the nations. These patterns include modernization, professionalization, and institutionalization of military organizations. These terms are often used casually, even interchangeably in the literature dealing with the military, and it is therefore important from the outset to clarify how these terms are being used here.[4]

By modernization I mean primarily the adoption of more sophisticated weaponry, tactics, and resources by military organizations, largely through the importation of technologies and materials developed for military purposes elsewhere. Modernization increases the potential effectiveness of military organizations in the technical sense and makes it easier and more efficient for them to complete their assigned tasks. New weapons, new communications systems, new tactics such as counterinsurgency, even new branches or divisions, such as air forces, fall into the general category of modernization.

By professionalization I mean primarily the training of personnel for their respective roles in the military, either as officers or as recruits, but particularly in the case of Central America, the former. Professionalization presumes formal education, in Central America as in most developing areas specifically the use of both national military academies and foreign (local and overseas) military training assistance. Professionalization increases the efficiency and skills of individuals, but it also inevitably changes their orientation to their roles, inculcating them with new values and commitments that both change and standardize their perceptions of themselves, again by changing and stand-

131

ardizing the processes through which they are recruited and rewarded or advanced within the organization. Professionalization produces more bureaucratic and potentially at least more stable processes than the traditional relationships in which the bonds are familial, patrimonial, or associational, and tends to reward (again, at least in principle) achievement or attainment and performance rather than personal loyalties and commitments.[5]

By institutionalization I mean a process whereby military organizations assume a life of their own in the sense that they develop their own processes for renewal and regeneration which transcend specific military leaders. They command principal loyalties and allegiances from those associated with them, and they establish a common bond of identifications, values, expectations, and interests. There are of course many conceivable (as well as actual) patterns for institutionalizing military organizations, which define variably in the process of institutionalization the relationships between the military personnel, their organizations, and their civilian counterparts. Military institutions may evolve so as to be subservient to civil sectors of society, equal to or competitive with them, or dominant over them. All of these patterns have emerged at various times in Central America.[6]

These three processes, which have changed and continue to change civil-military relations in Central America, are closely related, but I think it is essential to separate them analytically. They have tended historically to be somewhat sequential in their effect: Military organizations in the region began to modernize first, some as early as the mid-nineteenth century. Professionalization came, or is coming, later. Few have progressed very far along the path of institutionalization, but the influence and pressures to do so are clearly visible and important. In all instances, what has emerged are organizations which are complex mixtures. They are mixed in terms of the balances between the three processes—the levels that have been attained in each—and they are mixed in the sense that many very traditional characteristics remain and may even dominate these processes of change. None of the military organizations in Central America have reached high levels in any of the processes, not even by Latin American standards, let alone standards common to industrial countries. But these three long-term processes are influencing military organizations in the region, and more to the point civil-military relations there. They represent one important basis for characterizing those relations in each of the countries, and comparing contemporary realities with historical ones as well as with realities in the other nations. How, why, and when these processes were initiated, by whom, and under whose tutelage are important questions to raise in understanding the resulting patterns.

To the casual observer, the past half-century in all the Central American republics except Costa Rica has been one of military government, repeated processes if not cycles of coups and countercoups, and in general political instability. These conclusions are not inaccurate, but they are gross and breed more confusion than clarity. The military as a political factor has evolved and changed in each of the countries, as have the context and conditions under which they have participated, intervened, or controlled their nations' politics.[7] It is my purpose here to sketch briefly the organizational and environmental factors which affect the decision making of the military elites, and the changing relationships between civil and military groups in the region. Within the context of economic and social change in Central America, military organizations have been more responsive to adaptation and institutionalization than civilian ones have been. The central crisis is one of institutionalization, or rather the imbalances created by that process between civil and military organizations, a crisis that in and by itself can lead to revolution and political upheaval. The experience of El Salvador illustrates clearly and dramatically the changes identified, and for that reason the contest between the military and civil groups in that country will be used as a case study in the analysis.

Evolution of the Military as a Political Force in Central America

The origins of military politics and government in Latin America are well known and extensively analyzed. Essentially the tradition finds its roots in colonial Latin America, as the military was a principal instrument, in some areas the only effective one, for maintaining control over the indigenous peoples and the developing colonies. As was commonly the case at the time in European monarchies, the army and the crown (or government) were indivisible, and loyalties extended from the former to the latter through a complex and uncompromising series of legal and contractual bonds. The Central American republics were ruled prior to independence from the captaincy general of Guatemala, their peoples mostly Indian, with Creoles, *peninsulares*, and mestizos numbering no more than a few thousand. Following the example of Mexico, a paradigm that was to continue to exert influence on Central American leaders, the region declared independence in 1821, a move supported even by the captain general himself, Gabino Gainza. The landowning aristocracy in the region wanted independence principally because they believed it would be more profitable than continued subservience to Spain, and independence came with little violence once it had been proclaimed. The aristocracy was badly divided on regional, economic, and ideological grounds, producing throughout the region concentrations of interests that ultimately became known as "conservatives" and "liberals," a familiar story in Latin American history. These divisions acquired a military dimension, as the two groups mounted guerrilla armies that were fighting each other for control over the region's government agencies. The soldiers were untrained mercenaries paid by the aristocrats to wage war against their political enemies, in many cases mobilizing Indians who were pressed into military service by the landowners to whom they were indentured. The military, if one can extend that term to include these guerrilla groups, was an extension of aristocratic objectives and strategies and was totally under their control.[8]

Although the five weak republics went their separate ways after 1838, the idea of confederation, some sort of common regional union, stubbornly persisted, and regimes in the various republics—especially the three northern ones—continued to treat the internal political squabbles and conflicts in their neighboring republics as though they were affairs of their own. For several generations liberals and conservatives intervened to assist their like elites elsewhere in the region achieve victory over their opponents, and military actions became a standing tactic to achieve the political ends. The aristocracy did not directly involve itself in the daily control of the military organizations, nor did it directly provide leadership or an officer corps for the militia. As the aristocratic tendencies cloaked in the labels of conservative and liberal acquired the status of "parties" loosely conceived, strong, ambitious leaders, normally not from the landowning classes, emerged to control their countries, and military power became their chief instrument for rule. These men, dictators in the traditional sense of the term in Central America, were, like the guerrilla bands following independence, instruments for upper-class objectives in their continuing internecine political contests. The more effective of these dictators—like Rafael Carrera in Guatemala (1838–1865)—achieved a symbiotic relationship with the wealthy, sometimes overpowering them in resources based ultimately upon military power. The hallmark of these regimes was the traditionalism and lack of professionalization of their military forces. Leaders were dependent for their rank and privilege on the dictator personally, and their fate was ultimately tied to his. The military organizations in the region were instruments for control, not organizations that could by themselves control their nations' governments. Military strong men, if they were not members of the economic elite, sought its approval and membership in it. The relationship between the military strong men and the wealthy was mutually beneficial and reinforcing, and it is not surprising that the military rapidly became concerned in the nineteenth century in Central America with the preservation of privilege and the protection of wealth.

Another reality of the past century which affected the development of military and civil relations was decentralization, which evolved in the absence of effective central control from the capital city over the entire nation. This in turn allowed the development of local or regional caudillos, part of a system tied to the *latifundios* (large land holdings), which had effective control and coercion over limited areas within the country. In such small countries, and with relatively concentrated settlement in the nineteenth century, the reality of local caudillos was less significant than it was in larger countries, such as Mexico, Colombia, Argentina, or Venezuela. Nonetheless it did exist. In Nicaragua the regional divisions centered on the two rival cities of Granada and León, spatially polarizing the liberal-conservative division. Each community had its own military organization, which vied with each other for nominal control over the nation-state and its treasury.[9]

The inability or unwillingness of civilian elites to resolve their differences produced a half-century of near anarchy in the republics, relieved only by the imposition of a strong rule by individual dictators who could command sufficient military force to contain all opposition. The opportunity for economic development, which in each country meant the development of a viable export economy, increasingly placed a premium on stability and gave dictators at least a potential lever for political negotiation with the landowners, and ultimately with foreign corporations, which regarded political stability as an important prerequisite for cash investments. There was also the continuing threat of external invasion of the republics from their neighbors, and defense was a primary concern prompting the creation of more effective national military forces. These often coexisted with regional forces, performing largely police functions, and with private armies which continued to be organized and financed by many of the landowners.

Early Modernization of the Military. The earliest efforts at modernizing an armed force came by the middle of the nineteenth century, in often informal and modest ways. Representatives from larger Latin American nations were brought in to advise local military leaders.

Colombia provided some military assistance, for example, to El Salvador as early as the 1850s, and advisers from Chile, Spain, France, and other countries soon followed.[10] Along with this gradual modernization, there was a tenuous beginning of professionalization, in very limited ways, of the officer corps, the elites of the military, with the goal of more effective organization and command and greater tactical skills. But only slowly did there emerge the notion of a professional career soldier. The gestures toward professionalization did little if anything to change the internal dynamics of politics of the armies. They remained essentially traditional, loyalties based on personal bonds and *compadrazgo*, with leadership ultimately gravitating to the strongest and/or the most ruthless of the military officers.

Toward the end of the nineteenth century a pattern was set in Central American military organizations that was to persist until the last half-century or so, one which gave priority to building a more modern army and a somewhat more professional officer corps, for the armies had become an essential component for stability and continuity. The first half-century following independence, and particularly the period following the breakup of the United Provinces, was a time of civil wars, transnational interventions, and constantly threatening international and internal conflicts. Armed forces began to acquire a more national outlook, a symbol for national stability and viability in the face of chaos. In Nicaragua the party-inspired civil wars continued virtually unabated, but in Costa Rica there already were efforts to limit the army as a political factor. The Costa Rican constitution of 1948 provided for the abolition of the army and the creation of a civil guard as a permanent institution.

Apart from the need for a permanent modern army, the last half of the nineteenth century also saw the Central American republics increasingly able to afford such organizations, largely because of the development of their export economies. Economic development encouraged modernization, but as John J. Johnson observed, Latin American "nations often 'modernized' their fighting forces faster than they modernized other areas of their societies."[11] Justo Rufino Barrios, who controlled Guatemala from 1871 to 1885, was obsessed with technological development, and did much to build a more modern army, a more professional officer class in Guatemala. El Salvador, faced with the constant threat of peasant revolts in the last half of the nineteenth century owing to the confiscation of peasants' land for the sake of the wealthy coffee growers, established internal security forces which by 1895 had been extended by decree over the entire country. These "national" forces had emerged out of private armies organized and paid for by the coffee plantation owners, and along with the national army they constituted a growing if fragmented national force designed to maintain stability and control over a restless population. Honduras, sparsely populated and largely outside the experiences of economic development, alternated liberal and conservative regimes and dictators, but its army did not begin to modernize until much later, well into the twentieth century. The Honduran army was small, its officers untrained and poorly compensated, and it constituted little more than a praetorian guard to whoever was in control at the time.[12]

By the twentieth century the five Central American republics were on different courses in the development and evolution of their militaries. Three of them—Guatemala, El Salvador, and Honduras—shared many realities in common: the beginning of a modernized force and a somewhat professionalized military command, armies dependent on the lower stratum of society (in Guatemala, the Indian) for soldiers, a close and increasingly interdependent relationship with the landed elites, substantial decentralization in the command and control of the forces, and an active role in the nations' politics, providing a basis for recruiting dictators and a mechanism for their control.[13] In 1889 Costa Rica held its first free and honest election, after a half-century of rather authoritarian elitist regimes in which the army played an important role. From that time onward, the civilian institutions grew relatively strong, and the army, while still a variable in national politics, failed to dominate the country. Following the brief revolution of 1948, which ended the attempt to impose continuation of a regime, the resulting junta abolished the army altogether, replacing it with a national police and turning the main army barracks into a national museum. A different pattern emerged in Nicaragua, where party-sponsored armies continued to contest for national power through the nineteenth century. In 1912 the first group of U.S. Marines marched into Nicaragua, and remained in the country at varying levels of strength for nineteen of the following twenty-one years. In 1927 the United States established a national police or "National Guard" to replace the unreliable Nicaraguan army, an act which ultimately facilitated the rise to power of Anastasio Somoza and changed the course of Nicaraguan history.[14]

These experiences represent a different balance and emphasis in the growth of civil and military organizations in Central America during the twentieth century. In Guatemala and El Salvador the modernizing militaries by the early twentieth century and in Honduras by the mid-twentieth century had become the dominant organizations in the countries, and civil organizations for a variety of reasons were either overwhelmed by them or failed to develop apart from them. The gradual professionalizing of the military elites in these countries did not produce viable military institutions in the broader context but merely armed military organizations whose leaders were acquiring greater skills and resources that could further counterbalance or overwhelm civilian elites. The period produced personal dictatorships in these countries, which often endured over an extended period. Slowly, professional training and, more important, new generations of military officers did emerge, with a sense increasingly of collective—or institutional—responsibility for their nations' development and political viability.[15] These institutions became an important new factor in national politics following World War II.

Military control and intervention in national politics continued to be the dominant reality in all three countries, but the nature of that control and intervention was shifting from a strictly personal loyalty to a traditional strong man or dictator to a collective involvement, where individual leaders emerged out of a context of more bureaucratic organizational politics within the military organization. The individual dominance of these new military leaders over national politics never reached the levels of control characteristic of the earlier period. In the past thirty-five years in each of the three countries, military rulers have come and gone with remarkable regularity, though the military as an organization has remained in control of national government and politics.

The National Guard in Nicaragua under the Somoza regimes fits almost precisely what Max Weber described as a "patrimonial rule," a regime based on traditional authority under which a nation is ruled as though it were an extension of the ruler's household and in which the military is the personal representative of the ruler dependent for its rank, status, and welfare on the favors of the ruler and his extended household and obeys him out of regard for this traditional status.[16] The professionalization of such a household army was quite possible without institutionalizing it, and indeed for the Somoza family an institutionalized military could have been threatening. The model on which the Somoza regime depended at the national level was not much different from the models seen earlier in Guatemala, El Salvador, and Honduras, where wealthy landowners had created their own military forces in much the same way, though more limited spatially in the territory they controlled or dominated. Effective as the National Guard was under the Somoza regimes, it developed no sense of institutional identity apart from the family; such an institutional perspective would have been inimical to the interests of the regime. The demise of the Somoza family regime took with it the Guard, and left a vacuum which the revolutionary forces of the Sandinista regime have been trying to fill since 1979.[17]

Costa Rica's experience with military intervention, or rather lack of it, is unique, not only for Central America but generally. The durability of its democratic traditions and the abolishment of a formal army in 1948 sometimes obscures the role the army did play in the nation's history earlier, particularly in the nineteenth century, though it was rarely a dominant factor. The weakness of the military tradition in Costa Rica may be due more to a combination of special circumstances than the distinctiveness of the Costa Ricans. The conditions which prompted the growth of strong military organizations in the other states—divisive party warfare, imminent threats from external intervention by neighboring states, and political instability—these conditions were largely absent in Costa Rica. Its population was effectively isolated geographically from the remainder of the region, its population enjoyed a relatively prosperous condition and access to land, and its traditional elite was relatively cohesive and decidedly small; by the mid-nineteenth century there were still only about eighty thousand persons in the entire country, and most of these were living in a fairly compact area surrounding the capital city of San José. Strong civilian traditions, the same traditions which prompted the two-month "revolution" of 1948 to save the country from an imposed rule, were well developed, and the national police force so far has been sufficient to guarantee national stability. As will be argued later, this tranquil period in Costa Rican history may be coming to an end, and with it the unique dominance of the civil over military forces.

Recruitment, Class, and Training of Military Organizations

The significance of military institutions can be approximated by measuring and comparing their size and expenditures, though many factors distort such evaluations. Estimates for the Central American countries over the past quarter century vary significantly from one source to another, reflecting differences in the concepts used for measurement as well as the unreliability of the data. The size of the military forces is complicated by the fact that each of the republics divides its military forces into groups which often include regular armies, special police (which are in effect extensions of military power), militia, and reserves. Expenditures are obscured by the common practice of distributing them among several official ministries in the budget, as well as by the common practice of disguising expenditures to hide the actual amounts spent. When one compares data for the 1960s, however, the period preceding the emergence of revolutionary movements, most sources notwithstanding differences suggest that both the size of the military and expenditures on the military for Central

TABLE 6-1
SIZE OF THE MILITARY AND EXPENDITURES FOR THE MILITARY
IN CENTRAL AMERICA, 1965

	Guatemala	El Salvador	Honduras	Nicaragua	Costa Rica
			Manpower		
Per 1,000 sq. km.	82.6	280.4	44.6	50.1	0
Per 1,000 of working-age population	4.0	3.9	4.6	8.7	0
Rank worldwide per 1,000 working-age population of 119.5 countries	76.5	78	72	51	119.5
Total	9,000	6,000	5,000	7,000	0
			Expenditures		
Dollars per capita	3.5	3.42	3.06	4.83	1.40
As a percentage of GNP	1.0	1.3	1.4	1.4	0.3
Rank worldwide of 121 countries' GNP	105.5	99.5	95	95	119
Total (millions of dollars)	14	10	7	8	2

SOURCE: Charles L. Taylor and Michael C. Hudson, *World Handbook of Political and Social Indicators* (New Haven, Conn.: Yale University Press, 1972), adapted from pp. 30–37.

America were low by most standards. Some common estimates, if not necessarily accurate ones, are shown in table 6–1. All five nations rank relatively low by world standards in both the percentage of the gross national product spent on the military, a basis for comparison which equalizes nations for their size and wealth, and the total size of the military forces per thousand persons of the working-age population. Since none of these forces at the time were designed primarily for international defense, it can be assumed that their size and support are primarily for domestic security. Other estimates differ with these, some higher, some lower.

All these figures mask, however, the more critical question of how reliable, how useful, how responsive these forces are to command, to control, and to crisis situations, and here considerable differences exist within the region. My purpose here is to make such evaluations of the traditional military forces—that is, those preceding the most recent crises of the 1980s. The conclusions which seem inevitable are (1) that a major difference exists between the officer corps and the recruits, which is critical to evaluating the military; and (2) that professionalization of the officer corps to the extent that it has occurred in each nation has produced a "new class" in Central American politics which competes with the other classes in the traditional political confrontations.[18] It is a small but powerful and influential class that shares common economic and social interests despite conflicting and competing ambitions among its members, a class that functions to a large extent as an interest group—aware of its stake in the course of national politics and able and willing to defend its interests whenever and however necessary. This new class is often in competition if not in conflict with more traditional classes in the countries. It represents a relatively new development in the social structure and political systems of the region and is in effect the key to understanding the viability of the traditional political systems and their capacity to confront and contain frontal attacks by revolutionary movements. Such a class has yet to emerge in Costa Rica, but the pattern elsewhere is fairly clear. The establishment of a professional army in Costa Rica, or the transformation of the national police into a more military-oriented organization, would in time undoubtedly yield much the same results as have been seen in the other countries. The new class of military officers, including those who are active, those who are retired, and in some cases even those who are exiled, represents a tiny fraction of the total population, less numerous even than the traditional economic elites, but a formidable influence nonetheless. Like other classes historically in the region, its ultimate political leverage is force.

The past half-century has seen an increasing professionalization in the officer corps, increasingly as a result of U.S. military assistance and training, and also a slowly emerging institutionalization of the military in the sense that its internal processes, values, and rules have become more stabilized and clarified, and the body of officers who constitute the new class are more aware of those actions which fall within the accepted expectations of their group. These two processes have proceeded at different rates and to different levels in the five republics. In Honduras, one observer has characterized the change in the military as one of "creeping professionalization."[19] Under the Somozas, Nicaragua's military was professionalized but not institutionalized. In Guatemala and El Salvador elements of both can be found.

Professionalization has involved training officers in the skills and techniques of the military, which in the context of Central America has also meant basic education beyond the point of literacy. But it has also involved inculcation and indoctrination of values which support their professional status and the institution they serve, as well as a more regularized process for recruiting and promoting officers and establishing a career path for individuals who opt for a military career. The change has been away from the nineteenth-century practices, when military officers were commonly self-appointed generals, caudillos, or individuals who served entirely at the largess of warring party elites or traditional dictators, when a "career" in the military (if the experience can be so characterized) was unstable, unpredictable, and entirely dependent on personal relationships for its security. The motivation for professionalization came from the economic elites of the region who found military forces necessary to maintain control over opposition groups, foreign interests, and of course the masses. These elites rarely if ever chose a professional military career for themselves or donated a son for that purpose, as did by contrast the Argentine elite.[20] They would occasionally accept or take a high command position for a limited time and limited objectives, to guarantee their control over the armed forces.

The establishment of domestic military academies in the region is an approximate measure of at least the duration of the movement toward professionalization. The longest-surviving such institution—in all the countries there have been many examples of military academies that have been established and for whatever reasons subsequently abandoned or replaced—is the National Military Academy in Guatemala, which was founded in 1873. Cadets for the academy are selected at least nominally by competitive examination within each department of the country and are by background largely middle class.[21] In El Salvador, the first effort at professionalization came in 1868 with foreign assistance, a process described in detail below, resulting ultimately by 1929 in the Escuela Militar, the institution which has trained the current generation of Salvadoran officers in a program containing both military skills and a heavy indoctrination in military and nationalistic values, as well as skills in administration and finance.[22]

Honduras was slow to begin modernization, not to mention professionalization of its armed forces. The process was begun by the dictator Tiburcio Carías Andino (1933–1949) under guidance first from European advisers and subsequently from U.S. advisers during World War II. In 1946 a Basic Arms School was founded to train both officers and recruits, and in 1952, again under tutelage of the U.S. military mission in the country, the Francisco Morazán Military Academy was established. It is out of that institution that the present generation of Honduran officers has come.[23]

Nicaragua's military following occupation by U.S. Marines was simply destroyed in the early part of this century in an effort to "pacify" the country. It was replaced with the national police or "National Guard," whose leaders were entirely trained by the American forces. This practice continued in Nicaragua throughout the Somoza regime, which relied heavily on U.S. training for its professional military leaders, mostly training outside Nicaragua. A military academy was established in the country in 1928 and subsequently a domestic academy for police training (an indistinguishable division of the Guard) and a preparatory school of noncommissioned officers.[24] U.S. training remained the keystone for professionalizing the Nicaraguan as well as the Honduran forces and was a significant influence in both Guatemala and El Salvador.

Although the ratio of officers to recruits is extraordinarily high in the Central American republics, the bulk of the military is recruits, and the patterns and practices of generating soldiers for the officers to command may in the final analysis prove more critical in Central America than the professionalization of their leaders. All of the countries have compulsory military service, but with predictable results these universal military obligations have been enforced very selectively and in effect have remained relatively unchanged since the nineteenth century. The recruits come from the least advantaged sectors and regions of the countries, are poorly paid if at all, only marginally trained, and in service often out of fear for their lives. The offspring of families of even marginal status can avoid military service and indeed often view such service as only slightly less onerous than a prison sentence.[25]

Within a revolutionary context, the social and class backgrounds of the military are an important factor in assessing their behavior and capability. Again there is a clear and generally consistent pattern in the region. With professionalization the military has become the domain of those traditionally below the individuals and classes who own and control the wealth of the countries, depending on how far the professionalization of recruitment and promotion has gone toward opening up officer careers to individuals on the basis of ability rather than social status. In Guatemala, El Salvador, and Honduras, this has meant an officer class of middle-class origins (granting a broad range within that category) with forces recruited from the lower classes, particularly from rural areas. In Guatemala this has often been no more than pressing Indians into service for the military, as has been done for generations. In El Salvador, Honduras, and Somoza's Nicaragua young men from rural areas and small villages were used as recruits. Because of its higher levels of professionalization and institutionalization, the Salvadoran military can offer some marginal rewards to its recruits after they complete their mandatory service, including special favors such as lower prices for basic commodities which are provided to veterans by the Salvadoran military. These "veterans," rarely much beyond adolescence themselves, remain in the army reserves and in fact constitute the basis of a rather sophisticated network used by the army for internal espionage and intelligence, as well as providing the nucleus for government-organized terrorist squads which have operated in the rural areas. Likewise, under the Somozas those who served in the National Guard received special favors dispensed in the traditional patrimonial way by the Somoza family, as long as they remained loyal to the regime.

For officers military service has become both a career and an opportunity for personal advancement and, within otherwise closed and socially stagnant societies, an open, somewhat structured, and predictable course. Since none of the armies has achieved very high levels of professionalization, traditional bases for reward and punishment continue to exist and often dominate the modern practices. What professionalization means to officers, however, is at least the possibility of more equitable treatment and advancement based in part on ability and initiative and, perhaps more important, a common claim and a common stake in the military as an institution, an association which is both long term and, by comparison with other social and economic institutions, competitive. It is, in other words, the basis for a new class, an association which holds out the possibility of upward mobility for the officers who identify with it.

The distance between the officers and the recruits is quite literally a class difference, both in the traditional sense that they come from somewhat different backgrounds and regions and in the present sense that their expectations and claims upon the military as an institution are indeed different. The gulf between the commanders and the commanded is a serious threat to the viability of the armed forces in the region and one reason why too rapid and too extensive an expansion in the size of the military organizations, with a concurrent reduction in the ratio of officers to recruits, can be potentially threatening to the viability of the institutions. The loyalty of the recruits to the officers and their willingness to accept orders are perhaps the most critical of all variables in the survival of the military in a revolutionary context since the recruits potentially share more in common with the revolutionaries than they do with the officers. This awareness must inevitably influence the tactics of both sides in such a

TABLE 6-2
GRADUATES IN COUNTERINSURGENCY, SCHOOL OF THE AMERICAS, 1961–1964

Country	No. of Graduates
Guatemala	958
El Salvador	358
Honduras	810
Nicaragua	2,969
Costa Rica	1,639
Total for Latin America	16,343
Total for Central America	8,154

SOURCE: John Saxe-Fernández, "A Latin American Perspective on the Latin American Military and Pax Americana," in B. Loveman and T. M. Davies, Jr., *The Politics of Antipolitics* (Lincoln: University of Nebraska Press, 1978), p. 164.

conflict, for an army without loyal troops is no match for a revolutionary movement. The point at which certainty as to who will win becomes sufficiently clouded in the minds of the recruits may be the flashpoint at which the struggles will turn toward the revolutionaries and away from the officer class.

The importance of foreign training to the Central American military organizations is a critical factor in their professionalization. In the twentieth century this function has been largely an activity of the United States. Besides the U.S. influence through military missions within the countries, an influence that has been critical in Nicaragua under the Somozas, in Honduras since 1954, and in Guatemala since the U.S.-sponsored coup of 1954, training has also been provided by the United States at the School of the Americas, a training installation specializing in counterinsurgency, located in the Canal Zone.[26] As shown in table 6-2, about half of the students trained at this installation in the early 1960s for Latin America were from Central America, especially from Nicaragua. The influence of the United States is more than a technical one. The training experience has a socializing effect on the Central American officers, propagandizing them toward the values which have motivated the U.S. involvement in the first place: namely, maintenance of internal security, vigilance toward possible "Communist" subversion, a strongly pro-American international stand. Military aid, shown in table 6-3, in addition to instruction has tied these institutions to U.S. equipment, strategies, and standardization, making them dependent on the United States for their military resources, their future modernization, and perhaps their survival. The military organizations, through their exposure to foreign training

145

TABLE 6-3
U.S. MILITARY ASSISTANCE TO CENTRAL AMERICA,
VARIOUS YEARS, 1945-1984
(millions of U.S. dollars)

Year	Guatemala	El Salvador	Honduras	Nicaragua	Costa Rica[a]
1950-1960	4.3	1.1	2.2	3.8	0.8
1945-1963	30.3	7.8	10.3	16.6	1.9
1970	18.0	8.0	12.0	9.0	4.0
1980	0	5.9	3.9	0	0
1981	0	35.5	8.9	0	0.5
1982	0	82.0	31.2	0	2.0
1983	0.2	26.3	20.3	0	1.1
1984	10.2	86.3	41.0	0	2.1

a. U.S. military assistance to Costa Rica is virtually impossible to calculate, since much of it is not specifically classified as "military." Moreover, since 1978, U.S. aid has been channeled indirectly through other countries to Costa Rica to disguise the transfer; such countries have included Panama, Argentina, South Korea, and Taiwan, among others.
SOURCES: For *1950-1960:* John Saxe-Fernández, "A Latin American Perspective on the Latin American Military," *1945-1963:* adapted from Gary W. Wynia, *The Politics of Latin American Development* (New York: Cambridge University Press, 1978), p. 328; *1970:* G. E. Heare, *Latin American Military Expenditures 1967-1971* (Washington, D.C.: Department of State, 1973), p. 3; *1980, 1981, 1982:* Department of State; *1983:* Department of State (approved to date); *1984:* Department of State (requested by the administration).

and advisers, have increasingly specialized in counterinsurgency activities and planning, an area clearly encouraged by their U.S. mentors and in general by U.S. military assistance to the region. Counterinsurgency is by its very nature a concern with domestic political activity, with the objective of controlling the range of political options available domestically and the means to pursue them. This in turn has encouraged expansion of intelligence-gathering capabilities, a task again supported and encouraged by U.S. training and priorities and one which is perhaps endemic anyway in small countries with limited political participation.

The relationships between civil and military elites in Central America have changed over the past half-century. The general pattern has been one in which the military elites have overwhelmed civil ones in their organizational effectiveness, their resources, their specialized skills, and their growing individual and institutional incentives to prevail. The product of this unbalanced competition has been military intervention, an often misunderstood concept in the Central American context, and military dominance of government and political processes. The political dynamics that underlie military intervention have also changed and evolved over the past generations, and at this point it is important to consider them explicitly.

Political Dynamics of Military Intervention in Central America

Military intervention is a confusing experience in the Central American context for many outside observers, a confusion reflected in both professional and popular literature on the region. The confusion stems from the parochial but powerful premise of our own society that military intervention in civilian affairs of state is politically pathological, an anomaly that ought not to occur in any normal or properly functioning political order. But the confusion is more than just a conflict between this commonly held moral or philosophical premise and the realities of Central American politics. It is also a confusion resulting from the assumption that political processes in these nations "break down" or fail to function and that military intervention is either, at best, a symptom of that failure, or, at worst, the cause of it.[27] Those critical of the military see intervention as political instability, the reason why civilian institutions fail to take root in the region. Those who apologize for military regimes seem to feel compelled to explain intervention by invoking some higher value, such as political stabilization, containment of revolutionary movements and international conspiracies, or cold-war politics. But both sides accept the premise that military intervention is abnormal and must be either criticized or rationalized on the basis of that premise. The question of who controls the presidential office, civilians or military officers, becomes the critical, obsessive point, as is the task of designating regimes as *either* civilian *or* military.

A more realistic and perhaps useful approach is to view the military as just one of several politically viable interests in the region, functioning as a class of upwardly mobile individuals who share many common ambitions, aspirations, and values. Military intervention and influence are thereby conceived as a continuous, normal part of the political contests, distinguished by degree and kind of intervention rather than by their presence or absence from national politics. Military intervention in civilian affairs, in decision making regarding the allocation of scarce resources, occurs in virtually all societies, including our own.[28] In societies where such intervention is generally regarded as improper, it takes on subtle forms and processes and may—as in the case of our own society—be effectively contained in scope. In Central America, participants have different (and differing)

147

perspectives on the legitimacy of military political participation, but even when the official offices of government are occupied by civilians, intervention occurs as the result of natural political processes in which the military has emerged as a formidable political force, a class capable of political action, committed to its own objectives and goals—both self-serving and altruistic—and possessing extensive if somewhat unusual resources to pursue them.

In Central American politics intervention works in both directions in civil-military relations, in subtle as well as gross ways. The formal control of legal offices within the country is less important than the ongoing contest between civilian and military elites. Just as military elites intervene in civilian groups and try to influence or control their elites, civilian elites intervene in military organizations and try to influence or control their elites. This two-way contest is not limited to official government leaders, but rather includes all politically influential civilians whose attempts to influence the military are conditioned by their objectives but limited only by the political resources and skills they can mobilize to promote them. This two-directional political process depends ultimately for resolution on the creation of alliances, which in turn are forged by individuals, not institutions. It is this process of political alliance building that is critical to understanding military intervention in the region.

If one persists in defining the military as outside the political sphere, then civilian intervention becomes as normal and acceptable as military intervention is abnormal and unacceptable. If one defines the military as an inescapable component in Central American politics—not, I think, an unreasonable assumption under the circumstances—then the reality is an ongoing contest of mutual influence and intervention by one group and its elite in the affairs and ambitions of the other. It is a process in which political influence ebbs and flows in both directions. Political influence and intervention and their tactics are commonly rationalized by both civilian and military leaders by broader concerns and values, which permit them to act with the commitment and determination that are probably essential to any sustained political activity. Inevitably this creates confusion on both sides of the contest as to why the other side cannot be more reasonable in understanding "clearly justifiable" objectives and responsibilities, not to mention promoting confusion for outside observers who fail to grasp the essentially political nature of the process.

Intervention specifically requires the officer class to make alliances with other classes in the society, as well as to form coalitions within their own forces. One of the major consequences of professionalization for the military has been to encourage these political skills among its elite, skills based on both bureaucratic and patrimonial politics.[29] Bureaucratic skills have evolved within the military organizations as individuals jockey with one another for influence and position in pursuit of their own careers. These skills, which combine the traditional loyalties and protection, encourage military leaders to build alliances both personally and as advocates of their class with other significant elements in their societies, both domestic and international ones. The nature of this process is perhaps easiest to grasp as the officer class pursues its interests as a group through alliances with the upper classes, which are most immediately and profoundly able to improve its positions. But likewise, the upper classes pursue their vested economic interests and objectives by building alliances—again between both individuals and groups—with the military. This common, potentially powerful alliance has dominated others most of the time. It is clearly visible in the pattern of civil-military relationships in El Salvador over the past quarter-century, which will be explored subsequently in detail. The relationship is more complex than the simple traditional one assumed generally to exist between the wealthy and the military, a relationship which did persist almost unmodified in Nicaragua under the Somozas. But in Guatemala, El Salvador, and Honduras the alliance is one which neither can wholly control or dominate, and without which either's influence and ability to prevail politically can be seriously endangered. The military has other options for its class alliance, but the upper class does not.[30]

Intervention also requires coalitions, more traditional in nature, between sectors of the armed forces in the countries. There remains, partly as a remnant of earlier times, a good deal of decentralization and dispersion of control over groups within the military in Central America. In more advanced nations in Latin America this has often required coalitions between branches of the military (army, navy, air force, national police) and their leaders, as can be seen at critical times in Argentina and Chile, to give but two examples.[31] Because of the dominance of the army in Central America, such coalitions have been less important than intraservice coalitions between divisions in the command of the armed forces, divisions based either on region (reflecting decentralization) or between regular army and special forces aligned with the army. In El Salvador these special forces have included the National Guard, the National Police, the Treasury Police, as well as ad hoc groups coalesced around active as well as retired officers. The military organizations are far from monolithic structures, and internal coalition building normally involving a small number of individual officers has been necessary to facilitate intervention.

The motivations for political intervention by the military are found

149

in both group and individual interests. The more these overlap, the stronger the incentive for intervention and the easier the process. It would be tempting to dismiss group objectives and institutional motives as mere rationalizations for personal ones, but they doubtless do play a role and perhaps in critical times tip the scales in favor of intervention. The pursuit of stability—meaning both the absence of violence and often the maintenance of the status quo—appears to be the overriding institutional preoccupation of military officers. It is endemic to the trained military mind that nothing is more inconsistent with the responsibilities of a national military institution than growing political instability that can threaten the viability or survival of the nation-state.[32] Perceived threats to national security, whether real or not, are a primary factor increasing the chances for military intervention by facilitating the coalitions necessary within the military to pursue it.

At a somewhat lower level of priority but still important are national economic development and modernization, which to some officers are ends in themselves and to others a means of securing the primary value of national stability. Promoting and managing economic development are roles performed by military elites in many Latin American nations, including Argentina, Brazil, Peru, and in recent years Chile and Uruguay, and it is clearly a motivating force at the group level for officers in Central America.[33]

The personal incentives which encourage individual officers to participate in the political processes are equally strong if not always so overt. To the extent that the military organizations have become a career path for individuals, they are an avenue for social mobility, and for many officers the only practical one. Few officers can retire affluently on what they earn, and few can enrich themselves solely by robbing the national treasury, if for no other reason than it represents unfair competition for their peers. But there are many less obvious ways for increasing one's personal income as a military officer, and protecting these opportunities is a primary political motivation for many officers. Personal welfare for many officers is tied to their career and the organization that provides it, for the economic opportunities for unemployed Central American army officers are rather dismal. The insularity of the military organizations allows officers to engage in activities which for others would be illegal and far more risky. The range of activities for individual officers is probably limited only by their imaginations. Apart from the more obvious examples of political graft and corruption, income can be derived, albeit with discretion even within their own circles, from narcotics, illicit arms deals, organized prostitution, illegal gambling, all of which have been within the repertoire of officers in the region. In pursuit of increasing their influence in military elites, civilians have made the obvious connection between using their wealth and achieving useful military alliances with officers on a direct, personal basis. Such relationships are achieved by offering investment opportunities to officers, low-cost loans, real estate, automobiles, as well as a diversity of other incentives limited only by the fertile and far-ranging imaginations of the civilian elites.

Fear of exposure, fear of losing their comfortable incomes, and fear of retribution combine to make the officer class strongly motivated on a personal level to survive. For individual officers, those who have achieved status, rank, and influence within their organizations and those who aspire to achieve them, there is much at stake in the political welfare of the organization which translates clearly and directly into their own personal welfare.[34] In fairness, this is not entirely a system of their own design. On the one hand, it is the product of historical economic forces, changing political realities, and traditional cultural values which combine to create the system. On the other hand, whatever its causes or origins, it is an important reality defining the context of civil-military relations in Central America and the continuing pressures for military intervention there.

The viability of the armed forces, their political influence, and government control are determined by their relations and alliances with other groups as well as by the extent to which they can constitute and maintain workable coalitions within their organizations. The latter ultimately is the more critical, or at least the more immediate in its consequences, since there are many potential bases for division within the organizations. Apart from the personal rivalries of individuals trying to maximize their own political and economic positions, probably still the most divisive force, there are important divisions based on rank, generation, and class. As yet these have been secondary to the personal divisions that regularly emerge; but as professionalization proceeds, the likelihood that these secondary divisions will become more important increases. In El Salvador they may ultimately be decisive in that country's revolutionary experience.

The Evolution of Civil-Military Relations in El Salvador

The pattern of civil-military relations and the political role of the military in national life in El Salvador illustrate the general trends already discussed—namely, the modernization, professionalization, and gradual institutionalization of the armed forces, changes that have been reinforced if not traumatized by the conditions and events specific to El Salvador. El Salvador is perhaps a more extreme case than either Guatemala or Honduras; the trends have proceeded further, they have more deeply affected civil-military relations, and the context is more politically explosive and revolutionary than in the other Central American republics.[35]

The military is a complex mixture of organizations in El Salvador, a mixture of traditional and modern influences in the organizations and elites, which evolved out of a traditional context dominated by rural landowners who until 1931 had monopolized the nation's politics. The military consists of the "armed forces," the army's constitutional name, the National Police, the National Guard, and the Treasury Police—these are at least the formal organizations. Informal military organizations also exist, ranging from small-sized assassination squads to ad hoc personal armies commanded by ambitious military leaders and comprising both regular forces and reserves, "veterans" or recruits who have completed their military obligations. There is considerable controversy, both political and analytic, as to how much and in what ways these forces are unified, especially in terms of command.[36]

The so-called security forces (the National Police and the National Guard) are nominally in charge of internal security and control, the National Police in rural areas and the National Guard in cities and towns, though the spheres overlap. They emerged quite literally out of the private armies established in the period following independence by landowners to control those in their private domain—workers, tenants, villagers, Indians—and became increasingly important as the nation developed coffee as an export crop, a commodity which required land and labor to be profitable and, logically, effective control over each. These private armies were pooled or consolidated by landowners in the major coffee-producing areas of the country in the 1880s, into what were known as the Rural Police and the Mounted Police, which in turn were extended by decree over the entire country in 1895. These forces became the National Police.[37]

The National Guard was established in 1912, again for the purpose of internal security, with a highly centralized structure and command located in the capital city, and more clearly under the control of the national government. It was modeled on the equivalent organization in Spain and trained by Spanish advisers. The army, like its counterparts elsewhere in the region, remained a haphazard collection of self-styled generals or caudillos until the mid-nineteenth century, using peasants forced into service as troops. Slowly foreign advisers, originally from Colombia, then later from Chile and Europe, came to El Salvador to try to modernize the forces into a national army that could defend the nation against incursions from neighboring Central American republics. The army remained until well into the mid-twentieth century primarily a force for national defense, rather than a force for internal security, the responsibility for which lay with the National Police and the National Guard. Members of the oligarchy, who controlled the government agencies, retained titles as the highest-ranking officers in the army during the nineteenth century, which symbolized their control over it, and they also retained control over the finances of the country, which in effect paid the professional soldiers and provided their military resources. From the mid-nineteenth century until well into the twentieth, the army was freed to some extent from internal political conflicts under the tutelage of a consolidating oligarchy, for whom the newfound prosperity based on the exploitation of coffee provided an opportunity for greater cohesion. Under such conditions, a premium was placed within the army on modernization and the values of national (rather than partisan) commitments, and slowly as the quality of training and foreign military assistance improved, the organization began to produce its own corps of professionalized officers, the emergence of a new class in El Salvador.

The Treasury Police, the last of the formal military organizations, was established in 1936 as an elite force nominally responsible for enforcing national policies but also serving both investigative and intelligence functions for the government. A secret police also exists, the Agencia Nacional de Servicios Especiales Salvadoreños (ANSESAL), as does a small Customs Police.

There are several major branches within the army, including a small air force, a token navy, a signal corps, a cavalry regiment, three infantry brigades, and an artillery brigade, which in turn are headquartered in different locations around the country. Also within the general organizational structure of the army is the Acción Cívica Militar, a large and rather amorphous organization of reservists which is the largest of the military organizations. Although there are formal organizational structures and relationships to all these groups, they relate primarily to one another informally through their command structures, with individual commanders exerting influence approximately to the extent of their command, the size of their units and their potential force, and the loyalty they can command from other officers and recruits in their units.[38]

The residual influence of traditional and personalistic command in the Salvadoran military can be most clearly seen in the clandestine and paramilitary organizations. The most powerful of these in recent years was the so-called Democratic Nationalist Organization

(ORDEN), founded by Colonel Carlos Alberto Medrano in 1968. The organization had an official status under the Ministry of Defense and was affiliated directly with the National Guard, at least until 1979 when it was "officially" disbanded under pressure from the United States. ORDEN originally was designed as an intelligence operation with the specific responsibility of fighting left-wing terrorism, with its forces drawn from the active military, the reserves, and nonmilitary personnel. Under its mandate, the organization was authorized to carry arms, conduct searches of individuals, their homes and possessions, arrest individuals and hold them indefinitely for interrogation (which frequently involved torture), and in general operated without constraint. ORDEN was responsible for much of the government-sponsored terrorism and the deaths of thousands of Salvadorans, as Medrano expanded his organization's activities to include campaigns against all persons who opposed the regime. At its peak it could probably mobilize from twenty to fifty thousand troops or activists, and it operated secret jails and prisons throughout the country in which it held its prisoners.[39]

Another paramilitary organization was the White Guerrilla Union (UGB), led by Roberto D'Aubuisson while he was an active officer in the armed forces, which emerged on the scene about 1972. Known also as the White Hand because of its ubiquitous emblem, the UGB terrorized the poor and the peasants, executing them virtually at will, and had the support of other officers loyal to D'Aubuisson. Because D'Aubuisson's militia was financially supported by wealthy Salvadorans and not formally integrated into the armed forces, it constituted a threat to the military as an institution. Although many officers supported D'Aubuisson, he was expelled from the military after his alleged involvement in the assassination of Archbishop Arturo Romero in March 1980. Following this D'Aubuisson shifted his power base from the military to the civilian political arena. Even within the military an ad hoc group emerged known as the Armed Forces for Anti-Communist Liberation War of Elimination, the FALANGE, which assassinated both officers and soldiers who were believed to be sympathetic to the opposition political forces in the country. Finally, many landowners organized their own "death squads," essentially small groups of hired assassins, to intimidate peasants who tried to take advantage of the government's program of land reform. They were in a sense returning to a practice that had been used a century before by employing their own private military forces and executing their own concept of justice and retribution. These latter forces were never formally related to the regular army, though their existence, support,

TABLE 6-4
SALVADORAN ARMY OFFICERS BY RANK, 1978

Rank	Number of Officers	
General	6	(3 line officers; 3 public administrators)
Colonel	99	(20 line officers; 10 professional service officers; 69 public administrators and special service officers)
Lieutenant colonel	58	(15 professional service officers; 43 line officers, public administrators, and special service officers)
Major	56	(17 professional service officers; 39 line officers, public administrators, and special service officers)
Captain	113	(10 professional service officers; 103 line officers, public administrators, and special service officers)
First lieutenant	104	(9 professional service officers; 95 line officers, public administrators, and special service officers)
Second lieutenant	125	(2 professional service officers; 123 line officers, public administrators, and special service officers)

SOURCE: B. D. Moran, "Sectoral Transitions and Power Politics in El Salvador (Unpublished, Syracuse University International Relations Program, 1978), p. 19.

and acts of terror were well known to the military commanders, many of whom personally supported them.

As can be seen from the complexity of these organizations, just how large the Salvadoran military is depends on how and whom one counts. If only the formal military forces are counted, there are about six hundred active officers, distributed approximately by rank as indicated in table 6-4. Many of these are what is known as "professional service officers," such as physicians, lawyers, engineers, and public administrators, leaving somewhere around four hundred active officers in "line" positions of responsibility. The total manpower of the formal forces has risen over the past several years, from approximately thirteen thousand in 1978 to approximately eighteen thousand in 1982, of whom about half are in the regular army.[40] The reservists, organized through Acción Cívica Militar and affiliated formally with the armed forces, possibly number an additional one hundred and fifty thousand men. These forces are nominally responsible for protecting small rural communities in "times of national emergencies," as well as for supporting front-line troops when called upon to do so. They also work on public construction projects organized by the military commanders, most of which are a combination of public relations enterprises and patronage schemes for otherwise unemployed peasants. In exchange for these jobs, reservists are expected to perform security and surveillance functions in rural areas, reporting information back to the military commanders. They also have provided manpower for some of the government-initiated terrorist campaigns in rural areas during the current antiguerrilla operations. This organization is a rather ingenious network the military has established of former recruits after their return to the rural areas of their origin. The network is controlled through a traditional patronage system, in a sense an example of the new class exploiting an old one in familiar ways for the purpose of helping to maintain its control and influence.

The pay scale for the six hundred or so active officers in the country is modest, ranging from about U.S. $600 per month for second lieutenants to about U.S. $1,200 per month for colonels. Even granting the privileges and perquisites provided them, it is obvious most of the officers are not actually living on just their formal salaries.

Almost without exception the officers are graduates of the Escuela Militar, the present source of training and professional indoctrination for the military elite. This academy was established in the late 1920s under the control of Salvadoran officers and had emerged from a long line of military institutions established with foreign assistance, beginning in 1868 with the Colegio Militar, a school designed to teach officers the technical skills of warfare. The *colegio* was run by Spanish cavalry officers for about twenty years, when it was replaced by the Escuela Politécnica, which in turn was run by the Spanish artillery officers. Around the turn of the century, the Escuela Politécnica Militar was founded, directed originally by French army engineers and subsequently by Chilean infantry officers. Since the establishment of the nationally controlled Escuela Militar, one of the persistent divisions among the officers has been based on generation, and in fact even more specifically divisions based on loyalties to each year's graduating class or *tanda*. Sharing an important common experience at an impressionable age, these graduates maintain informal networks of communication, patronage, and commiseration throughout their careers, and it is not coincidental that critical examples of military intervention in El Salvador have been organized by younger officers of the same generation, from 1931 to the present. With the founding of the current military academy, formal control for professional training of officers has resided within the Salvadoran armed forces. Foreign advisers since then have been primarily from the United States, but have played an advisory rather than an administrative role in the institution.[41]

The political role of the army began on its present course on December 2, 1931, when a coup d'état was staged by the army, led by a small group of young officers who deposed the constitutionally elected Arturo Araujo and put an end to the country's brief democratic experiment, as well as to the popular uprisings that had accompanied it. Although the events of that period are beyond the scope of this analysis, it should be noted that peasant uprisings had occurred periodically in El Salvador, specifically in 1832 and at least five times in the last quarter of the nineteenth century. The seizure of power by the young officers precipitated a military regime and indeed initiated an uninterrupted period of military rule which continues today.[42] But it did not bring the military to power as an organization, as an institution. The regime was headed by Maximiliano Hernández-Martínez, a general and the country's vice-president, who ruled until he was overthrown in 1945 by the military, with support from the oligarchy and popular demonstrations. The Hernández-Martínez regime, while ultimately based on military power, was nonetheless a traditional dictatorship for which the professional military elite was a mechanism for control. The regime was personalistic, incompetent, and for many officers backward looking, at least when compared with what they believed was occurring in Mexico, a country that has often been used as a benchmark by Salvadoran officers for appraising their country's progress.

An abortive attempt to remove Hernández Martínez in 1944 provoked the dictator to execute several dozen army officers, using the internal security forces against the army. Not only did this action strengthen the resolve of the army officers to remove Hernández-Martínez, but it also strengthened their resolve not to be put in such a position again. These events culminated in 1948 when the army again seized power, again under the leadership of young officers. The 1948 coup was the critical time at which the army as a corporate body assumed direct control over the government, which it has retained ever since. Individual officers have come and gone, and none of them has lasted very long in power. But these changes have been controlled and orchestrated within the bureaucracy and politics of the military itself and represent the ultimate control of the nation by the military as an institution.[43]

Since 1948 the military has continued to govern El Salvador, advocating and consolidating its own class interests and those of its allies. There have been elections, most of them either controlled or fraudulent, with the military candidates selected by the institution winning the presidency in 1950, 1956, 1962, 1967, 1972, and 1979. Controlled elections have also been held for local and legislative offices. The military has staged several coups, which in effect have been military coups against military regimes, reflecting the divergencies and conflicts within the organization. Besides the 1948 coup, coups have occurred on October 26, 1960, January 25, 1961, March 25, 1972 (ending in failure), October 15, 1979, and for months thereafter a sort of "creeping coup" that eventually eliminated reform elements within the army who had led the coup of October 15. Many more coups were organized but not executed.

The coups that have occurred in El Salvador reflect generational and ideological divisions within the army, a modest but important difference between those officers who see development and modernization historically as the primary objective and some equalization of society as possibly an inescapable necessity to achieve stable development, and those principally younger officers who see equalization as a self-justifying goal. Within the context of a revolutionary confrontation, the objective of stability has now been substituted for development by both groups, since modernization is clearly impossible until the country is politically stabilized. These divisions represent confusion and tensions within the army as a class as to where its natural allies in the country are. In terms of social-economic origins, it would seem that some of the officers and certainly those of lower rank, as well as the recruits, would identify principally with the lower classes, urban and rural, for it is from those sectors that many of them have come. It would also seem reasonable, however, for officers to identify more with the middle-class sectors in the urban areas, for it is with them that they share most in common in terms of occupational status and nominal income. It is also from the middle classes that the most visible alternative political leadership has emerged over the past twenty-five years, notably from the Christian Democratic party.[44] Yet most of the time the military, under guidance of the older and senior leaders, has identified its interests primarily with the upper class and has indeed through its actions not only failed to support middle- and lower-class movements and leaders, but has actively repressed them at critical junctures in the nation's recent history.

The class alliance between the officers and the wealthy is a relationship which neither finds entirely comfortable and yet which both see as essential to their own survival and well-being. For the military, the wealthy have seemed essential for continued economic development, for it is their wealth, capital, investment, and entrepreneurship that have stimulated the process historically. To attack or destroy them or force them into exile would leave the country in difficult straits in terms of economic development, or so their argument goes. For the upper class, which through its own political ineptitude lost control of the country's government in 1931 to a dictator and in 1948 to the military as an organization, the military is a fact of life as well as the only viable source of protection for their wealth and well-being. The association has been mutually profitable for the individuals involved, particularly the officers who promoted it, but it has never been more than a relationship of mutual advantage, since the military leaders and their upper-class counterparts share virtually nothing in common in terms of social background, education, class, or families—all important bases for association in traditional Salvadoran society. As officers have aged, they have become more conservative, more integrated into the established system, and more nervous about the younger officers who have seemed impatient with their own organization's failure to seize opportunities for restructuring the society.[45]

The individual motives of the officers for cooperating with the upper class are more easily understood. They have found the relationship profitable in terms of their own wealth and income, and payments to officers by the wealthy have become a necessary business expense for the upper class. These payments encompass a broad range of payoffs, including among others outright gifts (cars, houses, cash), privileges (vacations, credit), and favors such as loans in which the principal is often left "uncollected" as long as the personal relationship remains cordial. Some of the more enterprising officers, under the shield of legal immunity from prosecution and political immunity from investigation, have generated their own profitable enterprises, including such activities as organized prostitution, narcotics, illegal gambling, smuggling and contraband, illegal arms sales, and even paid assassinations. The more outrageous enterprises have been primarily the domain of retired officers, since those on active duty, if discovered, could lose leverage among their peers through blackmail if not outright sanctions. One observer has characterized this process of self-aggrandizement, patronage, and mutual protection of the officers as filling a void commonly associated with organized crime in other countries.[46] Such practices by military officers are not unprecedented in Latin America; similar activities were organized by Cuban army officers under Batista and are the principal source of income for Bolivian army officers who today facilitate the lucrative international distribution of cocaine.

Criminal activities—or what at least in other countries and even nominally in El Salvador would be criminal—provide an important explanation for why army officers so involved are not eager to see radical changes in the system, especially new political leaders, for such changes not only might end their profitable ventures but also might lead to their expulsion from the army, an end to their career, and perhaps even criminal prosecution. Knowledge of these activities gathered by the secret police as well as by some military officers themselves produces dossiers on career officers that provide useful leverage in the process of internal coalition building within the army, adding a common bond of fear to the already substantial common interests of that organization.

Over the past five years under the growing threat of revolutionary activity, which the army finds difficult to contain let alone eliminate, the officer class has increasingly functioned under siege with a bunker mentality which has encouraged their leaders to "stonewall" the situation, hoping for some solution that will at least preserve their own class interests and status. In the absence of a single tyrant who can become the target of the revolution—a role performed effectively by Batista and Somoza in earlier conflicts—the officer class has been linked with the upper class, its reluctant ally in the past, as the principal target of the revolution, which, if successful, could sweep not only the present military leaders out of power but the whole institution itself, along with those who have associated with it as a class. In a very real sense, then, the conflict in El Salvador, perhaps even more than was the case in Nicaragua or Cuba, is a class war and is increasingly so perceived by both sides.

Others have characterized the ongoing political contest in El Salvador and the role of the military as a cyclical pattern, and indeed there is considerable evidence to support that interpretation.[47] But there is also a critical evolutionary dimension to it. El Salvador has changed dramatically over the past half-century, the result of economic growth and modernization more generally. These changes began to produce by the 1960s a politically viable and visible urban middle class, and with it an opportunity for a new alliance between the military and a broader-based politically active group. That alliance never materialized. The country also experienced increasingly higher levels of social mobilization, as the effects of modernization slowly spilled over into lower sectors of the society. Economic development has created an almost predictable and steady increase in class differentiation, which has come with the accumulation of wealth and land, especially within the context of rapid population growth and the absence of government policies to temper or reverse the trend. Over the same period, the Salvadoran military has also changed, continuing to modernize and professionalize its elite and gradually institutionalizing its self-perceptions and behavior. The failure of the military to form alliances with newly emerging sectors of the population toward the end of expanding and renovating civilian institutions in the country has increasingly isolated it as the only remaining institution in an increasingly revolutionary environment. In effect the pattern of institutional growth in the country has created an imbalance between civil and military institutions, which can be corrected only by countermilitary, that is, revolutionary, means or—should there still be time—by a new alliance between the military and a broader-based civilian sector.

Evolutionary Patterns in Civil-Military Relations in Central America

Both common patterns and distinctive patterns of civil-military relations have emerged in Central America, a result of the interaction of traditional indigenous political realities and the influence of economic growth, modernization, and international interests. The emergent civil-military relations in the five republics span a range from civilian dominance in Costa Rica to military dominance in El Salvador and Guatemala, but include two basic patterns. In the first, which characterizes Guatemala, El Salvador, and Honduras, the military began to modernize fairly early, more gradually to professionalize its leadership elites, and finally to institutionalize its organizations. Modernization began earlier in Guatemala and El Salvador than it did in Honduras, and El Salvador has been the most affected by professionalization—Honduras the least affected—of the three. None of the three has highly institutionalized militaries by comparison with the more advanced nations of South America, but the process has affected all three of them, again most significantly the military in El Salvador.

In the second pattern, which includes Costa Rica and Nicaragua, there was no institutionalization of a military organization. In the case of Costa Rica indigenous realities, both political and economic, made military force less essential than elsewhere in the region, allowing civilian institutions to develop relatively freely, encouraged by a basically harmonious civilian elite. Under the Somoza regime, the Nicaraguan military was modernized and professionalized in a distinctive pattern which encouraged partrimonial values and relationships with the ruling family, a pattern more traditional than modern and one that

161

placed no priority on nor left any room for an autonomous military institution to develop. With the exhaustion of the Somoza regime, an institutional vacuum was created which the National Guard was incapable of filling, and relatively modest revolutionary force was required to destroy it and replace it with a new order. The incipient military institutions in the first pattern have created a new class of military officers, a class which is armed to protect itself and its interests in any ensuing conflict. These military organizations are partly bureaucratized, partly traditional, and pervasively political in their very nature and the relationships within them. They are a class that dominates a state and maintains its control both by force and through alliances with other classes in those states. The old alliance between the military class and the upper class has been, is, or most certainly will be challenged by the new class interests as they emerge, congeal, and begin to pursue their own antagonistic objectives. The tensions within the military, perhaps most visible in El Salvador over the past quarter-century, are more strategic than philosophical, different perceptions of how alliances should be formed between their own class and others in the society. Overlaid on this pattern are the complex personal motivations of individual officers, ranging from opportunities for personal gain to fear of personal loss—of money, opportunities, careers, status, even perhaps life.

Both nations in the second pattern, Costa Rica and Nicaragua, are particularly vulnerable to military threats to their security. For Nicaragua, the threat is primarily external; for Costa Rica, it is both external and internal. Neither has as yet an effective military force, let alone one that is modern, professional, or institutionalized. The Sandinistas are rapidly moving in that direction, with considerable foreign assistance. The dilemma plagues the Costa Rican regime, for to move in such a direction is contrary to its established traditions, yet not to do so might be threatening to the very survival of its civilian institutions.[48]

The prospects for armed terror in El Salvador and Guatemala seem, at least on the basis of this analysis, far greater than they were for Nicaragua or even Cuba. The Salvadoran military is engaged in an armed class conflict, in which it is an unwitting participant. The same basic situation exists in Guatemala, where it is exacerbated by racial divisions which reinforce those of class. Class divides the military organizations internally as well as separates their officers from other political groups in the nations.

Within the context of a revolutionary struggle which to one extent or another faces each of the countries in the first pattern, it is likely that the officer classes will maintain some degree of unity, if for no reason other than a siege mentality that is created by a common perceived threat to them all. The critical question is whether they can maintain the unity of their organizations, given the differences which exist between them and their troops, should their final military victory ever be widely perceived to be in doubt. Their ultimate political leverage as a ruling elite has been based on force, a dominant historical theme in the region since independence, yet the increasing use and dependence on that force suggest a growing institutional weakness or decay, just as they did in simpler times with traditional dictators. The political imbalances created by uneven institutional growth in civilian and military organizations in the region seem to be creating their own mechanisms for correction. The human and economic costs of these corrections are likely to be tragically high.

Notes

1. Social mobilization is used simply to connote the aggregate changes in value and behavior patterns of individuals as they are affected by social and economic changes generated by modernization; see Karl Deutsch, "Social Mobilization and Political Development," *American Political Science Review* (September 1961), pp. 493–514.

2. The expanding need for institutions within the context of a modernizing country is discussed by Samuel P. Huntington, *Political Order in Changing Societies* (New Haven, Conn.: Yale University Press, 1968), pp. 8–31.

3. All the Central American republics except Costa Rica conform to what Huntington calls a "praetorian culture" (ibid., p. 237), in that the military has traditionally been involved in politics. The purpose here is to describe the changing context and motivations of military intervention in the region.

4. The distinction between the three processes—modernization, professionalization, and institutionalization of the military—appears in much of the literature dealing with the military in Latin America, though they are not always conceptually differentiated. See John J. Johnson, *The Military and Society in Latin America* (Stanford, Calif.: Stanford University Press, 1964), pp. 244–52.

5. Professionalization in the Latin American context is further discussed by Charles D. Corbett, "Politics and Professionalism: The South American Military," in Brian Loveman and Thomas M. Davies, Jr., *The Politics of Antipolitics: The Military in Latin America* (Lincoln: University of Nebraska Press, 1978), pp. 14–22.

6. The development of the military as a political institution in the Middle East is discussed by Fuad I. Khuri and Gerald Obermeyer, "The Social Bases of Military Intervention in the Middle East," in Catherine McArdle Kelleher, ed., *Political-Military Systems: Comparative Perspectives* (Beverly Hills, Calif.: Sage, 1974), pp. 70–72.

7. The process of military institutionalization in the region is embryonic, far from what has been described within the context of "bureaucratic-authoritarianism" found in the Southern Cone countries of South America. See Fernando Henrique Cardoso, "On the Characterization of Authoritarian Regimes in Latin America," in David Collier, ed., *The New Authoritarianism in Latin America* (Princeton, N.J.: Princeton University Press, 1979), pp. 33–57. Viewing the military as an integral part of the larger political process is advocated by Alfred Stepan, *The Military in Politics: Changing Patterns in Brazil* (Princeton, N.J.: Princeton University Press, 1971), pp. 8–10.

8. The emergence of the armed forces following independence in Latin America is reviewed by Edwin Lieuwen, *Arms and Politics in Latin America* (New York: Praeger, 1960), pp. 17–35.

9. This distinctive pattern in Nicaragua is discussed by Thomas W. Walker, *Nicaragua: The Land of Sandino* (Boulder, Colo.: Westview Press, 1981), pp. 13–20.

10. European military advisers in Central America were less common than elsewhere in Latin America. Frederick M. Nunn, "Effects of European Military Training in Latin America: The Origins and Nature of Professional Militarism in Argentina, Brazil, Chile and Peru, 1890–1940," *Military Affairs* (February 1975), pp. 1–7.

11. Johnson, *Military and Society*, pp. 62–63.

12. The lack of institutionalization in the Honduran army until very recently are described by Steve C. Ropp, "The Honduran Army in the Sociopolitical Evolution of the Honduran State," *Americas* (April 1974), pp. 504–28.

13. The divisions within the Guatemalan military between officers and enlisted men are discussed by Richard N. Adams, "The Development of the Guatemalan Military," *Studies in Comparative International Development*, vol. 4 (1968–1969), pp. 91–110.

14. Walker, *Nicaragua*, p. 23.

15. This "corporate" orientation of the Guatemalan officers, in large measure as a result of increased perquisites, is observed by Adams, "Development of the Guatemalan Military," p. 94.

16. Reinhard Bendix, *Max Weber: An Intellectual Portrait* (Garden City, N.Y.: Doubleday, 1962), p. 341. Riordan Roett, in *Brazil: Politics in a Patrimonial Society* (New York: Praeger, 1978), uses the concept of patrimonialism to characterize Brazilian politics, though as he clearly suggests, the military in that country is institutionalized and hence does not fit Weber's more precise use of the concept.

17. Walker, *Nicaragua*, p. 40, points out that the Carter administration, in the final hours of the Somoza regime, tried to bargain, without success, with the revolutionaries for the maintenance of the National Guard in a "revised" form after Somoza's departure.

18. Adams, "Development of the Guatemalan Military," p. 95, uses the term "caste," as have others, to characterize the military, and since profession or occupation is their distinctive bond, the term is appropriate. I have chosen, however, to use the concept of "class" because I believe it more appropriately fits into the social structure of these nations and more accurately describes the

behavior and values of officers as they relate to other groups in society.

19. Ropp, "The Honduran Army," p. 509.

20. In his study of the Argentine army and air force generals, de Imaz concluded that 73 percent came from families belonging to the well-to-do upper middle class. See José Luis de Imaz, Los Que Mandan (Albany: State University of New York Press, 1970), pp. 61–62.

21. John Dombrowski, ed., Area Handbook for Guatemala (Washington, D.C., 1970), p. 315.

22. Brian D. Moran, "Sectoral Transitions and Power Politics in El Salvador" (Syracuse University International Relations Program, 1978), p. 14.

23. Ropp, "The Honduran Military," p. 509.

24. Walker, Nicaragua, p. 111, argues that "the National Guard was the most heavily U.S.-trained military establishment in Latin America."

25. Adams, "Development of the Guatemalan Military," p. 95, observes: "To be liable for conscription is a good index of one's lack of power to avoid it." For further information see Jerry L. Weaver, "Political Style of the Guatemalan Military Elite," Studies in Comparative International Development, vol. 5 (1969–1970), pp. 63–81.

26. The U.S. Army School of the Americas is described in detail by Loveman and Davies, Politics of Antipolitics, pp. 148–52.

27. This position is forcefully argued by Samuel P. Huntington, "Political Development and Political Decay," World Politics (April 1965), pp. 386–430.

28. Typologies of military intervention in Latin America abound but seem unnecessary for the limited purpose here. See particularly Gino Germani and Kalman Silvert, "Politics, Social Structure, and Military Intervention in Latin America," Archives europeennes de sociologie, vol. 2 (1961), pp. 62–81; Lyle N. McAllister, "Civil-Military Relations in Latin America," Journal of Inter-American Studies, vol. 3 (July 1961), pp. 341–50 ; also de Imaz, Los Que Mandan, pp. 49–53.

29. These changes are discussed by Marion J. Levy, Jr., Modernization and the Structure of Societies: A Setting for International Affairs (Princeton, N.J.: Princeton University Press, 1966), especially chapter 4, "Armed Force Organization," pp. 571–605.

30. The confusion and divisions in the Guatemalan military about its alliances with emerging groups in the society are described for a critical period in that country, the overthrow of General Jorge Ubico, in Kenneth J. Grieb, "The Guatemalan Military and the Revolution of 1944," Americas, vol. 32 (April 1976), pp. 524–43.

31. The process of interservice coalition building is described within the context of the final days of the Allende regime in Chile by Frederick M. Nunn, The Military in Chilean History: Essays on Civil-Military Relations, 1810–1973 (Albuquerque: University of New Mexico Press, 1976), pp. 271–79.

32. This attitude is encouraged by the growing emphasis on counterinsurgency, which in turn is advocated by U.S. military assistance and training. The effect on Brazil is convincingly established by Stepan, The Military in Politics, pp. 126–33.

33. The economic motivation is given greater priority by Martin Needler,

"Political Development and Military Intervention in Latin America," *American Political Science Review*, vol. 60 (September 1966), pp. 616–26.

34. This is also the conclusion of Edwin Lieuwen, *Generals versus Presidents* (New York: Praeger, 1964), pp. 101–7.

35. Two general introductions to El Salvador are David Growning, *El Salvador: Landscape and Society* (Oxford: Clarendon Press, 1971), and Alastair White, *El Salvador* (Boulder, Colo.: Westview Press, 1973).

36. A recent analysis, which views the military largely as a right-wing conspiracy controlled or dominated by the "most conservative elements of the army," is Tommie Sue Montgomery, *Revolution in El Salvador: Origins and Evolution* (Boulder, Colo.: Westview Press, 1982), pp. 159–60.

37. Ibid., p. 43.

38. Moran, "Sectoral Transitions," pp. 13–21.

39. Montgomery, *Revolution in El Salvador*, pp. 84, 207.

40. These figures are estimates obtained from sources within El Salvador which cannot be identified.

41. The role of U.S. advisers, as well as U.S. assistance, has rapidly escalated since 1981.

42. These events are extensively discussed by Thomas Anderson, *Matanza: El Salvador's Communist Revolt of 1932* (Lincoln: University of Nebraska Press, 1971).

43. A useful analysis of this period is Robert Elam, "Appeal to Arms: The Army and Politics in El Salvador 1931–1964" (Ph.D. diss., University of New Mexico, 1968).

44. For a discussion of the emergence of the Christian Democratic party, see Stephen Webre, *José Napoleón Duarte and the Christian Democratic Party in Salvadoran Politics, 1960–1972* (Baton Rouge: Louisiana State University Press, 1979), pp. 31–68.

45. The conservative drift induced by senior officers, what Montgomery describes as *derechización,* (moving to the right) is particularly evident in the events since the 1979 coup. Montgomery, *Revolution in El Salvador,* pp. 159–68.

46. Moran, "Sectoral Transitions," p. 18.

47. The case is argued persuasively by Montgomery, *Revolution in El Salvador,* pp. 55–79.

48. The dilemma for the Costa Ricans is further tangled by U.S. pressure on them to improve their military capability and by the rapidly increasing U.S. military assistance and training for Costa Rica. See Dial Torgerson, "U.S. to Send Costa Rica Military Trainers, Gear," *Los Angeles Times,* October 16, 1982.

7
Revolutionary Movements in Central America: The Development of a New Strategy

ERNEST EVANS

Introduction

The makers of American foreign policy have always had considerable difficulty in formulating effective policies to deal with revolutionary change in other countries. To be sure, responding to revolutionary change is a difficult foreign policy problem for any country, but in the case of the United States the difficulties inherent in this problem are magnified by a key characteristic of American political history. Since the end of the period of the Civil War and Reconstruction (1861–1877) the major issues in the American political system have been dealt with through procedures such as elections, lawsuits, demonstrations, and lobbying: that is, by procedures that do not directly involve the use of violence (though there can be and usually are acts of violence that are the indirect result of such procedures, such as the violence directed against many civil rights workers in the South in the 1960s). Put differently, in the past century there has not been very much explicitly political violence in the United States. Moreover, what political violence there has been has generally been "pro status quo" violence— violence against movements, such as the labor movement, the civil rights movement, and the Socialist party, that are attempting to make changes in the social, economic, and political structures of American society.[1]

A country such as the United States, which has had very little revolutionary violence in its own recent political history, will inevitably have major difficulties in understanding revolutionary change anywhere else in the world. In the specific case of revolutionary change in Latin America, this general lack of understanding is reinforced by a widespread lack of knowledge on the part of most Americans of the history, politics, and culture of Latin America.

The United States has been, therefore, poorly prepared to respond to the problems created for its foreign policy by the violent upheavals in Central America that began to take place in the late 1970s. For example, the merits of U.S. policy toward the Nicaraguan revolution of 1978–1979 have been hotly debated, but virtually all analysts of this policy would agree that the United States had a poor understanding of the major groups involved in the revolution and of the dynamics of the revolutionary process. Specifically, when the revolution began, the United States overestimated Somoza's strength and underestimated that of the Sandinistas; after it realized the weakness of Somoza's government, it overestimated the chances of creating a moderate (that is, non-Sandinista, non-Somoza) government; and in the final stage of the revolution it overestimated its ability to force the Sandinistas to moderate their proposed government and political program.[2]

The purpose of this article is to try to clear up some of the confusion and misunderstanding concerning contemporary revolutionary movements in Central America. The central arguments that will be developed in this article can be summarized as follows: The current revolutionary movements in Central America are significantly different from the earlier generation of Latin American revolutionary movements. The time frame of this earlier generation was 1960–1977. These earlier movements either were Guevarist in their strategy (that is, the "foco" theory) or were pursuing a strategy of urban terrorism. The new wave of revolutionary movements are pursuing a different strategy for seizing power. This new strategy has profound implications for the way that the revolutionaries engage in guerrilla warfare and terrorism, for the violence and terrorism engaged in by both the revolutionaries and the pro-status quo forces in the region, and for the ability of the United States to influence the course of events in Central America.

The Earlier Generation of Revolutionary Movements

The victory of Fidel Castro's guerrillas in Cuba in 1959 led to a number of attempts to duplicate his revolution elsewhere in Latin America.[3] In 1962–1964, radical groups in Venezuela tried unsuccessfully to overthrow the government of Rómulo Betancourt. In Peru in 1962–1965, there were a series of uprisings in rural areas that had to be put down by the Peruvian military. Guerrillas in Guatemala in the 1960s launched several unsuccessful campaigns in an effort to overthrow the Guatemalan government.[4]

The death of Che Guevara and the destruction of his guerrilla foco in Bolivia in 1967 was a major turning point for revolutionary movements in Latin America.[5] Guevara's defeat, together with the earlier defeat of rural guerrillas in Argentina, Brazil, Colombia, Guatemala, Peru, and Venezuela, convinced many revolutionaries that the countryside was not the best arena for revolutionary movements. The result was a shift toward urban guerrilla warfare.

The results of these urban guerrilla campaigns were often spectacular. In 1969, the U.S. ambassador to Brazil was kidnapped by Brazilian terrorists. In Uruguay, the Tupamaro guerrillas became world-famous because of a series of widely publicized political kidnappings and assassinations. In Argentina, the various urban guerrilla movements became so powerful that when the military took power in 1976, the country was in a state of civil war.

Yet these urban guerrilla movements also ended in failure. The Brazilian military successfully crushed the urban guerrillas in the early 1970s. In Uruguay, the military successfully destroyed the Tupamaros in an intensive campaign in the spring and summer of 1972. In Argentina, the military was able to destroy the urban guerrillas within two years of taking power.[6]

In assessing the reasons for the failure of the rural and urban guerrillas of the period 1960–1977, it must be remembered that the failures of these movements were not due entirely to their own mistakes. To a considerable degree, these movements failed because the governments that they were up against were more efficient, better prepared, and more determined than was Batista's government in Cuba. Put differently, the governments of Latin America and the U.S. goverment *also* learned certain lessons from the Cuban Revolution. And (like the losing side in many wars) they were often far more perceptive in assessing the lessons of the Cuban Revolution than the revolutionary movements of Latin America were.[7]

There can be no doubt, however, that the revolutionaries of the period 1960–1977 made a number of major mistakes. Before analyzing these mistakes, it is necessary to understand that the errors of these revolutionary movements stemmed from the pervasive belief among Latin American revolutionaries that Latin America was "ripe for revolution"—that is, that the oppressed classes in Latin America (peasants, workers, and the urban and rural poor) were ready and eager to support revolutionary change and that the ruling classes were divided and demoralized and hence incapable of halting the revolutionary wave that would soon sweep through Latin America.

169

The assumption that Latin America was soon to be radically transformed shows up repeatedly in manifestoes by revolutionary movements and statements by guerrilla leaders. In its first manifesto in February 1963, the Venezuelan FALN (Armed Forces of National Liberation) stated: "The situation is ripe and there should not be a moment's delay in bringing together all patriots. . . ."[8] In Peru, Hugo Blanco, a radical who was organizing peasants in the countryside, wrote a letter to friends in 1962 in which he stated: "I am writing to you with the happiness the combatant feels as he sees that triumph in the war is near after fighting in a hundred battles."[9] A 1965 communiqué by the Peruvian MIR (Movement of the Revolutionary Left) stated: "The armed MIR calls on all sectors of the people to fight. Victory is ours. The guerrillas are spreading. Armed fighting is sweeping the country. Liberation is at hand."[10] In 1964 the Guatemalan group MR13 (Revolutionary Movement of November 13) issued a declaration which began: "The year 1965 will be of great importance. The Guatemalan Socialist revolution will make an enormous leap forward. The conditions for it exist and are mature."[11]

The assumption that revolutionary change was imminent in Latin America led to five major errors on the part of the rural and urban guerrillas:

1. There was a lack of emphasis on building popular support. Since it was felt that popular support for the guerrillas already existed, the guerrillas put little emphasis on efforts to mobilize and organize the population. Instead, the guerrillas assumed that all that was needed to mobilize popular support was for the guerrillas to launch their campaigns against the established governments. As Che Guevara says at the beginning of his book *Guerrilla Warfare*:

> We consider that the Cuban Revolution contributed three fundamental lessons to the conduct of revolutionary movements in America. They are:
>
> 1. Popular forces can win a war against the army.
> 2. *It is not necessary to wait until all conditions for making revolution exist; the insurrection can create them.* [Emphasis added.]
> 3. In underdeveloped America, the countryside is the basic area for armed fighting.[12]

In his "Minimanual of the Urban Guerrilla," Carlos Marighella stated:

> The rebellion of the urban guerrilla and his persistence in intervening in public questions is the best way of insuring

public support of the cause we defend. We repeat and insist on repeating: *it is the best way of insuring public support.* As soon as a reasonable section of the population begins to take seriously the action of the urban guerrilla, his success is guaranteed. [Emphasis in original.] [13]

When the Peruvian MIR launched its campaign in 1965, it issued a communiqué which closed with the following sentence: "What today is a spark, tomorrow will be a fire which will consume all false patriots, all liars, all hired thugs, all the torturers, all the hypocrites, all those who are behind the crimes and abuses our people have suffered." [14]

Put differently, these rural and urban guerrillas had a "militaristic" strategy. Because they assumed that popular support for them already existed, they concentrated their efforts and energy on the strictly military aspects of guerrilla warfare. In both Che Guevara's *Guerrilla Warfare* and Marighella's "Minimanual" the great bulk of the texts deal with the tactics and technical aspects of guerrilla warfare (care and use of weapons, staging ambushes, organization of guerrilla units, logistics, and so forth). As Marighella put it quite forcefully in the "Minimanual": "The urban guerrilla's reason for existence, the basic condition in which he acts and survives, is to shoot." [15]

2. Little effort was made to win support from existing political organizations (parties, unions, peasant movements, and so forth). The guerrillas regarded such organizations as lacking in any genuine popular support and as led by opportunistic leaders whose loyalty and commitment could not be counted on; and hence they saw no advantages in making an effort to get the support of such groups. Camillo Torres, a Colombian priest who had been radicalized, made strenuous efforts in 1965 to put together a broad coalition of student groups, unions, and left-wing political movements and parties to provide political support to the guerrillas fighting against the government of Colombia. Torres's efforts ended in failure, in large part because so many of the guerrillas saw no need for such a coalition. [16] One Colombian guerrilla group issued the following attack on Torres's United Front:

> A United Front cannot be set up by making flimsy alliances between the discredited heads of factions with revolutionary aspirations, nor by means of simply stirring up the masses, nor by defining as the masses sectors other than poor workers and peasants who attract other sectors by their seriousness and numbers. Working for alliances between individuals and not making a serious attempt to

organize an alliance of the exploited classes which is the essence of the United Front will only stimulate the ambitions and pretensions of many of the present unscrupulous and opportunistic leaders of left-wing factions.[17]

In his book *Revolution in the Revolution?* Régis Debray argued that while it was true that the Communist parties of Latin America were not willing to mobilize the population to support revolutionary change, this lack of support by the local Communist parties was not an insurmountable obstacle to successful revolutions. He pointed out that in Cuba Castro's and Guevara's guerrilla movement had been able to win despite the fact that it did not get any support from the Cuban Communist party until quite late in the struggle against Batista.[18]

In the diary he kept during his campaign in Bolivia, Debray's friend Che Guevara recorded his lack of concern at the refusal of the Bolivian Communist party to support his guerrilla movement: "The party is now taking up arms against us and I do not know what it will lead to, but it will not test us, and it may in the long run prove beneficial (I am almost certain of this)."[19]

3. The guerrillas adopted military strategies that isolated them from the population. The rural guerrillas of the 1960s were basically pursuing the strategy of the foco. As expounded by writers like Debray and Guevara, the foco theory held that the guerrillas should base themselves in a remote part of the country, gradually build up their military strength, and then come "down from the Sierra Maestras" and engage and defeat the regular army in a series of conventional battles.[20] (This theory was based on a very selective account of the events of the Cuban Revolution, an account that ignored the role played by the urban insurgents in the Cuban Revolution and instead gave virtually all of the credit for the victory over Batista to Castro and Guevara.)

A major problem with the foco strategy was that the remote regions where the guerrillas would try to establish focos were usually thinly populated (and often the population that was there was culturally very different from the guerrillas) and often quite inaccessible to the rest of the country. The result was that the guerrilla foco had enormous difficulties in expanding because it could not easily recruit from the local population, nor could it count on getting many recruits or supplies from the populated regions of the country.

The problems with the foco strategy often led to a vicious circle for the guerrillas. Because the guerrillas were seen as weak and hence as not likely to win, they had difficulty getting popular support, which would further erode their chances of success. In Guevara's Bolivian diary, he concluded each month with a summary of the progress of the campaign. The entries for July, August, and September (he was killed in October 1967) graphically illustrate the operation of this vicious circle:

July 1967
The most important characteristics are:
1. The total lack of contact [with other groups in the country] continues.
2. The lack of incorporation of the peasants continues to be felt. . . .

August 1967
The most important characteristics:
1. We continue without any contacts of any kind and without reasonable hope of establishing them in the near future.
2. We continue without any incorporation on the part of the peasants.

September 1967
The characteristics are the same as those of last month, except that now the army is showing more effectiveness in action, and the mass of the peasants does not help us at all and have become informers.[21]

The strategy of urban guerrilla war also resulted in isolating the revolutionaries from the population. An urban guerrilla group must operate in conditions of great secrecy. For the guerrillas to be known to too many people means that they are extremely vulnerable in the event of a major crackdown by the police and the military. For example, one of the reasons for the relative ease with which the Uruguayan military crushed the Tupamaros in 1972 was that in the previous year the Tupamaros had greatly expanded their membership and had built a number of sizable "people's prisons," weapons caches, and hiding places, thereby making it much more difficult to maintain secrecy. In other words, the Tupamaros were successful as long as they were a fairly small group that was isolated from the population; as soon as they tried to expand and break out of this isolation, they were quickly destroyed by the security forces.

The dangers of isolation from the population that are present in a strategy of urban terrorism and guerrilla warfare have been recognized by a number of major revolutionaries. In 1902, for example,

Lenin wrote the following criticism of the terrorism carried out by the rival Socialist Revolutionaries: "No verbal assurances or invocations can disprove the unquestionable fact that modern terrorism as it is practiced by the Socialist Revolutionaries is not in any way linked with work among the masses. . . ."[22]

4. The guerrillas committed acts of terrorism that alienated public and international support. As Lenin's statement indicates, many revolutionaries have realized that terrorism is a tactic that if improperly applied can be counterproductive. In *Guerrilla Warfare*, Che Guevara stated:

> It is necessary to distinguish clearly between sabotage, a revolutionary and highly effective method of warfare, and terrorism, a measure that is generally ineffective and indiscriminate in its results, since it often makes victims of innocent people and destroys a large number of lives that would be valuable to the revolution.[23]

The terrorism practiced by Latin American revolutionaries frequently alienated the population from the guerrillas. For example, Abraham Guillen, a revolutionary theorist who wrote a book entitled *The Strategy of the Urban Guerrilla*, which was widely read in Latin America, argued that many of the acts of terrorism engaged in by the Tupamaros had cost them public support. He maintained, for example, that holding individuals for months in "people's prisons" merely served to convince the public that the Tupamaros were as capable of repression as was the government, that in executing hostages they had acquired the image of assassins, and that in demanding large ransoms for hostages they had acquired the image of a "political Mafia."[24]

The large number of diplomatic kidnappings engaged in by the urban guerrillas destroyed the chances of any significant international support for the revolutionaries. The countries whose diplomats were kidnapped were obviously not going to be sympathetic to the revolutionaries, and even those countries whose diplomats were not targeted could hardly be expected to be eager to support revolutionary movements that violated one of the key ground rules of international conduct—namely, the principle of the inviolability of diplomatic personnel.

5. Military recklessness was another major error. The rural and urban guerrillas often engaged in costly, counterproductive military operations because they were convinced that victory was imminent and hence that they should feel free to undertake very risky opera-

tions. After the defeat of the guerrillas in Venezuela, one of the guerrilla leaders, Douglas Bravo, acknowledged that:

From the military point of view, our most serious mistake was being too adventurous. Although we talked a lot about a prolonged, long-drawn-out war, at the time we were using shock tactics, as for a *coup*. We wanted to overthrow Betancourt in a few hours, in one or two battles. This resulted in very far-reaching defeats, and prevented us from getting down to building a guerrilla army. We were throwing far too many forces into a hopeless struggle.[25]

Other revolutionary movements were equally reckless. The 1969 kidnapping of the U.S. ambassador to Brazil was a Pyrrhic victory for the Brazilian urban guerrillas. They undertook this kidnapping at a time when their organization was poorly prepared to survive intensive repression, and hence they suffered major reversals (including the death of Carlos Marighella) when the Brazilian government instituted harsh repressive measures in the aftermath of the kidnapping of the U.S. ambassador.[26] And the Tupamaros made a fatal mistake when they staged a series of spectacular assassinations in April 1972. These assassinations did not seriously damage the government or the military; what they did do was to provide the Uruguayan military with the rationale it needed to launch its all-out campaign against the Tupamaros. Soon after the assassinations, the parliament of Uruguay declared a "State of Internal War," thereby in effect giving the military the right to use "any means necessary" to crush the Tupamaros. By the end of the summer of 1972, the military had destroyed the Tupamaros.[27]

In sum, by pursuing policies that isolated themselves from both domestic and international support and by engaging in military strategies based on the delusion of a quick and easy victory, the rural and urban guerrillas in Latin America in the period 1960–1977 seriously eroded whatever chances they might have had to overthrow any of the governments that they were fighting against.

Contemporary Revolutionary Movements in Latin America

A number of catastrophic military defeats have been due to a tendency of militaries to "fight the last war"—that is, to assume that the sort of strategies, tactics, and military units that were successful in one conflict will be equally successful in the next conflict. After the brilliant military career of Frederick the Great, the Prussian military saw little reason to innovate, and this lack of any innovation was a major factor in its crushing defeat by Napoleon at the battle of Jena in 1806. In 1940, the French army felt that World War II would essentially be a repeat of World War I, and hence was totally unprepared for the sort of mobile armored warfare that the Germans unleashed against France in 1940. In 1943 at the battle of Kursk, the Germans themselves paid the price of the overconfidence born of their spectacular successes in 1939–1941. Failing to appreciate how much the Russians had improved their military capabilities since 1941, the German attack at Kursk resulted in massive losses that gravely weakened the German army.

Yet, although successful militaries often tend to "fight the last war," in many cases defeated militaries have been eager to innovate and try new ideas precisely because they do *not* want to "fight the last war." After the Prussian defeat at Jena in 1806, for example, there were a series of major reforms in the Prussian military. These reforms produced a revived Prussian army that inflicted a series of defeats on Napoleon in 1813–1815. After the German defeat in World War I, the German military was significantly more open to suggestions for changes and reforms than was the French military; and hence it is not surprising that in 1940 the Germans were far more sophisticated in their use of tanks and aircraft than the French were.[28]

Revolutionaries are also inclined to "fight the last war." Specifically, there is a tendency among revolutionaries to try to duplicate in their own country the strategy that proved successful in another country. In 1919 and 1920, the German Communists staged a number of urban uprisings in an effort to duplicate the Bolshevik October 1917 revolution; social and political conditions in Germany, however, were quite different from those in Russia, and hence these uprisings failed.[29] In 1948, the Malayan Communists launched a guerrilla campaign in Malaya hoping to repeat the success of the Chinese Communists; here again the Communists were defeated because there were major social and political differences between Malaya and China.[30] At the time that they launched their campaign against Israel in the mid-1960s, the leaders of the Palestinian movement seriously underestimated the difficulties involved in destroying the state of Israel, because they modeled their strategy against Israel on that of the Algerian National Liberation Front (FLN) against the French. Hence, they were not sufficiently cognizant of the fact that in their struggle against Israel they suffered from many difficulties and problems that the FLN did not have in its struggle against France.[31]

Still, like military establishments, revolutionary movements are capable of learning from their own failures and from the failures of other revolutionaries. In China, Mao Tse-tung's strategy of peasant-based guerrilla warfare was adopted as the official strategy of the Chinese Communist party in the late 1920s after a series of unsuccessful urban uprisings made it clear that the Bolshevik strategy of concentrating on organizing among the urban proletariat would not work in the Chinese context.[32] In their post-mortems on their unsuccessful 1956–1962 guerrilla campaign in Northern Ireland, the leaders of the Irish Republican Army agreed that a key reason for their failure was a lack of support among the Catholic population of Northern Ireland. Hence, in 1969–1971 as they were laying the groundwork for their campaign to drive the British out of Northern Ireland, the Provisional IRA went to considerable lengths to build a significant base of support among the Catholic population of Ulster.[33] In planning his own revolution, Castro carefully studied the reasons for the overthrow of the Arbenz government in Guatemala. (Perhaps the single most important lesson he drew from Arbenz's downfall was that a revolutionary government must immediately destroy the old military and create a new revolutionary army, a policy he immediately undertook when he came to power in Cuba.)[34]

The changes in strategy on the part of contemporary revolutionary movements in Central America are in large part the outcome of a process of reassessment similar to that undertaken by a number of other revolutionary movements that have suffered repeated failure. In order to understand the changes in strategy that resulted from this process of reassessment, it is first necessary to discuss the specific case of the evolution of the strategy of the Sandinista movement in Nicaragua. Although this process of reassessment has been taking place elsewhere in Central America as well, the spectacular victory of the Sandinistas has made them, in effect, the new "model" for a successful revolution, and hence the debates on strategy among Central American revolutionary movements have been massively influenced since 1979 by the victory of the Sandinistas over Somoza.

At the time of the Sandinista National Liberation Front's (FSLN) victory in 1979, it had been in existence for eighteen years. During these years, the FSLN went through what can be called three "learning processes" whereby it gradually evolved the revolutionary strategy that led to its victory in 1979:

• *The heritage of Augusto Sandino.* The Sandinistas studied the political ideas and military tactics of Augusto Sandino in his campaign against the U.S. Marines in 1927–1933. Sandino was fundamentally a nationalist rather than a radical leftist, and hence he was willing to work with anyone who was opposed to the American military occupa-

177

tion. Moreover, Sandino was a shrewd guerrilla commander: After an early defeat in which he tried to storm a U.S.-held strongpoint, he adopted the classic hit-and-run tactics of guerrilla warfare. In other words, Sandino avoided two of the major mistakes of the Latin American rural and urban guerrillas of the period 1960–1977—loss of popular support because of an extremely radical political program and military recklessness.[35]

• *The aftermath of Guevara's defeat in Bolivia.* The Sandinistas felt that one of the key lessons to be learned from Guevara's defeat in Bolivia was the disastrous consequences for a rural guerrilla movement lacking any support from the peasantry and not having any contacts with the urban areas. So in the period 1967–1974, they de-emphasized military activities and instead concentrated on organizing among the urban and rural population.[36]

• *Their own set of experiences.* The fact that by the late 1970s the Sandinistas had been an ongoing movement since 1961 and that there were individuals (such as Tomás Borge) who had been members of the movement since its founding meant that, unlike the earlier revolutionary movements, most of which were quite short-lived, many of the leaders of the Sandinistas had learned through personal experience the problems associated with various types of strategies and tactics. Tomás Borge, for example, recalled after the revolution that the FSLN's first attempt in 1963 to wage rural guerrilla warfare failed because of lack of proper political and military preparation: "We committed the error of moving into the zone without first undertaking preparatory political work, without knowing the terrain, and without creating supply lines."[37]

From these various learning experiences, the Sandinistas developed a strategy for taking power that differed quite markedly from the strategies pursued by the early Latin American revolutionary movements:

• The Sandinistas were quite cautious in their military operations. As was noted previously, after Guevara's disaster in Boliva in 1967, they essentially pulled back from military operations and concentrated on building their rural and urban popular base. When it became clear that they did not have sufficient arms to prevail in the September 1978 insurrection, they withdrew from the urban areas to build up their military strength for their successful offensive in the spring and summer of 1979.[38]

• Although the core elements of the FSLN were quite radical, they felt that victory over Somoza required a broad coalition of organized support. The political program of the FSLN that was put forward during the insurrection demanded many far-reaching social and political changes, but it had little of the Marxist-Leninist ideology and rhetoric that was so pervasive in the statements and manifestoes of the earlier generation of rural and urban guerrillas.[39] Moreover, the Sandinistas went to considerable lengths to get support from organized groups such as unions, political parties, and professional associations. They did not ignore or belittle such groups the way the guerrillas of the period 1960-1977 had tended to do.

• The Sandinistas made strenuous efforts to get a broad array of international backing. The earlier generation of Latin American revolutionaries had tended to feel that support from non-Communist countries was unnecessary (since revolution all over Latin America was imminent) and undesirable (since the price of such support could be compromising the radical goals of their movements). The Sandinistas, on the other hand, felt that such broad international support was essential for two reasons. First, they realized that, given Castro's fear of provoking the United States and given his ongoing efforts to "normalize" his relations with Latin America, there were real constraints on his willingness to assist their movement.[40] Second, they felt that a major constraint against U.S. intervention against them would be if they were supported by a broad range of countries in Latin America.[41] Third, they believed that it was important to get as much support as possible from sympathetic groups in the United States; they felt that a badly divided American public would tend to immobilize U.S. policy toward Nicaragua.[42]

These efforts to secure international support paid off. The Sandinistas were actively supported by Costa Rica, Mexico, Panama, and Venezuela, as well as by Cuba. When in June 1979 the United States proposed that the Organization of American States (OAS) create a peace-keeping force for Nicaragua, the American proposal was not supported by a single other nation in the OAS.[43] In the United States the Sandinistas were supported by many Catholic organizations, by a number of the more liberal Protestant churches, and by many academics who specialized in Latin America. This support was reflected in the Congress: When in September 1978 a group of seventy-six congressmen sent a letter to President Carter calling on him to increase aid to Somoza, another group of eighty-six congressmen sent a letter to Secretary of State Cyrus Vance urging that all aid to Somoza be terminated.[44]

The two countries in Central America which currently have the largest revolutionary movements are El Salvador and Guatemala. In both countries, the effect of the "Sandinista model" is a very important factor in the sort of new strategies that these movements are pursuing. It must be recognized, however, that in both El Salvador and Guatemala the current revolutionary movements antedate the victory of the Sandinistas in 1979, and that the process of reassessment of strategy and tactics that went on among the FSLN also went on among the revolutionary movements in El Salvador and Guatemala. In other words, the modifications in strategy by these various revolutionary movements are not simply a result of slavishly imitating the Sandinistas. On the contrary, the various learning experiences that the Sandinistas went through have also characterized these other revolutionary movements. They are aware of certain key figures and events in their national histories, of the successes and failures of the various guerrilla campaigns of the 1960s and 1970s, and of the lessons that they have learned in the course of the guerrilla warfare campaigns that they have waged in recent years.

The combined effect of their own learning experiences plus the victory of the Sandinistas in 1979 have led the revolutionary movements in El Salvador and Guatemala to adopt a strategy of revolution that is broadly similar to that of the FSLN.

The first component of the strategy is military caution. The guerrillas in both El Salvador and Guatemala are much less likely to engage in the sort of military recklessness that characterized the earlier generation of revolutionary movements. Instead, many of these guerrillas are committed to a strategy of gradually building up their own strength while eroding that of the governments that they are fighting. For example, the largest of the guerrilla groups in El Salvador, the Popular Forces of Liberation—Farabundo Marti (FPL)—is pursuing a strategy it calls "prolonged people's war." (In adopting this strategy, the FPL was heavily influenced by the example of the Vietnamese revolution.)[45]

Like all armies, guerrillas can at times delude themselves that they are on the verge of victory and hence there is no longer any need to exercise restraint. In the war between the French and the Vietminh in Indochina, for example, the Vietminh inflicted some major defeats on the French in 1950 in the area of Vietnam just south of the Chinese border. Emboldened by this success, the Vietminh announced that they would soon drive the French out of Hanoi. In their attack on Hanoi in early 1951, the Vietminh were decisively defeated and suffered heavy losses. Their military forces were not yet strong enough to defeat the French in large-scale conventional battles.

Given this inherent tendency among revolutionary movements to develop delusions that they are on the verge of victory, it is not surprising that the contemporary generation of Latin American revolutionary movements occasionally abandons its policy of military caution. Witness, for example, the "Final Offensive" that the El Salvadoran guerrillas launched in early January 1981 in an attempt to defeat the government before the Reagan administration came into office. On balance, however, the contemporary revolutionary movements in Central America exercise much more caution and restraint in their military operations than did the early generation of Latin American revolutionaries.

The second component of the strategy of revolution is the building of broad-based opposition coalitions. In El Salvador the revolutionaries have tried very hard (not always with complete success) to build a broad, unified opposition coalition to the government of El Salvador. In April 1980 a number of unions, peasant organizations, and political parties that were opposed to the current government in El Salvador formed the Democratic Revolutionary Front (FDR). In October 1980 the various guerrilla armies formed the Farabundo Marti Front for National Liberation (FMLN); the military operations of this front are coordinated through the Unified Revolutionary Directorate (DRU). The FMLN and the FDR are linked by a seven-person diplomatic commission. The head of this commission is Guillermo Ungo of the Social Democratic National Revolutionary Movement (MNR).[46]

The Guatemalan revolutionaries have made similar attempts to build a broad opposition coalition. In January 1981 the major guerrilla organizations issued their first joint communiqué. The guerrillas have also made attempts to form alliances with unions, peasant organizations, student groups, and political parties.[47]

The third component of the strategy of revolution is international support. In addition to their ties to the Soviet Union and Cuba (which will be discussed later), the new generation of revolutionary movements has tried to get support from a number of nations and international organizations. The El Salvadoran MNR is that nation's member of the Socialist International (SI), and hence the leadership of the MNR has lobbied for support (with some success) among the other member parties of the SI. A number of these parties are now heading their governments: The ruling parties in Spain, France, Greece, Costa Rica, Austria, and the Dominican Republic are all members of the SI. Many Catholic clergy, religious, and laity from Central America have lobbied for support for the revolutionaries among Catholics in the United States, Latin America, and Western Europe.

In their campaign to get as much international support as possible, the revolutionaries in Central America have benefited from a series of reports by various human rights groups and humanitarian

181

organizations that have been strongly critical of the governments of El Salvador and Guatemala. In 1982, for example, the American Civil Liberties Union (ACLU) and the Americas Watch Committee issued two reports on human rights in El Salvador that strongly criticized the human rights practices of the El Salvadoran government. Oxfam-America, a famine relief group, has published an unfavorable evaluation of the land reform program in El Salvador. Amnesty International has issued a number of quite critical assessments of the human rights record of the governments of Guatemala and El Salvador.[48]

A final respect in which the contemporary revolutionary movements in Central America differ from the earlier generation of revolutionary movements concerns their relationship with Cuba and the Soviet Union. In the late 1960s, Castro began to scale down his support of revolutionary movements in Latin America. This was partly because of a desire to concentrate on pressing domestic problems (in particular the weak Cuban economy) and partly because both Castro and his Soviet ally felt a need for Cuba to reduce its isolation in the hemisphere. So, without abandoning his support for revolutionary movements, Castro began according support for these movements a lesser priority than Cuba's domestic problems and the need to establish good state-to-state relations with other countries in the Western Hemisphere.[49]

This reduction of Cuban aid to Latin American revolutionaries was duly noted by the current revolutionary movements in Central America and significantly influenced their attitude toward receiving Cuban support. Specifically, the revolutionaries were quite willing to take whatever support Castro was willing to give them; what they were *not* willing to do is rely exclusively on Cuba (or any other country) as their only supporter. One point comes through quite graphically in Che Guevara's Bolivian diary—namely, the desperate position Guevara's foco found itself in once all chance of significant outside support was lost by the refusal of the Bolivian Communists to cooperate with him. So, although the contemporary revolutionary movements in Central America have received a significant amount of arms and training from Cuba, their dependence on Cuban support is less than was the case with the earlier rural and urban guerrillas of Latin America.[50]

The Soviet Union, in contrast to Cuba, has played a *more* important role with respect to the contemporary generation of revolutionary movements than it did with the earlier generation of revolutionary movements. The Soviet hostility toward this earlier generation stemmed from four factors:

• Many of these revolutionaries were considered doctrinally unorthodox. Trotskyism has played a larger role in Latin American politics than in the politics of any other region in the world, and hence it is not surprising that many Latin American revolutionary movements have been dogmatically Trotskyist or at least heavily influenced by Trotskyism. Many of the members of the revolutionary movements in Peru in the early 1960s were Trotskyists (including Hugo Blanco).[51] One of the major urban guerrilla groups in Argentina, the People's Revolutionary Army (ERP) was created by a group of Argentine Trotskyists.[52]

• The revolutionaries were often quite hostile to the local Communist parties, which they considered as fundamentally "reformist." Given that most of the Communist parties in Latin America are Moscow-line parties, the Soviets obviously were distrustful of movements that were hostile to these parties.[53]

• The Soviets were skeptical of the chances of success of the guerrillas. They were afraid that the only result of the violence by these guerrillas would be to bring very conservative, strongly anti-Communist governments to power that would repress the local Communist party and be hostile to the Soviet Union. In the period of the Allende government in Chile, for example, both the Soviet Union and the Chilean Communist party attacked the terrorism of the MIR (Movement of the Revolutionary Left) on the grounds (which, ultimately, proved to be quite correct) that such terrorism would lead to a military coup.[54]

• Finally, for reasons very different of course from those of the United States, the Soviets also desire to avoid "another Cuba." Specifically, as the Soviets told Allende quite bluntly, they have no desire to acquire another client state in the Americas that will require the sort of economic subsidies that Cuba needs.[55] Put differently, while the Soviets would like to have pro-Soviet revolutionary governments in the Western Hemisphere, their enthusiasm for revolutionary governments is constrained by fears of being put in a position of having to provide massive subsidies to the new government.

With respect to the new generation of revolutionary movements in Central America, many of these Soviet concerns have been mitigated. These new revolutionary movements are quite willing to include the local Communist parties in their broad opposition coalitions (the Communist parties of El Salvador and Guatemala are both currently supporting the guerrillas).[56] Moreover, these revolutionary movements have a number of international backers, and hence in the event of victory the new governments can look to sources besides the Soviet

183

Union for assistance. Nicaragua has received considerable economic assistance from Brazil, Mexico, and Venezuela.[57] Finally, the Soviets feel that these revolutionary movements have a significant chance of success. Given their claims to be the world's leading revolutionary power, the Soviets obviously want to be able to claim at least some of the credit for any successful revolution. Moreover, the Soviets are aware that failure to support a revolutionary movement early enough can aggravate relations with the new government. The Soviet failure to support the FLN until late in the Algerian war has inclined Algeria to keep a certain distance from the Soviet Union in its foreign policy.[58]

As for the contemporary Central American revolutionaries themselves, they are much more inclined to seek Soviet support than were the earlier generation of revolutionaries. Feeling that they are faced with a long struggle to achieve and consolidate power, these current revolutionary movements are attracted by the "assets" (arms, training, propaganda, international support) that the Soviet Union has at its disposal. So the upshot of this limited "convergence" of the Soviets and the Latin American revolutionaries is that the Soviets have given some direct aid (arms and training) to these revolutionaries and have also used their extensive propaganda structure to help mobilize political support for the revolutionaries.[59]

Patterns of Violence

The new strategy and tactics of the contemporary generation of revolutionary movements in Central America have meant that the violence which has resulted from these movements' military campaigns differs in three key respects from that of the earlier generation of revolutionary movements:

1. The violence is much more prolonged. The delusions of easy victory that were so pervasive among the earlier guerrilla organizations meant that quite often these organizations were so militarily reckless that they were quickly destroyed. In the 1965 guerrilla uprising in Peru the three separate foco lasted six months, four months, and one month, respectively.[60] Che Guevara's foco in Bolivia lasted eleven months.[61] And an Argentine foco set up in the spring of 1963 was destroyed in February 1964.[62]

The military caution that characterizes the contemporary Central American revolutionary movements reduces the chances that the governments of the region can score quick, crushing victories over them. Instead, what occurs are long, drawn-out insurgencies: The guerrillas in El Salvador began their campaign in the early 1970s; the guerrillas in Guatemala revived in the mid-1970s; and the FSLN's struggle against Somoza lasted from 1961 to 1979.[63]

2. The level of violence is much higher. In several of the earlier guerrilla campaigns there were large numbers of people killed and wounded in the course of the fighting. For example, both the Peruvian military's campaign against the 1965 guerrilla uprisings and the Guatemalan military's 1966–1968 offensive against the guerrillas resulted in thousands of people being killed and wounded.[64]

In the current guerrilla campaigns, however, the level of violence has been much higher than in these earlier campaigns. One reason for this increased violence is that, unlike in the foco period, the fighting now often takes place in populated areas rather than in thinly settled mountains and jungles. (In this connection, it should be mentioned that El Salvador has a population density of 600 people per square mile; it is the most densely populated nation in the Western Hemisphere.[65]) Also, the very fact that the current revolutionary movements are more powerful than their predecessors means that their capability of causing violence is greatly increased. And because those political forces opposed to the revolutionaries see them as more powerful (and hence more likely to seize power), they are quite prepared to increase repressive measures in an effort to defeat the guerrillas.

The grim "statistics of violence" powerfully illustrate the magnitude of the violence taking place in El Salvador. It is of course true that any figures on fatalities in a civil war must be treated with great caution, because many of those making the estimates are in no sense impartial. In El Salvador, however, there is complete agreement that thousands of people have died in the civil war. The disputes concerning these figures are chiefly over the degree of responsibility that different groups have for the violence. The State Department in its February 1981 White Paper estimated that 10,000 people had been killed in El Salvador in 1980.[66] There have been a variety of estimates of the total number of fatalities in 1981 and 1982; all of these estimates agree, however, that in these two years thousands more El Salvadorans were killed.[67]

3. A final difference concerns violence against foreigners. The urban guerrillas of the late 1960s and early 1970s often achieved spectacular publicity with their kidnappings and assassinations of foreign nationals and diplomats. Yet, there were also real political costs entailed in such kidnappings: The country whose nationals were victimized could hardly be expected to be sympathetic to the guerrilla organizations involved. In 1970, for example, the West German ambassador to Guatemala was kidnapped and later assassinated by one

185

of the Guatemalan guerrilla organizations. The West German government was quite angry over the incident, their diplomatic establishment in Guatemala was reduced to a minimum, and the Guatemalan ambassador was asked to leave Bonn.[68] Given that the contemporary revolutionary movements have made major efforts to get support from the Socialist International (in which the German member party, the Social Democratic party, or SDP, plays a very important role), they would be most unlikely to victimize a West German national because they would be afraid of alienating public and government opinion in West Germany.

Interestingly, while the revolutionaries have de-emphasized terrorism against foreign nationals, individuals and groups on the extreme right have engaged in a significant amount of such terrorism in recent years. The targets have included foreign clergy (the most well-known case, of course, being that of the murder of three American nuns and a lay worker in El Salvador in December 1980), American government officials, and foreign journalists. The right is engaging in such terrorism because it believes certain foreign organizations and countries are the allies of their political opponents, and hence they retaliate by using violence against individuals from these organizations and countries. At one point in the war in El Salvador, for example, the extreme rightist White Warriors Union (UGB) warned all Jesuits to leave El Salvador on penalty of death for their alleged aid to the revolutionary movements.[69]

Conclusion: Implications for U.S. Foreign Policy

The most important implication for U.S. foreign policy of the strategies being pursued by the contemporary generation of revolutionary movements in Central America is that these strategies greatly increase the difficulties involved in any sort of U.S. military intervention in Central America. Put differently, there are four reasons why any U.S. military intervention against these current revolutionary movements will involve much higher costs and risks than were involved in the U.S. military interventions against the earlier generation of revolutionary movements:

1. The weaknesses of the earlier generation of guerrilla organizations meant that small advisory teams and limited amounts of military aid were all that was required to help local governments defeat these guerrillas. When it became known, for example, that Che Guevara was in Bolivia, the United States sent down a small advisory team to retrain a Bolivian battalion in ranger tactics. When its training was

finished, the battalion was sent out after Guevara's foco and fairly quickly located it and destroyed it.[70] (An evaluation of Guevara's diary reveals the effectiveness of this ranger unit; in the first few months of the time period covered by the diary Guevara's foco scores a number of easy victories over the Bolivian army, while in the diary's final weeks the foco is progressively destroyed by a series of crippling defeats.)[71] In Guatemala, U.S. military aid averaged close to $2 million annually between 1962 and 1969.[72] An evaluation of the effectiveness of this aid written in 1977 stated:

> Over the past twenty years, U.S. military aid to Guatemala, even in its comparatively small scope, has contributed to institutional improvements in the Guatemalan armed forces. These forces are now better organized, equipped, trained, and staffed; they are more capable of fulfilling their military function.[73]

The much stronger contemporary guerrilla movements mean that in order for the United States to carry out any sort of effective military intervention, it must be prepared to commit much higher levels of resources. In March 1981, for example, the Reagan administration sent $25 million in military aid to El Salvador; for fiscal year 1982 it requested $26 million in military assistance to El Salvador; and in February 1982 it requested an additional $55 million worth of military assistance.[74]

2. Effective military intervention will be more difficult. The "militarism" that was so typical of the earlier generation of guerrillas simplified the task of the U.S. military personnel sent to various Latin American countries. Basically, all that these advisers were required to do was to improve the technical competence of the local militaries in counterguerrilla operations and, as noted previously, were often quite successful in doing so. But although the U.S. military has proved quite capable in the strictly military aspects of counterguerrilla warfare, the war in Indochina showed that the U.S. military finds it much more difficult to respond to the sort of wars now under way in Central America—namely, the sort of revolutionary warfare in which political and military factors are equally important and are inextricably enmeshed with each other.

For both doctrinal and organizational reasons revolutionary warfare goes deeply against the grain of the U.S. military. The doctrinal problem is that in the U.S. military there has always been a widely shared belief that military issues are and should be kept separate from political issues.[75] The organizational problem is that the U.S. military is a big-unit, high-technology military. Wars against guerrillas, however, for the most part, require small units and fairly simple technology. Although the U.S. military could, of course, modify its organizational patterns, the war in Vietnam demonstrated that the U.S. military is extremely reluctant to modify its big-unit, high-technology orientation.[76]

The "bottom line" of the U.S. military's problems with responding to revolutionary warfare can be summed up as follows: Unless and until the United States makes the effort to develop a significant capability to conduct counterguerrilla warfare, increasing the U.S. military presence beyond a fairly low level in a country combating an insurgency may well do more harm than good. As Robert Thompson, a British expert on guerrilla warfare, stated with respect to the American intervention in Vietnam: "The trouble with you Americans is that whenever you double the effort you somehow manage to square the error."[77]

3. Another factor is domestic American politics. The contemporary revolutionary movements are very skillful in building public support for their cause in domestic U.S. politics. They have learned how to use both the media and sympathetic groups in the U.S. to mobilize public opinion against any U.S. military intervention in Central America.

The revolutionaries' ability to mobilize U.S. public opinion against intervention is made easier by certain changes in American society in the past two decades. First, memories of the Vietnam War are still a significant factor in the political views and beliefs of large numbers of Americans. Tragically, even the memorial for the Americans who died in Vietnam became enmeshed in a bitter political controversy. Second, under the influence of the Watergate scandal, U.S. media today stress investigative journalism. Since wars always provide opportunities for such journalism, it is very doubtful that any U.S. military intervention in Central America would long remain a so-called secret war. (In the modern world, *very* few wars are genuinely secret; wars that are called such are almost always in the category of what used to be called forgotten wars. Apparently the term secret has caught on because it sounds mysterious and exciting, whereas the term forgotten can lead to the obvious assumption that maybe it was forgotten because it was unimportant and uninteresting.)

4. The United States must also consider the reaction of the international community. The contemporary revolutionary movements have made major efforts to gain support from other countries and international organizations. Hence, any U.S. military intervention in Central America will aggravate U.S. relations with a number of coun-

tries. Both Mexico and Venezuela, for example, are supporters of certain of the revolutionary movements in Central America; hence, the ongoing U.S. military intervention against these movements has caused strains in U.S. relations with these major oil producers.[78] Given the strength of the peace movement in Western Europe, the current U.S. military intervention in Central America has resulted in frictions between the United States and its European allies because these allies are very reluctant to aggravate their own domestic problems by supporting such intervention. Any large-scale U.S. military intervention would seriously aggravate these strained relations.

In conclusion, the difficult foreign policy problem that the United States must deal with in respect to the contemporary revolutionary movements in Central America can be summed up as follows: The strength of these movements increases the chances that they will eventually come to power; and at the same time this strength means that any sort of U.S. military intervention in Central America will have much higher costs and risks than was the case with the U.S. military interventions against the earlier generation of revolutionary movements.

Notes

1. Richard Hofstadter and Michael Wallace, eds., *American Violence: A Documentary History* (New York: Vintage Books, 1970), pp. 9–11.
2. William LeoGrande, "The United States and the Nicaraguan Revolution," in Thomas Walker, ed., *Nicaragua in Revolution* (New York: Praeger Publishers, 1982), pp. 66–71.
3. The revolutionary movements that followed the Cuban Revolution came in two basically distinct waves. The first was a series of attempts at rural guerrilla warfare; this wave lasted from approximately 1960 to 1967. The second wave was a series of urban guerrilla movements; these movements enjoyed their high point in the earlier 1970s but were for the most part destroyed by the late 1970s. Roughly, therefore, one can say that the time frame of the earlier generation of revolutionary movements was 1960–1977.
4. For histories of several of these rural guerrilla movements, see Richard Gott, *Guerrilla Movements in Latin America* (Garden City, N.Y.: Doubleday, 1971).
5. For Guevara's personal account of the Bolivian campaign, see Ernesto Che Guevara, *The Diary of Che Guevara* (New York: Bantam Books, 1968).
6. For a discussion of some of the most important of the urban guerrilla movements in Latin America, see James Kohl and John Litt, *Urban Guerrilla Warfare in Latin America* (Cambridge, Mass.: M.I.T. Press, 1974).

7. Douglas S. Blaufarb, *The Counter-Insurgency Era: U.S. Doctrine and Performance, 1950 to the Present* (New York: Free Press, 1977), pp. 279–86.
8. Gott, *Guerrilla Movements*, p. 163.
9. Ibid., p. 316.
10. Ibid., p. 369.
11. Ibid., p. 497.
12. Ernesto Che Guevara, *Guerrilla Warfare* (New York: Vintage Books, 1961), pp. 1–2.
13. Carlos Marighella, "Minimanual of the Urban Guerrilla," appendix in Robert Moss, *Urban Guerrilla Warfare* (London: International Institute for Strategic Studies, 1971), p. 40.
14. Gott, *Guerrilla Movements*, pp. 369–70.
15. Marighella, "Minimanual," p. 23.
16. Gott, *Guerrilla Movements*, pp. 275–92.
17. Ibid., p. 286.
18. Régis Debray, "Revolution in the Revolution?" in Walter Laqueur, ed., *The Guerrilla Reader* (New York: Meridian Books, 1977), pp. 214–18.
19. Guevara, *Diary*, p. 57.
20. Guevara, *Guerrilla Warfare*, pp. 8–12.
21. Guevara, *Diary*, pp. 150, 164–65, 185–86.
22. V. I. Lenin, "Why the Social Democrats Must Declare Determined and Relentless War on the Socialist Revolutionaries" (1902), in Stefan Possony, ed., *Lenin Reader* (Chicago: Henry Regnery, 1966), pp. 470–71.
23. Guevara, *Guerrilla Warfare*, p. 15.
24. Abraham Guillen, "Strategy of the Urban Guerrilla," in Laqueur, *Guerrilla Reader*, pp. 229–37.
25. Gott, *Guerrilla Movements*, pp. 149–50.
26. Kohl and Litt, *Urban Guerrilla Warfare*, pp. 48–50.
27. James A. Miller, "Urban Terrorism in Uruguay: The Tupamaros," in Bard O'Neill, William R. Heaton, and Donald J. Alberts, eds., *Insurgency in the Modern World* (Boulder, Colo.: Westview Press, 1980), pp. 171–74.
28. For an account of the German army's innovations in armored warfare between the two world wars, see the memoirs of Heinz Guderian, *Panzer Leader* (New York: Ballantine Books, 1965), pp. 7–27.
29. Gordon A. Craig, *The Politics of the Prussian Army* (New York: Oxford University Press, 1964), pp. 354–82.
30. Blaufarb, *The Counter-Insurgency Era*, pp. 40–49.
31. Y. Harkabi, *Fedayeen Action and Arab Strategy* (London: International Institute for Strategic Studies, 1969), pp. 18–19.
32. Blaufarb, *The Counter-Insurgency Era*, pp. 2–11.
33. Don Mansfield, "The Irish Republican Army and Northern Ireland," in O'Neill et al., *Insurgency in the Modern World*, pp. 64–71.
34. Cole Blasier, *The Hovering Giant: U.S. Responses to Revolutionary Change in Latin America* (Pittsburgh, Penn.: University of Pittsburgh Press, 1976), pp. 177–78.

35. Neill Macaulay, *The Sandino Affair* (Chicago: Quadrangle Books, 1967), pp. 74, 214, 226, 265.

36. Harry E. Vanden, "The Ideology of the Insurrection," in Walker, ed., *Nicaragua in Revolution*, pp. 50–54. The El Salvadoran rebels also learned from Guevara's defeat, as the following quotation shows: ". . . most of the Salvadorian revolutionaries had learned an important lesson from Che Guevara's disastrous experience in Bolivia. Guevara and his band of followers made little or no effort to build support among the population. Thus when U.S. Special Forces went looking for Che in the jungle there was no network to warn him and no one to hide him." Tommie Sue Montgomery, *Revolution in El Salvador: Origins and Evolution* (Boulder, Colo.: Westview Press, 1982), pp. 142–43.

37. Ibid., p. 50.

38. Thomas W. Walker, *Nicaragua: The Land of Sandino* (Boulder, Colo.: Westview Press, 1981), pp. 37–39.

39. John A. Booth, *The End and the Beginning: The Nicaraguan Revolution* (Boulder, Colo.: Westview Press, 1982), pp. 145–47.

40. Ibid., pp. 133–34.

41. Ibid., pp. 130–34, 165–68, 175–80.

42. LeoGrande, "The United States and the Nicaraguan Revolution," pp. 63, 66–67; Booth, *The End and the Beginning*, pp. 128–30.

43. LeoGrande, "The United States and the Nicaraguan Revolution," pp. 69–70.

44. Ibid., p. 67.

45. Enrique Baloyra, *El Salvador in Transition* (Chapel Hill: University of North Carolina Press, 1982), p. 161; idem, *El Salvador: Beyond Elections* (New York: North American Congress on Latin America, 1982), p. 28.

46. Baloyra, *El Salvador in Transition*, pp. 154, 161–62.

47. Daniel Premo, "Guatemala," in Robert Wesson, ed., *Communism in Central America and the Caribbean* (Stanford, Calif.: Hoover Institution Press, 1982), p. 83.

48. Americas Watch Committee and American Civil Liberties Union, *Report on Human Rights in El Salvador, January 26, 1982* (New York: Random House, 1982), and Americas Watch Committee and the American Civil Liberties Union, *July 20, 1982, Supplement to the Report on Human Rights in El Salvador* (Washington, D.C.: Americas Watch Committee, 1982); Laurence R. Simon and James C. Stephens, Jr., *El Salvador Land Reform 1980–1981: Impact Audit* (Boston, Mass.: Oxfam-America, 1981); for a sample of the criticisms made by Amnesty International of the governments of El Salvador and Guatemala see *Amnesty International Reports for 1979, 1980, 1981, 1982* (London: Amnesty International Publications), sections on El Salvador and Guatemala. These reports are an annual summary of the human rights situation in each of the countries of the world.

49. Carmelo Mesa-Lago, *Cuba in the 1970's: Pragmatism and Institutionalization* (Albuquerque: University of New Mexico Press, 1978), pp. 117–18.

50. The Kurdish revolt in Iraq in 1974–1975 is an example of what can happen to a revolutionary movement that is dependent on only one or two outside sources of aid. When the United States and the Iranians cut off aid to the Kurd rebels in early 1975, they were quickly defeated by the Iraqi army. Paul Viotti, "Iraq: The Kurdish Rebellion," in O'Neill et al., *Insurgency in the Modern World*, p. 202.

51. Gott, *Guerrilla Movements*, pp. 321–29.

52. Walter Laqueur, *Terrorism* (Boston: Little, Brown, 1977), pp. 203–4.

53. In the Algerian war, a major reason for the Soviet coolness toward the Algerian revolutionaries was that both the French Communist party (PCF) and the Algerian Communist party (PCA) had ambivalent attitudes toward the Algerian revolution. The ambivalence of the French Communists was due to the fact that the PCF realized that the French working class was to a considerable extent hostile to the Algerian cause, whereas the ambivalence of the Algerian Communists stemmed from the commitment of the PCA to defend the interests of the workers among the French settlers in Algeria. Alistair Horne, *A Savage War of Peace: Algeria, 1954–1962* (New York: Penguin Books, 1977), p. 405.

54. Paul Sigmund, "The USSR, Cuba, and the Revolution in Cuba," in Robert Donaldson, ed., *The Soviet Union in the Third World: Successes and Failures* (Boulder, Colo.: Westview Press, 1981), pp. 37–40.

55. Joseph L. Nogee and John W. Sloan, "Allende's Chile and the Soviet Union: A Policy Lesson for Latin American Nations Seeking Autonomy," *Journal of Inter-American Studies and World Affairs*, vol. 21, no. 3 (August 1979), pp. 339–68.

56. Premo, "Guatemala," pp. 82–83; Baloyra, *El Salvador in Transition*, pp. 161–62.

57. Booth, *The End and the Beginning*, p. 212.

58. Horne, *A Savage War of Peace*, p. 559.

59. In February 1981 the State Department issued a White Paper entitled "Communist Interference in El Salvador." The White Paper argued that the Soviet Union and certain of its allies had provided military aid to the guerrillas in El Salvador. The conclusions and the documentation of the White Paper have been widely criticized. It is important, however, to understand that very few critics deny that the Soviet bloc has provided military aid to the rebels; rather, the critics maintain that the amount of aid is less than the White Paper claims and that the White Paper is wrong in claiming that the Soviet bloc created and controls the revolutionary movement in El Salvador. For the text of the White Paper, see *Department of State Bulletin*, March 1981, pp. 1–7.

60. Gott, *Guerrilla Movements*, pp. 366, 371, 379.

61. Ibid., pp. 420–22, 474–76.

62. Luis Mercier Vega, *Guerrillas in Latin America: The Technique of the Counter-State* (New York: Frederick A. Praeger, 1969), pp. 115–17.

63. Baloyra, *El Salvador in Transition*, p. 161; Premo, "Guatemala," pp. 82–83; Booth, *The End and the Beginning*, p. 139.

64. Gott, *Guerrilla Movements*, pp. 99–101, 361–62.

65. Thomas P. Anderson, *Politics in Central America* (New York: Praeger Publishers, 1982), p. 63.

66. *Department of State Bulletin*, March 1981, p. 1.

67. See Baloyra, *El Salvador in Transition*, p. 191, for some of these various estimates.

68. Carol Baumann, *The Diplomatic Kidnappings* (The Hague: Martinas Nijhoff, 1973), pp. 99–100.

69. Baloyra, *El Salvador in Transition*, pp. 64–65.

70. Gott, *Guerrilla Movements*, pp. 450–51, 474–76.

71. Guevara, *Diary*, pp. 92–93, 120–21, 181–82, 186.

72. Brian Jenkins and Caesar D. Sereseres, "U.S. Military Assistance and the Guatemalan Armed Forces," *Armed Forces and Society* (Summer 1977), p. 578.

73. Ibid., p. 588.

74. Montgomery, *Revolution in El Salvador*, p. 221; Baloyra, *El Salvador in Transition*, p. 166.

75. Richard K. Betts, *Soldiers, Statesmen and Cold War Crises* (Cambridge, Mass.: Harvard University Press, 1977), pp. 130–31.

76. Brian M. Jenkins, *The Unchangeable War* (Santa Monica, Calif.: Rand Corporation, 1970), p. v; Blaufarb, *The Counter-Insurgency Era*, pp. 55–56, 78–79.

77. Robert Thompson, "Squaring the Error," *Foreign Affairs* (April 1968), p. 449.

78. Booth, *The End and the Beginning*, pp. 132–33, 211–13.

PART THREE
International Dimensions
of the Crisis

8

Soviet Strategy and Policies in the Caribbean Basin

JIRI VALENTA AND VIRGINIA VALENTA

From 1979 to 1983 there has been constant upheaval in some countries of the Caribbean basin—a geostrategic concept encompassing both the Caribbean island nations and such littoral nations as Mexico, Venezuela, and Colombia. This has occurred primarily in the countries of Central America as opposed to the majority of the relatively small, English-speaking Caribbean islands which appear considerably more stable. In Nicaragua and Grenada a revolutionary transformation has been underway since 1979, while in several other countries—Guatemala, Honduras, and even democratic Costa Rica—guerrilla groups have posed a serious challenge to existing regimes. Meanwhile a devastating civil war continues in El Salvador.

An understanding of this activity has frequently been obscured by the perception of conflicts in the area as strictly national in nature. As a result, greater regional and international trends have been either confused with national issues or ignored. The sources of instability in the countries of Central America are not always contained within each country. The conflicts tend to assume a regional dimension and thereby threaten to pit one grouping of countries against another. In addition, a strong Soviet and Cuban presence in the region has given these local problems international significance; for Cuba, backed by the U.S.S.R., without causing these problems, has played a pivotal role in their maintenance by assisting the revolutionaries.

Conditions internal to these Central American countries have set the stage for current problems. In most of them the middle classes remain weak and underdeveloped, resulting in polarization between a very small upper class and a very poor majority. The long-entrenched autocratic system of governing by past and present regimes has usually been oppressive. The decay of these outmoded authori-

An earlier and much shorter version of this paper appeared in A. Adelman and R. Reading, *Confrontation in the Caribbean Basin: International Perspectives on Security, Sovereignty and Survival* (Pittsburgh, Pa.: University of Pittsburgh Press, forthcoming).

tarian political, economic, and social structures has caused Central America to be the most disturbed and potentially destabilized area of the Caribbean basin, if not the entire Western Hemisphere. Several decades of U.S. hegemony and shortsighted policies, ranging from intervention to benign neglect, have contributed to a nationalist reaction in the region.

Contrary to the belief of many analysts, Soviet and Cuban policies in the region continue to have an important impact. According to one school of thought, the area is unimportant to the Soviet Union; the Soviets' "initial bravado [after the Nicaraguan Revolution] gave way to indecisiveness."[1] While the revolutionary turmoil in the basin would not simply disappear were the Soviet Union and Cuba to withdraw their support, their disengagement would render the crisis much more manageable by the solo or cooperative mediation of concerned local actors such as the United States, Mexico, Venezuela, Costa Rica, Colombia, and Jamaica. On this initial premise we agree with the assessment of analysts in the Reagan administration.

On other points and certainly in emphasis, however, this analysis may differ from some other arguments that have been articulated. First, as regards the nature of Soviet and Cuban strategy in the region, it is rather simplistic to assume that its prime objective is the creation of Leninist regimes. Should Leninist regimes modeled on Cuba's eventually materialize from the struggle, they would be bonuses, unexpected but welcome. However, the less bold, short-term Soviet goal is to achieve a number of specific "anti-imperialist" (that is, anti-U.S.) ideological, political, economic, and security objectives.

The second widely accepted premise to which we take exception is that Cuba and more recently Nicaragua are the main external sources of turbulence in other countries of the region. This view, often found in government and scholarly analyses concentrating on Cuban (and lately Nicaraguan) activities in the Caribbean basin, tends to isolate the phenomenon from the all-encompassing Soviet-Cuban relationship and fails to perceive these activities within the overall framework of Soviet strategy.[2] According to adherents of this perspective, the Caribbean basin is of "only peripheral interest" to the Soviets. As one policy-level State Department official bluntly put it: "I don't think the Soviets give a damn about Nicaragua. There's nothing to demonstrate their willingness to put a lot of resources in there."[3]

The leaders of some Caribbean nations are more realistic in their appraisal of Soviet intentions and interrelationships in the region. In the words of former Mexican President López Portillo, the Caribbean basin has been converted into a "frontier" between the United States and the Soviet Union: "The U.S. problem is not with Nicaragua or with Cuba. . . . The U.S. problem is with the Soviet Union."[4] Although perhaps he overstated, López Portillo identifies our central concern. The task of the analyst, then, is to correlate Cuban and recent Nicaraguan activities with Soviet strategy in the region—including Soviet support for Cuba which makes possible Cuba's revolutionary activities.

This essay tries to capture the actual Soviet reading of the situation and not the Western mirror imaging of Soviet views and behavior. First, we briefly trace the history of Soviet policies in the region, showing how they have undergone three major changes and may be in the process of changing again. Second, we name the primary factors that have influenced these policy shifts—presence of opportunity, degree of Soviet and Cuban concurrence regarding joint strategy, internal Soviet and East European politics, and Soviet perceptions of the correlation of forces with the United States. Finally, we state the long-term, more or less permanent Soviet strategic objectives in the region which are ideological, political, military, and economic in nature. We discuss Cuba's role in the fulfillment of these goals and how Soviet policies vary according to Soviet perceptions regarding the various regimes with which they deal—"revolutionary," "progressive," "bourgeois-liberal," and "reactionary." In conclusion we discuss prospects for Soviet-Cuban policies in the near future and the corresponding strategy of the United States.

Unlike Cuba, the Soviet Union has no longstanding cultural, political, or commercial ties with the countries of the Caribbean and Latin America. It began to develop such ties only as recently as the 1960s. This was initially due to the area's geographic remoteness and therefore marginal importance to the Soviet Union and also to traditional U.S. hegemony in the region.

The element of geographic remoteness has been an asset to the Soviet Union. Like the United States in Eastern Europe, the Soviet Union does not have a strong imperial record in Central and South America. Comintern and Soviet officials have traditionally been cautious about the prospects for communism in these areas. Like Marx and Engels, they have displayed a certain Eurocentric disdain for Latin leaders and peoples and have viewed the countries within a colonial framework under firm U.S. command.* Until the Cuban Revolution

---

* It is interesting that Marx and Engels favored the United States in the war against Mexico in 1848. Later Marx wrote a very unflattering essay on Simon Bolívar, which was based on the recollections of the French soldier of fortune Ducoudray Holstein. Marx's negative evaluation of Bolívar colored Soviet writings on Latin America until the 1950s.

the Communist Party of the Soviet Union (CPSU) had had only spo-
radic contacts with the Latin American Communist parties, and these
contacts were solely through individual party and Comintern officials.

Shifts in Soviet Policies, 1960–1982

The turning point in Soviet relations with the Caribbean basin nations
came in 1959–1960 after the Cuban Revolution. When U.S.–Cuban
differences became unbridgeable and the United States withdrew
from Cuba, the Soviets tried to fill the political and economic and,
ultimately, security vacuums thereby created. Since this time there
have been three major historical shifts in Soviet polices in the Caribbean basin. These were influenced by a number of interacting factors,
among which the most crucial were (1) Soviet-perceived opportunities
in countries of the region, (2) the status of the Soviet-Cuban alliance in
general and in the Caribbean in particular, (3) the dynamics of Soviet
internal politics and East European politics, and (4) changing Soviet
perceptions of the "correlation of forces" with the United States.

1. As suggested by actual events, Soviet activities in the Caribbean basin tend to reflect optimism or pessimism, depending on and
corresponding to observable trends in the region—that is, the presence or absence of local revolutionary activities, deteriorating socioeconomic conditions, and anti-U.S. nationalism. Soviet optimism
about promising revolutionary opportunities in the region reached
two highs following the revolutions in Cuba in 1959–1962 and in Nicaragua in 1979–1981. Their exemplary success led to a certain euphoria
on the part of the Soviets, who became hopeful about the revolutionary potential of other countries in the region.

The Cuban missile crisis in 1962, however, soon reminded the
Soviets of the limits of their power in the area. The resolution of the
crisis had a sobering effect on Soviet perceptions about the potential
for revolution in the Caribbean basin. The failure of Cuban-backed
guerrilla revolutionaries in the 1960s in Guatemala, Nicaragua, Colombia, and Venezuela, as well as in Bolivia and Peru, further in-
grained this attitude. Moreover, in the late 1960s and early 1970s the
Soviets were preoccupied with developments in other regions:
Vietnam War in Southeast Asia, the deepening Sino-Soviet dispute,
and conflict in the Middle East. The overthrow of Salvador Allende in
Chile in 1973 further quelled their enthusiasm. In the middle and late
1970s the Soviets were less preoccupied, but there were no immediate
revolutionary opportunities in Latin America. The contrary was true
in Africa, where the Soviets intervened with Cuba in Angola in 1975–
1976 and in Ethiopia in 1977–1978.

Soviet perceptions regarding the climate for revolution in the Caribbean basin changed again dramatically in 1979–1980. The Nicaraguan Revolution, the coup in Grenada, the growth of the insurgency movement in El Salvador, and the considerable worsening of socioeconomic conditions, particularly in Central America, brought about this third shift. It was characterized by active support of the more militant aspects of anti-imperialism, in which the pivotal role was played by Cuba. What makes the latest shift in Soviet policies intriguing is that it occurred when the Soviets had also become preoccupied with crises in Afghanistan and Poland closer to their borders. Thus it appears to have been motivated not only by simple opportunities but also by a strategic desire to preoccupy the United States in its "strategic rear" and thus direct attention away from troubled Poland and Afghanistan.

2. The dynamics of Soviet-Cuban relations is yet another important variable conditioning the shifts in Soviet policy. Beginning with Cuban dissatisfaction over Soviet behavior during the missile crisis, the Soviets and Cubans had profound disagreements about which strategy to pursue in Latin America. Castro, who was in favor of a "genuinely revolutionary road," criticized the Soviet Union for dealing with capitalist governments in Latin America. In adhering to Ernesto "Che" Guevara's concept of guerrilla-peasantry insurgency, Castro's strategy in the Caribbean basin and elsewhere in South America in the 1960s contradicted and even challenged the Soviet doctrine allowing for diversified roads toward socialism. The Soviets in the late 1960s were unwilling and unable to sponsor Castro's call to create "two or three" and even "four or five more Vietnams" for the United States in Latin America. As a result of these doctrinal and tactical differences, Soviet-Cuban relations in the late 1960s were unsatisfactory, at times strained almost to the breaking point.

After the death of Che Guevara in 1967, when most of the guerrilla movements in Latin America were wiped out, the Cubans soon came to realize the need for overcoming their differences and coordinating their policies with Moscow. By making mutual concessions, the Soviets and Cubans were able to arrive at a compromise strategy in the 1970s. It is misleading to suggest, as was common practice in the 1970s, that the Soviet Union and Cuba had given up the notion of supporting revolutionary movements in the region. Their posture was pragmatic, but it was not acquiescent. Neither the Soviets nor the Cubans entirely renounced the viability of armed revolution against unfriendly anti-Communist political forces and governments. The Soviets approved support for selected guerrilla activities in some Latin American countries with extremely pro-American and anti-Communist regimes, while the Cubans agreed to pursue diplomatic, commercial, and cultural channels with other friendlier, "progressive" (independent, with anti-American undertones) regimes. The growing Cuban dependency and Sovietization of Cuba helped merge the strategic visions of both countries in the 1970s and resulted in their basic agreement on the dialectics of "anti-imperialist" strategy in the third world in general and in Africa and the Caribbean in particular.

3.   Changes in Soviety strategy and tactics have also been conditioned by the dynamics of Soviet and East European internal affairs. It is fairly accurate to say that the Soviets have been more constrained in their behavior abroad when they were experiencing severe internal problems such as succession and power struggles in the Kremlin and/ or crises in Eastern Europe. This was true in 1953–1957 after Stalin's death and again in 1964–1968 after Khrushchev had been forced from power. Conversely, conditions were propitious for Soviet global activity when there was strong leadership in the Kremlin and there were no serious domestic and East European problems. This happened to an extent (even though Khrushchev's globalism was premature) after Khrushchev had crushed the Hungarian Revolution in 1956 and defeated his rivals in the Politburo in 1957. Subsequently, Brezhnev's successful policy of selective globalism followed his consolidation of power in the wake of the Soviet invasion of Czechoslovakia in 1968 and the dismissal of various rivals in the early 1970s.

4.   Finally, but not least important, Soviet policies in the Caribbean basin are influenced by the state of the Soviet-American global relationship and Soviet perceptions of the balance of power. Judging from the historical record, it appears that the worse Soviet-American relations are, the more the Soviets tend toward an activist posture in the basin. This was true during the Soviet-American confrontation over Berlin in 1958–1961 when the Soviets sought vigorously to exploit opportunities in Cuba and (with the Cubans) elsewhere in the region and again in 1980–1981 when Soviet-American relations deteriorated following the Afghanistan invasion and the Soviet intimidation of Poland. To qualify this assessment, the Soviets have pursued assertive policies in other third-world nations during times when Soviet-American relations were more cordial. Détente in the 1970s did not prevent their bold military aid to Arab clients in the Middle East War of 1973 or the joint Soviet-Cuban military interventions in Africa in 1975–1978.

Within the framework of Soviet-American relations, what appears to matter most is the Soviet perception of the correlation of forces or balance of power between the Soviet Union and the United States. During Stalin's time, the Caribbean basin's geographic remoteness and limited Soviet sea- and air-lift capabilities made the region of only marginal importance. Gradually the Soviet Union evolved from a basically regional and premature global power in the 1960s under Khrushchev to a fully developed, globally oriented superpower under Brezhnev. The acquisition of strategic parity with the United States in the early 1970s and immeasurably improved conventional capabilities helped to make possible the Soviet-Cuban ventures in Angola and Ethiopia and support for Nicaragua and other clients. In the second part of the 1970s the Soviets demonstrated time and again a more assertive strategy in third-world countries by means of direct or indirect military intervention and increasing military aid. Cuba's emergence as a pivotal player in Africa and the Caribbean in the 1970s, which unfolded within a context of global interaction between the Soviet Union and the United States, was possible mainly because of growing Soviet military and economic power.

Of the shifting Soviet perceptions concerning the balance of forces since the mid-1970s, the most significant has been the image of declining U.S. ability to counter Soviet activity in the third world in general and the Caribbean basin in particular. This contrasts sharply with the image held by the Soviets in previous decades when U.S. policy makers were believed to have not only the power to obstruct Soviet plans but also the will to use it. This image was shaken only briefly during the short period marking the transition from Eisenhower's to Kennedy's administration and the unsuccessful Bay of Pigs invasion shortly thereafter. Khrushchev's appraisal of Kennedy as "weak" and "inexperienced"* led the Soviets to conclude prematurely that the Kennedy administration was unable to curtail revolution in the Caribbean. The humiliating defeat suffered by the Soviet Union a year later dampened for a long time to come Soviet enthusiasm for the revolutionary aspects of their strategy in the basin. Soviet perceptions regarding U.S. strength and conviction were reconfirmed by the U.S. intervention in the Dominican Republic in 1965, when the motto "Never a Second Cuba" became the imperative for U.S. policy in Latin America through the early 1970s. Since the mid-1970s the Soviets have observed a weakness on the part of U.S. policy makers which they attribute to the defeat in Vietnam and the subse-

---

* President Kennedy himself formed this impression while negotiating with Khrushchev in Vienna in 1961 after the Bay of Pigs invasion attempt. As James Reston, who interviewed Kennedy after the summit, reported: "Khrushchev had assumed, Kennedy said, that any American president who invaded Cuba with inadequate preparation was inexperienced and a president who then didn't use force to see the invasion through was weak. Kennedy admitted Khrushchev's logic on both points."

quent fear on the part of the American public and Congress of slipping into a new Vietnam quagmire; the damaging political and economic effect of the 1973 oil embargo; and the weakening of the office of the U.S. presidency during the Watergate scandal. Numerous Soviet writings point to these phenomena as having weakened the U.S. will and propensity to resist "anti-imperialist" trends in the Caribbean basin. Thus U.S. support for proxies (Guatemala in 1954) as well as the direct use of military force (the Dominican Republic in 1965) were viewed as improbable measures or at least much more difficult to stage in the late 1970s and early 1980s.

Soviet Strategic Objectives

By the 1970s the Soviet Union and Cuba had arrived at a coherent strategic vision with regard to the third world in general and the Caribbean basin in particular, according to which their actions have been orchestrated. After almost a decade of discord, there is now an integrated, though flexible, and long-term plan of action aimed at achieving specific ideological, political, security, and economic objectives.[5]

Ideology. As discussed, it is misleading to assume that the Soviets support revolutionary movements in the Caribbean basin solely as part of a grand design to create Leninist regimes. Still, ideology cannot be discounted among their motives. The Cuban trajectory in the 1970s, resulting finally in conformism to true Leninist development and Soviet recognition of Cuba as a member of the socialist community, is one the Soviets would like to see emulated by other radical regimes in the region. Because of numerous bad experiences in the 1960s and 1970s, however—when many such radical regimes in various parts of the third world, including Latin America, were overthrown, and others substantially reduced the Soviets' presence and influence—the Soviets feel compelled to exercise caution in making commitments to would-be Leninist regimes.

With the probable exception of Cuba, the Soviets in the early 1980s hardly view the new radical regimes in developing countries as truly Leninist, in the Soviet understanding of the term. For the moment it is enough that Soviet officials in the Central Committee responsible for dealing with Caribbean basin revolutionary regimes see fit to refer to them as progressive, anti-imperialist, and, at most (in the case of Nicaragua and Grenada), as on "the path toward socialist orientation" (without yet being truly "Leninist" or "socialist"). This cautious terminology reflects the Soviets' guarded expectations, conditioned by Cuba's long and arduous evolution toward real Leninist development, and the desire that there be no confusion as to which is the model regime embodying the most advanced and mature form of socialism—that is, the Soviet. At the same time, the Leninist inclination of the new regimes in Nicaragua and Grenada cannot but be appreciated and applauded by the Soviets, who are thereby better able to justify to their domestic constituencies and allied Communist countries the aid extended to these regimes.

Disillusioned over the prospects for revolution in Latin America after the fall of Salvador Allende in Chile in 1973, the Soviets did not anticipate the revolution in Nicaragua or the coup in Grenada or the momentum of various other revolutionary struggles throughout Central America. They did recognize, however, the potential in these events for promoting Soviet ideological interests, both abroad and at home. The Soviets see the revolutionary process in the Caribbean basin and elsewhere in the third world in the context of the worldwide struggle between capitalism and communism. Because these conflicts are "tipping" the global balance of power "in favor of the socialist camp," argues Victor Afanasiev, who is editor in chief of *Pravda* and a member of the Central Committee of the CPSU, the Soviet Union "will spare no support or sympathy for these countries seeking [revolutionary] transformation."[6]

Politics. The Soviets' most important political objective in the basin is to ferment and further forces and regimes which they consider progressive. Because the Soviets view the region as the strategic rear or internal security zone of the United States, their policy has been cautious, until recently respecting in action if not in word the Monroe Doctrine. This attitude changed in 1960 when Khrushchev stated that "the Monroe Doctrine has outlived its times" and that U.S. acceptance of the Cuban Revolution was proof that it had died a "natural death."[7] Still, because of a number of constraints Soviet strategy in the Caribbean during the past two decades has continued to be refined and subtle, allowing for revolutionary transformation by violent and/or peaceful means (the parliamentary road to socialism—a prolonged political process during which anti-American forces build national coalitions to challenge U.S. hegemony). The choice of means is dictated by internal, national conditions, which vary from country to country, and by a number of external variables, the most important among them being the state of Soviet-American relations.

The criteria for deciding which tactics to employ in each country were clearly delineated in Soviet behavior throughout the 1970s. During this decade, peaceful, diplomatic channels were pursued avidly vis-à-vis the late Omar Torrijos's military yet "progressive" Panamanian regime and the likewise "progressive" regime of Michael Manley in Jamaica (until Manley's electoral defeat in 1980). The Soviets also courted the liberal-democratic regimes—Mexico's more intensely and those of Costa Rica, Colombia, and Venezuela in lesser degrees. It is important to note that until Somoza's overthrow in Nicaragua became imminent, the Soviets dissuaded at least some of the local Communist parties and other more radical leftist groups from trying to overthrow the mentioned regimes, encouraging them rather to expand gradually their influence and work toward the greater goal of building anti-imperialist coalitions and the wide popular support necessary to sustain the revolution should the revolutionaries take power. The Soviet strategy in Central American countries having pro-American, anti-Communist regimes—that is, Nicaragua (before the fall of Anastasio Somoza in 1979), El Salvador, Guatemala, and, to a certain extent, Honduras—was to give steady encouragement to revolutionary struggle, though not necessarily by fostering terrorism.

Soviet strategy changed in the late 1970s when, in the Soviet view, the correlation of forces began to shift worldwide because of U.S. setbacks in Vietnam, Angola, Ethiopia, and Afghanistan. The growing wave of radical anti-U.S. sentiment in Central America was, for the Soviets, another manifestation of this change. Furthermore, the 1973 ouster of Allende in Chile seems to have caused the Soviets to doubt the feasibility of following the purely parliamentary path toward socialism in Latin America. "In contrast with the usual 'parliamentary' path," the Chilean revolution "through peaceful means" was "nothing else than a form of class coercion by a majority of the revolutionary people." This path is not the "only possible one."[8] Because of these perceptions and propitious global and regional conditions, the Soviets in the late 1970s once again began to promote, though guardedly, the more militant aspects of the struggle by revolutionary forces. The successful revolutions in Nicaragua and Grenada increased Soviet confidence in the militant path. Still, Soviet tactics followed two tracks, with the Communist parties' role continuing to be one of gradually building coalitions among all revolutionary forces while positioning themselves in the vanguard of the struggle.

In the early 1980s the Soviets appear to have further conceptualized and perfected their anti-imperialist strategy in the Caribbean basin. Careful research of Soviet sources suggests that in the Soviet view there exist four different kinds of regimes in the Caribbean: (1) revolutionary, pro-Soviet, Leninist regimes or regimes evolving along a Leninist course—actually Soviet clients; (2) capitalist, yet progressive, anti-imperialist regimes that are basically friendly toward the

Soviet Union and willing to stand up to U.S. "imperialism"; (3) capitalist, liberal, bourgeois regimes of a democratic character that depend, some more and others less, on the United States; and (4) reactionary, right-wing military regimes, generally not liked yet supported by the United States.

Revolutionary regimes. The first class of regimes, consisting of Soviet clients such as Cuba, Nicaragua, and Grenada, are either developing closely along Leninist lines or, in the case of Cuba, have already achieved a Leninist identity. The Soviets support these regimes using all available means, with heavy emphasis on political, economic, and military aid and advisory assistance. Their political and economic support and cautious arms transfers to Nicaragua and Grenada are patterned after their relationship with Cuba and express faith in the eventual Leninist transformation of these countries.

Progressive regimes. These are nonsocialist countries in the Caribbean basin, such as Mexico and Panama, which, for a variety of reasons, have conducted policies independent of and sometimes contrary to those of the United States and which the Soviets therefore describe as anti-imperialist. Because of their size, large population, plentiful resources, or strategic location, they are seen as important nations worthy of being courted in every fashion. In these countries, for the moment, the Soviet Union and Cuba do *not* support armed insurgency but rely exclusively on political, cultural, and, to a lesser degree, economic instruments to gain influence. (Through both Mexico and Panama, however, the Soviets and Cubans coordinate the military and other activities of Communist parties and insurgents from other Caribbean basin nations.)

Liberal, bourgeois regimes. In dealing with the democratic regimes of larger countries having plentiful natural resources and policies independent of those of the United States, revolutionary means, including armed insurgency, are not entirely excluded by the Soviets and Cubans, though legal means of gaining influence are preferred. Yet in countries such as Costa Rica, Colombia (until 1982), and Jamaica, and perhaps also the Dominican Republic—which are viewed by the Soviets as being less significant because of their size, population, resources, and, most important, perceived dependency upon the United States—the Soviets see little jeopardy to their interests stemming from their tacit support of Cuban efforts to aid the revolutionaries in these countries. This represents an important readjustment in Soviet thinking from the late 1960s and 1970s when the Soviets seemed to prey only upon "right-wing" regimes. Now apparently "liberal" regimes can also be subjected to revolutionary tactics. The fact that Cuba, and not the Soviet Union, *appears* to be the main coordinator of insurgency activities in these countries has enabled the Soviets to continue, though in a more limited fashion, diplomatic and economic intercourse with Costa Rica and Colombia.

Reactionary regimes. Soviet policy toward what they call reactionary regimes—those that are traditionally anti-Communist—is to promote violent revolutionary tactics, which, since the late 1970s, include acts of terrorism. The regimes in El Salvador, Guatemala, and Honduras, which are hostile toward the Soviet Union and Cuba, if possible, should be overthrown. Some of these regimes are the worst offenders of human rights in all of Latin America, making it attractive for the Soviets to support the guerrilla movements there. Backed by the Soviets, the Cubans have played a pivotal role in uniting splinter movements and providing at least a minimal amount of arms and training to insurgents in these countries. The continuation, scope, and intensity of this policy depend on available opportunities and the perceived costs and risks of such a strategy for both the internal situations in these countries and the overall state of Soviet-American relations. Although Cuba is apparently an autonomous actor in the coordination and support of armed insurgency, this activity would not have been possible without continuous Soviet economic and military aid to Cuba and to new clients in Nicaragua and Grenada, as well as Soviet strategic coordination through local Communist parties. (In August 1981, for example, such strategic coordination and planning took place in Panama City during the visit of a senior CPSU official who discussed regional strategies with Cuban officials and the leaders of local Communist parties.[9])

One of the motives for the modification in Soviet strategy between 1979 and 1982 (support of armed as opposed to peaceful revolution in democratic countries of the Caribbean basin) is to preoccupy the United States in its strategic rear and divert a degree of U.S. attention from the Soviet periphery, where the Soviet Union's western and southern guard (Poland and Afghanistan) are embroiled in unresolved conflict. Soviet officials view the already deeply troubled Caribbean basin as pregnant with a potentially unending series of conflicts. Thus, Georgi Arbatov, member of the Central Committee and director of the USA and Canada Institute, suggested to visiting American scholars that the Caribbean region confronts the United States with a series of "delayed-fuse land mines" which the United States will no more be able to defuse than those in Iran. According to him, the Soviet Union has "great sympathy for the struggle" in that region.[10] The deputy director of the institute, V. Zhurkin, declared, furthermore, that the Soviet Union "will not accept the Monroe Doctrine" in the region; and yet another adviser to high Soviet officials warned that Soviet policies in the Caribbean basin will ultimately "reflect the overall state of U.S.–Soviet relations."[11]

Security. Another important component of overall Soviet strategic vision regarding Central America and the Caribbean is oriented to security matters. The primary Soviet security objective is gradually and cautiously to secure access to and maintain naval facilities in the Caribbean basin so as to improve the projection of Soviet power while undermining that of the United States and its allies. The basin constitutes a key passage zone for oil and other vital raw materials from Guatemala, Venezuela, and the Caribbean islands to the United States, as well as for all seagoing vessels using the Panama Canal. About 1.1 billion tons of cargo pass through the Caribbean annually, of which almost half originates in ports of the Gulf Coast of the United States. In addition, the region would assume crucial strategic importance if the United States were to be engaged in a conventional war. A substantial Soviet military presence in the basin would endanger logistical support for U.S. allies in Europe and the delivery of oil and other strategic materials to the United States. During war time Cuba, though highly vulnerable, might serve as a forward base for submarines and aircraft carriers. According to Soviet Air Force Lieutenant Viktor Belenko, who defected to the West in 1976, the Soviets view the island as their "aircraft carrier" in the Caribbean.[12]

Yet this argument must be qualified. So far, the Soviet military presence in the region is limited by the lack of facilities and logistical support necessary for the permanent deployment of a fleet. Moreover, Soviet warships scheduled for deployment in the Caribbean must pass first through NATO checkpoints. To date, the only significant Soviet military presence is in Cuba. This includes modern docks and repair facilities; airport facilities for reconnaissance craft; satellite stations and the most sophisticated intelligence facilities (outside the Soviet Union) for monitoring U.S. satellite and microwave conversations, U.S. ship and air movements, and advanced NATO weapons testing in the Atlantic. The presence of crates of new Soviet aircraft detected at an airfield outside Havana in early 1982 suggests that the Soviets may be deploying the MiG-27, a bombing version of the MiG-23 "Flogger," which is capable, after some modification, of carrying nuclear weapons. Since 1975, Soviet Tu-95 "Bear D" long-range reconnaissance planes have been periodically deployed from José Martí Airport in Havana for missions monitoring U.S. naval activities in the Atlantic. (In September 1972 Tu-95s were observed for the first time being deployed from Cuba for the purpose of reconnoitering U.S. naval units off the East Coast of the United States.[13]) These aircraft often cross the Atlantic and refuel at Soviet facilities in Luanda, Angola. The Africa-based "Bear-D" was also used to conduct reconnaissance of the British task force deployment toward the Falkland Islands in the 1982 war.

Overall, the Soviets do not now have sufficient strength in the region to be able to disrupt important sea lanes to the United States, a scenario feared by some analysts. Moreover, they would probably attempt such action only in case of all-out war, and then probably closer to Europe or the Persian Gulf. Although they proceed with caution, the Soviets would undoubtedly like to see the quality of their naval presence in the Caribbean upgraded and expanded. This has been indicated by Soviet plans to make permanent use of the facilities of Cienfuegos, which were partly shelved in 1970 because of vociferous U.S. protests. Unfettered, the Soviet Union is likely to establish additional facilities in the region in order to create a stronger and more permanent military presence than it now has. This trend is suggested by recent Soviet tactics in Nicaragua and Grenada, countries that the Soviets view as being the most anti-imperialist in the region, and whom the Soviets hope will follow Cuba's lead to becoming future clients.

Given the Soviets' awareness of the basin's paramount importance to the United States, Soviet naval activities in the area, including regular visits by warships, until now have seemed rather scaled down in comparison with U.S. naval visits to areas in Western Europe close to the Soviet Union. They are probably designed to establish the legitimacy of a Soviet naval presence. There have been twenty-two such visits by Soviet naval task groups to the Caribbean Sea in the past twenty years, all of which made Cuban port calls (except that of August 1979). The most recent took place between December 2 and December 20, 1982. The Soviets deploy not only warships but also intelligence, merchant, oceanographic, space supporting, salvage and rescue, and fishing vessels, many of which also have intelligence missions. (Soviet intelligence collectors, under the pretext of fishing, patrol off the U.S. East Coast almost continuously—in the vicinity of Norfolk, Kings Bay, Charleston, and Narragansett Bay—as well as in the Caribbean basin.) The increasing Soviet deployment of such vessels, which can visit ports prohibited to warships, is a cause of concern to some Caribbean countries.* Soviet naval visits of this kind are

* The Netherlands asked the Soviets to curb future visits by research ships to the harbor at Willemstad, the Netherlands Antilles, to only one oceanographic vessel per month. The reason cited was "insufficient harbor capacity." In reality, however, The Hague acted exclusively on security considerations.

designed to help encourage long-term political and economic transformation of the area along the lines of what Admiral Sergei Gorshkov, commander in chief of the Soviet navy, refers to as "progressive changes" offshore.

Economics. Economic objectives play a more minor role in Soviet strategy in Central America. Soviet trade, investment, and credits in early 1982 were limited to Cuba, Mexico, Costa Rica somewhat, and the new clients Nicaragua and Grenada. Since they generally must pay for imports in hard currency, the Soviets probably do not view the Caribbean as a priority interest in strictly economic terms. However, their patient nurturing of the Caribbean market may be expected to pay off in the future, barring unforeseen changes in the international economic order. Most Soviet exports are to the South American countries, especially Brazil and Argentina, which accounted for 60 percent of total Soviet exports to South America in 1979. Strictly in terms of foreign trade, the Caribbean basin countries are of much less importance to the Soviet Union than the countries of South America. In Central America Soviet trade is low in absolute and relative terms.

The presence of vital natural resources, however—particularly in Mexico, Venezuela, and elsewhere—has doubtless spurred increasing interest in the basin. Thus the Soviets are working with the Mexicans on long-term cooperation in oil matters and may be interested in similar cooperation with other oil producers in the region. Mexico has also agreed to supply crude oil to Cuba and, in the future, to assist with Cuba's oil exploration efforts. Meanwhile, Venezuela is presently supplying Cuba with some oil. Soviet and Eastern bloc trade and economic aid to client regimes such as Nicaragua and Grenada, not to mention Cuba, encourage the Soviets' strategy in the area.

Soviet Policies toward Revolutionary Regimes: Cuba, Nicaragua, and Grenada

Cuba. The Soviets' gradual involvement in Cuba spanning the past twenty-three years, in spite of ups and downs, suggests a well-conceived plan to assure survivability and development of a revolutionary regime along Leninist lines. Cautious commercial and diplomatic ties preceded military aid and security involvement. Thus, although Castro came to power on January 1, 1959, the Soviets did not begin to provide economic aid to Cuba until early 1960. Soviet loans and other economic aid such as donations, technical assistance, and trade agreements, including provisions for the Soviet purchase of Cuban sugar, were not forthcoming until a full year later. Diplomatic relations were reestablished even later, in May 1961.* At the same time the Soviet Union and other East European countries signed a number of diplomatic, commercial, scientific, and technical treaties with Cuba. By 1961 transactions with the countries of the Council for Mutual Economic Assistance (COMECON) accounted for 75 percent of Cuba's total trade.

After the period of ups and downs in Soviet-Cuban relations between 1962 and 1969, the Soviet Union and Cuba reached an understanding on the coordination of their foreign policy strategies, which was somehow related to the Soviets' continuing economic and security support of the island. Cuban economic dependency on the Soviet Union grew substantially during the late 1960s and 1970s and was one of the factors influencing Castro's decision to compromise with the Soviets on foreign policy matters. As of the early 1980s, the Soviet Union supports the Cuban economy with an estimated $8 million per day, and this is thought to be a low estimate. Annually this amounts to about $3 billion and is equivalent to approximately 25 percent of Cuba's gross domestic product. This amount is roughly five times the total U.S. aid to Latin America.

Because of the active Cuban role in the Soviets' anti-imperialist strategy in Africa and in the Caribbean from the mid-1970s through the early 1980s, Cuba gained the status of a privileged ally, or what Soviet officials call "the first socialist country in the Western Hemisphere," and was able to insist on further adjustments in Soviet-Cuban economic relations, mainly commodity subsidies and credits to bolster the Cuban sugar and nickel industries. For the planning period 1981–1985, for example, COMECON gave the faltering sugar industry a major injection of economic credits equivalent to $643 million. Another $451.2 million should be made available between 1985 and 1990. The Soviets also subsidize petroleum prices, enabling the Cubans to purchase oil at roughly one-third of the world market price. They have pledged to supply Cuban oil needs at least until 1985. According to Konstantin Katushev, the Soviet ambassador to Cuba and former member of the Secretariat of the Central Committee of the CPSU, the extent, depth, and high level of Soviet-Cuban cooperation in 1982 were demonstrated by the Soviet-Cuban joint spaceflight, the inclusion of Cubans in the Soviets' scientific expedition to Antarctica, and Soviet construction of the first nuclear power plant in Cuba.[14] Without privileged Soviet treatment the Cubans simply could not sustain their operations in Africa and the Caribbean basin.

---

* The Cuban dictator Fulgencio Batista had broken relations with the Soviet Union in 1952, following his coup d'état.

Significant Soviet military aid to and involvement in the security affairs of Cuba followed the establishment of economic and political ties and actually commenced after a secret agreement was signed in the fall of 1960. In early 1961 the Cuban armed forces openly displayed Soviet- and Czechoslovak-made weapons, and since the summer of 1962 the Soviets have maintained a military presence in Cuba—an advisory group of a few thousand military intelligence specialists and a few thousand ground forces (ascertained in 1979 as a brigade of 2,600). In 1962 the Soviets also deployed the missiles which led to the October crisis with the United States. As shown in figure 8-1, Soviet seaborne arms transfers to Cuba reached the highest peak in 1962, the year of the crisis. They declined and reached the lowest point in 1968, a time when overall Soviet-Cuban relations were at a correspondingly low level. Arms transfers increased slightly in 1969 and remained constant until 1974. The new increases in the 1970s coincided with the Soviet-Cuban interventions in Angola and Ethiopia.

In 1981–1982 the Soviet arms transfers to Cuba reached the highest level since the missile crisis. As in 1962, this increase was intended as a manifestation of the Soviets' commitment to a client and of their determination to give military support during a period when, in the Soviet view, the U.S. threat to Cuba was greater than at any time since 1962. Because of the perceived threat posed to Cuba by officials of the Reagan administration, who threatened to "go to the source" of the Caribbean basin problem, Castro decided to enlarge Cuba's territorial militia from 500,000 to 1 million men, with a corresponding increase in arms. There was probably another reason for the sharp increase in Soviet seaborne military deliveries to Cuba in 1981–1982: the future need to supply Nicaragua and Grenada and other revolutionary forces in the basin from Cuban stockpiles.

In the whole of Latin America the armed forces of Cuba (population 10 million) are second in size only to those of Brazil (population 120 million). They number 225,000 regulars, of which 200,000 are army, 15,000 are air force (not including the formidable airborne contingent and assault brigade of 3,000 special troops), and 10,000 are navy. (The last number includes a small yet elite marine corps.)

Soviet modernization of Cuba's armed forces with sophisticated weapons has made them, in terms of both size and equipment, the most formidable force in the Caribbean basin, with the exception of the United States. Although the Cubans do not have sufficient air- and sea-lift or amphibious assault capabilities to conduct on their own an invasion of any Central American country or large island nation such as Jamaica, they could effectively intervene in small islands like Grenada in support of "fraternal" regimes. With Soviet assistance the

213

FIGURE 8-1
SOVIET SEABORNE MILITARY DELIVERIES TO CUBA, 1962-1982

Thousand metric tons

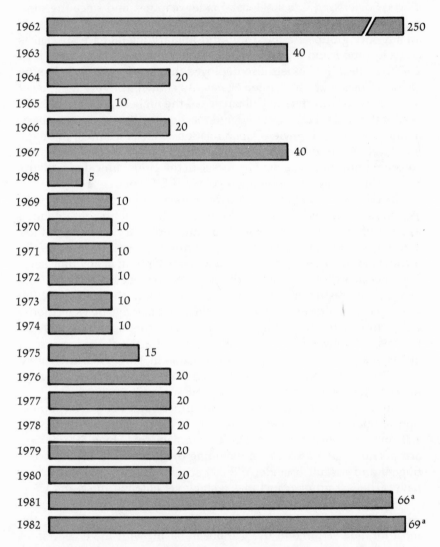

1962 250
1963 40
1964 20
1965 10
1966 20
1967 40
1968 5
1969 10
1970 10
1971 10
1972 10
1973 10
1974 10
1975 15
1976 20
1977 20
1978 20
1979 20
1980 20
1981 66[a]
1982 69[a]

a. Approximate figure.

SOURCES: U.S. Department of State, *Cuban Armed Forces and the Soviet Military Presence*, Special Report No. 103, Washington, D.C., August 1982. The figure for 1982 is taken from U.S. Department of Defense, *Soviet Military Power 1983*, 2nd ed. (Washington, D.C., March 1983).

214

Cuban armed forces in the early 1980s reached a significant level of limited interventionist capability throughout the region. Enhancing this capability in the Cuban inventory at this time are, among other items, 200 MiG fighters, two squadrons of MiG 23 "Flogger" type jet fighters, several AN-26 short-range transport planes, and seven Il-62 long-range jet transport aircraft. The army's inventory includes sophisticated weapons such as Soviet T-62 tanks and Mi-24 HIND-D assault helicopters.

The Soviets have also helped Cuba to build small, yet modern and efficient naval and merchant fleets. In the past few years they have equipped the Cubans with nine guided-missile attack boats of Osa and Komar class and Turya class hydrofoil patrol boats, as well as an antisubmarine frigate, mine sweepers, several landing craft, and two Foxtrot class torpedo attack diesel-powered submarines. In 1981 the Soviets delivered the largest vessel in the Cuban navy, the 2,300 ton Koni class frigate. Although this ship is considerably smaller than the new classes of U.S. frigates, it is viewed as a major improvement in Cuban naval inventory and may, in larger numbers, enable Cuba to project its power into the Caribbean basin and intimidate its neighbors. The Soviets have helped to enlarge Cuban ports and update the Cuban merchant marine with passenger ships, oil tankers, and container ships.

Obviously the essentially defensive Cuban navy cannot challenge U.S. naval power in the Caribbean basin. Yet given U.S. confrontation with the Soviet Union in another region (the Persian Gulf or Europe), the Cubans could put constraints on U.S. mobility and capacity to respond, causing significant delays in U.S. deployment. Moreover, if unchallenged, Soviet-backed Cuban forces could provide decisive military aid to revolutionary forces in other countries of the Caribbean region.

Cuba is not totally subservient to the Soviet Union in the Caribbean and at times appears to be even more assertive and activist than its mentor. Castro undoubtedly exercises some autonomy in formulating policy toward other countries in the region and provides inputs into Soviet policy making. One of the authors has discussed these mutual constraints and leverages in detail elsewhere. It is not possible to dwell at length here on the complex personality of Castro, who appears to be more Machiavellian than Leninist, and more Bonapartist and Bolivarian than socialist in his ambitions and perceptions of the payoffs to be gained by maintaining close Soviet ties. Despite Castro's biases and interesting personality, however, the bottom line is that overall Cuban economic and military dependency on the Soviet Union makes it unthinkable for the Cubans to initiate any major overt or covert support operation for guerrilla forces in the Caribbean basin without Soviet approval and assistance. Such operations, furthermore, would be impossible without Soviet strategic cover and commitment to protect Cuba in the event of an attack on the island. Obviously there exists a basic agreement between Cuba and the Soviet Union regarding the coordination and implementation of their strategy in Africa and the Caribbean basin. The Soviet Union, however, plays the dominant role.

Cuba's great vulnerability to Soviet economic coercion was used by the Soviet leaders to their advantage in the late 1960s when they slowed down the supply of oil and arms in order to encourage Castro to appreciate the subtleties of Soviet anti-imperialist strategy. The Soviets are likely to use this leverage again should the need arise. On the Cuban side, Castro himself made it clear to American officials during secret negotiations that although he desires better relations with the United States, he "cannot abandon his friends, the Soviets, who have supported his revolution unequivocally."[15] Although day-to-day Cuban policies in the Caribbean region are not subordinated to those of the Soviet Union, there is, as Cuban leader Carlos Rafael Rodríguez admitted, "a high level of agreement" with the Soviet Union in foreign affairs, and Cuba is "always willing to subordinate its national interests to the interests of socialism as a universal aspiration." In 1982 Castro's brother and deputy, Raúl Castro, declared that Soviet-Cuban relations are the "cornerstone" of Cuban foreign policy and that these relations were at "the highest level ever recorded in the past two decades."[16]

Nicaragua. For the Soviets, the triumph of the Sandinistas in Nicaragua in July 1979 signaled an important juncture in what they consider the progressive transformation of the Caribbean basin, equal in importance only to the victory of Castro in Cuba twenty years earlier. In both cases, the United States was perceived by the Soviets as suffering humiliating political defeat.

Before and shortly after the Sandinistas' victory, the Soviets exercised a great deal of caution and were typically guarded in their willingness to make commitments to the new regime, as they had been originally in 1959 in Cuba. In contrast to the situation in Cuba in 1959–1962, however, in Nicaragua in 1979–1982 the Soviets were in a better position to provide support because of Cuba's proximity to Nicaragua and role as a middleman, coordinating the transport of military aid in the decisive phase of the Nicaraguan Revolution. As the revolution took hold, the Soviets gradually assessed their options and decided to pursue their anti-imperialist strategy in Nicaragua. In 1980–1982 the

Soviets and their East European allies concluded, as earlier in Cuba, a variety of economic, technical, and trade agreements with Nicaragua. These mainly concerned fishing and marine affairs, water power resources, mining and geological surveys, communications, and scientific and cultural cooperation. After establishing initial commercial contacts, the Soviet Union opened its first diplomatic mission in Managua in March 1980. The Sandinista Liberation Front (FSLN) and the CPSU also agreed on future party-to-party contacts, along the same lines pursued by the Soviets with Castro and other revolutionary forces in Angola and Ethiopia.

In 1980–1982, as earlier in Cuba, the Soviets used donations and credits to further their influence in Nicaragua. First, in 1980, they donated 14,000 tons of wheat, followed by $21 million in industrial grants for various agricultural and industrial projects. In 1981 and 1982 they granted the country $80 million in credits and $30 million in aid. As in Cuba, the Soviets also agreed in 1982 to assist Nicaragua by committing themselves to buy large quantities of agricultural products and to provide long-range economic and technical aid. In 1982, there were 700 Nicaraguan students and fifteen teachers in the Soviet Union, and in 1982–1983 the Soviet Union will provide an additional 300 scholarships for students and fifteen grants for professors to study there.[17] Furthermore, in 1983 the Soviet Union will assist in building, as it did in Cuba in the 1970s, a ground station as part of the Inter-Sputnik system—an international telephone network having direct communication with the Warsaw Treaty Organization countries.

Credits granted to Nicaragua by other Soviet allies in 1981 included $30 million from Czechoslovakia, $20 million from Bulgaria, $10 million from East Germany, and $10 million from Hungary. Cuba granted Nicaragua $3.6 million in credits, and economic aid estimated at $60 million in 1980–1981 and $85 million in 1982. The Cubans also have sent 2,000 teachers and several hundred medical personnel, as well as technicians and other workers, bringing the total number of Cuban civilian personnel in Nicaragua to approximately 3,800.[18]

As in Cuba, the arms transfers to Nicaragua were preceded by the formal establishment of economic and political ties. In contrast to Cuba, however, Soviet security relations with Nicaragua so far have been more low key, avoiding any move that could directly provoke the United States. Nevertheless, military aid to Nicaragua from the Soviet Union and its allies is in full progress. The $28 million worth of Soviet, East German, and Cuban arms transferred to Nicaragua in 1981–1982 included at least fifty or more T-54 and T-55 tanks (according to former Sandinista leader Eden Pastora, the number is eighty), many armored personnel carriers, two helicopters, heavy artillery, surface-to-air missiles, and large quantities of automatic rifles. Preparations for delivery of MiG jet fighters seemed to be under way in 1982, though they had not been delivered at the time of writing. The Soviets may be waiting for the outcome of the 1984 U.S. presidential elections. East Germany has delivered 800 military trucks. According to Sandinista leaders, this military equipment was purchased in response to "the danger of U.S. invasion."

There were also about 3,000 Cuban security and military advisers in Nicaragua by the end of 1982. In addition, there are reportedly 98 Soviet advisers, 50 East Germans, 30 Bulgarians, 28 North Koreans, 20 Vietnamese, and 10 Palestinians of the Palestine Liberation Organization who have been training the 22,000-man Nicaraguan army and state security forces.[19] Nicaraguan pilots are being trained to fly Soviet planes in Cuba and Bulgaria. Meanwhile, with Soviet and Cuban assistance, the Nicaraguans are building new runways at four airfields, probably to accommodate Soviet MiG fighters.

Nicaragua, like Cuba, may soon serve as an important transit center for guerrilla warfare experts. In Nicaragua Cuban military advisers are running limited yet advanced training programs for guerrillas destined for El Salvador and other countries in the region. These operations are more significant than might appear, since the guerrilla movement in Central America can be sustained and exported more easily from Nicaragua than from an island such as Cuba. Indeed, between October 1980 and February 1982 Nicaragua became the staging center for a large Cuban-coordinated effort to conduct arms transfers and prepare a major offensive in El Salvador.

The Soviet Union is promoting maritime cooperation with Nicaragua, which, if Cuba is a precedent, will be closely followed by naval cooperation. The two nations have signed agreements calling for joint fishery and oceanographic research programs, the training of Nicaraguans at Soviet fishing schools, and Soviet aid in repairing Nicaraguan vessels. Soviet ships equipped to conduct studies in oceanography, fishing, and marine biology are already conducting research in Pacific and Atlantic waters adjacent to Nicaragua. At San Juan del Sur, a shipyard and dock manned with Soviet technicians will be installed whose main functions will be to repair Soviet fishing boats in the Pacific Ocean.[20] With Cuban assistance the Nicaraguans are finishing a major highway linking the Pacific and Atlantic coasts. These projects, like others, might become militarily valuable to the Soviet Union, if they are not already so.

Some U.S. officials believe that the sequence of events suggests that Nicaragua is becoming a "second Cuba." Although this is not the place for a comprehensive analysis and comparison of Cuban and Nicaraguan postrevolutionary development, the Nicaraguan pattern of rapid revolutionary transformation and Soviet involvement in the early 1980s is very reminiscent of the Cuban pattern in the early 1960s. Indeed, according to the Nicaraguan Ambassador to the United States Francisco Fiallos Navarro, as of 1982, there is the "threat of a leftist dictatorship" in Nicaragua similar to the one that developed in Cuba in the early 1960s. At this writing, we do not know whether the Soviets and Nicaraguans have signed a secret military agreement, yet Soviet Ambassador to Nicaragua German Shliapnikov already pledged Soviet support for the Nicaraguans' "defense of their fatherland."[21]

There are some differences between Cuba and Nicaragua. Given their bitter experience during the 1962 missile crisis, the Soviets have exercised greater caution in extending provocative military aid or establishing an overt Soviet military presence in Nicaragua. Moreover, in Nicaragua, unlike Cuba, the regime still continues to tolerate, to some extent, a mixed economy, private agriculture, a powerful Catholic Church, and limited political pluralism, symbolized, in particular, by the newspaper *La Prensa*, which operates independently of the junta and in spite of protests by Soviet diplomats.

Whether Nicaragua will become "a second Cuba" depends on many factors, some of which cannot yet be determined. Certainly the Soviets have expressed the hope that Nicaragua will become another "starlet" of anti-imperialist strategy in the Caribbean. During his visit to Moscow in May 1982, Nicaraguan leader Daniel Ortega was treated with all the respect accorded a leader of an allied Leninist country and Soviet leaders pledged continuous economic aid to Nicaragua.

Grenada. The Soviets and Cubans have established a foothold in the minuscule island of Grenada, which is strategically located close to the oil-producing nations of Venezuela and Trinidad-Tobago. Grenada's revolutionary prime minister Maurice Bishop came to power in 1979 through a successful coup d'état conducted by a radical group with Leninist inclinations which calls itself the New Jewel Movement. Bishop is a close friend and admirer of Fidel Castro, and members of the New Jewel Movement were trained by the Cubans. The political importance of Grenada for the Soviets and Cubans became obvious after the electoral defeat of Prime Minister Manley by Western-oriented Edward Seaga in Jamaica in November 1980. Grenada then became the only Caribbean island under strong Soviet and Cuban influence.

The Soviet and Cuban involvement in Grenada, including military and economic assistance, has followed the pattern of Soviet-Cuban involvement in Nicaragua, though on a much smaller scale. Obviously the Soviet commitment to Grenada is less than to the larger and more populous Nicaragua. In Grenada the Cubans appear to be playing an even more pivotal role than in Nicaragua, though certainly with full support of the Soviets, who favor "the progressive social transformation" and "political vanguard" in Grenada—that is, of course, Bishop and the Leninist New Jewel Movement.[22] Typically, the Soviets first exercised caution while the Cubans, since 1979, became vigorously involved by supplying military and other forms of aid. Hundreds of Cuban workers and technicians have begun building a new international airport at Point Saline and another "executive" airstrip nearby.* When completed, both will be capable of handling all types of Soviet and Cuban heavy jet aircraft. Moreover, in Grenada, which has a population of 110,000, more than fifty Cuban military advisers are helping to build a new revolutionary army of some 1,500 to 2,000 men. Like Cuba and Nicaragua, Grenada's population is organized into a people's militia which conducts periodic maneuvers in preparation for a possible invasion of the island. To equip the militia, Cuba has supplied Grenada with several thousand AK-41 rifles and other equipment. In addition, there are several hundred Cuban military and civilian advisers and doctors serving in Grenada.

When there were indications that the revolution was taking hold, the Soviets decided to make a formal economic commitment to the island in August 1982 during the visit of Premier Bishop to the Soviet Union. At this time the CPSU and the New Jewel Movement agreed to cooperate along the same lines pursued by the Soviets with the Sandinistas. Thus the Soviet Union decided to establish its first diplomatic mission in Grenada and with Bishop signed a number of economic, scientific, cultural, and technological agreements as well as a five-year trade agreement. Military assistance might have been discussed as well during this visit. The Soviets also gave Grenada a $1.4 million grant to buy 500 tons of steel and has donated 400 tons of flour; $7.7 million in credits were pledged over a ten-year period to purchase other equipment.[23] As in Nicaragua, the Soviets are now assisting to build and promote a fishing industry in Grenada for which the Cubans have supplied six trawlers in the past two years. This aid, as Bishop explained, was intended to help Grenada "disengage" from the capitalist world. The pro-Soviet orientation of

---

* Grenada also received aid for the airport from Libya, Syria, Algeria, Iraq, and the European Economic Community.

Grenada was already demonstrated in 1980 when Grenada supported
the Soviet Union in the international forum by voting against condem-
nation of the Soviet invasion of Afghanistan. (Even Nicaragua abstained from this vote.)

Soviet Policies toward "Progressive" Regimes:
Mexico and Panama

Mexico. Mexico traditionally has been viewed by the Soviets as one
of the most friendly countries in Latin America and as one of the most
important owing to its independence, large physical size and population, and location at the southern frontier of the United States. Because of what Mexico considers to be its vulnerable position vis-à-vis
its powerful neighbor to the north, it has sought traditionally to counterbalance U.S. hegemony in the area by pursuing friendly relations
with great powers outside the Western Hemisphere: with Germany
during World War I and World War II and with the Soviet Union
thereafter. The Soviets' main channels of involvement in Mexico are
diplomatic and, to a lesser degree, economic.

The Soviet Union first established diplomatic relations with Mexico in 1924. Relations were severed in 1930 but were reestablished in
1942 and have not been interrupted since. The largest Soviet embassy
in Latin America, outside of Cuba, is in Mexico City. Before the Cuban
Revolution, it was the main base for expanding Soviet influence in the
Caribbean basin and South America.

Because of Mexican geography, revolutionary historical experience, and traditionally independent posture with respect to U.S. foreign policy, the Soviets see Mexico as a progressively oriented country
which should be treated in a special fashion. Certain facets of Mexico's independent foreign policy have further influenced this Soviet
stance: Mexico was one of the few countries not to break diplomatic
relations with the Soviet Union in 1947 and the only Latin American
country not to cut off diplomatic ties with Cuba in the 1960s (though
Mexico did demonstrate basic support of the U.S. embargo by halting
most of its trade with Cuba in 1962), and Mexico spoke against U.S.
policies in Guatemala in 1954 and the U.S. intervention in the Dominican Republic in 1965. These policies and others were understood by
the Soviets to signify that Mexico was more than just independent of
the United States and that it was in fact anti-imperialist. In addition,
the Soviet and East European embassies in Mexico City function as
centers of liaison with and coordination of support for Communist
parties and guerrilla activities in the Caribbean basin. (One important
meeting between the Salvadoran guerrilla leadership and Soviet and

East European officials reportedly took place in the Hungarian embassy in March 1981.) For these reasons, both the Soviets and the Cubans have refrained from supporting revolutionary struggle by the Mexican left against what they see as the liberal and bourgeois, yet essentially progressive, regime in Mexico. They have always stressed the democratic orientation of the Mexican Communist party and applauded López Portillo's 1978 decision to remove obstacles to its legalization.

The Soviets have consistently tried to promote closer economic cooperation with Mexico through a variety of bilateral economic, technical, and scientific agreements and through multilateral cooperation with COMECON. Indeed, Mexico was the only Latin American country (aside from Cuba) to sign a formal agreement with COMECON (1975). Mexico has also agreed to help Cuba with oil exploration in the 1970s, though this agreement has not yet materialized. Mexico has signed a number of scientific agreements with the Soviet Union and Cuba that include provisions for the training of personnel. In spite of Soviet efforts, Soviet-Mexican economic cooperation and trade have remained relatively low in volume throughout the 1970s and early 1980s.

In the realm of security, the Soviets and the Cubans developed cordial relations with the Mexican armed forces during the 1970s. Although there are exchange visits by military leaders and some scholarships are offered, there are no nondiplomatic Soviet or Cuban military and security personnel stationed in Mexico (as there are in Cuba, Nicaragua, and Grenada). Furthermore, Mexico's armed forces do not depend for arms on the Soviet Union.

With the Mexican oil boom of the 1970s and the increasing tendency of Mexican leaders to become involved in the interregional politics of the unstable Caribbean basin independently of the United States, the Soviets have come to appreciate Mexico even more. Correspondingly, Cuban-Mexican relations improved considerably in the 1970s. Mexico's independent position was again demonstrated during the wave of revolutionary activities in the basin following the Nicaraguan Revolution of 1979, when Mexico offered financial assistance to the new Sandinista regime in 1981 and pledged future aid. In El Salvador Mexico supported the guerrilla organization of the Democratic Revolutionary Front of the Farabundo Marti National Liberation Front by donating money and allowing the FDR-FMLN government in exile to operate out of Mexico. Together with France, Mexico attempted to mediate between the government in El Salvador and the FDR-FMLN. These policies were cautiously applauded by the Soviet

Ambassador to Mexico Rostislav Sergeiev, who in 1982 described Mexico's foreign polices as a "great contribution to peace in the world."[24] Sergeiev said that despite the difficult economic situation, Mexico has "ample resources to forge ahead." The grave economic crisis in Mexico ($81 billion foreign debt, 100 percent inflation, and 50 percent unemployment), however, may bring unforeseen shifts to the radical right or left and corresponding challenges and opportunities.

Panama. The Soviets see Panama as an important country for its strategic location and nonaligned, even progressive (as they see it) orientation. In Panama, as in Peru in the 1970s, the armed forces are determining what the Soviets consider the basically anti-imperialist foreign polices of the country. This was certainly true until the death in 1981 of General Omar Torrijos of the National Guard, who had been the real power in Panama beginning in 1968. Torrijos was able to put pressure on the United States to relinquish control gradually over the Panama Canal. (Torrijos claimed that he had given orders for the National Guard to attack and blow up the canal if the U.S. Senate rejected his agreement with President Carter.*) Torrijos was perceived by the Soviets and the pro-Soviet People's Party of Panama (Communist Party of Panama) as a "patriotic officer" and leader of "the national liberation" process aimed at liquidating the colonial enclave at the Canal.[25] The Panamanian regime under Torrijos also maintained cordial relations with Cuba (Torrijos had a close personal relationship with Castro) and gave strong support to Nicaragua's Sandinistas before the overthrow of Somoza. Shortly before his death, however, Torrijos apparently became concerned about what he saw as increasing Cuban and Nicaraguan interference in Central America.

As of 1983 there has been no indication of Soviet or Cuban support for radical elements *inside* Panama, mainly because the People's Party of Panama had been legalized and was supportive of Torrijos's "anti-imperialist" regime. In the year following Torrijos's death, the People's Party of Panama has been supporting the military government in Panama. Furthermore, Panama, where the Cubans maintain their second largest embassy, has served as a point of liaison for Soviet-Cuban coordination of revolutionary activities in other countries of the region.[26] Possibly some Panamanian revolutionaries are being trained in Cuba, though none have yet been observed conducting revolutionary activities in Panama. Another reason for the con-

---

* In Torrijos's words, "we would have started our struggle for liberation, and possibly tomorrow the Canal would not be operating anymore." Carter, *Keeping the Faith* p. 178.

straint witnessed until now is probably the Soviets' desire to establish diplomatic relations with Panama, which Torrijos was reluctant to move on until the completion of canal negotiations with the United States.

The post-Torrijos leadership has expressed the wish to conduct diplomatic relations with the Soviet Union "eventually," but in 1982 this was still not apparently "a priority."[27] In the meantime the Soviets continue to court Panama on other levels by promoting commerce, educational exchanges, and cultural ties. Thus between 1980 and 1982 the Soviet Union gave thirty-five scholarships to Panamanian students and Cuba gave twenty-nine.[28]

The death of Torrijos has created political uncertainties. This was confirmed by the subsequent power struggle and government reshuffling which led to President Aristides Royo's resignation and replacement by Vice President Ricardo de la Espriella. The National Guard officials have called for a reorganization of the government. Continuation of the problems linked to the succession of Torrijos and a worsening of Panama's current economic difficulties may jeopardize the country's stability and call into question implementation of the Canal Treaty negotiated with the Carter administration in 1977. Such a development could lead to unforeseen changes in Soviet and Cuban perceptions and policies regarding Panama.

Soviet Policies toward "Bourgeois-Liberal" Regimes: Venezuela, Costa Rica, and Colombia

Venezuela. This is a democratic country run by a liberal-bourgeois (both in the Soviet sense) regime which, nevertheless, the Soviets perceive as displaying some independent features, though not to the same degree as Mexico. Soviet relations with Venezuela were established in 1970, and growing Soviet interest in this country parallels its ever-increasing importance in the third world in general and in the Caribbean basin, where, along with Mexico, it is one of the chief producers of oil. In the 1970s Venezuela was also eager to pursue better ties with the Soviet Union and Cuba in order to strengthen, as Mexico seems to have succeeded in doing, its position toward the United States. Thus in 1975 Venezuela played a key role in the process which led the OAS to lift most sanctions against Cuba and in the late 1970s gave substantial financial support to the Sandinista revolutionaries in Nicaragua.

The Soviets have tried to develop closer economic ties with Venezuela in the past decade, although these have not grown significantly. One success of negotiations between the two countries was the 1976 agreement by which Venezuela now supplies some oil to Cuba, while the Soviet Union supplies the equivalent amount to Spain, thus saving transportation costs to the Soviet Union, Cuba, and Venezuela. However, unlike Mexico and Panama, Venezuela is not viewed by the Soviets as an anti-imperialist oriented country, particularly given the changes in Venezuelan policies with the entry of the COPEI (Comité de Organización Política Electoral Independiente—Christian Democratic party) administration of President Luís Herrera. The Soviets obviously are not pleased with Venezuela's support for the Salvadoran regime and the Central American Community (El Salvador, Honduras, and Costa Rica) or Venezuela's deteriorating relations with Cuba (Cuban diplomats were ordered to leave Venezuela in 1980) and with Nicaragua, where Venezuela supports the democratic forces and is increasingly critical of the Sandinista junta. Yet, the Soviets and Cubans so far have either discouraged or curbed support for leftist guerrillas who would oppose violently the democratically elected government in Venezuela.

As argued earlier, between 1979 and 1981 there was a reassessment of Soviet and Cuban policies toward at least two countries whose democratically elected regimes are viewed as liberal and bourgeois but which, unlike the so-called progressive regimes of Mexico and Panama and oil-rich Venezuela, have had strong ties to and have been dependent (in the Soviet view) on the United States—Costa Rica and Colombia. This was an important shift.

Costa Rica. The Soviets and Cubans established diplomatic relations with Costa Rica in the early 1970s. They viewed this country as a tranquil exception to the right-wing dictatorships of Central America, and until 1979 the small, pro-Soviet Costa Rican Communist party, the Popular Vanguard party, favored only peaceful means for coming to power. There are various reasons for this. Costa Rica is the only Central American country which has had a democratic government since 1948, and it has had no army since that year. Since 1974 the Soviets have been developing a small trade relationship with Costa Rica based primarily on the exportation of small amounts of coffee and other agricultural products. Overall, however, the Soviets view Costa Rica as only marginally important because of the lack of economic resources (unlike Mexico and Venezuela) and its nonstrategic location (unlike Panama). Furthermore, Costa Rica has been traditionally friendly toward the United States and never sufficiently anti-imperialist as are, for example, Panama and Mexico.

This picture of Costa Rican tranquillity changed in the late 1970s and early 1980s. The high cost of oil imports and the lowering of world prices for coffee, sugar, and other agricultural commodities contributed to Costa Rica's most serious economic crisis in thirty years. With a foreign debt of $2.6 billion in 1982 the country is, in the view of its leadership, on the "edge of bankruptcy." This problem was complicated by the Cuban-supported network of guerrilla activity throughout Central America and terrorism inside Costa Rica.

As concluded by the Costa Rican legislature in an inquiry published in May 1980, it is obvious that the Cubans were running a very extensive covert network in 1978–1979, supplying arms and other aid from Venezuela to the Sandinistas in Nicaragua through Costa Rica. With the termination of the civil war in Nicaragua the arms traffic network, now originating mainly in Cuba, was redirected toward El Salvador directly or indirectly through Honduras, all under the supervision of Cuban diplomats and facilitated by the Costa Rican left.

The Cubans, with Soviet backing, appear to have been giving ideological and military training in Cuba to a group of urban terrorists from Costa Rica. Until recent terrorist acts against the Costa Rican police and U.S. embassy personnel in San José, terrorism was virtually unknown to the country. Two of the terrorists arrested in connection with these acts were trained in the Soviet Union. Others received training in Cuba and Nicaragua.[29] Some of those arrested have belonged to the MRP, or Revolutionary Movement of the People, a Leninist group with close ties to Cuba (not to be confused with the Popular Vanguard party, which is still less inclined to favor violent means for coming to power) which implicitly approves the antigovernment terrorism.

The Cubans originated the arms transfer through Costa Rica, but this could not have happened without Soviet knowledge and approval, since the Soviets have an embassy in San José. The Soviets probably did not initiate the terrorist attacks in Costa Rica. Yet they must have known of them, and if they did not approve them, at least they decided not to oppose them. (After the terrorist attack on personnel of the U.S. embassy, the Soviet embassy asked the Costa Rican police for protection.) The Soviet-Cuban-sponsored guerrilla activities in Costa Rica have cost the Soviets, though not so dearly as the Cubans, whose diplomatic mission was shut down after the aforementioned Costa Rican investigation. Because of this interference and Soviet involvement in local labor problems, including support for the Communist labor union (some of the Soviet diplomats were linked to a banana strike), there has been a cooling of diplomatic relations and the technical and economic aid agreement with the Soviet Union, concluded earlier, was renounced. Moreover, Costa Rican officials have indicated that they do not plan to increase trade with the Soviet Union and that if more evidence of Soviet involvement in terrorism in

Costa Rica becomes available, relations with the Soviet Union may be broken. As of the fall of 1982, the number of officials at the Soviet embassy in San José was reduced from twenty-five to eight, and Soviet-Costa Rican relations were at a low ebb. The post left vacant by Soviet Ambassador Vladimir Chernishov in June 1981 was not filled for sixteen months. Two men proposed for the post by the Soviets were supposedly rejected by the Costa Rican government, and only in December 1982 was Yuri Pavlov accredited as the new Soviet ambassador in the capital city of San José.[30] The Soviets, while complaining about recent Costa Rican hostility, do not view as significant their losses in Costa Rica, since the government of Costa Rica's President Luís Alberto Monge is viewed as subservient to the United States and Costa Rica is seen as not having substantial economic benefits to offer the Soviet Union.

Colombia. In Colombia the Soviets and Cubans have also revised their tactics, at least temporarily. The February 1980 seizure of the Dominican Republic's embassy in Bogotá by guerrillas (who were later flown to Cuba) was followed by a sharp increase in leftist guerrilla activities.*

Cuba has had excellent contacts with Colombian revolutionaries, who have been training in Cuba since the 1960s. Leaders of some of the guerrilla groups in Colombia have also attended schools in Moscow. During the 1970s, when Cuba established diplomatic relations with Colombia, Cuba limited its contacts with these groups—the urban April 19 Movement (M-19), the People's Liberation Army (ELN), and the Revolutionary Armed Forces of Colombia (FARC). After 1979, when Colombia ran against Cuba for the Latin American seat on the United Nations Security Council, Cuba, with Soviet backing, renewed its assistance to the Colombian guerrillas and in the summer of 1980 made efforts to unite these organizations or at least ensure their cooperation on a practical level. Although a united strategy was not achieved, the groups did agree to cooperate. Moreover, there is some evidence that Cuba played a prominent role in organizing and providing intensive training for some of the M-19 guerrillas (who came to Cuba via Panama) and, beginning in 1979, provided them with money for the purchase of arms (via Panama) to be used in the 1981 spring offensive.

---

* Curiously, diplomats from Communist countries left the party en masse before the seizure, leaving the diplomats from other countries to be taken hostage. It appears they were warned beforehand. At least this is the impression of the former U.S. ambassador to Colombia, Diego Asencio. See his and Nancy Asencio's *Our Man Is Inside: Outmaneuvering the Terrorists* (Boston, Mass.: Little, Brown and Co., 1982), p. 7.

This offensive was planned so as to coincide with a scheduled civil strike which, it was hoped, would lead to a nationwide insurrection. Some guerrillas of a large group which was sent by ship to Colombia in February 1981 were intercepted while attempting to land on Colombia's Pacific coast. One member confessed that the group had been trained and armed in Cuba. Later in 1981 a ship carrying weapons for the guerrillas was sunk by the Colombian navy in Colombian territorial waters. (According to Colombian authorities, Nicaragua is the source of many of the weapons captured from Colombian guerrillas, and there is an indisputable link between the Communist Party of Colombia [PCC] and at least one of Colombia's guerrilla groups, FARC.[31]) In response to this attempt, Colombia broke diplomatic relations with Cuba in 1981. The Colombian guerrilla groups continued to engage in a number of ambushes and terrorist operations against military units until the amnesty of 1982.

As in Costa Rica, in Colombia the Soviets must have known about the Cubans' renewed support for the guerrilla movement. Although Soviet trade with Colombia has been growing, in Soviet calculations Colombia, though larger than Costa Rica, is probably not a very significant country in terms of resources or location. More important, Colombia in 1980–1982 was hardly a country the Soviets could characterize as having anti-imperialist policies on important international issues. Thus in terms of economics, security, and politics the Soviets have little to lose by antagonizing the Colombians. Furthermore, by allowing Cuba to play a pivotal role in these operations the Soviet Union can deny responsibility and minimize the costs.

The Colombian offensive—like the guerrilla operations in Costa Rica and most importantly, as we shall see, the large guerrilla offensive in El Salvador—was planned to coincide with U.S. presidential elections in November 1980 and the period shortly thereafter in order to put the United States and its allies on the defensive in the U.S. strategic backyard during the vulnerable period of transition from one president to another. The timing and implementation of all these operations betrayed a large element of planning and preparation. Although not in charge of the training and military operations on a daily basis, the Soviets must have been kept informed and certainly must have approved these operations.

The new Colombian administration of President Belisario Betancur is downplaying the Cuban and Nicaraguan support of revolutionary activities in the Caribbean basin, not only to demonstrate independence from the United States, but also because insurgency activities subsided in Colombia in 1982. In a rather surprising move the new president refused to isolate Cuba and Nicaragua from the

OAS during President Reagan's visit in November 1982 and proposed that Colombia join the nonaligned group of nations, perhaps hoping thereby to dissuade the Soviets and Cubans from promoting further havoc and perhaps retaliating against the Reagan administration for what he saw as slighting his country in the Caribbean Basin Initiative.

Soviet Policies toward "Reactionary" Regimes: El Salvador, Guatemala, and Honduras

El Salvador. The Sandinista victory in 1979 prompted the Soviets to anticipate a chain reaction of leftist upheavals and revolutions throughout Central America and contributed to a shift in Soviet policy. After Nicaragua, the Central American country singled out by Soviet writers at that time as being most pregnant with revolutionary opportunities was El Salvador, which the Soviets see as occupying an important strategic position in the region.[32] Like Nicaragua, and perhaps even more so, El Salvador has a strong heritage of instability caused by a rigid class structure, unequal distribution of wealth, and high unemployment (30 percent). In El Salvador, the smallest yet most densely populated country in Latin America, socioeconomic conditions are determined by an oligarchy of wealthy families protected by military strong men who control the country's politics. The civil war, in which at least 20,000 have died, continues to ravage that country.

Cuban assistance to Salvadoran guerrillas increased sharply after 1979 when the Cubans helped to unite the various revolutionary groups under the Farabundo Marti National Liberation Front (FDR-FMLN), already referred to. At this time also the Cubans increased greatly their training of Salvadoran guerrillas. Although originally very cautious, the Soviets, after a meeting of the various guerrilla groups organized by Castro in Havana in December 1979, decided to back the Cuban plan and to help supply weapons.[33] In the spring of 1980 the Soviets also agreed to provide for the training of a few dozen Salvadoran youths. This change in tactics was reflected when the pro-Soviet Communist party of El Salvador (PCES) endorsed violent revolution at its seventh national congress in May 1980. This was a very important shift, since the PCES leader Shafik Jorge Handal in the past had broken with some of his colleagues who had advocated these tactics and had been critical of such tactics in the Soviet press. Up to that time the PCES had participated in several presidential and legislative elections and had opposed armed struggle and terrorism in favor of peaceful tactics. In the fall of 1979, though jubilant over the victory in Nicaragua, Handal was cautious about commenting on prospects for revolution in El Salvador. In April 1980, however, he became much more optimistic and, according to Soviet sources, expressed "confidence" in the "defeat of internal reaction, despite the fact that the latter is backed by imperialist forces."[34] The fact that this important shift in Handal's line was well advertised in the Soviet press means that the Soviets gave it their support.

The example of Nicaragua and the changing relationship between the superpowers, however important, were not the only motives for the changing tactics of the PCES and the Soviets in the spring and fall of 1980. Both the Soviets and the Cubans probably feared that if the PCES did not use violence to implement its anti-imperialist strategy, it would soon be overtaken by its more radical rivals, who were quickly gaining popular strength. The PCES, they likely reasoned, should not be suddenly surprised by successes of non-Communist guerrillas and deprived thereby of credit for the victory. Thus Cuban and Soviet tactics since the spring of 1980 have been directed at transforming the numerically small PCES into a leading force in the guerrilla struggle in El Salvador.

It appears that the Soviet backing of the Cuban involvement in El Salvador, though not the main cause of the civil war, has significantly strengthened the guerrillas in El Salvador. If nothing else, Handal's search for arms in the East, which is well documented by the U.S. administration in its White Paper,* began around the time of the seventh congress of the PCES, during which a passive line was exchanged for one of organized violence intended to topple the government. After the congress, as Castro later admitted, the Cubans took charge of coordinating the delivery of weapons to guerrillas in El Salvador, and Castro actively assumed the role of broker in unifying the various revolutionary groups. (The Cuban involvement in the civil war in El Salvador is well documented by Jorge Dominguez.[35]) In June and July 1980, with the assistance of Soviet officials responsible for third-world affairs in the Soviet Secretariat (such as K. Brutens and his deputy M. Kudachkin), Handal visited the Soviet Union and several East European countries and obtained American-made weapons (such as M-14 and M-16 rifles, M-79 grenades) as well as other U.S. equipment from Vietnam and Ethiopia. Thus by proceeding with caution, the Soviet Union could deny its involvement if accused. Obvi-

---

* Having carefully analyzed the White Paper, we agree with Mark Falcoff that all errors therein—and there are several that have been pointed out by its critics—are irrelevant to the document's authenticity and its political significance. See Mark Falcoff, "The El Salvador White Paper and Its Critics," *AEI Foreign Policy and Defense Review*, vol. 4, no. 2 (1982), pp. 18–24. The Soviet and Cuban role in El Salvador was further confirmed by captured guerrillas who were trained in Cuba. *El Mundo* (San Salvador), March 20, 1981.

ously, the Soviets did not wish to appear involved, and this is why they were "helpful" in arranging Handal's visit to Vietnam and Ethiopia. Without Soviet sponsorship the East Europeans and very likely the Vietnamese and Ethiopians would not have cooperated.

The Soviets' East European allies (except Poland and Romania) promised to provide additional weapons, communications equipment, uniforms, and medical supplies, while the Soviets helped to arrange for the transport of the weapons, with Cuban assistance, to Nicaragua, and from there directly by ship, air, or land (through Honduras) to El Salvador. Following the U.S. presidential elections, Cuban experts, with cautious yet active Soviet backing, played a key role in the arms transfer and preparation of the "final" guerrilla offensive originally scheduled to coincide with the transition of power in Washington in January 1981.

The Soviet-backed and Cuban-coordinated arms transfer to guerrillas in El Salvador is not the only and perhaps not even the main source of support for the guerrillas. They also receive arms from internal sources in El Salvador, including disloyal troops. Although evidence about the exact quantity of the Soviet and Cuban arms transfer is incomplete, the evidence about Soviet and Cuban aid and support for revolutionary forces in the Caribbean basin in general and in El Salvador in particular is more solid than some critics would like to acknowledge. Costa Rican and other Central American sources as well as Colombian sources have substantiated the basic premises of the U.S. White Paper. The flow of arms in March–April 1981 was reduced and then increased somehow again before the new offensive of August. The arms transfer by way of small ships[36] and by surface and air continued in 1982, though, it seems, at a minimal level.

To be sure, the Soviets' original hope for rapid revolutionary advances following the general offensive in El Salvador was overly optimistic. In the Soviet appraisal as of 1981, the difference between the current situation in El Salvador and the pre-revolutionary situation in Nicaragua was that the Salvadoran bourgeoisie were still stronger than their Nicaraguan counterparts; the Salvadoran left had mass support yet was unable to exploit it fully.[37] Nevertheless, the Soviets still expressed belief in eventual victory of the guerrilla movement. For in spite of the guerrillas' inability to disrupt the 1982 spring elections or even prevent a large turnout, the results of the elections were probably viewed in Moscow as a U.S. political defeat. They did not legitimize centrist rule by the Christian Democratic party's President José Napoleón Duarte, despite U.S. support. The elections brought to power a coalition of several right-wing parties whose policies might lead to a reversal of reforms such as land redistribution. This could lead to further radicalization of El Salvador's society and place additional limits on U.S. assistance to the country. (There were fifty-five U.S. military advisers in El Salvador in 1982, as opposed to a much larger number of Soviet and Soviet-allied advisers in Nicaragua.) The successful guerrilla offensive leading to the brief capture of the city of Berlin in February 1983 and indications of deep divisions within the Salvadoran military are viewed as clear signs that the war in El Salvador will continue. The Soviets still support the revolutionaries in El Salvador, though perhaps more cautiously than in 1980–1981, taking care not to provoke what they view as the "unpredictable" Reagan administration.

Guatemala. Since the overthrow of the "progressive" government of Jacobo Arbenz with CIA participation in 1954,[38] the Soviets have viewed each successive regime in Guatemala as reactionary. Judging from their sources, they are aware of the deteriorating socioeconomic conditions in Guatemala. The economy of this most populous country in Central America, like that of its neighbors, is in disarray. As elsewhere in the region, agriculture, which is the basis of Guatemala's economy, has been seriously affected by the recent worldwide decline in coffee, cotton, and sugar prices. Although it is growing, the industrial sector is still weak and unable to incorporate the impoverished and ever more radicalized Indian population which comprises more than half of the total population. (U.S. officials estimate that eight out of every ten insurgents are Indian.) Guatemala, unlike El Salvador, however, has attractive reserves of oil which, if developed, will provide an excellent source of foreign exchange.

The worsening socioeconomic conditions in Guatemala, coupled with the effects of guerrilla warfare in neighboring countries, have contributed to the radicalization of Guatemalan society. Economic conditions worsened particularly following the loss of transport routes through Nicaragua (whose use was denied Guatemala by a hostile Nicaraguan regime) and the destruction of the Pan American highway in El Salvador. Incredible violence by factions right and left, which goes back to the mid-1950s, intensified with the upsurge in guerrilla movements in the 1970s and exacerbated this situation. In the late 1970s and early 1980s, under the oppressive rule of General Romeo Lucas, violence on the part of the extreme right (the famous death squads) and extreme left further harmed the country. Because of the Guatemalan regime's extremely violent tactics in dealing with both guerrillas and political dissidents and because of the large emigration of those fleeing the violence, the United States has declared a ban on military sales to Guatemala. Yet in the early 1980s conditio in Guatemala were less ripe than in El Salvador for a popular revolution of the Nicaraguan style.

While the United States has suspended its arms transfer and military advisory assistance to the Guatemalan government, the Cubans, with Soviet backing, have stepped up their military aid to the guerrillas, whom they have supported since 1960. The pattern of Cuban aid resembles the course followed in Nicaragua and El Salvador. First the Cubans insisted on unification of the four leading guerrilla groups, one of which has close ties to the Guatemalan Communist party. The unity agreement was signed in Managua in November 1980 in the presence of high Cuban and Nicaraguan officials. The Guatemalan guerrilla leaders still continue to meet in Managua. Later the agreement was presented to Castro. Although the revolutionary groups did not agree at first to establish a unified political front, they did agree on a joint military strategy, including an increase in insurgency activities. The political unification of these groups, apparently modeled after the Nicaraguan and Salvadoran examples, was achieved in Cuba in March 1981 under the banner of the Guatemalan Nationalist Revolutionary Unity. Then the Guatemalan Labor (Communist) party, which in the past had advocated cautious resistance to military rule, also came to advocate "clandestine methods" in the struggle since, as their leader explained, "all the legal ways are closed."[39] Later the Cubans increased their training and military assistance to the revolutionaries. More than 2,000 guerrillas are being trained in Cuba. Meanwhile the arms transfer from Nicaragua via Honduras continues, though on a smaller scale. There is also a degree of collaboration between the Salvadoran and Guatemalan guerrillas, though the actual insurgency in Guatemala is conducted on a smaller scale than in El Salvador. The guerrillas themselves admit that they suffered a setback in late 1982.

The latest developments in Guatemala may be decisive in the outcome of the guerrilla war in that country. An apparently fraudulent election in March 1982 led to the election of General Angel Anibal García as president. Anibal García in turn was overthrown by a three-man junta led by General Efraín Ríos Montt, who decided to annul the results of the Guatemalan vote. Ríos Montt in turn was overthrown by General Oscar Humberto Mejía Victores in August 1983. Given the long succession of rapid political turnovers, it seems likely that the trend toward instability and political polarization will continue. As in El Salvador, the Cubans, backed tacitly by the Soviets, are expected to try to continue, even if only moderately, their support for revolutionary forces in Guatemala.

...duras, one of the poorest countries in the Caribbean ...ing through a dramatic economic and financial crisis, ...debt of almost $1 billion. Although the army has played ...t role in the politics of this country, described by the ...aving a "soft dictatorship," this may change with the new ...adership of the popular country doctor Suazo Cordova (the ... ...ian president in a decade), who was elected in November 1981 ...nd inaugurated in January 1982.

As elsewhere, the Cubans have sought to encourage the domestic revolution in Honduras, urging the unification of revolutionary groups, which are much smaller than in El Salvador and Guatemala, and providing them in 1981 with some arms and instruction in Cuba and Nicaragua. The guerrilla insurgency in Honduras is still very limited. Because of the country's strategic geographic position bordering Nicaragua, El Salvador, and Guatemala, Honduras plays an important role in Soviet-Cuban tactics. It has served as a logistical bridge (over air and surface) for support of insurgency in all these countries. In 1980, with Soviet and Cuban support, the small Communist party of Honduras organized the Committee for Solidarity with the Struggle for the Central American Peoples, which helped to enlist support for the revolutionary struggle in El Salvador and aid to Nicaragua. This effort has been coordinated with other Communist groups in the region and with Panama and Mexico.[40] Because of its very strategic position, Honduras may become the key to stability in the Central American region.

Regional Conflict in the Caribbean Basin?

Although we have limited ourselves primarily to examining Soviet and Cuban policies as they affect stability in the Caribbean basin, we have tried to show that the instability stems from internal sources as well. In addition, there is an interregional dimension which goes back to old territorial disputes and new political and security problems. Thus Nicaragua refuses to recognize the 1919 treaty acknowledging Colombian sovereignty over the Caribbean islands of San Andrés (where Colombia is building a naval base), Providencia, Roncador Cay, and the Serrana Keys. Nicaragua also disputes the Cañas Jerer Treaty of 1858, which was ratified by the Cleveland Resolution and gives Costa Rica freedom in perpetuity to navigate the San Juan River on Nicaragua's borders.

Venezuela's claim to two-thirds of Guyanese territory goes back to the 1899 Treaty of Washington, which involved Great Britain as arbiter. Guyana has declared its readiness to accept military aid from

234

Cuba in case Guyana is attacked by Venezuela. There also exists a serious problem of demarcation between portions of the borders between Venezuela and Colombia. A significant part of the new state of Belize (former British Honduras) is claimed by Guatemala, which professes to need a large port on the Caribbean coast. Guatemala has claimed this territory almost since it became an independent state in 1821. In the future strong pressure from Guatemala against Belize may cause this small country, with a population of only 140,000, to move closer to Cuba and Nicaragua in search of allies and protection.

In the recent past some countries of the Central American isthmus were invaded by their neighbors. Thus in 1954 the CIA financed and backed the invasion of Guatemala simultaneously from both Honduras and El Salvador. Then there is the old border dispute between Honduras and El Salvador which led to the so-called Soccer War in 1969. There are also a number of trade disagreements among various countries in the basin, even those which are ideologically and politically close to one another like Honduras and Guatemala.

The new revolutionary policies of the Sandinistas in Nicaragua have compounded the existing interregional problems. This is manifested in the Central American arms race, which began with the Sandinistas' planned military buildup and was publicly announced in the spring of 1980. This is a very important point, since it is often argued that the Nicaraguan military buildup was begun only in response to Reagan's tough policies. More than any other factor the Nicaraguan buildup has destabilized the region. The supply of heavy tanks, in particular, which are not included in the inventory of Nicaragua's neighbors Honduras, El Salvador, and Guatemala, has fueled this race. While the Nicaraguan armed forces by the end of 1982 could count at least fifty T-54 and T-55 tanks in their arsenal, the Central American nations combined possessed in 1982 approximately twenty small Sherman and Scorpion tanks. The large-scale deliveries of sophisticated weapons to Nicaragua from the Soviet Union and its allies, but also from France and Algeria, is accompanied by the Sandinistas' effort to build, with Cuban help, one of the largest standing armies (with a goal of 50,000 men, making it second only to the armies of Cuba and Mexico) in the region. The Nicaraguan armed forces have grown from 8,000 under Somoza to 22,000 (not including 4,000 state security police and 60,000 militia reserves) at the present time. This number already far exceeds the level needed for Nicaraguan self-defense. If realized, the goal of 50,000 will exceed greatly the combined strength of the armed forces of Nicaragua's neighbors, which can be broken down as follows: Guatemala, 18,000, El Salvador, 5,000, Honduras, 14,000, and Costa Rica, 0.

The race is on. In response to their own internal problems but also to what they perceive as the threat from Nicaragua, Honduras, El Salvador, and Guatemala have begun making large-scale arms purchases, particularly to upgrade their air forces, but also including antitank missiles and helicopters. Even Costa Rica, which has no army, is trying to upgrade the training of its 5,000-man guard and plans to form special antiterrorist units.

A third source of regional instability is the forced migration from Nicaragua of various large groups who have settled in the proximity of the Nicaraguan borders. A few thousand supporters of the former dictator Somoza, mainly members of his national guard, have settled along the borders of Nicaragua, especially in Honduras but also in Costa Rica, and have undertaken occasional military forays into Nicaraguan territory (from Honduras). In 1981–1982 some ex-guardsmen began to cooperate with the growing anti-Sandinista organization of exiled Nicaraguans known as the Nicaraguan Democratic Force, which operates both in Honduras and inside Nicaragua. It consists of a wide spectrum of opponents to the Managua regime, including ex-Somozistas, ex-Sandinistas, deserters from the Sandinista army, and many others. Their raids against Sandinista military bases have succeeded in destroying some Soviet military equipment.

Although the migration of Somoza's supporters is clearly an after-effect of the civil war which preceded the Sandinistas' assumption of power, the migration of other groups from Nicaragua is caused by the Sandinistas' postrevolutionary policies. This migration concerns 200,000 mostly English-speaking Misurata Indians (Miskito, Sumo, Rama), 8,000 to 10,000 of whom had already been forcefully removed by Sandinista troops from border areas adjacent to Honduras. The Sandinista government claims that the eviction was necessary because of intrusions into Nicaragua by former Somoza guardsmen. During the removal, about 100 Indians were killed. Afterward some 3,000 Miskitos fled to Honduras, and many others were murdered by the Sandinistas.[41] The flight of Indians from the border areas and in 1982 the flight of thousands of other Nicaraguans from areas throughout the country has exacerbated the tension with Honduras.

The Sandinistas, assisted by Cuban coordination and Soviet economic backing, have supported insurgency and terrorism in El Salvador and recently, to a lesser degree, in Honduras, Costa Rica, and even Colombia. This activity has also contributed to regional instability in Central America. Because of a long common frontier with Nicaragua and because of mutual accusations and hostilities on both sides, the threat of war is greatest between Honduras and Nicaragua. Honduras has claimed thirty-three border violations and violent acts by the Sandinistas in the period from January 30 to August 20, 1982.[42] Honduran violations also are cited often by Nicaraguan leaders who talk about "a real state of war" along the borders with Honduras. As a result, in November 1982 Nicaragua imposed martial law in the border areas with Honduras which has been extended through 1983. Both sides have increased their military presence along the borders, with Honduras deploying 10 percent of its armed forces in these areas. Honduras, which had been receiving Argentine aid in the past, is now receiving U.S. aid to upgrade its military capability and airport facilities. The forty U.S. military advisers in the country and Honduran troops conducted joint military exercises near the Nicaraguan borders in the summer of 1982. The growing fear of war between Nicaragua and Honduras was heightened in the summer of 1982 when both governments recalled their respective ambassadors, charging each other's troops of border violations, kidnappings, and preparations for war.

There is also border unrest on the Costa Rican–Nicaraguan frontier. Costa Rican officials, who originally supported the Sandinista Revolution, share the concern of their Honduran counterparts about the tense situation on their borders, which, in their view, was created by continuous Nicaraguan incursions into Costa Rican territory. Nicaraguan support for insurgency in Costa Rica is another serious concern.

In short, the conflict in the Central American isthmus may polarize even further the countries in the Caribbean region. Honduras, El Salvador, Costa Rica, and Guatemala formed a political alliance—the Central American Democratic Community (CDC)—in early 1982 to isolate the Sandinista regime in Managua. (Costa Rica, however, objects to establishing an economic or military alliance within this grouping.) Even Mexico became concerned in 1981 over the widening conflict in Central America. Following the influx of thousands of Guatemalans into their country, the Mexicans created a 4,000-man quick reaction force to respond to unrest on its borders with Guatemala. As feared by some Central American leaders, the tension in the region as of 1982 has reached a dangerous level, and any incident can transform the conflict with uncontrollable consequences. Should the conflict between Honduras and Nicaragua rapidly escalate into war, the regime in El Salvador, if not besieged by its own guerrillas, would very likely come to the aid of Honduras, both politically and militarily. Already units of the Salvadoran army occasionally cross into Honduran territory to conduct attacks against Salvadoran guerrilla sanctuaries there. Costa Rica, though it has no army, would probably help Honduras in some limited way. Meanwhile Nicaragua might call for aid from Cuba, with Honduras and El Salvador asking for increasing military assistance from Israel and the United States. This in turn could precipitate increasing military involvement on the part of both superpowers.

Future Soviet-Cuban Strategy in the Caribbean Basin

We have outlined at least four major factors which in the past visibly affected Soviet and Cuban policies in the Caribbean basin: (1) the presence of opportunity, (2) the degree of Soviet and Cuban concurrence regarding joint strategy, (3) the conditions and dynamics of Soviet and East European internal politics, and (4) U.S. ability and willingness to counter Soviet and Cuban tactics. As illustrated, at times the absence of exploitable opportunities, disagreement with Cuba about overall strategy, unfavorable internal conditions in the Soviet Union and Eastern Europe, and a firm U.S. response have acted against successful implementation of Soviet strategy. In attempting to decipher future trends in Soviet and Cuban tactics, we must consider these same variables.

Opportunities for Exerting Influence. As concerns local opportunities in the English-speaking Caribbean islands, where it was early feared there would be repetitions of the revolutionary coup in Grenada, prospects for the Soviets and Cubans are rather unfavorable. Recently the islands of Dominica, St. Lucia, St. Vincent, and St. Kitts-Nevis rejected in democratic elections the radical, leftist orientation. It appears that the Soviets and Cubans, like some Western scholars, have underestimated the efficacy of the parliamentary tradition and the system of legitimate self-government in countries of the English-speaking Caribbean. The most crucial setback, as admitted by the Soviets, was the electoral defeat of socialist Prime Minister Michael Manley in Jamaica in October 1980. He lost to the more pro-Western Edward Seaga, who then expelled a host of Cuban diplomats, some of whom were intelligence operators.

This is not to conclude that Soviet and Cuban policies toward the Caribbean islands were jeopardized in the 1980s. Grenada's revolutionary regime remains strong and marshaled significant economic aid from the Soviet Union in 1982. A slow economic recovery in the industrial world is being accompanied by seriously deteriorating socioeconomic conditions in the Caribbean region. As in the past, a worsening of these conditions might lead to radicalization, thereby making conditions propitious for Soviet and Cuban activity. Such changes cannot be excluded even in a country with democratic traditions such as Jamaica or the democratically ruled Dominican Republic, both of which are facing severe economic problems. With the possible exception of Haiti, where poverty is coupled with severe political oppression, in 1982 possibilities for revolutionary upheaval seemed less abundant in the Caribbean islands than in Central America.

Revolutionary upheaval seems to pose more of a threat to Central America for several reasons. First, the Central American political culture, in contrast to that of the English-speaking Caribbean, is deeply rooted in the Hispanic-Catholic tradition of powerful caudillos and often violent authoritarianism. Second, as demonstrated, in the early 1980s, socioeconomic conditions continue to deteriorate everywhere in Central America and have reached a critical point, even in Costa Rica. This trend has often been accompanied by violence.

Perhaps the success in Nicaragua has again led the Soviets and Cubans to overestimate the revolutionary potential in Central America. However, the possibility for the continuation of this success in El Salvador and perhaps in Guatemala, is still a matter for conjecture. Certainly up to 1983 the guerrilla offensive in El Salvador failed to spark a popular insurrection of the kind seen in Nicaragua, in part because of some rather significant differences in political developments in the two countries. Nicaragua's revolution was genuine in that it expressed the will of a majority of the people in overthrowing the hated Somoza dictatorship. El Salvador's revolution is much less so. Until recently, both the Soviets and the Cubans committed their resources to the cause there in the absence of considerable returns that would warrant such investment. In such other countries as Costa Rica and Colombia, Cuban support for the guerrillas has had damaging consequences for diplomatic relations. Judging from Soviet sources, it seems that the Soviets in 1982–1983 were somewhat less enthusiastic than they were in 1980 about the prospects for revolution in Central America.

Yet, because of the continuously deteriorating socioeconomic conditions, which are combined in some countries with a shift to the antireformist right (El Salvador) or with unrelenting violence and insurgency (El Salvador and Guatemala), unforeseen opportunities may arise for Soviet-backed Cuban activity. The deep socioeconomic cleavages, which are the main source of the ongoing crisis, are especially pronounced in countries located in the northern tier: El Salvador, Guatemala, and, to a lesser degree, Honduras. The more southern countries of Costa Rica and Panama do not have such marked social problems, but they do face severe economic difficulties (particularly Costa Rica), making them candidates for social upheaval in the future. Even countries where so far there has been little or no violence, such as Mexico and Panama, are worrisome. The severe economic crisis in Mexico, which imposes additional hardships on the already impoverished masses, could lead to great unrest, radical shifts in Mexican policy, and massive new waves of immigration to the United States. The death of Torrijos makes Panama's future likewise unpredictable. New revolutionary upheaval in Suriname on the South American coast may yet be exploited by the Soviets and Cubans. The most immediate and critical problem in 1982 is the almost warlike situation on Nicaragua's borders with Honduras and the dangerous arms race in the region.

Relations between the Soviet Union and Cuba. The state of relations between these two countries is the second important factor contributing to or mitigating against Soviet strategy in the region. Their joint strategy for dealing with third-world countries in the late 1960s and 1970s was not necessarily designed to create Leninist regimes in these countries, but rather to achieve a variety of anti-imperialist ideological, political, security, and economic objectives. Soviet and Cuban strategies have not always been identical. As recent Soviet-Cuban policies in Africa and Central America attest, however, most of these differences have been overcome. In spite of past disagreements and existing differences, the Soviets and Cubans are in unison on third-world strategy, a subject of contention in the 1960s. Although Cuba is not subservient to the Soviet Union, for a variety of reasons its foreign policies in Africa and the Caribbean are basically dependent on Soviet support. The Soviets and Cubans seem to have the same objectives regarding the Caribbean basin. Although the Soviets are newcomers, with Cuban help they have been able to exploit the socioeconomic malaise there and characteristic anti-U.S. sentiment. In doing so, their tactics have been violent or peaceful, but more often a combination of both.

It is very unlikely that during the remainder of the 1980s serious differences will create fissures in the Soviet-Cuban alliance, as happened in 1962–1968. Naturally one cannot exclude some disagreements on day-to-day tactics, but differences in strategy are unlikely. The forecast for the Soviet-Cuban alliance precludes any meaningful rapprochement between Cuba and the United States, which Cuba sees as a natural enemy. In response to two different overtures from U.S. policy makers, the Cuban leaders indicated clearly the impossibility of forgoing their alliance with their friends the Soviets. In the past, U.S. moderation such as manifested in acceptance of the violent overthow of Somoza's regime or the conciliatory approach toward

Cuba in 1975 and again in 1977 did not lead to appreciable changes in Soviet and Cuban policies. The overture of 1975 preceded the Soviet-Cuban intervention in Angola; the one in 1977 was followed by the intervention in Ethiopia; and U.S. moderation in Nicaragua was followed by more assertive Cuban policies in El Salvador.

The Soviet-Cuban alliance has produced tangible benefits for both countries. Moscow has an indispensable ally who is willing to deploy troops or coordinate insurgency activities in strategic areas of the third world. Moscow has made enormous ideological, political, security, and economic investments in Cuba. To turn its back on Castro's regime now would seriously undermine Soviet strategy in Africa and Central America.

Likewise, Soviet security, economic, and political support is essential to Cuba. Cuba is too dependent on the Soviet Union to try to alter the relationship and still too committed to revolutionary change to consider trying. Castro can hardly afford to turn his back on revolution, whose activities in part are designed to compensate for failed domestic experiments and mishandled Cuban internal politics. To forgo the alliance with the Soviet Union and move closer to the United States would undermine the very rationale of Castro's regime. Short of a very unlikely anti-Castro coup, in the 1980s there is probably very little possibility for polarizing change in the Soviet-Cuban alliance. Even Castro's death would not likely lead to profound changes in Cuban policy. His replacement by the number two man, who is Fidel's brother, Raúl Castro, would result in Cuba's becoming even more subservient to the Soviet Union.

Soviet and East European Internal Politics. As in the past, Soviet strategy and tactics in the Caribbean basin in the 1980s also will be influenced by Soviet domestic politics and economic conditions internal to the Soviet Union and Eastern Europe. In the early 1980s overall economic conditions in the Soviet Union and Cuba are not propitious for large economic commitments or revolutionary undertakings. As illustrated, however, Soviet and Cuban economic problems in the 1970s did not keep the Soviets and Cubans out of Africa or the Caribbean. It is particularly remarkable that Cuba, despite deep economic problems, until 1983 maintained and even extended its commitments in Africa and the Caribbean. The Soviets throughout have backed Cuba's pivotal role and have given significant economic support to Nicaragua and Grenada, though it is unlikely that they can afford to take on new revolutionary clients in the foreseeable future. Unlike Cuba, the Soviet Union is a superpower with global responsibilities and obligations not only to its clients in Asia, Africa, and the Caribbean but also and primarily to its hard core of allies in Eastern Europe, where economic conditions in the 1980s are rapidly going from bad to worse. Bankruptcy and continuous unrest in Poland and signs of coming crises in other East European countries as well as the continuing war in Afghanistan will force the Soviets in coming years to center their attention, as in the mid-1950s and late 1960s, on their own strategic backyard. Adding to these problems of instability was the death of Brezhnev in November 1982 and the attendant period of political uncertainty marking political succession in the Soviet Union.

The cumulative effect of all these conditions may be forced Soviet constraint in the Caribbean basin, for at least a few years. To be sure, it would be overly optimistic to conclude that the Soviets will cease the arms transfer and economic support necessary for the survival of existing revolutionary regimes in the region. Their support for Cuba, Nicaragua, and Grenada, in fact, intensified in the early 1980s. Yet in several years to come they will very likely be more cautious about giving new or significant support to struggling revolutionaries because of necessarily increasing preoccupation with their own domestic problems and problems at their periphery. The Soviets, who determine the limits of Cuban assertiveness, may likewise moderate future Cuban activities while waiting for new, low-risk opportunities.

The Balance of Power between the Superpowers. The final and most crucial variable in the formulation of Soviet strategy and tactics in the 1980s will be the overall balance of power between the Soviet Union and the United States and, within this framework, U.S. willingness and ability to respond to Soviet ventures in the Caribbean and elsewhere. In the wake of the Vietnam War, Cuban and Soviet assertiveness was not constrained by the United States because of unwillingness to do so by the American public and Congress. Thus the Soviets and Cubans had a free hand in Angola and Ethiopia. The sometimes fickle rhetoric of President Jimmy Carter, who in 1979 suddenly classified as "acceptable" what was first an "unacceptable" Soviet brigade, did not help deter Soviet and Cuban military activities in the Caribbean basin.

The election of Ronald Reagan to the presidency in 1980 was indicative of a shift in the American public mood. Rightly or wrongly, both the Soviets and the Cubans view President Reagan as unpredictable and a hard-liner. President Carter, though also perceived as unpredictable, was deemed less dangerous than his successor, whose hard stance was displayed as early as the presidential campaign of 1980 when he threatened to retaliate against the Soviet invasion of

Afghanistan by blockading Cuba.* As shown, it was no coincidence that the Cubans made every effort to coordinate and time the guerrilla offensives of 1980–1981 in El Salvador, Colombia, and Costa Rica for the period shortly following the transition from Carter to Reagan. The three-pronged offensive was very likely intended as a means of "beating Reagan to the draw," preempting his proclaimed tough response to Cuban activities in the Caribbean basin and placing him in what could have been an embarrassing defensive position during the delicate period initiating his tenure.

Although President Reagan has yet to weave his policies in the Caribbean basin into a coherent strategy, his policies so far have made the basin a major issue in the East-West context, causing some moderation of Soviet and Cuban revolutionary tactics in the region. The Reagan administration wisely did not rule out the use of a blockade or other military force against Nicaragua or, as former Secretary of State Haig put it, "going to the [Cuban] source" to prevent further Cuban involvement in El Salvador. Until Haig's departure, however, the administration unwisely engaged in some unneccessary talk which, because it was confrontational at the same time that it was unaccompanied by actions, lost some of its effectiveness.

As of the early 1980s, the Soviets have increased their military and economic aid to existing revolutionary regimes and continue to cultivate anti-imperialist trends in Mexico and Panama. U.S. support for Great Britain in the Falkland Islands War in 1982 served the ends of both the Soviets and the Cubans, who supported the Argentines and skillfully exploited the heightened anti-Americanism on the Latin American continent. U.S. efforts to work with the Argentines to moderate the situation in Central America were spoiled as a result of this war. The Soviets will probably proceed cautiously in the Caribbean so as not to provoke the United States into some drastic action in the next few years. As during similar periods in the past, a lessened emphasis on violence will not mean they have forgone their worldwide anti-imperialist strategy, in which support for revolution plays an integral part. The Soviets know that, short of a direct and unprovoked challenge to U.S. physical security, the Reagan administration will probably continue to have difficulties mobilizing U.S. public support for possible military action against revolutionary forces in the Caribbean, particularly if clear evidence of Soviet involvement is lacking.

Overall, any bold changes in Soviet strategy can be expected to wait until the results of the presidential election in 1984. Should a candidate less decisive or less committed to curbing Soviet expansion-

---

* George Kennan, a man the Soviets view as a "dove," suggested likewise.

ism be elected, one can expect the Soviets to take advantage by insti-
gating another round of well-planned offensives.

Toward a New U.S. Strategy

The task of U.S. policy makers in the 1980s is to develop a strategy
which would multiply and intensify the constraints on Soviet and
Cuban strategy in the Caribbean. First, the United States should establish limits beyond which it will not tolerate Soviet-Cuban involvement in the Caribbean and on the Pacific side of Central America—
clearly and unambiguously drawn "red lines." Such constraints
would be applied against the deployment of offensive weapons such
as medium-range missiles capable of carrying nuclear warheads or the
establishment of permanent facilities for Soviet submarines having
the same offensive capability. The Kennedy-Khrushchev agreement
worked out after the Cuban missile crisis (1962) and the Nixon-
Brezhnev understanding after the Cienfuegos incident (1970) provide
some precedent for setting such boundaries. The Soviets should be
made to know unequivocally that disregard for these limits in Cuba,
Nicaragua, or elsewhere in the region is unacceptable.

Obviously, the Soviet and East European arms transfer to the
Nicaraguan army does not pose the same direct national security
threat as did the Soviet missile deployment in Cuba. Beyond this,
however, a permanent Soviet military presence, even of the conventional type (a Soviet brigade), or major naval facilities in the basin—
and one must not distinguish between the various countries, since in
this respect all are equally important—should be treated as having,
though not immediate, the same potentially detrimental consequences as the first two conditions. In other words, a significant Soviet military presence in Nicaragua or Grenada would be the precedent for a similar buildup elsewhere in the region. If the phenomenon
is accepted in one locale, it will become difficult to oppose in others.
Thus spreading Soviet military facilities in geographic proximity to the
United States could make a major difference in wartime by tying up
U.S. forces needed in other theaters. As ever, U.S. physical security
depends on the ability to prevent the military involvement of potentially hostile powers in countries on its southern flank.

The United States must be able to distinguish between Soviet-
Cuban fomented strife in the region and revolutionary situations that
are indigenous to the countries. Carter's decision not to try to rescue
Somoza's dictatorship was correct in that the opposition to Somoza
was internal, vehement, and widespread. To regret this decision for
its possible linkage to developments in Nicaragua in the past three

years is to ignore that the consequences of any revolution are unpredictable and full of risk. Each revolution must be judged independently. There are times when U.S. policy makers will necessarily feel compelled to give military and economic aid to authoritarian military regimes when these are undermined by guerrilla or civil war with strong evidence of Soviet and Cuban support for opposing revolutionary forces. In deciding when or when not to lend U.S. military support, the red lines or limits of tolerance may not always readily apply.

Should the United States consider a military response if the influx of Soviet and Cuban military advisers and the conventional arms transfer to revolutionary forces in the Caribbean basin continue and reach critical proportions? Doubtless such a response will be considered. In doing so, U.S. policy makers would need to weigh carefully the potential benefits and adverse effects of military action on the American public, which remains at the time of writing adamantly opposed to the use of U.S. combat troops in what is viewed as a Vietnam-type conflict. This mood was still reflected in late 1982 when both houses of the U.S. Congress voted for an amendment to the Department of Defense budget barring the use of government funding for groups seeking to overthrow the Nicaraguan government.

Any eventual deployment of U.S. combat forces in the Caribbean basin may be opposed by the Congress and, more important, cause domestic polarization that could in turn undermine the Defense Department's efforts to counterbalance the Soviet strategic and conventional buildup elsewhere in the world. If there were a concentration of U.S. forces in the Caribbean basin, it could jeopardize U.S. ability to resist Soviet diversions in other areas. A naval blockade of any country in the region, though perhaps less risky than outright military intervention, could also be difficult. There are inherent risks in blockading any Central American nation, as opposed to the blockade of an island such as Cuba. Furthermore, a blockade at the present time would be much more difficult than in 1962 when the U.S. Navy was larger. Not surprisingly, it was, at that time, the Department of Defense officials who reportedly opposed the military actions in the region often suggested by Secretary of State Alexander Haig in 1980–1982.[43]

U.S. policy makers could forgo the risky option of direct military intervention for the less risky one of giving military aid and economic support to opposition forces, including armed units aiming to overthrow or destabilize regimes which are or may be planning to develop military ties with the Soviet Union and Cuba. This was the rationale behind CIA support for anti-Arbenz forces in Guatemala in 1954. According to press reports, it is also the motive as of 1982 behind CIA

245

support for anti-Sandinista elements in Honduras who are harassing the Nicaraguan regime and destroying Soviet military equipment supplied to the Sandinistas. U.S. aid to democratic forces in the Caribbean basin should be carefully prepared and selected so as not to promote unpopular and discredited political forces. In Honduras the forces led by former Sandinista commander Eden Pastora and such former members of the Nicaraguan junta as Alfonso Robelo and Arturo J. Cruz are a more logical choice for U.S. support than the Somozistas. Support for the latter might be counterproductive, leading to the consolidation of Sandinista power in Nicaragua and significant support for them abroad.

There are other possible military measures short of direct intervention or blockade that should be used to strengthen long-term U.S. policies in the Caribbean basin. The U.S. Navy would play a substantial role in such activities. The United States should continue efforts to expand its naval presence in the Caribbean, acting on but surpassing President Carter's 1979 decision to establish a Caribbean Contingency Joint Task Force (CCJTF) in Key West, Florida, and President Reagan's December 1, 1981, decision to upgrade and redesignate the CCJTF as a U.S. military command for forces in the Caribbean. These additional measures could include building new naval and also air facilities to monitor ship and air movements in the Caribbean basin; continuous surveillance of the Pacific coast of Nicaragua and El Salvador as long as the civil war in El Salvador continues; and possibly other measures such as assignment of permanent forces to the U.S. military command in the Caribbean and the scheduling of occasional, if not regular, deployments of a U.S. aircraft carrier battle group in the basin. The navy should increase air surveillance operations and conduct more ship visits to Caribbean countries to show the flag, and, if possible, hold more regular surface combatant task group exercises.

In short, the United States should heed the writings of Admiral S. Gorshkov and Admiral Alfred Thayer Mahan, both of whom stress the use of naval power during peacetime to further political objectives. The United States has been successful in conducting regular deployments in the Mediterranean Sea and Pacific Ocean for quite some time. A regular schedule of bilateral and multilateral* exercises with its Latin American allies could be initiated along similar lines. Naval exercises with amphibious landings, such as Ocean Venture 1982, should be conducted periodically to show foe and friend alike the viability of U.S. power. In light of advanced Soviet weapons trans-

---

* For various reasons, including border disputes, the Latin American allies favor bilateral exercises with the United States.

246

fers to Cuba and lately to Nicaragua, the United States has little choice but to arm friendly regimes in the Caribbean basin.

As long as Soviet support for Leninist forces does not cross the limits of U.S. tolerance, primarily diplomatic and economic means should be used to counter Soviet and Cuban strategy in the Caribbean. The United States should continue and should increase financial assistance to non-Sandinista political forces in Nicaragua to try to effect a change from within in the policies of the Nicaraguan government. As argued earlier, Nicaragua has not yet become Cuba of 1962, and the United States has several options available for trying to ensure that the democratic process there survives.

It is of enormous importance that while resisting Soviet-Cuban activities, the United States not lose track of the complex nature of the various conflicts in the region. As argued earlier, the present crisis in the Caribbean cannot be attributed solely, as is sometimes done, to Cuban and Soviet interference. Socioeconomic polarization and the decay of specific political and economic structures have triggered the rise of internal and intraregional conflict as have the oppressive policies of right-wing regimes in the region. It is the responsibility of the United States to discourage the excesses of both the left and the right in the region. Both are enemies of economic progress and political liberty.

As the Cuban and Soviet setback in the Jamaican elections of 1980 suggests, the U.S. approach, patience together with vigorous support for democratic forces, can be fruitful for U.S. policy. It is important that each country in the region be treated as a special case and that the wide-ranging cultural, social, and political diversity in the area be appreciated. If necessary, military aid should be further upgraded to countries such as El Salvador, Honduras, and Guatemala, and this in addition to comprehensive economic aid. The main roots of the various conflicts in the region are socioeconomic, and their resolution calls for a major economic program to support beleaguered and often weak democratic forces. This effort should be coordinated multilaterally with countries having strong regional interests like Mexico and Venezuela and other democratic countries in the region like Colombia and Costa Rica.

Although, as we have discussed, it would be naive to expect Castro to negotiate his alliance with the Soviet Union or his revolutionary image with the United States, diplomacy should be sought before confrontation. Even though the Soviet-Cuban alliance remains solid, the United States can play upon future tactical differences between the Soviet Union and Cuba, the Soviet Union and Nicaragua, and Nicaragua and Cuba. Meanwhile, the establishment of Radio Martí

247

would be a step forward, since Nicaragua and Cuba are vulnerable to criticism via U.S. broadcasts regarding treatment of their dissidents and lack of respect for human rights. This should be followed by wide-ranging cultural and scholarly exchange programs aimed at demonstrating the failures of the Cuban political and economic systems and Cuba's dependency upon the Soviet Union.

Like Poland, both Cuba and Nicaragua belong on the list of the world's most indebted countries. Both, and particularly Cuba, with a $3.5 billion debt to the West, are bankrupt at present, in spite of Soviet economic aid. In a dramatic policy shift, reflecting the seriousness of the economic problems, Cuba launched a plan in 1981 to attract foreign investors. This situation provides the United States with an opportunity to use positive and negative economic incentives to further peaceful change. As with the credits to Eastern Europe and the Soviet Union, the U.S. government should do its utmost to coordinate Western credit policies toward Cuba and Nicaragua. The United States should try to ease Castro's and the Nicaraguan junta's financial difficulties only if Cuba and Nicaragua agree to curb significantly their support for revolutionary activities in the Caribbean. The United States should indicate to the Soviet Union, Cuba, and Nicaragua, and also to the East European countries—some of whom, like East Germany, vigorously support Soviet anti-imperialist strategy—that moderate policies will be rewarded. Meanwhile, the succession of Andropov and the new period of transition in the Soviet Union may provide the opportunity for new diplomatic initiatives. Although Andropov's succession might turn out to be a breakthrough for U.S.–Soviet relations by dissipating a stalemate, one should not expect striking results from new U.S.–Soviet negotiations. A more significant and challenging task for the United States both at the bargaining table and in the world arena is to overcome its own domestic constraints, particularly the paralyzing legacy of Vietnam.

The main instrument of U.S. policy capable of constraining Soviet and Cuban strategy is economic leverage. The Reagan administration's Caribbean Basin Initiative (CBI), which included emergency aid for El Salvador, Costa Rica, Honduras, Jamaica, and the Dominican Republic totaling $350 million, as well as preferential, duty-free treatment of exports and significant tax incentives to attract investment by American entrepreneurs, is only a first, modest step toward a much needed massive economic program, including technical and scholarly exchanges and perhaps even a "Good Neighbor Corps" structured along the lines of the Peace Corps. The CBI is a small package in comparison with the Soviet aid program to Cuba which includes not only funding but also great numbers of personnel. Unfortunately, even getting approval for the CBI was a major undertaking in terms of U.S. domestic politics. The protectionist opposition in the U.S. Congress to the portion of the CBI plan providing for duty-free access to U.S. markets and the search for exclusions* suggest clearly that the development of a successful U.S. counterstrategy in the Caribbean basin presupposes, first, overcoming the protectionist mentality and predisposition of many Americans regarding the economic aid and assistance which are vitally in the interest of their country and, second, radical improvement of the U.S. economic situation caused by the recent recession.

As argued earlier, the main problems of the Caribbean basin are miserable living conditions, hunger, and unemployment, which in turn invite violence and revolution. If unresolved, the socioeconomic problems in the Central American isthmus, exacerbated by current U.S. economic difficulties, might sooner or later engulf the United States in a conflict of overwhelming dimensions. The Soviets and Cubans see very clearly these economic and social difficulties, and they count on their continuation to provide heightened opportunities for their own self-serving role in the Caribbean basin. It would be a tragedy and failure of the Western democracies to allow the Soviets ostensibly to champion the cause of political and economic justice, the traditional undertaking of democracies, while in the long run furthering the political, military, and social objectives of totalitarianism. Military concerns about arms levels in the region alone will not lead to resolution of the systemic social and economic crisis visited on those least able to bear the burden. Successful containment of Soviet initiatives in the Caribbean basin depends on the equitable distribution of wealth and burdens within all nations of the region. What is required finally is a balanced approach to the problems which can prevent the widening of the conflict in the basin and its exploitation by the Soviet Union and Cuba.

---

* These proposals died during the lame-duck congressional session in late 1982. At the time of writing the Reagan administration has vowed to fight for the proposals in the Ninety-eighth Congress in 1983.

Notes

1. For the most convincing interpretation of this kind see Richard Feinberg, "Central America: The View from Moscow," *Washington Quarterly*, vol. 5, no. 2 (Spring 1982), pp. 171–75.
2. Even sophisticated and well-prepared reports and policy papers like *Cuba's Renewed Support for Violence in Latin America* (Special Report No. 90) and *Strategic Situation in Central America and the Caribbean* (Current Policy No. 352),

both published by the U.S. Department of State, Bureau of Public Affairs, Washington, D.C., December 14, 1981, do not integrate adequately Cuban strategy in the Caribbean basin with that of the Soviets. The same is true of some otherwise good scholarly analyses. See, for example, Max Singer, "The Record in Latin America," *Commentary*, vol. 74, no. 6 (December 1982), pp. 43–49.

3. Feinberg, "Central America," p. 174.

4. *New York Times*, March 12, 1982.

5. For a more detailed discussion of the formulation of Soviet-Cuban strategy see Jiri Valenta, "The USSR, Cuba and the Crisis in Central America," *Orbis*, vol. 25, no. 3 (Fall 1981), pp. 715–46.

6. An interview conducted by Yomiuri Shimbun (Tokyo), April 13, 1980, as reported in *Foreign Broadcast Information Service* [hereafter cited as FBIS]— USSR, April 16, 1980. Also see an analysis of candidate Politburo member and CPSU Central Committee Secretary Boris Ponomarev, "Joint Struggle of the Workers and National-Liberation Movements against Imperialism and for Social Progress," *Kommunist*, no. 16 (November 1980), pp. 30–44.

7. TASS (Moscow), July 12, 1960. For an elaboration of Soviet strategy see M. F. Kudachkin, *Velikii Oktiabr' i Kommunisticheskie partii Latinskoi Ameriki* (The Great October and Communist parties of Latin America) (Moscow: Progress Publishers, 1978). Soviet anti-imperialist strategy has also been put forward in numerous articles published in *Latinskaia Amerika* (Moscow) in the 1960s and 1970s. There were, of course, some significant disagreements in formulating this strategy. These are well analyzed in a forthcoming book by Jerry Hough, to whom we are indebted for his comment.

8. See an important essay of Yu. N. Korolev, "The Timeliness of the Chilean Experience," *Latinskaia Amerika* (Moscow), September 1980, pp. 5–14.

9. U.S. Department of State, *Cuba's Renewed Support for Violence in Latin America*, p. 3.

10. Feinberg, "Central America," p. 173.

11. Ibid.

12. Viktor Belenko, in John Barron, *MiG Pilot: Final Escape of Lieutenant Belenko* (New York: Readers' Digest Press, 1980), p. 65.

13. See U.S. Naval Institute, *Proceedings*, May 1973, p. 351.

14. Figures on COMECON economic credits were reported by *CANA* (Bridgetown), September 1, 1981; in *FBIS–Latin America*, September 2, 1981; and in Katushev's speech on Radio Havana, October 29, 1982, *FBIS–Latin America*, October 29, 1982.

15. Jimmy Carter, *Keeping the Faith: Memoirs of a President* (New York: Bantam Books, 1982), p. 480.

16. Rodriguez's statements were reported in *Granma Weekly Review*, February 21, 1982, and Radio Madrid, April 7, 1982, *FBIS–Latin America*, April 8, 1982. Raúl Castro's statement was reported in *Prela*, November 8, 1982.

17. Figures regarding aid and scholarships were provided by the Soviet Ambassador to Nicaragua German Shliapnikov on Radio Sandino (Mana-

gua), November 1, 1982, *FBIS-Latin America*, November 1, 1982, and by Nicaraguan Ambassador to the Soviet Union Jacinto Suarez, *Barricada* (Managua), September 2, 1982.

18. Radio Sandino (Managua), March 27, 1981, *FBIS-Latin America*, March 30, 1981; Radio Sandino, April 6, 1982, *FBIS-Latin America*, April 7, 1982.

19. Voz de Honduras (Tegucigalpa), April 8, 1982, *FBIS-Latin America*, April 15, 1982.

20. *El Nuevo Diario* (Managua), November 14, 1982.

21. Shliapnikov's statements reported by AFP (Paris), December 6, 1981, *FBIS-Latin America*, December 6, 1981.

22. K. Khochaturov, "Changes on the Island of Spices," *Pravda* (Moscow), August 17, 1981. Khochaturov stressed that the New Jewel Movement was developed on the principles of "democratic centralism," that is, Leninism.

23. CANA (Bridgetown), July 28, 1982, *FBIS-Latin America*, July 28, 1982.

24. *Notimex* (Mexico City), September 16, 1982.

25. An interview with Ascanio Villalaz, national executive member and second deputy of the general secretary of the Revolutionary Democratic Party of Panama, by Feliex Dixon, member of the People's Party of Panama (PCC) in the Soviet-sponsored *World Marxist Review* (Prague), vol. 23, no. 11 (November 1980), pp. 49-50. Dixon is the PCC's representative on the *World Marxist Review*.

26. *La Republica* (Panama City), October 16, 1981.

27. Foreign Minister Juan Amado III, *Critica* (Panama City), August 24, 1982.

28. *La Estrella de Panama* (Panama City), September 10, 1982.

29. U.S. Department of State, *Cuba's Renewed Support for Violence in Latin America*, p. 8, and *La Republica* (Panama City), February 7, 1982.

30. *La Nación* (San José), May 9, 1981, and September 23, 1982. An interview with President Luís Alberto Monge, Radio Reloj (San José), April 6, 1982, *FBIS-Latin America*, April 7, 1982.

31. *El Tiempo* (Bogotá), February 21, 1982, and *El Espectador* (Bogotá), November 19, 1981; *Latin* (Buenos Aires), August 26, 1981, and November 1, 1980, and Bogotá, Emisoras Caracol Network, October 9, 1981, *FBIS-Latin America*, October 20, 1980.

32. V. Korionov, "El Salvador: The Struggle Sharpens," *Pravda*, December 30, 1981.

33. U. S. Department of State, *Communist Interference in El Salvador*, Special Report No. 80, February 23, 1981.

34. For more extensive discussion, see Jiri Valenta, "The USSR, Cuba and the Crisis in Central America."

35. See Jorge Dominguez's essay in the forthcoming volume edited by A. Adelman and R. Reading, *Confrontation in the Caribbean Basin: International Perspectives on Security, Sovereignty and Survival* (Pittsburgh, Pa.: Pittsburgh University Press).

36. *El Mundo* (San Salvador), April 3, 1982.

37. Feinberg, "Central America," p. 172, and private interviews.

38. Rusland Tuchin, "Guatemala: Reign of Terror," *New Times* (Moscow), no. 14 (April 1980), pp. 9–10.

39. Antonio Castro and Guillermo Toriello, "Guatemala: A Step toward Unity," *World Marxist Review,* vol. 24, no. 3 (March 1981), pp. 66–68. Castro is Central Committee Political Commission member of the Party of Labor; AFP (Paris), December 11, 1981, *FBIS–Latin America,* December 14, 1981.

40. Milton R. Paredes, "Solidarity with Revolutionary Peoples," *World Marxist Review,* vol. 23, no. 8 (August 1980), p. 15; *La Prensa* (Tegucigalpa), September 25, 1981; *Voz de Honduras* (Tegucigalpa), April 20, 1981, *FBIS–Latin America,* April 20, 1981.

41. *La Nación* (San José), July 11, 1982, and *The Daily Telegraph* (London), September 15, 1982; an interview with Roberto Guillén, who before his defection served as deputy chief of military counterintelligence for the Ministry of Defense under the Sandinistas; *Time,* January 24, 1983.

42. Documents and the introductory notes by the Honduran foreign secretary which were sent to the UN Security Council. Tegucigalpa Radio, August 24, 1982, *FBIS–Latin America,* August 25, 1982.

43. *New York Times,* January 25, 1983.

9

European Socialism
and the
Crisis in Central America

Eusebio Mujal-León

One of the most notable consequences of the Central American crisis has been the opportunity it has afforded a number of transnational, regional, and extra-Continental powers to become involved in an area traditionally considered a reserve and special zone of influence for the United States. An especially notable example of this internationalization has been the willingness and desire of major European Socialist parties such as the West German Social Democratic party (SPD), the French Socialist party (PS), and the Spanish Partido Socialista Obrero Español (PSOE)—in power and out, acting individually as well as through the Socialist International—to adopt positions and promote outcomes to the Central American conflict that are at variance with those of the United States and especially the Reagan administration. Their involvement in Central American issues represents a significant departure for parties that, at least from the early 1960s, were either uninvolved in international affairs or were broadly supportive of U.S. foreign policy initiatives.

This chapter will explore European Socialist efforts to influence the course of events in that region. The first section analyzes the reasons for renewed European interest in Latin America and considers some of the changes that have occurred in the past two decades that affect the triangular U.S.–West European–Latin American relationship. The second section discusses the contexts out of which PSOE, PS, and SPD policies toward Latin America have developed.

I would like to thank Philip Newell, Afshim Pedram, and Réné Romain for their help in the research of this chapter. I have also benefited from the comments and suggestions of John Bailey, Enrique Baloyra, Karl Cerny, William Douglas, David Scott Palmer, and Pete Vaky. Errors are, of course, my responsibility.

The third section foçuses on European Socialist activities in Central America (particularly in El Salvador and Nicaragua) since the Reagan administration took office. It explores the proposals advanced by the Socialist International with respect to the situation in the region and discusses its efforts to collaborate with regional powers such as Mexico and Venezuela. The conclusion, in assessing the effect European Socialist activity has had on events in Central America and on European-American relations, speculates on the limits and prospects for those parties' efforts to exercise greater influence in the region.

I

European Socialist involvement in Latin America (and especially in Central America) is not a spontaneous phenomenon. Rather it is a consequence of an evolution in the self-perception and role of the United States, Latin America, and Western Europe in the international system. The most important and mutually reinforcing characteristics of this process have been the erosion of American leadership in the West and in Latin America, the growth of nationalism in Latin America and the search for greater economic and political independence from the United States, and growing European political and economic assertiveness as manifested by the activities of individual countries and the European Economic Community as well as by those of Socialist and Christian Democratic parties and foundations.[1]

Renewed European interest in Latin America signaled the end of a historical parenthesis that began with the consolidation of American influence over Latin America and Western Europe earlier in this century. The expansion of American power in relation to Western Europe occurred during and after World War II. The postwar devastation led European countries to concentrate their energies on domestic political and economic issues and to rely on the United States for their security needs vis-à-vis the Soviet Union. A similar process occurred with respect to Latin America, where the United States began to compete actively with European economic and political influence in the first two decades of this century and to displace it after World War II. In the case of Spain, for example, this was not a difficult task; after the loss of its empire (and the Spanish-American War represented the final, bitter nail in this process), that country turned inward, being consumed by virulent political quarrels that ended in civil war from 1936 to 1939. The British and German economic and political presence in Latin America declined more slowly, with British investments being larger than total U.S. investment in Latin America until the depression.

New opportunities for the reassertion of European influence did not develop until the late 1960s when weakened American self-confidence (compounded later by Watergate) and diminishing U.S. influence over Europe and Latin America became evident. The Vietnam War provoked a crisis of confidence in the United States and the growth of a neoisolationist movement; it also alienated important sectors of West European public and elite opinion and raised doubts in others about American judgment. Pursuit of détente in the meantime increased fissiparous tendencies within the Atlantic alliance. At first, some Europeans feared that détente would lead to a superpower condominium. Later, in the wake of Afghanistan and the declaration of martial law in Poland, many saw the growing confrontation between the United States and the Soviet Union as narrowing their room for maneuver vis-à-vis the two superpowers.

U.S. relations with Latin America also underwent a shift in the late 1960s in the wake of the unfulfilled expectations aroused by the Alliance for Progress. U.S. concern with Latin America waned under the Nixon and Ford administrations; their policy of benign neglect and of reliance on "regional influentials" to safeguard stability put Latin America on the backburner, while allowing the United States to focus on Vietnam. Under Carter, the United States assumed a more activist posture toward Latin America, with the human rights campaign, the Panama Canal treaties, and overtures to Cuba; but the policy had the effect of weakening American influence over a number of traditional allies. American policy in the late 1970s also had a defensive orientation, aimed at damage limitation. The Carter administration saw fundamental changes in Latin America and an erosion of U.S. influence in the region as inevitable; some even saw such a reduced American role as necessary.

The decline of American influence coincided with and contributed to the shift from a bipolar order in the 1970s, opening up new opportunities and challenges for Western Europe and Latin America in the process. The European Economic Community emerged during this period as a major force in the international economy; so did Germany and France, which assumed political prominence as well. European dependence on imported raw materials, energy, and exports (in 1973, 22 percent of the EEC's gross domestic product was trade related) added some urgency to the European quest for an international role.[2]

Joined to such economic activism was greater European political assertiveness. It transcended ideology, becoming a shared value of Gaullists, Social Democrats, Christian Democrats, and even some Communists, especially in Italy. European involvement in the Middle

255

East and in negotiations with South Africa over Namibia, not to mention the arms control and disarmament issues that have convulsed the Atlantic alliance since the late 1970s, have been indicative of the growing assertivenes of those countries.

European interest in Latin America grew out of this reality. The economic foundations of this interest lay in the potential of a continent that includes 350 million people, has a gross domestic product of approximately $250 billion, and is one of the most advanced regions in the third world. Nevertheless, European economic ties with Latin America did not grow as rapidly as some hoped when the nascent European Economic Community sent a memorandum in 1958 to Latin American countries urging closer ties. Indeed, although the value of Latin America's exports to the European Economic Community has increased in nominal terms, its share of that market has dropped from 11 percent in 1958 to 5.5 percent in 1976.[3] In this period, the trade balance became markedly favorable to the EEC. This trend has been reinforced by European ties to their former colonies, the growing protectionism of the EEC, and the continued importance of the United States as a market and source of imports for Latin America.[4]

On a more positive side, Europe is the second largest market for Latin American exports;[5] France, Germany, Italy, and the United Kingdom became the largest arms suppliers to Latin America, accounting in the period 1975–1979 for an estimated $2.2 billion in arms sales, compared to $725 million for the United States in the same period.[6] Brazil, Mexico, Argentina, Venezuela, and Colombia have become important trading partners for Europe, with the EEC absorbing nearly one-third of total Brazilian exports.[7]

What is more, even though trade and development assistance from European countries to Latin America is not large, the flow of European investment into Latin America (especially in the banking and manufacturing sectors) has been significant: Latin America has absorbed more direct European investment than any other region in the developing world.[8] Even though Spanish exports to Latin America represent only 10.6 percent of Spain's total exports, by the late 1970s Spanish investments totaled close to $800 million (54 percent of total Spanish direct foreign investment), and Spanish banks had lent over $10 billion to Argentina, Brazil, Mexico, Venezuela, and Cuba.[9] For its part, Germany also developed a strong economic relationship with Brazil, Argentina, Mexico, and Venezuela—these four countries accounted for over $3 billion in 1979 or 70 percent of German exports to the region.[10] More notably, through 1979, 47 percent of German foreign investment in developing countries was in Latin America.[11]

The Europeans have viewed Latin America from a perspective

that mixes conviction with convenience. On the one hand, there is the sense that Latin America is perhaps the most "European" area in the third world, with institutions and attitudes that in many respects resemble those of southern European countries. Latin America confronts many of the same problems they experienced in the late nineteenth and early twentieth centuries. The role of the state and of the Catholic Church in Latin American societies certainly parallels the southern European experience. Europeans view the establishment of closer relations with Latin America as a way to modify the bipolar logic of the international system and to increase the autonomy of both regions. Criticism of American policy toward El Salvador and Nicaragua as well as of American "cultural imperialism" (the latter, a chord struck by French Minister of Culture Jack Lang at the July 1982 meeting of the United Nations Educational, Scientific, and Cultural Organization in Mexico City and by the Socialist head of the Spanish Instituto de Cooperación Iberoamericana in early 1983) can occasionally provide a useful diversion from domestic problems and pacify leftists who could otherwise criticize the reformist behavior of Socialist parties at home.

Latin America's transformation from a safe, strategic rearguard of the United States to an area increasingly susceptible to non-American influence, both economic and political, emboldened the Europeans. The Cuban Revolution opened the door to large-scale Soviet activity in the hemisphere and provided an example of a successful nationalist movement that could, despite its new dependence on the Soviet Union, flout the United States. The resurgence of Latin American nationalism during the 1960s and 1970s further weakened the role of the United States in the inter-American system. The emergence of middle subregional powers such as Mexico, Brazil, Venezuela, and Argentina testified not only to the weakening of the old inter-American systems but also to the growing multipolarity of the international one.

Latin America's economic and trade relations diversified in the process. While the United States remained a major trading partner, its proportion of manufactured exports dropped for Central and South America between 1970 and 1978.[12] By the late 1960s, private nongovernment institutions and international organizations were providing more loans and economic assistance to Latin America than was the United States. The establishment of closer Latin American economic links with Western Europe and Japan further weakened the U.S. presence. On the other hand, the decay of powerful political and social institutions (the most striking example of which has been the realignment of important sectors linked to the Catholic Church) undermined traditional domestic power structures and broadened the possibilities for domestic change. For modernizing Latin American elites, the European connection promised an alternative source of economic capital and greater political flexibility to be used in lessening the influence of the United States.

II

The triangular relationship between the United States, Western Europe, and Latin America has been strongly affected by the shift from bipolarity in the international system as well as by the growing political and economic ties between Latin America and Western Europe. Current European Socialist efforts in Latin America—and particularly the role that Socialist parties have played in Central America—is part of this phenomenon.

European Socialists share certain attitudes about the third world and the United States that have special relevance for Latin America. They believe that: (1) narrowing the gap between the rich and the poor nations has become "the social question of the [twentieth] century";[13] (2) the United States does not understand (or, in its more extreme form, cannot and will not understand) what is happening in the third world; (3) many conflicts in the third world are locally generated and result from indigenous social and economic causes; (4) the United States is eager to bring the East-West conflict into third-world arenas in part because it is eager to reassert its faltering hegemony over the Western alliance; and (5) East-West confrontations in the third world will torpedo vital negotiations over arms control and disarmament, ultimately weakening Europe.

The European Socialist and Social Democratic parties with which we are concerned—the Spanish PSOE, the French PS, and the German SPD—do not all hold these views with the same intensity; nor do they approach the United States and Latin America in the same way. A number of factors condition their specific policies. Most are obvious. It matters, for example, whether a given party is in the government or in the opposition or whether it rules in a coalition. Significant, too, is the party's degree of ideological and political cohesion and the traditions out of which it operates. There is, moreover, the question of how deep a party's ties are to Latin America as well as of the instruments at its disposal for exercising influence in the region. Finally, the nature of the party's (and its country's) relationship to the United States is important and affects both its outlook and the American position.

The PSOE and its First Secretary Felipe González have become prominent figures on the Latin American scene in the past decade.

Because of its own experience under Francisco Franco's nearly forty-year dictatorship and the role it played during the transition to democracy, the PSOE has felt a special responsibility for contributing to the democratization of those Latin American countries ruled by authoritarian regimes. The Socialists partake of a longstanding Spanish desire (whether expressed in the form of a neocolonialist concept of *hispanidad* under Franco's dictatorship or in its more recent variant of *hispanismo democrático*) to extend Spain's cultural and political influence in the New World. There is, of course, a commercial dimension to this nascent relationship, as is suggested by the sizable investments and loans Spain has made in several Latin American countries since the early 1970s. For the Spanish Socialists, however, the political dimension is the more important, with Latin America providing an opportunity for the Spanish to assert and confirm the historical importance of their own accomplishment.

The PSOE's foreign policy operates in a domestic environment that is marked by a tradition of isolation and isolationism, growing Europeanization, latent anti-Americanism, and a desire to function as a bridge to the third world.[14] Prior to reaching power the PSOE emphasized its strong "neutralist" convictions, and numerous statements by Socialist spokesmen contained sharp criticisms of the United States. By the October 1982 election, the party significantly moderated its foreign policy rhetoric and, since then, has pursued very pragmatic international policies. Felipe González, who, since the twenty-ninth PSOE congress in September 1979, has been the unchallenged leader of his party and the architect of its foreign policy, has played a key role in this moderation.

González's authority is enhanced because the PSOE, having won a majority of 202 out of 350 seats in the October 1982 elections to the Spanish Congress of Deputies, need not accommodate itself to any coalition partner. González has been especially active with respect to Latin America, visiting the region more than a dozen times since 1976 and heading the Socialist International's Committee for the Defense of the Nicaraguan Revolution. Generally speaking, González and the PSOE have been critical of U.S. policies in Central America, but by expressing his opinions without virulence and understanding U.S. concerns about the militarization of Nicaragua, González has earned the grudging respect of the Reagan administration and has been a valuable interlocutor for both Secretaries of State Alexander Haig and George Shultz.

Under the Socialists, Spain has become quite active in Central America. González has traveled to the region, urging convocation of a regional peace conference and the establishment of multilateral development projects there. There was a flurry of diplomatic activity in early 1983 involving the Spanish government, which included Assistant Secretary of State Thomas Enders' unauthorized effort to sound out González on his willingness to play a role in facilitating negotiations in El Salvador.

Nevertheless, although flattered by the attention and eager to extend Spanish influence and prestige, the González government has been careful about its involvement in Central American issues. For one thing, influence develops only slowly, and the danger exists that too prominent a role could lead countries in the region to resent the Spanish presence. An overly assertive posture could also bring Spain into conflict with the United States, something the González government wishes to avoid given the fragility of Spanish democracy and the sensitive foreign policy issues (such as Spanish participation in the North Atlantic Treaty Organization, the Gibraltar question, and the defense of Ceuta and Melilla from possible Moroccan attack) that Spain must address in the next few years.

Spain also lacks the instruments to influence events in Central America decisively. The Instituto de Cooperación Iberoamericana, for example, now under the direction of former PSOE Foreign Relations Secretary Luis Yañez, would like to develop a major presence in Latin America, but the budget of this government-run department is quite low; it totaled less than $13 million in 1982, 60 percent of which was spent on administrative costs in Spain itself.[15] Having been clandestine for a long time, moreover, the PSOE has no strong institutional ties with parties outside the European continent.

A second European Socialist actor of significance in Central America has been the French Socialist party. The PS came to power in mid-1981, when François Mitterrand won election as president and dissolved the legislature. Thereupon, his party won an absolute majority of the seats in the National Assembly. The French Socialists came to power in a context deeply marked by the Gaullist presidential style and by the ideological nature of French politics. Socialist doctrine called for the radical restructuring of the international economic system as well as the gestation of a new internationalism based on solidarity with "oppressed" and "progressive" peoples.[16] To many French Socialists, the United States was in fundamental opposition to these policy directions and, almost as noxiously, was the purveyor of an international consumerist and philistine culture. Once in power, however, the Socialists have pursued an increasingly Atlanticist foreign policy—to the point, that during Mitterrand's address to the German Bundestag in January 1983, he warned Germany to resist neutralist temptations and to remain strongly tied to the Atlantic alliance.

The Mitterrand government has given a more radical flavor to French policy on third-world issues, but even here, despite the use of more radical, romantic rhetoric, there have not been many significant policy departures. France, for example, favors a "planetary new deal" to develop the countries of the South and has called for the creation of an international energy agency, the restructuring of lending agencies and requirements, and a stabilization of commodity prices.[17] These demands have found an echo in a number of Latin American countries. And yet, though Mitterrand's government has sought to develop closer economic ties with Mexico and Venezuela, the French economic relationship with Latin America has not been especially strong. Although the volume of French exports to Latin America has increased during the past decade, French trade with the region represents a very small part ($686 million or 3.6 percent in 1980) of France's total trade volume,[18] and Latin America's share of French trade with less developed countries is much lower than the European Community average.[19] In contrast to West Germany, which has diversified its official development aid in Latin America, France directs over 90 percent of its aid to overseas departments such as Martinique and Guadeloupe.[20] The strongest trade link that the French have established with Latin America is in the area of arms sales with the performance of the Exocet missiles and the Super Etendard fighter aircraft in the Falklands War already resulting in increased sales.

France has much stronger political and ideological ties with Latin America. French ideology (and particularly the traditions arising out of the French Revolution) have had an important effect on Latin American political discourse and culture. Mitterrand played to this revolutionary myth in his October 1981 speech in Mexico City:

> To all combatants for liberty, France sends its message of hope. She sends her salute to men, women and even children who . . . in this moment fall throughout the world for a noble ideal. Salutations to the humiliated, to the emigrés, to the exiles in their own lands who want to live, to live free. . . . To all France says: Courage! Liberty shall overcome.[21]

This speech, such symbolic gestures as seating Salvador Allende's widow in a prominent place during Mitterrand's inauguration, the appointment of Régis Debray as personal adviser to the president, and other more concrete political acts—such as the Franco-Mexican declaration on El Salvador—are indicative of French interest in exercising greater political influence in Latin America. The region is an area of ideological but not excessively practical concern for the French Socialists, however. Ongoing cultural programs sponsored by the Alliance Française are one way of extending French influence in the region, but more explicitly political instruments and vehicles (such as those available to the SPD) have been lacking.

Although some French Socialists hope to promote changes that will dramatically diminish U.S. influence in the third world, others are equally, if not more concerned with Soviet expansionism in the third world. As we shall discuss later in this chapter, the tone of French Socialist statements on Central America changed after less than a year in power. In part this reflected the French Socialist fear that the United States, if dragged further into the Central American morass, would become distracted from the more important task of redressing the strategic imbalance in Western Europe. The support of French Socialists for Great Britain during the Falkland Islands crisis and their disagreement with Socialist International calls for Puerto Rican independence also suggest the limits to an excessively ideological posture by the PS. Both cases involved a "colonial" problem for a French ally. In both cases, the Socialists were setting precedents for the defense of their own "colonial" enclaves in various parts of the world, particularly in the Caribbean.[22]

The Spanish and French Socialist parties thus share a number of characteristics. With respect to foreign policy issues, both parties are strongly nationalistic (though the French party is more vehement in its views than the Spanish and has a better articulated view of what France's role in the world should be) and incline toward "third-worldist" rhetoric. The PS and the PSOE have only recently come to power, however, and neither has had a very significant role in shaping foreign policy over the past quarter century. Their lack of government responsibility and the absence of public funding for international activities have meant that these two parties have had a limited effect beyond their borders.[23]

More central and significant in extending European Socialist influence in Latin America has been the work of the German Social Democratic party. When Helmut Schmidt lost a motion of confidence vote in October 1982, the SPD lost the dominant role it had had in German politics since the late 1960s. During that period, Germany under SPD leadership had become increasingly assertive in international affairs, both economically and politically. Catapulted to a position of preeminence in the world economy by 1980, the Federal Republic of Germany had become the second largest exporter in the world behind the

United States, with 62.4 percent of its trade going to less developed countries. Germany embarked on an ambitious program to expand its markets and influence: Official development assistance reached $3.35 billion (with an additional $3.43 billion from private sources) and investments in foreign countries reached DM 18 billion in 1979.[24] German economic involvement in Latin America grew substantially, with nearly half of German private investment in the third world since the mid-1950s directed to Latin America. Ironically, German economic expansion also increased its vulnerability and dependence on foreign trade as well as supplies of raw materials: These became important considerations in determining the country's foreign policy.

The expansion of German influence abroad also had a distinct political dimension. The Federal Republic of Germany and the SPD took the lead in developing relations with Eastern Europe and the Soviet Union (what became known as *Ostpolitik*) and became driving forces behind an energized European Economic Community; they played a prominent role during the transitions to democracy in Spain and in Portugal. From its vantage point as a party of government, the SPD used German state influence to encourage reformist elements in both countries (Helmut Schmidt, for example, dealt directly with King Juan Carlos and Premier Adolfo Suárez at various points during the transition) and in 1975 put together an emergency economic package for Portugal totaling $750 million. The SPD was also active in funding and developing the organizational infrastructure for the Spanish and Portuguese Socialist parties—the latter having the distinction of having been founded in October 1973 at a Friedrich Ebert-Stiftung school outside of Bonn. Its success in the Iberian peninsula encouraged the SPD's political activism in other parts of the world, notably in Latin America.

During the 1970s, there emerged within the SPD three distinct orientations with respect to the third-world issues. The first, associated with Schmidt and Georg Leber, was dominant in a coalition government that included the Free Democrats; it had a moderately conservative orientation and opposed those formulas—indexation, debt moratoria, and the like—which were at the core of demands for a new international economic order.[25] Their approach was to isolate third-world conflicts so that these did not affect the global balance and to provide political and development assistance to countries as a way of stabilizing their political and social situations. Achieving the latter objective necessitated, in their view, a certain openness (though certainly not naiveté) toward revolutionary movements in the third world, with a view to dissuade their more "moderate" elements from aligning with the Soviet bloc. Because there were groups in the third

263

world with whom the United States could not or would not establish ties, Germany could play a useful role in reaching out to them.

The second group crystallized around former Chancellor and Nobel laureate Willy Brandt and included (at the risk of some oversimplification) individuals such as Egon Bahr and Uwe Holtz. Broadly speaking, this group felt a much greater urgency about North-South issues—Brandt himself chaired the Independent Commission on International Development Issues, which published the famous *North-South: A Programme for Survival*—and they chafed under what was perceived as the superpowers' intention to hold Germany and other countries hostage to their hegemonic ambitions.[26] This group was especially active in articulating development policy for the SPD and used the Socialist International, of which Brandt was president after 1976, as a forum for galvanizing world public opinion in favor of global negotiations.[27] Egon Bahr expressed their position on political change in the third world thus:

> The SPD is for supporting liberation movements that obviously are supported by the populace or that are recognized by the United Nations as spokesmen for those concerned. These movements deserve not only humanitarian but also political and economic aid—with the consideration in mind that training which is provided behind the battle lines often is important in discharging future responsibilities. Here we need to realize that even given a clear delineation that rules out weapons and munitions, any other commodity or any financial aid facilitates the armed struggle. But that is the point of support in a battle, to assert the hitherto-withheld human rights of the majority.[28]

An even more aggressive perspective on third-world issues was to be found among the neo-Marxist elements close to the SPD and its youth branch, the JUSOS, which endorsed the dependency school argument about U.S. imperialism.[29] Their political importance was slight, but as the factional squabbling within the SPD intensified during the late 1970s and a neutralist movement developed in Germany, they gained ground in some local SPD organizations and became especially vocal in expressing their opposition to American policy in Central America.

The divisions within the SPD, German economic interests, and the demands of a coalition government led the German government to adopt differing postures with respect to Latin America. There was, for example, an emphasis on developing economic ties with a number of countries in the region, most especially Brazil, with whom the

Federal Republic of Germany signed a $5.5 billion nuclear power plant contract in 1975. With respect to Central America, the German government approved an aid program to the Sandinista government immediately after the fall of Somoza and suspended approximately $14 million in aid to El Salvador in early 1980 on the grounds that the safety of German administrators involved in the projects could not be guaranteed. The latter measure provoked a row between the Foreign Ministry (headed by Free Democrat Hans Dietrich Genscher), which urged resumption of the aid, and the Overseas Development Ministry, whose director, Rainer Offergeld, opposed it.[30] There the issue remained until the SPD left the government in October 1982. Schmidt, for his part, never became overly involved in the debate. Asked his opinion of the crisis in Central America, Schmidt laconically replied:

> It is a regional crisis with factors connected with the cold war. Soviet influence in Cuba and Cuban influence in Central America should not be underestimated. But I really do not want to become involved in that question. I have too many problems to become involved in other people's.[31]

The SPD has had several vehicles other than the government for exercising political influence in Latin America. One such instrument was the Friedrich Ebert Stiftung, one of several German foundations with ties to specific political parties. As part of an official effort to encourage a private role in domestic and foreign policy, these organizations—and others, such as churches—receive funds directly from the government for their activities. The Ebert Stiftung is closely, if unofficially, tied to the SPD, and the members of its board of directors (chaired by Heinz Kühn, former member of the SPD presidium and former ministerpräsident of the North Rhineland-Westphalia government) are either party or trade union activists.[32]

With over two hundred collaborators worldwide and a 1980 budget of approximately $75 million (of which nearly half went for international projects), the Ebert Stiftung has an international presence which rivals that of many foreign ministries. Because it is a private foundation and is not required, according to German law, to publish detailed annual reports, the Ebert Stiftung's activities are shrouded in secrecy. One of its avowed objectives in Latin America is to develop ties with "parties of Social Democratic tendencies" and unions that have "a minimum of independence and maneuvering room."[33] Its principal activities consist of channeling funds from the SPD to sister parties in the region (this is done either directly or by asking Latin Americans who become involved in a project under foundation auspices to become consultants) and of sponsoring conferences and seminars at various schools it has in Costa Rica, Venezuela, Ecuador, and Brazil. There, trade union and party activists receive political and ideological training. The formal Ebert Stiftung budget for Latin American activities is estimated at over $7 million annually, the bulk of which goes for approximately fifty annual meetings (lasting from a few days to a week) involving some two thousand people held at the Centro de Estudios Democráticos de América Latina (CEDAL). The Ebert Stiftung provides financial and organizational support for branches of the Instituto Latinoamericano de Investigaciones Sociales and for the Asociación Latinoamericana de Derechos Humanos headquartered in Quito. Among its other activities, the foundation publishes the journal *Nueva Sociedad*, which describes itself as a "magazine open to all currents of progressive thought . . . advocat[ing] the development of political, economic and social democracy."

The most problematic aspect of the Ebert Stiftung's activities in Latin America has been its financial support for groups (such as the Frente Sandinista in 1978–1979)[34] which, although fighting against odious dictatorships, could hardly be described as having a "social democratic" orientation. A similar criticism may be made with respect to those invited to several conferences that the foundation sponsored in Costa Rica. *Nueva Sociedad* has also made its pages available to views that are certainly not in the mainstream of "social democratic" thought. Thus, for example, the report it published at the conclusion of a Seminar on International Security with the Nicaraguan People in May 1979 not only called for "unity" between democratic and non-democratic elements of the Latin American left (an idea that the SPD would hardly endorse in West Germany) but also pointedly excluded Cuba from the list of those countries in the Caribbean region that "suffered from open or covert dictatorships."[35]

CEDAL and the other institutes as well as *Nueva Sociedad* provided forums for establishing indirect contacts with a wide range of individuals and groups with whom the German government or the SPD might prefer not to develop direct relations. To many in the SPD, this indirect approach made tactical sense (especially since the Ebert Stiftung is not only independent of the government but also once removed from the SPD as well) and could pay longer-term dividends in moderating groups that were not as radical and undemocratic as they might at first glance appear. But there are significant dangers inherent in this approach as well. For one thing, it presumes a substantial knowledge and understanding of Latin American realities. What is more, legitimating groups with which social democracy had little, if anything, in common obviously weakens the democratic left and sows ideological confusion in its ranks.

Another nongovernment institution used by the SPD in its quest for greater international influence was the Socialist International, a descendant of the nineteenth-century International Workingman's Association once headed by Karl Marx.[36] A loosely organized "association" which, in distinction to the Communist International, did not seek to impose a common policy or orientation on its member parties, the Socialist International languished during much of the 1960s, retaining its preeminently European character.

This began to change in the early 1970s, however, as the SPD became more prominent in European affairs and itself developed an interest in the Socialist International. The election of Willy Brandt as president of the Socialist International in November 1976 was a major turning point for the organization. Henceforth, in the words of Richard Löwenthal, "it endeavor[ed] systematically to become relevant for the Third World and its problems."[37] Brandt impelled this quest for "relevance." Under his mandate, the Socialist International became "internationalized": It sent fact-finding missions to the Middle East and southern Africa, tried to mobilize world public opinion on disarmament and North-South issues, became increasingly critical of American foreign policy toward the third world, and took steps to attract members outside of Western Europe.

Although several Latin American parties (such historical mainstays of the regional democratic left as Acción Democrática in Venezuela, and the Partido de Liberación Nacional in Costa Rica) had been admitted to "observer" status at the May 1966 Socialist International Congress, the Socialist International was not very visible in Latin America until the mid-1970s. By then, the SPD's growing international assertiveness, the role Social Democratic parties played in the transitions to democracy in Spain and Portugal, and the emergence of Mexico and Venezuela as wealthy oil producers (and of their respective parties, the Partido Revolucionario Institucionalizado, PRI, and Acción Democrática, AD, as regional powerbrokers) opened up new opportunities.

An important first move in expanding the Socialist International's presence in Latin America came in May 1976 at a meeting in Caracas (called the Reunión de Dirigentes Políticos de Europa y América en Pro de la Solidaridad Democrática Internacional) hosted by AD.[38] The meeting had no formal connection with the Socialist International, but thirteen Socialist International and European Social Democratic leaders were present. They and the representatives of sixteen political parties and movements from Latin America (among them the Mexican PRI, the Argentine Radicals, and a faction of the Liberal party in Colombia) issued a statement that, while not mentioning socialism as a goal, did insist that "the ideals of justice and solidarity required concerted action by our parties in Latin America and Europe."

Brandt, Portuguese Socialist leader Mario Soares, AD president Gonzalo Barrios, and PRI president Porfirio Muñoz Ledo then created an ad hoc committee to give organizational continuity to this effort. Several rounds of bilateral and multilateral meetings led to a March 1978 trip by Soares, who headed a thirteen-man delegation to Mexico, Jamaica, the Dominican Republic, Costa Rica, and Venezuela with the purpose of developing a comprehensive policy toward Latin America. That trip laid the groundwork for yet another conference, held in Lisbon in October 1978, whose theme was "Processes of Democratization in the Iberian Peninsula and Latin America."[39] Again, the Socialist International was not the ostensible organizer of a conference that brought together thirty-three parties, only eight of which were European, but it was the Ebert Stiftung and the SPD that provided funds to the Portuguese Socialists for the event. Among the participants at this meeting were the Movimiento Nacional Revolucionario Independiente and Movimiento de Izquierda Revolucionaria from Bolivia as well as the Frente Sandinista de Liberación Nacional from Nicaragua.

An important component of the Socialist International's strategy was the promotion of close links with the Mexican ruling party, the PRI. Its leaders participated in SI-sponsored conferences, and Willy Brandt worked to increase collaboration between his organization and the Conferencia Permanente de Partidos Políticos de América Latina (COPPPAL), the latter being an organization founded in October 1979 under the aegis of the PRI which brought together twenty-three "democratic, nationalist, socialist, and anti-imperialist" parties.[40] By joining forces with the PRI and COPPPAL (several Latin American parties belonged to both COPPPAL and the SI), the Europeans hoped to make the Socialist International a more acceptable partner for left-wing, nationalist groups in Latin America. The relationship was also useful to the PRI, increasing its visibility in the area and further legitimating its rule in Mexico.

Although the Mexicans were wary of European intentions (as many in Central America were about those of Mexico) and the PRI did not become a member of the Socialist International, Mexico had an agenda that coincided in many respects with that of the SI. Both wanted to keep the East-West conflict from becoming the principal axis of conflict in Central America and hoped to prevent overt American intervention there. Both also viewed revolutionary change in Central America (for obvious reasons, Mexico excluded Guatemala from this analysis) as necessary and inevitable. For its part, the Mexican position was the product of a unique synthesis that combined cynicism, realism, and anti-Americanism with a domestic need to appear aligned with "progressive" international causes.[41] It led the PRI under Presidents Luis Echevarría and López Portillo to identify the United States—not leftist insurgents or Cuba—as Mexico's principal adversary in the region and the weakening of American influence there as its most important objective. By discreetly supporting insurgent movements and by giving the Cubans less excuse to become involved, the Mexicans hoped to prevent overt American intervention and to insulate their country from the "revolutionary virus" sweeping the region. Because such changes would inevitably weaken U.S. influence, they would in turn increase Mexico's leverage.

This outreach effort, which aimed at expanding the influence of the Socialist International and incorporating more Latin American parties into its membership, had the desired result. Collaboration with the PRI, Venezuela's AD, and the Costa Rican PLN increased. Moreover, whereas in December 1975 the SI had three full members from Latin America, by its Vancouver congress in October 1978 the number had grown to seven (including the Movimiento Nacional Revolucionario from El Salvador), and four more full members joined in late 1980. Along with this membership expansion came a relaxation of the rules on observers and guests (with the effect that groups that stood clearly outside the Socialist International, such as the FSLN, attended most meetings after 1978) and the creation of the SI Regional Committee on Latin America and the Caribbean. The latter began to function in early 1979 under the chairmanship of José Francisco Peña Gómez, secretary general of the Partido Revolucionario Dominicanó, but with former Venezuelan President Carlos Andrés Pérez playing a key role from his position as regional vice-chairman.

III

The Socialist International's effort to expand its presence in Latin America and the Caribbean drew a favorable response from a number of center-left parties in the region. Impressed by Socialist successes in Spain and Portugal and by the vigor that Brandt was bringing to his crusade for North-South dialogue, many of these parties were also flattered that such an exclusive "first world" club as the Socialist International was now paying attention to them. Some parties viewed the SI's appearance in Latin America with special favor; AD, the PLN, and several others hoped it would provide new life to that earlier tradition of center-left transnational cooperation in which prominent personalities like Rómulo Betancourt, José Figueres, and Luis Muñoz Marín had been involved. For the most part, however, those parties that sought to develop ties with the Socialist International did so less out of ideological affinity than out of their eagerness to lessen Latin American dependence on the United States and to negate the extreme left's critique of them as pliant tools of American imperialism. With the colonial era long over and with Western Europeans in no position to impose their will, contacts that would previously have been denounced as "intervention" were now welcomed as solidarity. Individual leaders (Carlos Andrés Pérez is an example, but much the same could be said of Peña Gómez and Daniel Oduber in Costa Rica) used the SI connection to bolster their prestige and influence at home and to project themselves onto the regional and even the international scene.

As the Socialist International's involvement in Latin America increased, so did its ideological assertiveness (some described it as moral posturing) and its criticisms of U.S. policies in the region. The resolution approved at the May 1976 Caracas meeting had spoken out against "all foreign interference in matters which affect the sovereignty of peoples or obstruct their right to progress" and referred to "economic, political or ideological imperialism," but it had not mentioned the United States expressly.[42] By March 1980, when the Socialist International conference in Santo Domingo met, a distinctly anti-American tone had crept into the resolutions. The latter even warned against "any attempt through subterfuge or under different names, to keep Puerto Rico in its present colonial status. . . ."[43]

Paralleling these increasingly sharp attacks on the United States were the Socialist International's overt demonstrations of support for insurgent movements in Central America. We have already noted the admission of the MNR to the SI as well as the presence of Sandinista representatives at numerous meetings hosted by the Socialist International and/or the Ebert Stiftung. These contacts had increased as the crisis in Central America became more intense. SI declarations against the Somoza dictatorship became especially sharp edged, with an October 1978 statement (following the lead of countries like Venezuela and Costa Rica) calling for the suspension of all economic and financial assistance as well as the "elimination of all political and diplomatic support for Somoza."[44] Beginning in mid-1978, the Socialist International and its European member parties undertook to give financial and organizational support to the Sandinistas. Bruno Kreisky, premier of Austria, headed the national Committee of Solidarity with Nicaragua; and at the Ebert Stiftung's school in Costa Rica, the Sandinistas prepared their blueprint for government. Shortly after Somoza's downfall, an SI delegation headed by Soares visited Nicaragua, where it expressed "unconditional political and material solidarity" with the new regime.[45] The Socialist International followed up this demonstration of support at its 1980 Madrid congress by creating a Committee in Defense of the Nicaraguan Revolution under the direction of PSOE First Secretary Felipe González.

The Socialist International saw the Somoza overthrow as opening up possibilities for the democratization "not only of Nicaragua but of the whole of Central America."[46] Convinced that radical change was sweeping the region, the SI became an active supporter of revolution in Guatemala and El Salvador. Whereas at the SI 1978 congress there had been no explicit mention of El Salvador, by mid-1980 that country received prominent treatment. The MNR had in the meantime withdrawn from the Salvadoran junta in December 1979, with Guillermo Ungo and his collaborators charging that, with the military condoning right-wing violence and with the government powerless to stop it, a reformist strategy would not work in El Salvador. The March 1980 SI regional conference held in Santo Domingo then adopted a resolution condemning the junta's program of "reforms and repression."[47] A few months later with the MNR participating in the Frente Democratico Revolucionario (a political front allied to the guerrilla umbrella organization, the Farabundo Marti Front for National Liberation, or FMLN) the Socialist International became more explicit. At its Oslo bureau meeting in June, the SI indicated it "fully support[ed] the struggle of the FDR for freedom and democracy in El Salvador" and declared that "U.S. support for the present junta is not a viable solution and will not prevent further bloodshed."[48] By late 1980, the SI's rhetoric had become even sharper; it described the junta as "a despotic regime whose activities [had] led to a state of civil war" and, paralleling its earlier statements of support for the Sandinistas, the SI pointedly called for "*active* solidarity [emphasis supplied]" with the FDR.[49]

There was an ideological matrix which, though not universally shared, (and, as time went by and the stakes in Central America increased, a number of moderate Latin American as well as European Socialist parties made their differences more explicit) undergirded these positions.[50] Its proponents represented the left wing of international social democracy. They believed that the path to reform in Central America (and perhaps elsewhere on the continent) had been decisively blocked. Neither the incorporation of the traditional right into democratic politics nor the professionalization of the armed forces was possible. U.S. support for the "moderate" solution was not only utopian but would also in the end strengthen the more radical guerrilla elements while increasing the likelihood of Cuban intervention.

The United States, according to this view, should simply learn to live with radical change. The democratic left in these countries (parties like the MNR in El Salvador or the PSD in Guatemala) had to resort to violence, and there was no alternative to their collaborating with the Communists and other groups farther to their left; the exigencies of resistance to quasi-fascist regimes demanded it. Many erstwhile Marxist radicals were either capable of being turned around to more "democratic" views or, fearing a national and international backlash, could be persuaded to "honor their commitments . . . to respect pluralism [and] the mixed economy." [51] To press for greater assurances, however, would be counterproductive, lessening what "credibility" the Socialist International (and its member parties) had developed among leftists in Latin America.

From this perspective, the Cuban role in Latin America had to be reappraised. Cuba, one prominent Swedish Social Democrat insisted, "constitutes a factor of moderation in [the region]." It had not "for many years provid[ed] military support in Latin America"; and, where the Cubans had intervened (as in Africa), "the sins of colonial Europe and of the Western powers [had] created the need for external aid." [52]

Linked to this was an argument about the nature of democracy in the third world. It was not definable in terms of parliamentary rule, checks and balances, or based on institutional electoral uncertainty. Democracy, rather more simply and vaguely, should be based "on legality and on the respect for human rights." [53] Single-party states (such as the one that might develop in Nicaragua under the FSLN) were not by definition undemocratic, since the "Westminster" model of parliamentary democracy was inapplicable to most third-world countries.

The Socialist International's growing involvement in Central America provoked much criticism in the United States (both within and outside the government) and did little to further American relations with the SPD-led West German government. At one level, the position of the Carter administration toward Latin America was not so different from that of the SI: In a memorandum sent to a number of embassies in mid-1980, the Carter administration argued that since "change [in the region] was . . . both natural and inevitable," the United States should "define itself as the ally of progressive, democratic forces." There was, it said, "considerable uncertainty as to [Nicaragua's] ultimate direction, [but] the withdrawal of support by Western democracies and [the] failure to assist the government financially could guarantee a Cuba-style dependence on Soviet assistance and ensuing Soviet-backed adventurism from a Central American base." [54]

Where the Carter administration parted company with SI was in the analysis it made of the situation in El Salvador.[55] The situation there had deteriorated in early 1980 with the resignation of the MNR representatives from the junta and with mass demonstrations sponsored by the newly formed Coordinadora Revolucionaria de Masas. In the ensuing weeks, even as the new junta was announcing a program of structural reforms to include land reform and the nationalization of the banking system, the spiral of violence continued. Several European countries (among them West Germany) withdrew their diplomatic representatives and suspended development assistance projects, and the Socialist International stepped up its criticism of the Salvadoran regime.

The Carter administration had viewed the evolving SI position and European Socialist support for the FSLN in Nicaragua with misgiving; it reacted to the hardening SI position on El Salvador (as manifested publicly in the March 1980 Santo Domingo Declaration) by expressing its deep concern to several Latin American and European parties with whom the United States had close relations. The SPD came under particular pressure.[56] Just before the 1980 Santo Domingo SI meeting, Ambassador Walter Stoessel had a lengthy interview with Willy Brandt. Thereafter, expressions of concern were relayed to Chancellor Schmidt and Foreign Minister Genscher and in July 1980 then SPD Vice-Chairman Hans-Jürgen Wischnewski, a close aide to Schmidt, traveled to Washington and discussed the issue with National Security Adviser Zbigniew Brzezinski.[57]

The effect the Carter administration's efforts had on the SPD and the German government is difficult to assess. More moderate elements like Genscher, who were in any case amenable to being convinced, urged a resumption of aid to El Salvador.[58] But the effort to change the German government's policy bore little fruit. Schmidt could not (and perhaps would not) impose such a course on his increasingly divided party. Although it would yet win a landslide victory in the October 1980 Bundestag elections, the SPD had become increasingly factionalized. Many in the SPD were disdainful of the Carter administration; the more leftist among them, already bristling over American policy on East-West issues as these affected Western Europe, were even less ready to support the United States on El Salvador.

The SPD's relationship with the Socialist International had also changed in the years since Brandt became president. The SI's organizational expansion in Latin America had occurred with the support of a significant part of the SPD. But as the Socialist International expanded, it became much more diffuse organizationally. The Latin

American parties, once peripheral, had become by the late 1970s an increasingly autonomous force within the organization—to the point that it was they who became responsible for the formulation of SI statements on Central American issues.

Although the SPD remained a major force within the Socialist International, other European Socialist parties were also gaining international prominence. An especially competitive relationship developed between the SPD and the French Socialists once the latter emerged as a major national force in the late 1970s.[59] The Mitterrand victory in May 1981 occurred as the fortunes of the SPD entered a sharp decline, and divergences between the two parties became more evident once Mitterrand took power. The French Socialist party viewed the SI as a vehicle employed by the SPD for extending German influence in Latin America. They found the Socialist International's accommodation to "anticolonialist" movements in the Caribbean particularly worrisome. Prodded by this concern and eager to act as a counterweight to the SPD, once in power the French Socialists became more active in the Socialist International, urging a tightening of criteria for membership in the organization and a reduction in the autonomy of the Regional Committee for Latin America and the Caribbean.

European Socialist involvement in Central American issues intensified after Ronald Reagan's election to the presidency of the United States. The European Socialists viewed the incoming administration and its promise of a more competitive relationship with the Soviet Union with dismay. Fearful of the consequences that a sharp escalation of tensions would have internationally, many of them also believed that the return to confrontation advocated by the new administration (even if justified to some extent by Soviet behavior in the third world since the mid-1970s) betokened an unspoken strategy aimed at reasserting American hegemony over an increasingly independent Western Europe. What was at stake, as the Final Resolution of the November 1980 Socialist International congress declared, was nothing less than Western Europe's capacity for developing "its own interests and responsibilities in all spheres."[60]

To many European Socialists, the Reagan administration's argument that instability in Central America and the Caribbean had been caused or catalyzed by Soviet- and Cuban-sponsored subversion (and because of this East-West dimension threatened vital American and, indirectly, European security interests) was not only analytically incorrect but also threatened to undo the patient European Socialist efforts during the previous decade to flesh out a "third way." Acquiescence to (much less support for) the Reagan administration's policies in Central America would undermine the credibility of their efforts to build bridges to and establish ties with left-wing Latin American parties.

European Socialist leaders, themselves confronted by restive left-wing elements for whom American behavior in Central America was reminiscent of Vietnam and comparable to Soviet intervention in Afghanistan and Poland, were unconvinced that a military solution was at all possible in the region without the massive commitment of American troops—a course that was of itself undesirable. For them, a negotiated settlement in El Salvador and U.S. accommodation to Nicaragua were the only realistic alternatives. Numerous European Socialist leaders and Socialist International missions traveled to Central America during the first year of the Reagan administration hoping to attain these objectives.

European Socialist efforts to mediate in the Central American conflict occurred against a backdrop of a sharply deteriorating situation in El Salvador, where the guerrillas had launched a "final offensive" in January 1981. Undertaken in the last weeks of the Carter administration, its objective was to bring about a decisive shift in the balance of power in El Salvador, handing a *fait accompli* to the incoming Reagan administration. Responding to this crisis, President Carter announced the resumption of arms shipments to El Salvador, which had been suspended after the assassination of three American nuns and a layworker in early December 1980. The Reagan administration endorsed the arms shipments, itself substantially increasing military and economic aid to El Salvador several weeks after taking office in response to what the administration described as a "textbook case of indirect Communist aggression." Opposed to negotiations with the guerrillas, the new administration favored elections, in which the opposition could participate, as the vehicle for ending the Salvadoran civil war. Distrustful of Sandinista intentions and angered by Nicaraguan support for the guerrillas in El Salvador, American policy makers hardened their line toward Nicaragua, also suspending economic aid in April 1981.

At its November 1980 congress, the Socialist International had endorsed the Salvadoran MNR and lauded "the victory and the accomplishments of the Nicaraguan revolution [as] reflect[ing] our hopes for social change in the entire region,"[61] but its real *mise en scene* in Central America came with the launching of the January rebel offensive in El Salvador when a few days after Reagan's inauguration, SI President Brandt and Secretary General Bernt Carlssen issued a statement that not only reiterated their support for the MNR (and more broadly the FDR) but also endorsed "revolutionary change" in

El Salvador, now that "all attempts at peaceful political change had been blocked by violence and fraud."[62] A subsequent statement issued at the March 1981 meeting of the SI's Regional Committee for Latin America and the Caribbean described the FDR as "*the* legitimate representative of the Salvadoran people" [emphasis supplied][63] and then later in the year, the SI bureau pointedly referred to the FMLN guerrilla coalition as "an important political representative force" which should participate in any "comprehensive political solution" and attacked the United States for engaging in "military intervention [that] only leads to further terror and death."[64]

Joined to this rhetoric was the Socialist International's oft-repeated offer to act as a mediator in bilateral and multilateral negotiations between the United States and the Salvadoran junta on the one hand, and the FDR/FMLN and the Sandinistas in Nicaragua on the other.

There were three prominent mediation efforts during the first half of 1981. One involved the SPD-led West German government. This initiative featured an effort by Brandt and other SPD figures—themselves in touch with the German Christian Democratic Union (which had long provided political and financial support to the Salvadoran Christian Democrats) and Italian Christian Democratic leader Mariano Rumor—to bring about a face-to-face meeting between Guillermo Ungo and José Napoleón Duarte.[65] Shortly thereafter, the SI's Regional Committee for Latin America and the Caribbean asked Brandt to offer himself directly to President Reagan as a mediator in the conflict.[66]

Hans-Jürgen Wischnewski, vice-chairman of the SPD and an individual with a knack, one German newspaper said, for "tackl[ing] problems without an ideological bias,"[67] headed up the second mediation effort, traveling to Central America, Mexico, and Cuba in March 1981. During discussions with Salvadoran Foreign Minister Fidel Chavez Mena, he presented a negotiating proposal on the FDR's behalf, as well as a West German offer to sponsor private talks between the two sides. Wischnewski's visit to Cuba included a lengthy conversation with Fidel Castro. Castro apparently surprised the West German leader by confirming that Cuba had indeed supplied arms and war materiel to the Salvadoran guerrillas. He further noted that, if asked, Cuba would continue its aid. Failure of the Wischnewski mission did not deter a third initiative—led by Edward Broadbent of Canada's New Democratic party, in late May 1981—which also failed.[68]

European Socialist efforts to mediate in the Central American crisis during the first year of the Reagan administration were unsuccessful. That failure occurred as the SI and its member parties, while offering their services as mediators were at the same time increasingly involved participants in the dispute. As a result, they had only slight leverage over the FDR/FMLN and the Sandinistas and were, in some respects, themselves susceptible to pressure from those organizations.

In El Salvador, for example, the Socialist International used its influence with the MNR to convince the FDR/FMLN to drop its demand for direct negotiations with the United States (and to accept Duarte and other members of the junta as valid interlocutors), but it could not budge the hardliners on the FDR/FMLN's Political-Diplomatic Committee on a far more crucial issue: to agree, as the democratic elements supporting the junta asked, to a cease-fire before negotiations were begun. Moreover, while membership in the Socialist International gave the MNR clout in the FDR and with the FMLN, it also had a less favorable effect. Precisely because the MNR was a "valued" SI member, the Socialist International found itself endorsing positions adopted by the FDR/FMLN to which the MNR had agreed.

The dilemma facing the SI in Nicaragua was even sharper. Having played an important role in legitimating the Sandinistas before world public opinion, the Socialist International and its member parties were uneasy with developments in Nicaragua. Harassment of opposition leaders and the Catholic Church, media censorship and the adoption of economic measures directed specifically at the middle class, the use of aggressive Marxist-Leninist rhetoric by some Sandinista leaders, and the growing number of Cuban and East European advisers did not bode well for democracy there.[69] Many European Socialist leaders expressed their concern with these developments privately to the Sandinistas (and the SI communiqués always alluded to the need for political pluralism, a mixed economy, and nonalignment in foreign policy), but they only criticized the FSLN indirectly publicly, for fear of appearing to back the Reagan administration's policies. The Sandinistas, of course, exploited the SI's hesitation on this score, wasting no opportunity to put the Socialist International's public support on display.

Its continuing support for the FDR/FMLN and for the Sandinistas may have given the Socialist International access to and credibility with leftist movements in the region, but this also lessened its chances either for influencing American policy or for acting as a mediator in the conflict. The Reagan administration had entered office already distrustful of the SI; when some of its European member parties dismissed U.S. complaints about Soviet-Cuban involvement as mere cold war rhetoric and rejected the American strategy of isolating the guerrillas in El Salvador and the FSLN in Nicaragua, this distrust deepened. Although administration spokesmen continued to meet with SI representatives, American policy makers had virtually abandoned any hope of developing a joint strategy with the Socialist International, preferring instead to work in conjunction with Christian Democratic parties in the region, especially the Comite de Organización Política Electoral Independiente (COPEI) in Venezuela.[70]

A number of Latin American and European SI members had in the meantime begun to mark their distance from the official Socialist International position on Central America but especially on Nicaragua. The efforts of the Venezuelan Acción Democrática, the Costa Rican Partido de Liberación Nacional, and the Partido Revolucionario Dominicano of the Dominican Republic were particularly visible in this respect. AD and the PLN had had historically close ties, forged on a political and personal plane during the preceding three decades.[71] Active in the struggle for democracy and development in the Caribbean, AD and the PLN in conjunction with several other parties had organized (before the Ebert Stiftung and the AFL-CIO's American Institute for Free Labor Development had become prominent) the Inter-American Institute of Political Education in San José as a training school for party and trade union cadres. Because the two parties had been closely identified with the Latin American democratic left, their endorsement of the FSLN's struggle against Somoza in the late 1970s (they became the Sandinistas' most important suppliers of arms and materiel) had rallied many Latin Americans to the Sandinista side.

The honeymoon with the Sandinistas, however, did not last. Already in 1980, Daniel Oduber of the PLN (in conjuction with Portuguese Socialist leader Mario Soares) had lobbied within the SI to invite the Movimiento Democrático Nicaraguense led by Alfonso Robelo to become a member.[72] A few months later, the PLN formally disassociated itself from the January 1981 Socialist International statement on El Salvador. The Costa Ricans, in a pointed but indirect reference to Nicaragua, bitterly criticized the "trafficking in arms and violation of territorial sovereignty" taking place in the region. They went on:

> We support liberation movements; but in no manner do we accept, under the pretext of liberating a people, the attempt to subject them to ideologies of despotic communism or to other foreign interests. We repudiate violence in all its forms, whether of repressive military forces and of social injustice or of terrorism that causes material destruction and, more gravely, destruction of human life. In the case of Nicaragua, long tortured by dictatorship, we retain, with

profound respect for the decisions adopted by this neighboring country, the hope and the demand that its revolutionary process will be realized within the strict bounds of political and social democracy.[73]

Neither AD nor the PRD attended the July 1981 SI regional committee meeting at which Maurice Bishop (whose New Jewel Movement had joined the Socialist International in 1980) launched a vitriolic attack on the United States. Later in 1981, AD leaders talked with Ungo and Duarte in an effort to find a formula that would allow the opposition to participate in the upcoming Salvadoran elections,[74] and former Venezuelan President Carlos Andrés Pérez privately warned the Sandinistas against any further encroachments on political and civil liberties in Nicaragua. Significantly, before his death in July 1981, Panamanian leader Omar Torrijos had joined his voice to theirs in criticizing the Sandinistas as well as Castro's policies in Central America.[75]

Skepticism of the Sandinistas' intentions had also grown among European Socialist parties. Mario Soares, the Portuguese leader who had lived through a revolutionary period during which military radicals in alliance with the Communist party had tried to install a "popular democracy," had begun publicly to criticize the Sandinistas in early 1981. Soares objected to their presence as "observers" at SI meetings and urged a tougher SI line on Nicaragua. Using his party's International Affairs Foundation, he hosted Eden Pastora during the latter's visits to Western Europe in 1981 and 1982.

Because Soares had always had a reputation as a "moderate Social Democrat," however, his criticisms of the Sandinistas were not taken as seriously within the SI as those of his Iberian colleague Felipe González. González had been an early, enthusiastic supporter of the Sandinistas, becoming head of the SI's Committee for the Defense of the Nicaraguan Revolution in November 1980. His disillusionment with the Nicaraguan regime came after numerous trips to Latin America, where his Spanish background and experience allowed him to grasp the evolving situation in Central America.[76] He and Carlos Andrés Pérez visited Managua in late 1981 (shortly after the arrest of the Consejo Superior de la Empresa Privada leaders) and urged Brandt not to invite the Sandinistas to the upcoming SI meeting in Caracas. González became convinced that the more radical Sandinistas were fueling a "siege mentality" in order to consolidate their control. Although González was in close touch with Secretary of State Alexander Haig, he did not endorse American policies in Central America. Even so, the developing relationship with American representatives did encourage him to be more restrained in his public statements, making him as well somewhat sympathetic to the dilemmas facing the Reagan administration. More than other Europeans, González came to be seen as a viable interlocutor between the United States and opposition groups in Central America.

The most visible manifestation of the divergences developing within the Socialist International on Central America was the cancellation of the SI's Caracas meeting in February 1982.[77] Saying that the FSLN belonged "in another International, not ours," the host AD party refused to invite the Sandinistas. Miffed, Brandt responded by canceling the meeting, and a number of other European parties—notably the Dutch and Swedish Socialists—attacked AD (as well as the PLN and PRD) for having bowed to U.S. pressure. And yet, while it cannot be denied that American diplomats had become quite interested in SI activities since Somoza's overthrow and had intensified their contacts with moderate Latin and European parties since the Reagan administration had taken office, the position adopted by AD and a number of other parties reflected above all domestic political considerations and their very serious qualms with the course of Nicaraguan events. These parties certainly did not favor greater American military presence in the area; nor did they wish to encourage hardliners in the Reagan administration.

They did, however, want the Socialist International to increase public pressure on the Sandinistas, if only for the sake of its own self-respect. Although differences between and within the moderate forces existed on the issue of how hard to push Nicaragua, they felt that the SI had for too long been cowed into supporting the FSLN because to do otherwise was somehow to support the "enemies" of the Nicaraguan revolution. The more "progressive" groups within the SI (Michael Manley's Popular National party from Jamaica, sectors of the West German SPD, and the Swedish Social Democrats, among others) were rather more tolerant toward the Sandinistas (whom they saw as idealistic and romantic radicals), seeing U.S. policy as the villain in Latin America. Manley, of course, had had a running feud with the IMF and the United States. Some Swedish Social Democrats were reflexively neutralist and ill disposed toward the United States. And the SPD's left wing, galvanized by the peace and disarmament issue, had become quite assertive in foreign policy matters. Brandt was close to them and balked at doing anything that would appear as having been dictated by the United States. He not only was personally fond of several Sandinista leaders but also felt that direct criticisms of the FSLN would undercut much of what the Socialist International had accomplished in Latin America under his tenure.

The divisions within the Socialist International (which in some ways paralleled those that had developed over Middle East and disarmament questions) lessened its political effectiveness. So did the Reagan administration's growing activism in Central America. The broad array of initiatives undertaken by the administration in late 1981 and early 1982—which included the authorization of a $20 million program to arm and train anti-Sandinista guerrillas in November 1981; conversations between Secretary of State Alexander Haig and Cuban Vice Premier Carlos Rafael Rodríguez in Mexico at about the same time; pursuit of informal negotiation with the Cubans and Nicaraguans in March/April 1982 (and a not-so-secret meeting between Fidel Castro and General Vernon Walters in Havana); and the emphatic support given for the upcoming elections in El Salvador—underscored the importance the Reagan administration attached to developments in Central America.[78] Growing American involvement and concern narrowed considerably the role that the SI and the European Socialists could play as independent actors in the region.

Paradoxically, the diminution of the European Socialist role occurred as Central American issues were developing their own domestic momentum in Western Europe. Coupled to the equally emotional controversy over the deployment of nuclear weapons, they fueled anti-Americanism (particularly among the young) and further strained European-American relations. Seeking not to alienate domestic public opinion, many European governments—not just those in which Socialist and Social Democratic parties participated—marked their distance from the Reagan administration.[79] Most European governments, for example, voted against the United States in the United Nations' Third Committee when resolutions criticizing the Salvadoran government's handling of human rights were put forward; and only the United Kingdom voted with the United States against a January 1982 UN. General Assembly resolution that called for the suspension of aid to El Salvador. Again, of the Europeans, only the Thatcher government sent official observers to the March 1982 election in El Salvador. A similar pattern was evident in international lending agencies such as the Inter-American Development Bank, where a number of European governments supported the granting of loans and credits to the Nicaraguan government. Notably, through late 1983 no Western European country had cut off economic assistance to Nicaragua (or started it to El Salvador) in response to American requests. Those most responsive to Reagan administration arguments were the West German Christian Democrats whose government appointed an ambassador to El Salvador in November 1983 and reduced development aid to Nicaragua. Even so, both West Germany and the United Kingdom abstained (while France and Spain voted against the United States) on a United Nations General Assembly resolution condemning the October 1983 invasion of Grenada.

In an effort to accommodate the differences that had arisen among its members on Central American issues, the Socialist International coupled ambiguous and conditional statements of support for Nicaragua with calls for a negotiated settlement in El Salvador and criticism of American policies in the region. Thus, the SI presidium meeting in April 1982 declared: "The Sandinista government of Nicaragua must be supported in its commitment to pluralism and social justice, to democracy and to non-alignment and *must be supported by condemning any attempts from whatever source to de-stabilize or interfere with its sovereignty"* (emphasis supplied).[80]

At a bureau meeting in October 1982 the Socialist International ratified its "support for the *original* project of the Sandinistas for political pluralism, a mixed economy and non-alignment," and indirectly criticized the United States by "condemning the militarization of Central America and the plans for military aggression against Nicaragua and the staging of military maneuvers in the region which aggravate tensions . . ." (emphasis supplied).[81] Challenging the Reagan administration's position on the upcoming March 1982 Salvadoran elections more directly, the Socialist International insisted that "there [were] no . . . conditions for elections . . . [since these] are being held without the participation of major political forces who fear assassination if they present their names."[82]

Not surprisingly, the March 1982 elections in El Salvador elicited a negative commentary from the Socialist International. The "so-called elections," the SI presidium declared in early April, "provided no solution to the terrible ravages of the civil war. Terrorism can be eliminated and justice and peace can be achieved only by means of a comprehensive negotiated settlement involving all the political elements which will accept the democratic process. These must include the FDR/FMLN."[83] Press coverage in the United States and elsewhere focused on the statement's use of the phrase "so-called," interpreting it to imply a strong rebuke of American policy. There was undoubtably such a dimension to the statement; but equally as important, by coming out in favor of "a democratic process," the Socialist International had abandoned the revolutionary "triumphalism" shown by Brandt during the January 1981 guerrilla offensive. Although the statement called for a negotiated settlement, it was a far cry from endorsing the FDR/FMLN's claim to power.

The impressive turnout on election day (claims of fraud were never substantiated) had something to do with this. A number of

European Socialist leaders became convinced that the election showed the depth of sentiment in favor of peace and the limits of support for the guerrillas. They hoped that democratic elements on both sides would find the will to isolate the extremes and pursue negotiations. But the elections, in fact, foreclosed rather than opened these possibilities. Unexpectedly, they displaced José Napoleón Duarte and his Christian Democratic party from the center of power, shifting the balance of power to the right in El Salvador and encouraging those elements that betrayed no enthusiasm for political reform and democracy. In this, the extreme right found itself agreeing with radical guerrilla leaders who were unwilling to entertain proposals for a dialogue until they had recovered military and political momentum.

Already before the Salvadoran elections, the Socialist International and its European member parties had turned away from direct mediation efforts in Central America and toward providing behind-the-scenes support for negotiating proposals advanced by parties and governments from the region itself. Of course, collaboration among the Socialist International, the European parties, and regional groups had been ongoing. With Acción Democrática out of power in Venezuela and the Costa Rican PLN not very sympathetic to their activities, however, the Socialist International and its European member parties focused most of their attention on Mexico and the PRI. European leaders had been in close touch with the Mexicans during the various Socialist International mediating missions in early 1981; and France chose to make its first official incursion into the Central American quagmire at the hand of Mexico, signing the controversial August 1981 declaration that recognized a state of belligerence in El Salvador and declared the FDR/FMLN to be "a representative political force . . . [that should] legitimate[ly] participate in establishing the mechanisms of conciliation and negotiation."[84] But the symbiotic relationship that developed between the SI and Mexico had some less than salutary consequences, especially since the two often reinforced each other into taking more "progressive," and therefore less realistic, positions.

As the Europeans realized more and more the limits to their influence in Central America, they focused on Mexico as the cornerstone around which to pursue regional peace efforts. They may have misjudged on this score; for, while Mexico and its president José López Portillo desired such a role, they were not especially trusted by the Reagan administration. Whatever the case, the Socialist International and the European parties cooperated closely with López Portillo in early 1982 when he put forward a three-part Mexican proposal to negotiate a settlement in El Salvador and a nonaggression pact between the United States and Nicaragua, as well as to sponsor talks between Cuba and the United States.[85] As part of this effort, the Socialist International encouraged its member parties—AD and the PLN—to sign a COPPPAL-sponsored document known as the Declaration of Managua, which incorporated Nicaraguan proposals for bilateral nonaggression pacts with its neighbors and praised the Salvadoran "revolutionary and democratic" organization's desire for "a pluralist solution to the conflict." By late 1982, this initiative too had failed, victimized by Nicaraguan unwillingness to stop arms shipments to El Salvador or to engage in multilateral negotiations and by the United States' demand that these conditions be met before real negotiations were begun.

Despite this failure, the European Socialists continued to rally their efforts around region-based initiatives, supporting a new Mexican-Venezuelan proposal in October 1982 and, subsequently, the Contadora initiative that joined Venezuela, Colombia, Panama, and Mexico in the search for a negotiated solution that would secure borders and reduce foreign military presence in the area.[86] This was perhaps the most ambitious effort yet, but its chances for success were increased by the presence of several countries with which the United States had traditionally close relations and by the accession of Miguel de la Madrid to the presidency in Mexico. The latter development brought with it a less rhetorical style and a somewhat better understanding of shared U.S.-Mexican concerns with developments in Central America.

European Socialist support for such regional initiatives reflected not only a realistic assessment of the limits to their influence in Central America but growing Latin American assertiveness as well. The Falklands/Malvinas War had contributed to this process by catalyzing Latin American nationalism and driving a wedge between Europe and the New World. European support for Great Britain (over Irish and Italian opposition, the European Economic Community decreed a trade embargo against Argentina) alienated many Latin Americans, making more explicit their latent distrust of the Europeans.

The friction between Europeans and Latin Americans spilled over onto the Socialist International. In late April 1982 the SI Regional Committee for Latin America and the Caribbean had issued a first communiqué drafted by Carlos Andrés Pérez calling for mediation "to halt the war activity which was regrettably initiated by the British fleet"; it expressed "Latin America's active solidarity" with Argentina.[87] At the May 1982 bureau meeting in Helsinki, Carlos Andrés Pérez again spoke for the Latin Americans, offering a resolution approving the Argentine claim to the islands and criticizing the European Economic Community for "sanctions directed against all of Latin America." After a spirited rebuttal by French Socialist leader Lionel Jospin, who said the conflict was not a North-South issue nor one related to decolonization, the bureau approved an anodyne communiqué: "The Bureau reiterates the principle of the non-use of force as stated in the Charter of the United Nations. The use of force to solve a conflict cannot be accepted."[88] This wording artfully evaded even the question of who used force first. The matter did not end there. Political differences led to organizational disputes. The French PS and several other European parties insisted that the Regional Committee for Latin America and the Caribbean be subject to greater control by the Socialist International. But this turned out to be more a wish than an expectation, since the Latin American parties were unwilling to be reined in by the Europeans. The Falklands/Malvinas War thus compounded the earlier divisions over Central America, adding a North-South dimension to conflict with the Socialist International.

Not only had the European Socialist profile in Central America assumed a different, less assertive dimension by late 1982, but also the SPD, PS, and PSOE were themselves confronting new situations in their respective countries, with the result that their positions toward the conflict in the region had also varied. The West German Social Democrats had lost a motion-of-confidence vote in October 1982 and would lose the general election in March 1983. The party was in the opposition for the first time in sixteen years. Its ouster from the government provoked much soul-searching within the SPD, exacerbating its internal fragmentation and fueling debate over how best to recapture the political space lost on the right and left to the Christian Democrats and the antinuclear, pro-ecology party known as the Greens. With the burden of governmental responsibility lifted and its identity as an opposition party deepening, the SPD stepped up its opposition to Reagan administration policies in Western Europe and elsewhere. Linking up forces with the Evangelical churches (with whom they were often allied on the nuclear deployment issue), the SPD vigorously criticized U.S. policies in Central America, with some important party federations sponsoring solidarity campaigns under the slogan "Chile fights—Nicaragua lives" in midsummer 1983.

A different situation prevailed in France where François Mitterrand's Socialist government had abandoned much of its earlier activism and rhetoric. The Franco-Mexican declaration, Mitterrand's stirring speech on the occasion of his October 1981 visit to Mexico, and the signing of a $15.8 million arms accord with Nicaragua in December 1981 were, if not forgotten, at least not often remembered. The unfavorable reaction given by Venezuela, Colombia, and the Dominican Republic to the Franco-Mexican declaration (which they denounced as an "extremely grave precedent" and "interference" in Salvadoran affairs) had given the French government pause.[89] More important in encouraging a lowered French profile in Central America, however, was the desire not to strain relations with the United States where the Reagan administration had threatened retaliatory moves if the sale and delivery of weapons to Nicaragua were not stopped. Growing French restraint had already been visible on the occasion of the March 1982 Salvadoran election. Although the government did not heed American requests that observers be sent to monitor the vote, both it and the Socialist party handled the issue in very low-key fashion, with several party leaders conceding privately that they had overestimated the breadth of popular support for the guerrillas. In the meantime, French Socialist disenchantment with the Sandinistas was also growing and, during the July 1982 visit of Nicaraguan junta coordinator Daniel Ortega, Mitterrand bluntly demanded that the "originality of the Sandinista project" be protected and "authentic nonalignment" achieved.[90]

Although they remained critical of U.S. policies toward Central America, by early 1983 the French Socialists had too many other problems (among them, mounting economic troubles) and shared too much the Reagan administration's views on East-West issues to challenge the United States directly on questions that were, in any case, peripheral to French interests. The subtleties of the French position were aptly summarized by Foreign Minister Claude Cheysson in remarks before the National Assembly in February 1983:

> The government cannot follow the honorable member of Parliament when he recommends that more pressure be exerted on the Reagan Administration to make it change its policy in Central America. The French can, of course, deplore the fact that the trends it promotes are not taking place as rapidly as it hopes. But rather than exert pressure, it would prefer to continue its diplomatic action with respect to Washington, which it hopes to convince.[91]

Of the three parties with which we have been especially concerned in this chapter, only the Spanish Socialists were a force in the ascendant during this period. They were on their way to a stunning victory in the October 1982 parliamentary election that gave them 202 out of 350 seats in the Congress of Deputies. But the PSOE's proximity to power only increased its caution in foreign (as well as domestic) policy, and especially its desire to avoid conflict with the United States.

With González in office, Spain established a more visible presence in Latin America. During the first half of 1983, King Juan Carlos visited the region on two occasions, and both González and his foreign minister traveled there as well. Later, upon his return from an official visit to the United States, González was in almost daily contact with representatives of the Contadora group, hosting on one occasion meetings with Brandt, Carlos Andrés Pérez, Peña Gómez, José Napoleón Duarte, and Andrés Zaldívar (he was president of the Christian Democratic International) in the space of several days. While the Socialist government endorsed the Contadora initiative (the Central American crisis could be surmounted, the PSOE declared, by "change in social structures and the establishment of liberties and the principles of a representative system"),[92] it declined the role of mediator, a role for which, the Spanish government believed, Mexico and other neighboring countries were better suited. In keeping with this restrained approach, therefore, González mounted no direct challenge to Reagan administration policies in Central America, by and large limiting his criticisms to indirect references to what he termed "negative [U.S.] leadership" in Latin America.[93]

By this time, the enthusiasm that had accompanied the first European Socialist efforts in Central America had dissipated. Toward El Salvador, it had been replaced by frustration with the failure of negotiations to materialize. No European Socialist leader called for an outright guerrilla victory (in this, Nicaraguan events had provided a powerful lesson); most of them now pointedly coupled calls for negotiations in El Salvador with an endorsement of future elections to lay the foundations for a representative democracy there. The European parties continued to work at strengthening Guillermo Ungo and the MNR. By projecting him (in the words of the resolution of the April 1983 Socialist International congress) as the "leader" of the FDR, they hoped to increase his visibility and thereby his leverage with respect to the FMLN guerrilla movement.[94]

There was a glimmer of hope in midsummer 1983 that a settlement could be reached in El Salvador. The FMLN had experienced a bitter internecine struggle that left the three top leaders of one guerrilla group dead, and the victors showed a greater openness toward negotiations. Such tactical flexibility was encouraged by the Cuban and Nicaraguan governments which, themselves now subject to increasing American pressure, indicated a new willingness to refrain from supplying arms to the guerrillas. The Reagan administration was itself pursuing a two-track policy of increasing military (and economic) aid to El Salvador while encouraging conversations between the government (or, more exactly, the government-sanctioned peace commission) and the opposition.

The locus of the Central American conflict had shifted in early 1983 toward Nicaragua. The Sandinistas, although claiming that preparations were under way for elections in 1985, showed little interest in leading Nicaragua toward democracy. Curtailment of political, press, and trade union freedoms (the leaders of the Corinto port workers' union had been arrested in early June 1983 for the "crime" of disaffiliating their organization from the Sandinista-sponsored union), harassment of the Catholic Church both during and after Pope John Paul II's visit, and reliance on Cuban security and military assistance had spawned resentment and opposition among many sectors of the population.

The Reagan administration, in the meantime, stepped up its pressure on the Sandinistas. Besides reducing the Nicaraguan sugar quota, the United States increased its covert support to Nicaraguan opposition groups (the Fuerzas Democráticas Nicaraguenses launched several large-scale military operations from Honduras in the spring of 1983) and then conducted extended joint military maneuvers close to the Honduran-Nicaraguan border. The covert operations had the stated objective of pressuring the Sandinistas into cutting off supplies to the Salvadoran rebels, but it was also evident that the administration would not be displeased to see an insurgency gain ground in Nicaragua, eventually either overthrowing the Sandinistas or compelling them to negotiate with the armed opposition. The Reagan administration's refusal to rule out an even more active American military role in the region provoked a domestic furor, but such purposeful ambiguity may have prompted the Sandinistas to become more willing to stop arms shipments to El Salvador. As to the other dimensions of the conflict, although neither the FDN nor Eden Pastora's ARDE (which had also begun military operations in the south) seemed able to transform popular discontent into support for an armed insurgency, the October 1983 attacks on major economic targets (for example, the fuel storage tanks at Corinto) increased the pressure on the Sandinistas.

As events unfolded in Nicaragua, most European Socialists sought to maintain their equidistance from both the Sandinistas and the United States. Despite their growing disillusionment with the FSLN and its Marxist-Leninist rhetoric, many Socialist leaders clung to the hope that the Sandinistas could be persuaded or at least moved to adhere to their original statement of principles. A number of them tried to encourage the FSLN to reach some sort of accommodation with Pastora. Forthright admonitions to the Sandinistas also increased. Spanish leader González, for example, bluntly warned them that Spanish support was conditional on whether they maintained "the original plan of the process"[95] and (with Willy Brandt) then sent a public letter to FSLN leaders in July 1983 urging them to move toward the holding of elections and the establishment of democracy in Nicaragua. For his part, SPD presidium member Wischnewski displayed an uncharacteristic directness after a visit to Managua in June 1983:

> We call on the Sandinistas now politically responsible in Nicaragua not to hazard the sympathy and support granted them, but to advocate, even under aggravated conditions, the implementation of the revolutionary principles: mixed economy, political pluralism and nonalignment. The parties outside the Sandinista coalition need more freedom for their political activities. We were given a number of promises. We will closely watch how they are kept.[96]

Even as their skepticism of the Sandinistas had increased and their pessimism about the future prospects for Nicaraguan democracy had deepened, most European Socialist leaders still refused to support Reagan administration policies toward that country. Their objections to the administration's hard-line were twofold. On the one hand, they believed that U.S. policies would encourage the FSLN to adopt even more radical policies internally and to deepen their involvement with Cuba and the Soviet Union. But many European Socialists regarded such developments as well-nigh inevitable. What really impelled their opposition to the Reagan administration was the fear that, confronted with such a radicalization, the U.S. government would respond by sending in troops.

From their perspective as governing parties, neither the French nor the Spanish Socialists challenged the United States directly on these issues. The SPD, on the other hand, was less restrained. Virtually without exception, West German Social Democratic personalities criticized American policy in Central America generally and toward Nicaragua in particular, with the foreign policy spokesman of the SPD parliamentary party, Karsten Voigt, referring to U.S. policy as "gunboat diplomacy."[97] Wischnewski went further. Adopting a controversial idea that had been incorporated into the resolution of the April 1983 Socialist International congress, he called for a lobbying effort in the United States against the Reagan administration.[98] The idea was fraught with dangers and, if carried forward, would raise the level of polemics between the United States and European Socialist and Social Democratic parties to unprecedented heights.

IV

This chapter has analyzed the policies and the initiatives of a number of European Socialist and Social Democratic parties (in particular the German SPD, the French PS, and the Spanish PSOE) toward the crisis in Central America, placing these efforts in the broader context of the efforts of European political parties to expand their presence and influence in Latin America and to gain greater independence vis-à-vis the United States. Galvanized by the overthrow of Anastasio Somoza in Nicaragua and thereafter by the civil war in El Salvador, these parties used a wide array of instruments (party-to-party links, government-sponsored loans and credits, and aid from foundations and the Socialist International) to provide support for left-wing groups and movements in Central America.

European Socialist parties have played an important role in Central American conflict, internationally legitimizing the Sandinistas and (through their support of the FDR's alliance with the FMLN) the Salvadoran guerrilla movement as well. They have further provided useful contacts for parties like Venezuela's Acción Democrática and Mexico's Partido Revolucionario Institucionalizado and enhanced their opportunities for greater regional leverage. The criticisms of Reagan administration policies in Central America issued by individual Socialist and Social Democratic parties and governments as well as by the Socialist International have also been important in the political propaganda war that rages about conflict in the region.

And yet, despite the publicity and controversy generated by European Socialist efforts in Central America, the impact that these parties have had on events in the region should not be overstated. Western Europe has no significant military presence or projection in the region, and, given the present structure of international trade and commerce, individual European countries and even the European Economic Community are in no position to direct substantial economic assistance or benefits to Central American nations.

There are important limits to European Socialist political influence in the region as well. Those parties have established ties with numerous groups in Central America and the Caribbean during the last decade (ranging from traditional center-left parties like AD and the PLN to more controversial groups like the New Jewel Movement or the Sandinistas), but the development of these ties attests less to European influence than to the uses that such ties can have for Latin American parties and politicians. Some parties, it is true, have an ideological affinity with European social democracy, but they and certainly the others pursue the European Socialist connection primarily because it affords them greater leverage vis-à-vis the United States, reinforces their regional influence, and gives individual leaders a broader stage on which they can project themselves.

The European Socialists do not have much leverage over the positions adopted by Central American parties and movements. Some examples illustrate this point. As has been amply documented in the preceding pages, the Europeans have steadfastly supported a negotiated settlement to the conflicts in Central America. And, when a European leader calls for negotiations, he is praised by these parties for his statesmanlike position. And yet, the point is that while negotiations may be a laudable objective, the call for them has become a virtually meaningless slogan; it is a position with which everyone agrees, but which means quite different things to each involved party. What is more, the European Socialist call for negotiations does not carry much real weight; it reflects rather than influences the posture adopted by their homologues in the region.

Within the Socialist International, European Socialist and Social Democratic parties still represent a formal majority, but those parties have seen their influence in the organization eroded to the point that they play little or no role in the drafting of resolutions on Latin America, even though these are later presented as the position of the International. Moreover, as a number of documents seized from the New Jewel Movement in the wake of the Grenada invasion suggest, several SI members (among them the MNR, the Radical party of Chile, and the New Jewel Movement) have been in close touch with the Cuban and Nicaraguan leaders in an effort to further tilt the "balance of forces" within the SI Regional Committee for Latin America and the Caribbean in favor of more "progressive" elements. One document in particular discussed ways to exploit the "sharp divisions" that had appeared on Central American issues among European Socialist parties, and specifically identified the Portuguese Socialist and the Italian Social Democratic parties as "our principal enemies" within the International.[99]

The weakness of the European Socialists has been especially apparent with respect to Nicaragua. By refraining from public criticism of the FSLN, many European parties have hoped that they could more effectively encourage the Sandinistas to fulfill their earlier pledges to bring democracy to Nicaragua. For such a policy to work, however, the European parties would have had to act in concert and demonstrate the will to exercise pressure. In the Nicaraguan case, the European Socialist parties have shown themselves to be disunited and hesitant to exert what leverage they have over the FSLN forcefully, lest they be accused at home and abroad of lending moral support to counterrevolutionary efforts and of acting as instruments of American imperialism.

Most European Socialist and Social Democratic parties have been critical of U.S. policies in Central America, but the activism and sense of purpose they displayed during the Carter administration and into the first year of the Reagan administration have been replaced by the realization that there are no easy solutions to the crisis in the area and that their efforts to influence U.S. policies can have only a partial success. Over the past two years, these parties have downplayed their direct involvement in the area, preferring instead to work more discreetly in conjunction with parties and governments in the region. A number of considerations encourage the European parties (and especially the governments of which they form part) to eschew direct confrontation with the Reagan administration. For one thing, Central America is an area where the United States has been traditionally strong and in which vital American security interests are quite clearly at stake. For Europeans, on the other hand, Central American issues are preeminently symbolic. Needing to collaborate with the Reagan administration on other, more pressing foreign policy concerns, many European parties and governments wish to avoid overly sharp criticisms of the United States. Those parties in power, moreover, fear that, if the debate over American policy in Central America becomes a domestic European issue, it will limit their room for maneuver on other domestic and foreign policy questions. The call for negotiations in Central America (and the endorsement of initiatives like the one associated with the Contadora group) is likely to remain the centerpiece of European Socialist policies in the region. Moreover, if negotiations between the various parties are in fact begun, some European governments (notably the Spanish one) may be involved either as quasi mediators or as participants in a possible multinational peacekeeping force. Nevertheless, unless there is an unprovoked and massive American intervention in Central America, caution and restraint will continue to characterize European Socialist efforts in the region.

The European Socialist role in Central America, however, has longer-term implications than those discussed so far. The contacts and relationships that these parties have developed have laid the foundations for deepened involvement in Latin American affairs. To the degree that both Latin American nationalism and Europe's search for ways to assert its political and economic independence intensify over the next decade, such involvement will be reinforced. European Socialist and Social Democratic parties may, for example, play an important role in the development and consolidation of the democratic left in Latin America. This is a task for which the European parties are in some respects better placed than political groups in the United States. With the exception of the labor movement, few American organizations have the experience and tradition to contribute significantly to that enterprise. Although the European Socialist and Social Democratic movement has occasionally cooperated with groups whose commitment to democratic socialist principles is nonexistent, for the most part its adherents have a profound commitment to democratic values. Drawing on their extensive experience with nongovernmental forms of cooperation and assistance, their movement made a significant contribution to the peaceful transitions to democracy in Spain and Portugal, particularly to the rebuilding of the Socialist parties in those countries. They can do the same in a number of Latin American countries. Equally important, European Socialist and Social Democratic parties have access to movements in Latin America with which U.S. groups (because of lingering ethnocentrism on the one hand and Latin American distrust of the "Colossus of the North" on the other) would have a difficult time establishing cooperative relations.

Although the development of democratic institutions, parties, and trade unions is an objective that the United States shares with many European Socialists and Social Democrats, increased European activism in Latin America evidently carries with it the potential for conflict with the United States. Anticipating this, the U.S. government and American political forces can redouble their efforts for dialogue with the mainstream of European social democracy. Complete agreement between the two sides is neither a practical nor a desirable goal since American interests in Latin America are by no means identical to those of the European Socialists and, more broadly, Western Europe. But broad agreement exists on the importance of consolidating democratic structures (including democratic parties of the left and right) and halting Soviet and Cuban expansion in Latin America. Accommodation would involve on the European side greater discrimination and skepticism when dealing with "progressive" Latin American parties: Sharp anticapitalist and anti-American rhetoric hardly qualifies an organization as a member of the democratic socialist family. On the U.S. side, the focus should be on explaining more coherently American objectives in the region and stressing the commitment to a policy of reforms that, while not rejecting the use of military instruments to defend vital security interests, nevertheless relies more on political and economic forms of assistance. The search for such coincidences will weaken the influence of those more left-wing Socialists who not only view American policy in Latin America as profoundly misguided, but also believe the United States (not the Soviet Union or Cuba, not to mention the Sandinistas or the FMLN) is the real threat to the independence of Latin America and Western Europe. By lessening the chances for virulent conflict over Latin American policy, the search for common ground will serve to strengthen the bonds of the Atlantic alliance and also lay the foundations for a more cooperative U.S.–Western European relationship vis-à-vis Latin America during the coming decade.

Notes

1. A number of books and articles have dealt with these issues. Among the most useful: A. Glenn Mower, Jr., *The European Community and Latin America: A Case Study in Global Expansion* (New York: Greenwood Press, 1982); Bernard Lietaer, *Europe and Latin America and the Multinationals: A Positive Sum Game for the Exchange of Raw Materials and Technology in the 1980s* (New York: Praeger, 1980); Georges Landau and Harvey Summ, eds., *The European Community Enlargement and Latin America* (forthcoming); Gustavo Lagos, ed., *Las Relaciones entre América Latina, Estados Unidos y Europa Occidental* (Santiago: Instituto de Estudios Internacionales de la Universidad de Chile, 1980). Of the articles, several by Wolf Grabendorff have been especially helpful. See his "Las Relaciones entre América Latina y Europa Occidental: Actores Nacionales y Transnacionales, Objectivos y Expectativas," *Foro Internacional* (Mexico), vol. 23, no. 1 (July/September 1982), pp. 39–57; "The United States and Western Europe: Competition or Cooperation in Latin America," *International Affairs*, vol. 58, no. 4 (Autumn 1982), pp. 625–37; "The Central American Crisis and Western Europe: Perception and Reactions" (Research Institute of the Friedrich Ebert-Stiftung, 1982). Others include Roberto Aliboni, "Europe and Latin America: Toward a Non-Special Relationship," *Lo Spettatore Internazionale* (Rome), vol. 8, no. 3 (July/September 1973), pp. 179–98; Blanca Muñiz, "EEC–Latin America: A Relationship to Be Defined," *Journal of Common Market Studies*, vol. 19, no. 1 (September 1980), pp. 55–64; Francisco Orrego, "Europa y América Latina: Hacia un Rol Internacional Complementario?" *Estudios Internacionales* (Chile), vol. 14, no. 53 (January/March 1981), pp. 3–16; Simon Serfaty, "Atlantic Fantasies," in Robert W. Tucker and Linda Wrigley, eds., *The Atlantic Alliance and Its Critics* (New York: Praeger, 1983); and Simon Serfaty, *The United States, Western Europe and the Third World: Allies and Adversaries* (Washington, D.C.: Center for Strategic and International Studies, 1980).

2. For a general discussion, see ibid. Serfaty, *The United States, Western Europe and the Third World*. On Germany and France, see Michael Kreile, "West Germany: The Dynamics of Expansion," in *International Organization*, vol. 31, no. 4 (Autumn 1977), pp. 635–67; and Lawrence G. Franko and Sherry

Stephenson, *French Export Behavior in Third World Markets* (Washington, D.C.: Center for Strategic and International Studies, 1981).

3. Landau and Summ, *The European Community Enlargement*, p. 25; and Ricardo Eugenio Gerardi, "Posibles Tendencias del Intercambio Comercial de América Latina y la CEE," *Comercio Exterior* (Mexico), vol. 30, no. 5 (May 1980), pp. 463–72.

4. See Bernardo Grinspun, "Trade," in Landau and Summ, *The European Community Enlargement*, pp. 187–216.

5. See "Las Relaciones Externas de América Latina en el Umbral de los Años Ochenta" *Comercio Exterior*, vol. 29, no. 6 (June 1979), pp. 673–84.

6. *Miami Herald*, November 29, 1982.

7. Muñiz, "EEC–Latin America," p. 63.

8. Ibid.

9. Daniel Szabo, "Direct Investment and Financial Flows," in Landau and Summ, *The European Community Enlargement*, pp. 229–41; and *Financial Times* (London), November 10, 1981.

10. Statistical Office of the European Community, *Analytical Tables of Foreign Trade* (NIMEXE) (Luxembourg, 1976-   ), p. 117.

11. Cited in Peter Hermes, "Aspects and Perspectives of German Latin American Policy," *Europa-Archiv* (Bonn), vol. 34, no. 14 (1979), pp. 421–30. Also in *Politik der Partner*, (German Development Ministry, 1981), p. 134.

12. Raymond Mikesell and Mark G. Farah, *U.S. Export Competitiveness in Manufactures in Third World Markets* (Washington, D.C.: Center for Strategic and International Studies, 1981), p. 24, appendix table I-A.

13. Willy Brandt, lecture in St. Antony's College at Oxford University on May 27, 1980.

14. For a discussion of Spanish foreign policy objectives and concerns, see the author's essay "Rei(g)ning in Spain," in *Foreign Policy*, no. 51 (Summer 1983), pp. 101–17.

15. *El País* (Madrid), May 18, 1983.

16. See the discussion in Jean Touscouz, "Le Parti Socialiste Français et la Coopération avec le Tiers-Monde," *Politique Etrangère* (Paris), vol. 46, no. 6 (1981), pp. 875–89. Also Ricard Gombin, "Le Parti Socialiste et la Politique Etrangère—Le Programme de 1972," *Politique Etrangère*, vol. 42, no. 2 (1977), pp. 199–212. On the competing demands of "idealism" and "realism," see Dominque Moisi, "Mitterrand's Foreign Policy: The Limits of Continuity," *Foreign Affairs*, vol. 60, no. 2 (Winter 1981/82), pp. 347–57.

17. See, for example, Minister of Finance Jacques Delors' statement to a United Nations-sponsored conference on Least Developed Countries in September 1981 in *Le Monde* (September 5, 1981), and the memorandum circulated by the French government at the Cancún summit quoted in *Le Monde* (October 22, 1981). Also, the Mitterrand speech to the September 1981 meeting of the United Nations as reprinted in *Statements from France* 81/77, and the Cheysson speech to the United Nations General Assembly in the same month (ibid., 81/79), and Michael Harrison, "Socialist Foreign Policy for France?" *Orbis*, vol. 19, no. 4 (Winter 1976), pp. 1471–98.

18. United Nations Statistical Office, *Trade by Country and SITC Category,*

Computer Tapes (1981).

19. *Analytical Tables of Foreign Trade*, p. 122.

20. Landau and Summ, *The European Community Enlargement*, p. 321.

21. *Le Monde*, October 22, 1981.

22. This was a theme touched on in an article entitled "Nous aussi, nous avons nos Falklands" that appeared in *The Economist*, January 22, 1983, pp. 40–41.

23. Shortly after the PSOE took power in Spain, there was strong speculation about Franco-Spanish policy concentration toward Latin America. The idea found little support among the Spanish Socialists. *El País*, February 13, 1983.

24. Landau and Summ, *The European Community Enlargement*, p. 315, and *Politik der Partner* (1981), p. 134.

25. Serfaty, *The United States, Western Europe and the Third World: Allies and Adversaries*, pp. 20–31. For German statements, Helmut Schmidt's statement on behalf of his government to the Bundestag in *Foreign Broadcast Information Service*, Western Europe (February 29, 1980), pp. J1–J9; Hans-Dietrich Genscher, "Toward an Overall Western Strategy for Peace, Freedom and Progress," *Foreign Affairs*, vol. 61, no. 1 (Fall 1982), pp. 42–66.

26. Peter Bender (a writer who is close to Brandt) has argued: "If the cause from which a third world war could arise is to be found in the dualism between the Americans and the Russians, then the first thing that has to be done is to reduce the effectiveness of this dualism. Many parts of the world should remove themselves from the conflict of the superpowers or be removed from it. The Americans tend toward the globalization of their power struggle with Moscow, but for Europe the exact opposite is needed." *Das Ende des Ideologisches Zeitalters* (Berlin: Severin and Siedler, 1981), p. 194.

27. For example, Willy Brandt, "North-South Division," *Socialist Affairs*, nos. 3–4 (March/April 1979), pp. 95–98; Uwe Holtz, "SPD and the New International Economic Order," ibid., pp. 48–50. Also a number of the speeches delivered to an SPD conference in September 1977 reprinted in *Forum SPD* (Fachtagung "Entwicklungspolitik der SPD," am 1. und 2. September 1977 in Wiesbaden).

28. Egon Bahr, "From the Perspective of the SPD: Towards a Consensus on Basic Development Policy," a speech delivered in Bad Godesberg on January 25, 1979.

29. See, for example, former JUSOS leader and European Parliament Deputy Heidemarie Wieczorek-Zeul's statements vis-à-vis Latin America. In particular, her speech to the Asamblea Legislativa in Costa Rica reprinted in *Sozialdemokratischer Pressedienst*, vol. 37, no. 109 (June 11, 1982), pp. 8–9, and her "15 Thesen zum Verhaltnis EG-Lateinamerika und zu einer koharenten Lateinamerika-Politik aus sozialdemokratischer Sicht" (Manuscript). The local Hessen-South branch of the SPD approved a statement in early 1981 that described the FDR as "the legitimate representative of the broad majority of people in El Salvador" and "condemn[ed] the efforts of the US government" (Mimeograph).

30. *Der Spiegel*, August 18, 1982.

31. *Le Monde*, February 24, 1982.

32. The analysis presented in this paragraph draws on written and oral source material. The interested reader is referred to several articles in the *Washington Post*, July 24, 1979, and September 1, 1980; the Ebert Stiftung annual reports (*Jahresbericht* 1977–1982); *Der Spiegel*, April 16, 1979, "History, Objectives and Work of the Friedrich Ebert Stiftung," a report delivered to the Caribbean Congress of Labor in January 1977 (Mimeograph); and the journal *Nueva Sociedad* published in Costa Rica. The Ebert Stiftung is only one of several German foundations involved in work overseas. The others—the Konrad Adenauer, Hans Seidel, and Friedrich Naumann—are affiliated with the Christian Democratic, Christian Social Union, and Free Democratic parties respectively; they receive over 300 million DM from the German state as well as substantial amounts in unreported private donations. The Adenauer Stiftung has been almost as active as the Ebert Stiftung in Latin America. The Adenauer Stiftung and the Christian Democratic Union have made significant financial and organizational contributions to like-minded parties in the region. Another very active organization, an analysis of whose activities is beyond the scope of this essay, is the Swedish LO/TCO. The latter's Council of International Trade Union Cooperation had a 1980 budget of nearly $4.5 million; it has undertaken projects with unions affiliated with the Soviet-sponsored World Federation of Trade Unions. Another vehicle used by the Swedish Social Democratic party, the LO, and others is the International Center of the Swedish Labor Movement (AIC).

33. Friedrich Ebert Stiftung, *Jahresbericht 1978*, p. 103.

34. *Nueva Sociedad*, no. 40 (January/February 1979), p. 131 and no. 42 (May/June 1979), pp. 145–48.

35. The phrase is used in the communiqué published at the conclusion of a meeting on "Condiciones para una Democracia Efectiva en Centroamérica y el Caribe." It appeared in *Nueva Sociedad*, no. 42 (May/June 1979), pp. 204–9. See also *Nueva Sociedad*, no. 43 (July/August 1979), pp. 141–50 for a similar statement on trade union unity issued in June 1979 by a Workshop on Trade Unionism in Latin America.

36. For the Socialist International's basic statements of principle, see "Aims and Tasks of Democratic Socialism" (Frankfurt Declaration) issued in 1951 and "The World Today—The Socialist Perspective" (Oslo Declaration) from 1962. Published in *Socialist Currents*, vol. 3, no. 1 (April 1977), pp. 1–17.

37. Richard Löwenthal, "Democratic Socialism as an International Force," *Social Research*, vol. 47, no. 1 (Spring 1980), pp. 63–92. Also Reimund Seidelmann, "Die Sozialistische Internationale als Parteienbewegung und politischer Wegbereiter," *Europa-Archiv*, vol. 36, no. 21 (1981), pp. 659–68. For a left-wing critique, "The Socialist International in Africa and Latin America," *Socialist Thought and Practice* (October 1979), pp. 86–99.

38. Documents approved and speeches made at the Caracas meeting are in *Nueva Sociedad* (Costa Rica) (May/June 1976), pp. 67–93. Also Klaus Lindenberg, "Focus on Latin America—View from Bonn," *Socialist Affairs*, nos. 9–10 (September/October 1979), pp. 148–51.

39. The speeches and documents are published in Departamento Interna-

cional do Partido Socialista, *Procesos de Democratização na Peninsula Ibérica e na América Latina* (Conferencia de Lisboa de 30 de Setembro a 2 de Outubro de 1978). Also the articles in *Cuadernos para el Diálogo* (Madrid), October 14, 1978, pp. 32-34 and *Cambio 16* (Madrid) October 15, 1978, pp. 58-59.

40. *La Vanguardia*, March 20, 1982, carried an article on COPPPAL. Brandt remarked at the Oslo Bureau meeting (June 1980) that "the existing and developing forms [with COPPPAL] of cooperation are complementary and not competitive." *Socialist Affairs*, no. 5 (September/October 1981), p. 153. *Nueva Sociedad* reprinted many COPPPAL statements—not surprisingly since all Latin American members of the Socialist International belonged to it as well. As of March 1982, thirty-one parties had joined COPPPAL.

41. Mexico's position is discussed in several interesting articles. René Herrera Zuñiga, "México ante Centroamérica," *Nexos* (Mexico), (April 1980), pp. 3-9; Carlos Rangel, "Mexico and Other Dominoes: Forum and Substance in Mexican Foreign Policy," *Caribbean Review*, vol. 10, no. 3 (Summer 1981), pp. 8-11, 38; Anthony J. Bryan, "Mexico and the Caribbean: New Ventures into the Region," ibid., pp. 4-7, 35-36; *Vorwärts*, April 23, 1981.

42. *Nueva Sociedad*, no. 24 (May/June 1976), p. 68.

43. Quoted in an Associated Press dispatch, March 30, 1980. See also *Latin America Weekly Report*, no. 15 (April 18, 1980), p. 9; an article in the SPD's weekly *Vorwärts*, April 3, 1980; and an article by Daniel Waksman Schinca in *El Día* (Mexico), May 28, 1980.

44. *Procesos de Democratização*, p. 189.

45. *Nueva Sociedad*, no. 45 (November/December 1979), p. 295.

46. *Socialist Affairs*, no. 1 (January/February 1979), p. 28. The phrase is used in the Resolution on Latin America approved at the SI congress in Vancouver.

47. The text of the statement is in a magazine published by the SI Regional Committee for Latin America and the Caribbean. *América Socialista* (Santo Domingo), vol. 1, no. 2 (July 1980), pp. 59-60.

48. Quoted in Pierre Schori, "The Central American Dilemma," *Socialist Affairs*, no. 1 (January/February 1981), p. 36.

49. The text is in *Socialist Affairs*, no. 1 (January 1981), p. 23.

50. This paragraph synthesizes themes found in several articles. Among the most relevant, Willy Brandt, "Nuevas Perspectivas para América Latina," *Nueva Sociedad*, no. 45 (November/December 1979), pp. 72-76; Karl-Ludolf Hübener, "Vancouver Congress in Perspective," *Socialist Affairs*, nos. 1-2 (January/February 1979), pp. 20-22 and his "Is the Caribbean Going Cuban?" *Socialist Affairs*, nos. 5-6 (May/June 1980), pp. 156-59; Jean Ziegler, "Cuba, Castro and the Socialist International," *Socialist Affairs*, no. 4 (July/August 1981), pp. 134-35, and her "The New Challenge," *Socialist Affairs*, no. 2 (March/April 1982), pp. 76-77; and Pierre Schori, "Central American Dilemma," *Socialist Affairs*, no. 1 (January/February 1981), pp. 33-39. Also of interest is Hübener's "The Socialist International and Latin America: Problems and Possibilities," *Caribbean Review*, vol. 11, no. 2 (Spring 1982), pp. 38-41. For a biting riposte that directly challenged most of Ziegler's assumptions,

see the article by Rui Mateus, the Portuguese Socialist party's international relations secretary, entitled "Cuba No!" *Socialist Affairs*, no. 1 (January/February 1982), pp. 24–28.

51. Mario Soares, "Focus on Latin America—View from Portugal," *Socialist Affairs*, no. 5 (September/October 1979), pp. 146–48.

52. Pierre Schori, "Cuba en Africa," *Nueva Sociedad*, no. 36 (May/June 1978), pp. 94–104. Also Schori, "Central American Dilemma," p. 36, where he praises Castro for "hav[ing] accepted parliamentary democracy as a method, even after a revolutionary struggle for liberation."

53. For example, as argued by SI Secretary General Bernt Carlssen in "Democracia-Violencia-Socialismo," *Nueva Sociedad*, no. 43 (July/August 1979), pp. 107–13.

54. Cited in Schori, "Central American Dilemma," pp. 33–34. It is also quite likely that some lower-ranking members of the Carter administration sought to coordinate policy with the SI prior to 1980.

55. For an overview, see Thomas P. Anderson, *Politics in Central America* (New York: Praeger, 1982), pp. 76–106.

56. Constantine Menges, "Central America and the United States," *SAIS Review* (Summer 1981), pp. 13–33.

57. *Latin America Weekly Report*, no. 34 (August 29, 1980), p. 9. Also *Badische Zeitung*, August 5, 1980. For the SPD's position, see *Vorwärts*, especially two articles by Anton-Andreas Guha in the issues of March 27 and April 16, 1980.

58. *Der Spiegel*, August 4, 1980. An excellent interpretative article on the SPD and El Salvador may be found in the *Frankfurt Allgemeine Zeitung*, February 2, 1981.

59. The tensions between the SPD and PS reflected policy differences (over such issues as collaboration with Communist parties in Europe and commitment to structural changes) as well as personal antipathies. Mitterrand and Schmidt, for example, had less than cordial relations. See *Le Monde*, January 28, 1976; *Le Monde Dimanche*, November 2, 1980; and *Le Monde*, May 13, 1981. More recently, an article (with some inaccuracies) by Diana Johnstone in *In These Times*, December 8–14, 1972.

60. *Socialist Affairs*, no. 1 (January/February 1981), p. 22.

61. Ibid., p. 23.

62. Ibid., no. 3 (May/June 1981), p. 120.

63. Ibid., p. 121. Also the Associated Press story on March 2, 1981.

64. Statement of the Socialist International Bureau meeting in Paris (September 25, 1981).

65. *Frankfurter Rundschau*, March 6, 1981; *Der Spiegel*, March 9, 1981; *El País*, February 28 and March 3, 1981.

66. *SPD Press Release*, no. 104/81, March 4, 1981.

67. *Stuttgarter Nachrichten*, July 24, 1982. Wischnewski had served as minister for development aid from 1966 to 1969 and later was minister of state in the chancellor's office from 1976 to 1979 and again in 1982. He is best known for having directed the operation against the guerrillas who hijacked a Lufthansa jet to Mogadicio in 1977. On Wischnewski's efforts, see the articles in

Le Monde, October 13, 1981; *Latin America Weekly Report*, no. 18 (May 8, 1981), pp. 3–4; and an interview with him carried in *SPD Press Release*, no. 93/81, February 26, 1981.

68. United Press International dispatches dated June 2 and July 17, 1981. Also Broadbent's statement upon his return in *Socialist International Press Release*, no. 14/81, June 10, 1981. For a jaundiced view of the SI's "shuttle diplomacy," see Carlos Alberto Montaner, "The Mediation of the Socialist International: Inconsistency, Prejudice and Ignorance," *Caribbean Review*, vol. 11, no. 2 (Spring 1982), pp. 42–45, 57.

69. Minister of the Interior Tomas Borge, for example, allowed in an interview (*El País*, March 21, 1982) that the "subsistence [of the mixed economy was] due to the incapacity of the revolutionary State." For an overview of events during this period, the reader is referred to the periodic coverage in *Keesing's Contemporary Archives*.

70. A useful discussion of Christian Democratic policies may be found in Bernard Cassen, "La Democratie Chrétienne en Amerique Latine," *Le Monde Diplomatique* (February 1981); Mariano Rumor, "Christian Democratic Parties and Latin America," a speech delivered at Georgetown University, April 27, 1983; and *La Nación Internacional* (May 12–18, 1983). On Venezuela, Robert D. Bond, "Venezuelan Policy in the Caribbean Basin," in Richard Feinberg, ed., *Central America—International Dimensions of the Crisis* (New York: Holmes and Meier, 1982), pp. 187–200; Françoise Barthelemy-Febrer, "L'Offensive Venezuelienne dans les Caraibes: Continuité et Changement," *Amerique Latine*, no. 4 (October/December 1980), pp. 19–27; *Latin America Weekly Report*, no. 21 (May 28, 1981), pp. 4–5; *Expresso* (Lisbon), March 28, 1981; and David E. Blank, "Venezuela: Politics of Oil," in Robert Wesson, ed., *U.S. Influence in Latin America in the 1980s* (New York: Praeger, 1983), pp. 73–101.

71. Charles D. Ameringer, "The Tradition of Democracy in the Caribbean—Betancourt, Figueres, Muñoz and the Democratic Left," *Caribbean Review*, vol. 11, no. 2 (Spring 1982), pp. 28–31, 55–56.

72. Karl-Ludolf Hübener, "The Socialist International and Latin America: Problems and Possibilities," *Caribbean Review*, vol. 11, no. 2 (Spring 1982) p. 41.

73. *Socialist Affairs*, no. 1 (January/February 1981), p. 22.

74. *Le Monde*, October 13, 1981.

75. On the shift in Torrijos' position, see *Latin America Weekly Report*, no. 14 (April 3, 1981) and *El País*, August 9, 1981.

76. The discussion in this paragraph is based on interviews in Madrid and Washington in October–November 1982.

77. *Cambio 16* (Madrid), March 1, 1982; *Le Monde*, February 28–March 1, 1982; *Deutsche Allgemeines Sonntagsblatt*, February 21, 1982; and *Latin America Weekly Report*, no. 14 (April 2, 1982), pp. 7–8.

78. The reader is referred to other chapters in this volume and to newspapers like the *New York Times* and the *Washington Post* for daily coverage. About the various proposals, see the *New York Times*, April 15, 1982, and *Latin America Weekly Report*, no. 16 (April 23, 1982), pp. 7–8.

79. For sources relevant to this paragraph, the reader is referred to the *New York Times*, March 10, 1982; the *Report on the Election in El Salvador on 28 March*

1982 (April 7, 1982) submitted by the British observers Sir John Galsworthy and Professor Derek Bowett; and Rajeev Singh-Molares, "French Foreign Policy at the United Nations" (Manuscript, April 1983). On loans and credits to Nicaragua, see *Latin America Weekly Report*, no. 81-15 (April 10, 1981), p. 1, and no. 82-44 (November 12, 1982), p. 10. Also the *Washington Post*, July 30, 1983. On the CDU, see *Foreign Broadcast Information Service*, Western Europe (March 1, 1983), p. J6 citing Hamburg DPA. A German spokesman referred to the "lack of stability" in El Salvador but indicated that his government would generally coordinate its aid policies with those of the United States.

80. *Socialist International Press Release*, no. 12/82, April 2, 1981.

81. *Socialist Affairs*, no. 6 (November/December 1982), p. 241.

82. *Socialist International Press Release*, no. 8/82, March 5, 1982.

83. Ibid., no. 12/82, April 2, 1982.

84. *Le Monde*, August 30, 1981. See also *Latin America Weekly Report*, no. 35 (September 4, 1981), pp. 1-2. Economic interests also played a role in the initial French decision to join Mexico in this declaration. Specifically, France may have hoped to place itself in a better position to bid on several major projects such as the extension of the Mexico City metro and a large nuclear contract that had yet to be negotiated. *Latin America Weekly Report*, no. 27 (July 10, 1981), pp. 1-2.

85. See the text of the Managua Declaration published as a paid advertisement in the *Washington Post*, February 24, 1982. Also articles in *Le Monde*, February 23, and March 16, 1982, as well as a piece by Leslie Gelb in the *New York Times*, April 16, 1982.

86. On the Contadora initiative, see the *New York Times*, January 6, 1983, and *El País*, January 11, 1983. The Venezuelan government had in the meantime shifted away from its close identification with the United States. The defeat of Duarte in El Salvador, the Falklands/Malvinas crisis, and the impending presidential campaign contributed to its shift.

87. *Socialist International Press Release*, no. 14/82, April 27, 1982. France supported Great Britain but made a point of not backing its claim to sovereignty over the Falklands. *La Documentation Française, Textes et Documentes, Juin 1982* (Paris, 1982), p. 132. A leaked memorandum (apparently approved by Cheysson) nevertheless betrayed satisfaction with the problem Britain faced. See *Le Monde*, May 16, 1983.

88. *Socialist Affairs*, no. 4 (July/August 1982), p. 143. Also *Le Monde*, May 29, 1982; *El País*, May 26, 1982 (for an interview with Carlos Andrés Peréz); and my interviews in Washington and New York in March and April 1983.

89. *El País*, September 4, 1981, and the *Washington Post*, September 3, 1981. See also Michel Tatu's biting analysis of Mitterrand's policy in "La Position Française: Les Difficultés d'être un Bon 'Latino,'" *Politique Etrangère*, no. 2 (1982), pp. 319-24.

90. *Le Monde*, July 14, 1982. French policy in the region is discussed in interviews with presidential adviser Alain Roquié and critic François Bourricaud carried by *Caribbean Review*, vol. 11, no. 2 (Spring 1982), pp. 46-49.

91. The quotation is from Cheysson's reply to a written question in the French National Assembly. *Foreign Broadcast Information Service*, Western Eu-

rope (March 3, 1983), p. K2, citing Paris Diplomatic Information Service on March 2, 1983. On the caution of French policy toward Latin America, see *Le Monde*, February 27–28, 1983, and the *Miami Herald*, November 23, 1982.

92. *ABC* (Madrid), April 21, 1983. Luis Yañez pointedly remarked, "We are the first to know that the solution cannot come from Europe." *El País*, March 30, 1983. See the discussion in author's "Rei(g)ning in Spain."

93. *El País*, June 2, 1983. González maintained this approach during his state visit in mid-June 1983. At the same time, the Spanish government extended new credits to Nicaragua in March 1983 (totaling as much as 8 billion pesetas) and nearly 3 billion pesetas in credit to Cuba. *El País*, March 24, and May 23, 1983.

94. Summary of the Sixteenth Congress of the Socialist International (Albufeira, April 7–10, 1983), General Circular No. G4/83E, April 19, 1983, p. 65.

95. *Unomasuno* (Mexico City), May 28, 1983. González further marked his distance from the Sandinistas after October 1983 when Costa Rican police captured a Basque ETA terrorist commando team that was trying to assassinate Pastora and Robelo. Even though the FSLN argued there was no organized ETA presence in Nicaragua, other reports in the Spanish press suggested ETA and Palestinian commandos were receiving training in two camps outside Managua. The controversy was especially embarrassing for the González government because ETA had stepped up its attacks on Spanish military and security forces. *El País*, September 22, 1983.

96. Quoted in *Foreign Broadcast Information Service*, Western Europe (May 27, 1983), p. J5. Excerpt from a press conference in Bonn carried by Hamburg ARD television network.

97. Ibid. (July 27, 1983), p. J2, from an interview with the *Neue Osnabrucher Zeitung.*

98. Summary of the Sixteenth Congress of the Socialist International, p. 65.

99. See the *Report on the Meeting of the Secret Regional Caucus* (January 6–7, 1983) drafted by the New Jewel Movement representative, Chris de Riggs. Document No. 100446.

10
Mexico's Central American Policy: National Security Considerations

EDWARD J. WILLIAMS

A leading student of military strategy has it correctly that "no nation
. . . can afford to make overall foreign policy without reference to
considerations of national security; that is, after all, fundamental."[1]
However fundamental that maxim may be, the imperative of coordinating foreign and national security (or strategic) policies only now is
beginning to influence Mexico's decision makers. It is a novel problem
for the splendid reason that the two components of the relationship
are new to the Mexican milieu. Until relatively recently, Mexico had no
positive foreign policy, and only in the 1980s has it turned its attention
to the development of measurable military potential—a basic ingredi-
ent of a national security policy. Several factors obviously condition
the conundrum imposed upon Mexico's policy makers, but the threatening boil of the Central American caldron has catalyzed the issue. It
is the Central American nexus (and the Caribbean Basin, more generally) that melds Mexico's maturing foreign policy and its embryonic
national security policy.

This chapter describes and analyzes the conditions and the processes that contributed to the integration of national security considerations into Mexico's Central American policy. Two background factors
provide the context for this analysis and lead to its primary focus. The
first looks to the evolution of Mexico's positive foreign policy, with
special emphasis on Mexican initiatives in Central America and the
Caribbean. The discussion then examines the modernization of the
Mexican military, describing both the nuts and bolts of the process
and the tentative moves toward formulating strategic doctrine imply-

Much of the research and the initial draft of this study were completed while I served as
a visiting research professor with the Strategic Studies Institute of the U.S. Army War
College. Although none of the analysis in this study should be construed as an official
Department of the Army position, I do gratefully acknowledge the support of the
institute and the army. I also thank two of my colleagues at the institute, Dr. Keith
Dunn and Colonel William D. Staudenmaier, for their thoughtful critiques of this paper.

ing an embryonic national security policy. The primary focus of the study combines these two elements and centers on the synthesis of the two in Mexico's posture vis-à-vis Central America.

The chapter does not argue that there was at the beginning a direct and conscious link between the military's modernization program, Central American turmoil, and Mexico's foreign policy in the region. No such relationship existed at the outset of the modernization program during the last years of the 1970s. The argument is made, however, that the developments are logically intertwined. As the several parts of the larger whole crystallize, moreover, the relationships become increasingly clear.

Mexico's Positive Foreign Policy and Military Modernization

Foreign Policy. The recent evolution of Mexico's foreign policy from introspective and negative to outward-looking and positive has been well documented in the literature and wants no longish recitation here.[2] It is sufficient to offer a flavor of that development by way of understanding the context for the incipient integration of foreign and national security policies.

An active Mexican foreign policy is relatively new. Only within the past twenty years or so has the nation repudiated its traditional inward-looking, defensive attitude that proclaimed essentially negative dicta on anti-imperialistic policy positions designed to ward off transgressions from the "Colossus of the North." The nation's foreign policy, such as it was, posited the inviolability of principles such as the self-determination of nations, absolute sovereignty, and nonintervention. Overall national policy stated explicitly that Mexican interests were best served by concentrating on internal development. Reviewing Mexican foreign policy as late as the early 1960s, ex-foreign minister Jorge Castañeda signaled the inception of a more positive posture, while decrying the defensive tone of traditional foreign policy:

> The postwar attitude of Mexico toward the outside world is still, however, one of mistrust and partial disinterest, and its foreign policy is mostly defensive and anti-interventionist. Until the inception of the present administration [in 1958], when the international outlook of the country began gradually to change, Mexico's participation in the discussion of world political and economic problems has been, generally, reserved, cautious, and mainly defensive.

Drawing special attention to the Central American region, Castañeda continued that "the successive administrations made no great effort to assert a true political and cultural Mexican presence in Latin America or even Central America."[3]

As Castañeda implies, the first steps toward a more dynamic foreign policy were taken by President Adolfo López Mateos (1958-1964). The evolving policy was marked by several significant commitments, including a specific decision to affiliate with the Latin American Free Trade Association, a more implicit bid for expanded influence in Latin American affairs, the hosting of the 1968 Olympic games, and a move toward an increased role in third-world politics. In definite and theatrical form, the die was cast by President Luis Echeverría (1970-1976), who initiated a campaign for Mexican world leadership involving a series of measures including his sponsorship of the Charter of the Economic Rights and Duties of Nations, appearances at numerous conferences, visits to many third-world, Socialist, and European nations, and his regime's establishment of diplomatic relations with sixty-five new governments.

Although President José López Portillo (1976-1982) toned down his predecessor's flamboyant theatrics, he continued to pursue an active foreign policy. Parlaying Mexico's newly found petroleum power, López Portillo negotiated with leading world powers and established Mexico as a voice to be reckoned with in the larger global arena. Mexico's acceptance of a seat on the United Nations Security Council in 1980 and its hosting of a North-South summit meeting in 1981 symbolized the success of the positive policy launched by López Mateos in the 1960s and pursued by López Portillo in the 1980s. Domestic problems have preoccupied the present government of Miguel de la Madrid Hurtado, who took office in late 1982, but all indications affirm that Mexico will not forsake its increasing activity in foreign affairs, even as it deals with its domestic economy.

Mexico's interest in expanding its influence in Central America and the Caribbean covers about the same time period.[4] Early on, the emphasis centered on a concerted drive to diversify trade and increase export earnings. As Mexico's trade balance began to grow to serious negative proportions in the mid-1960s and as the Central American Common Market began to take on some coherence, Mexican decision makers set out a new policy to strengthen and increase relations with its immediate neighbors to the south (really, the southeast). President Gustavo Díaz Ordaz (1964-1970) launched in early 1966 the first goodwill tour of the Central American nations ever undertaken by a Mexican chief of state.[5] In early 1971, President Echeverría encountered "an unprecedented crisis in the Mexican balance of payments" and responded by meeting with the chief executives of Costa Rica, Guatemala, and Nicaragua to "explore the possibilities of increasing the exportation of manufactured products to Central America."[6] Shortly after his accession to power, President López Portillo followed the lead of his predecessors in conducting a series of bilateral meetings with his Central American counterparts looking to ongoing growth in Mexican exports.

Although Mexico's present policy anent Central America continues to reflect some degree of economic interest, it is really much more complex than the original contacts of the 1960s. The contemporary policy may well be dated from September 1978 when Mexico's embassy in Managua, Nicaragua, welcomed hundreds of political refugees fleeing an abortive insurrection against the Somoza dynasty. From that beginning, contacts matured and policy blossomed to involve a series of initiatives including diplomatic, political, and economic intercourse. The scenario is well known. On the diplomatic level, President López Portillo and Minister Castañeda pushed to act as "communicator" between the United States and Nicaragua and between the United States and Cuba. In another diplomatic move, Mexico joined with France in recognizing the leftist opposition in El Salvador as a "representative political force." In still other initiatives, the de la Madrid administration assumed the leading role in the peace proposals sponsored by the Contadora Group which included a wide-ranging series of measures encompassing all of the Central American nations in addition to Cuba and the United States. Meanwhile, Mexico lent continuing support to the Sandinista regime in Nicaragua; maintained cool relations with Guatemala; exchanged friendly visits with Fidel Castro; and enthusiastically backed the independence of Belize. In addition Mexico presided over the Conferencia Permanente de Partidos Políticos de América Latina in a measure calculated to increase its influence with political parties in a number of the nations of the Caribbean Basin.

Mexico's most important economic initiative involves joining Venezuela in supplying financial assistance to the nations of the Caribbean region through a system of cut-rate prices for petroleum linked to low-interest, long-term loans. In a series of further economic departures, Mexico has granted preferential access to its market for Central American products, opened lines of credit for the purchase of Mexican goods, and affiliated with the Caribbean Development Bank. In the area of petroleum, Petróleos Mexicanos (PEMEX), the national oil monopoly, has been engaged in several programs. In Costa Rica, PEMEX is exploring for hydrocarbons and offering technical advice; in Nicaragua, PEMEX has donated oil-drilling equipment. The oil monopoly is also assisting Cuba in exploration.

All of that, in sum, offers documentation of Mexico's increasingly vigorous foreign policy and that policy's special applicability to the Central American and Caribbean region. It should be emphasized, furthermore, that the policy is quite consciously designed to increase Mexico's influence in the area. The point has been captured by a Mexican scholar in a lengthy analysis of Mexico's Central American policy. After stating that "Mexico has neither an imperialistic vocation nor ambition in Central America," he allowed that the present situation does "permit [Mexico] to play the role of confidential interlocutor. . . ." The analysis proceeds to say that "in this context, Mexico is able to vigorously introduce its own national interests, taking advantage of the contradictions which overwhelm the United States."

In other sections of the discussion, the argument is even more clearly proposed. In one instance, the analysis holds that "the traditional historical-cultural considerations which have prevailed in Mexico's relations with its neighbors to the south have given way to political and strategic considerations." Again, the point is made that Central America is a zone which pertains "to the national security and international political prestige of Mexico."[7]

Castañeda used more measured tones in an interview discussing petroleum in Mexico's foreign policy, but the essential point was similar. The foreign minister cautioned that "energy sales cannot be reduced to the level of mere commercial transactions" and that Mexico "should obtain something more than their monetary value in return." He then listed several considerations, concluding with the criterion of "soberly-evaluated political benefits." Focusing on Central America, the foreign minister stressed that his interpretation of those considerations in foreign policy had guided Mexico's relations with the Sandinista government in Nicaragua. Reflecting those analyses on the contemporary Mexican scene, a foreign commentator reports that Mexico describes the Caribbean Basin as its "natural area of influence." Striking even closer to the specific national security theme of this paper, President Miguel de la Madrid Hurtado has proclaimed that Mexico's "destiny as a nation is indissolubly tied to what occurs in Central America and the Caribbean."[8]

Military Modernization. The second part of the foreign policy–national security policy relationship pertains to a contemporary initiative designed to expand and modernize Mexico's military establishment.[9] It is less well known; the military modernization program was launched only in the late 1970s and did not become clearly defined until the 1980s. The program involves a number of measures, including the numerical expansion of the armed forces, increased production of arms at home, purchase of additional military equipment abroad, and improvements in the military educational system. Along with upgrading the educational system, the initiatives also make significant new departures in the formulation of a national security doctrine.

Like Mexico's traditional foreign policy until the late 1960s, the nation's military was nondescript for more than a generation. Relative to the size of the national population, Mexico's military establishment was (and remains) among the smallest in the world. It claimed a minute portion of the national budget, was equipped with outmoded hardware, and was inadequately trained, and its officer corps was poorly educated. Thanks to the accident of geography which placed Mexico between the overwhelming might of the United States to the north and much smaller nation-states to the south, Mexico had little need for a large military establishment.[10]

The small military force which existed, in that sense, had little relevance to an external threat. Beginning in 1952, indeed, official military doctrine relegated to second place the mission of protecting the nation against foreign invasion. Reflecting a reality existing long before that time, the preservation of internal order became the armed forces' primary mission. The military functioned as a sort of national police force. It occasionally engaged in authentic antiguerrilla warfare (in the early and mid-1970s) but more usually supported Mexico's authoritarian political system by intervening against recalcitrant *sindicatos*, squelching rebellious peasants, disciplining dissident members of the middle class, and, as manifested at Tlatelolco in 1968, brutally neutralizing the challenges of protesting students. A study of the Mexican army written during the 1970s lends credence to the point in proposing that "there are no specific concentrations of forces or military installations in what might be considered national defense positions. Instead, the military is more concerned with being positioned properly in order to subdue any internal disturbances."[11]

As for the armed forces' mission of defending the nation against foreign aggression, the traditional posture was lacking in any clear definition as to possible threats and different strategies. In a vague way, the official doctrine continued to depict the United States as an ongoing threat to Mexico's territorial integrity, but the amorphous doctrine had no implication for the formulation of coherent strategy. As a contemporary Mexican scholar dryly understates, "the theme of national security does not occupy a privileged place in reflections upon Mexican political life." What doctrine existed proposed that internal socioeconomic development must lead to increasingly satisfied citizens, thereby defusing a threat of internal subversion, the only plausible threat to the nation or to the system.[12]

Beginning in the late 1970s, however, the Mexican military's posture began to change. It expanded its forces, updated its hardware, improved its educational system, and launched initiatives in thinking through national security and strategic policy. In 1968, the armed forces numbered 67,000. Over the next decade, 30,000 personnel were added. By 1982 the combined strength of the armed forces had increased to about 120,000, with projections for 220,000 by 1988.[13]

The qualitative improvement of the armed forces' hardware is an even more salient part of the larger modernization process. Mexico has acquired from Germany the rights to manufacture G3 automatic rifles, and they are now being mass-produced in the army's Military Industries facility in Mexico City. The government's Dina Nacional truck factory is manufacturing an armored car, with thoughts of upgrading it to a light tank. The Dina plant is also mass-producing a new three-quarter ton truck. The crowning glory of the nation's efforts is a series of short-range (three to twelve kilometers) rockets now being developed, some of them successfully tested by the early 1980s. Abroad, Mexico has purchased antitank vehicles from the French, with expectations of further acquisition of another type of military vehicle. From the United States, the army anticipates a large purchase of helicopters and a radar air defense system.[14]

The air force and navy are also being upgraded. The air force has ordered "an undetermined number" of transport planes from Spain and sixty Pilatus aircraft from Switzerland, with the probability of sixty more to come. Reports are that the air force is also shopping for a primary trainer. In the most publicized purchase, the air force bought twelve F5 fighter planes from the United States as part of a $130 million program that includes support equipment. The first batch of planes was delivered in mid-1982, and indications point to the possibility of Mexico's buying another dozen F-5s. The naval minister has announced that fully half of the present fleet will be renewed. The program includes the construction of more than thirty Azteca patrol boats for coastal and river duty. Six frigates are to be purchased from Spain. From the United States, the Mexican navy has received delivery of two Gearing-class destroyers, one LST, and an oceanographic research vessel. The economic crisis that struck Mexico in 1982 is slowing the implementation of the military's modernization program, but the commitment is made and the updating process continues.[15]

As the hardware of increased military potential is assembled in Mexico, the nation's decision makers have also turned their attention to upgrading the military's educational system. The military plans to improve the quality of education from top to bottom. Major facilities renovations have been undertaken at the Escuela Superior de Guerra, the Mexican military's second-level educational institution. Beyond the updating of brick and mortar, the curriculum has been improved to keep abreast of changes in military doctrine in the United States and elsewhere. A new emphasis has evolved to prepare the students against external as well as internal threats to national security, and war-gaming exercises have been introduced for the first time. Even more significantly, the armed forces founded in 1981 the Colegio de Defensa Nacional, a new departure in higher military education analogous to the famous Centro de Altos Estudios Militares in Peru and Escola Superior de Guerra in Brazil. The *colegio's* first class of about twenty army and air force officers was graduated in 1982.[16]

If one assumes the analogy between the Mexican institution and similar departures in other Latin American nations, the future development of the *colegio* may be expected to involve further progress on the elaboration of a coherent national security doctrine. A study of the Inter-American Security System suggests the scenario:

> The 'development decade' of the 1960s produced in Latin America a totally new and profoundly significant phenomenon which had great impact on the Inter-American Security System: the Latin American military reformer armed with the 'Doctrine of National Security and Development ....' Typically, these development plans emerged from the efforts of a dynamic group of mid-level and senior officers working out of their National War College which, unlike the U.S. counterpart, frequently became a think-tank and policy influencer as well as educational institution.[17]

But it is important for this analysis to emphasize that even now the Mexican elites have begun to move toward the formulation of a national security doctrine. General Felix Galván López, the former defense minister, catalyzed the discussion in a now-famous interview granted to *Proceso* in 1980. The incipient policy debate is mightily concerned with the implications of Mexico's new role as a petroleum power and its increasingly sophisticated industrial infrastructure. A modernized armed force is required for protection, of course, but so is a coherent strategic doctrine leading to a full-fledged national security policy. Springing from these considerations, Mexican leaders are engaged in discussions concerning the foundation of a formal deliberative and decision-making body designed after the National Security Council in the United States.[18]

In sum, the modernization of the Mexican military serves to posit the second contextual factor of the analysis. Combined with Mexico's activistic foreign policy in the Central American region, it suggests a possible linkage between the two. In mid-1982, former President Ló- pez Portillo defended the military's modernization program in declar- ing that "the impulse for the modernization and growth of the Armed Forces reflects a better guarantee of [Mexico's] national security." As- suming the validity of that declaration, it remains to probe the rela- tionship of Mexico's military modernization, its incipient national se- curity policy, and its foreign policy initiatives in the Central American region.[19]

Foreign Policy and National Security Policy:
The Central American Nexus

The connection between Mexico's foreign policy in Central America and its evolving national security policy can be analyzed on three related levels. The first, or most general, level defines the intrinsic connection between any nation's foreign and national security poli- cies. At the second level of analysis, the focus centers on the changing realities of Mexico's domestic political and socioeconomic system and on equally significant changes in the international political system of the Caribbean Basin. The third, or most specific, level of analysis fastens on several elements of the Mexican military's modernization program, including its incipient force structure and other concomitant security initiatives. That level of analysis pertains especially to Mexi- co's south, which borders on Central America, but also has potential for affecting policy toward Central America and the Caribbean.

Foreign Policy and National Security Policy. The first level of analysis is pristine in its simplicity and can be disposed of forthwith. A mili- tary force is intrinsically a part of any nation's foreign policy stance. Degrees of military strength and military preparedness form part of a larger foreign policy posture that inevitably adds to or subtracts from a nation's ability to pursue its foreign policy goals. In some instances, strategic calculations are consciously integrated into a sophisticated national security policy designed to complement other elements of overall foreign policy, but the argument here is less complex.

Pertaining to Mexico, the point is simply that increasing military potential implies that the nation will carry more weight as it maneu- vers in Central America. The point is well crystallized by two authori- tative sources. A leading work on military strategy has it correctly that "prestige springs partly from the fear that one is capable of instilling; particularly when dealing with emergent nations, 'face' plays a con-

311

siderable part." General Galván emphasized the same message in 1980 in defending the armed forces' modernization program. The former defense minister proclaimed that the program would make Mexico more "respected." "The strong are more respected than the weak," he declared.[20]

Although all of that is certainly elementary, it appears to have been little appreciated either within or without Mexico. Part of the explanation for the apparent disregard for the military's contribution to Mexico's Central American posture obviously stems from the government's distaste for the image. It is, after all, unseemly to rattle sabers, and especially so for a nation that has long prided itself on its commitment to a moral foreign policy tradition. More to the analysis at hand, however, the connection between military might and foreign policy objectives is diffuse in Mexico because of the unfamiliarity of the calculation. As was noted earlier, a positive foreign policy in Mexico is barely past its infancy, and measurable military potential is still embryonic. Hence, it is only now that Mexico's decision-making elites are beginning to think through the connection. Whether or not the relationship is consciously internalized, it exists. More importantly, as it becomes increasingly internalized, it will grow more significant in Mexico's posture anent the Central American region.

The Argument from Time and Place. In connecting Mexico's military modernization and its evolving national security concerns to its Central American policy, the second level of analysis centers more on the realities of time and place. It takes off from Samuel P. Huntington's analysis of change in the equation between foreign and national security policies.

Huntington posits that "only fundamental and permanent changes in a government's environment produce fundamental and permanent changes in its military policy." The dictum might be revised a trifle to read "environment and/or *ambition*" to fit some nuances of the Mexican case, but the point is well made. Huntington proceeds to pinpoint change in both domestic and foreign environments as contributing to a revision of the foreign policy–military policy equation. Domestic changes leading to a shift in military policy are exemplified by "the rise of new industries" and "the change from a predominantly rural to a predominantly urban society." In the external environment, causal factors include "a fundamental shift in the balance of power, the rise of new and threatening states," and "the decline of old and established empires."[21]

All of those changes, and more, are applicable to the analytical case at hand. A generation of markedly successful modernization has combined with Mexico's emergence as a petroleum power to trans-form the economic, sociopolitical, and psychological context of Mexi-co's domestic system. Economic growth and sociopolitical change have implications for Mexico's posture in the Caribbean Basin and inject national security considerations into the larger foreign policy nexus. Economic development catalyzed by the petroleum boom im-plies novel strategic imperatives. Sociopolitical mobilization conjures challenges to Mexico City, some with potential security connotations.

As luck would have it, moreover, both economic growth and so-ciopolitical change have significant foci in Mexico's southern region, bordering on Central America. In a somewhat different vein, domes-tic successes in Mexico have encouraged new ambition in foreign policy.

The international environment has also changed, both inviting and compelling Mexican participation. A mini–arms race in the region highlights Mexico's comparative military disadvantage. To make mat-ters worse (or better?), U.S. influence in the area has diminished, making it easier for Mexico (or compelling it?) to protect its interests and itself by tending more seriously to national security considerations.

Domestic considerations. Despite the serious problems attendant to the economic crisis of 1982, the post–World War II modernization process in Mexico has wrought dramatic changes in the nation's eco-nomic landscape. Writing even before the oil boom of the 1970s, one student exclaimed that "the whole apparatus of a modern economy was dropped into place within a generation: railroads, banks, heavy industry, stable currency, and gilt-edged national credit from abroad." Combined with Mexico's newly found petroleum riches, those do-mestic changes imply a new reality and force the nation's policy-making elites to frame different policies and programs. The petroleum bonanza has brought even further economic growth and has implied novel strategic imperatives in the area of national security policy.

Mexico's former defense minister made the point in explaining the military's modernization program. He emphasized that Mexico's in-dustrial growth had created new "necessities for protection and vigi-lance," making particular reference to the "vital installations" of Petró-leos Mexicanos and the Compañía Federal de Electricidad. "We have to give them security," he noted, and "for that reason we need more equipment, more means, and more soldiers."[22]

The location of the new petroleum reserves is especially salient to Mexico's Central American posture within the context of its evolving national security policy. The fields are located in the southeastern states of Chiapas and Tabasco. Both states border on Guatemala, and some of the fields are less than 100 miles from the frontier. Although less frequently mentioned, an additional strategic consideration in the south is the security of the transisthmian rail line, recently upgraded and destined to become a lucrative economic asset for Mexico as the 1980s unfold.[23]

Mexico's southern region also highlights the security implications of sociopolitical change attendant to the nation's rapid modernization. The troubled scenario of the south suggests a receptive host for the contagion of the revolutionary epidemic advancing from Central America. A bombastic journalistic metaphor may exaggerate the point, but it captures the essential security concern among some sectors in Mexico in declaring that "Central America is reaching northward toward Mexico like a knife pointing at the proverbial soft underbelly."[24] The most flaccid part of that underbelly is the nation's southern region.

In truth, the area has always been unsettled, and old problems have combined with new ones to exacerbate the situation. Traditionally, the nation's southern states have been Mexico's poorest and least developed region. The area also counts the nation's largest concentration of indigenous peoples, many of the same ethnic tradition as their brethren living in northern Guatemala. The retarded development of the region implies the continuing existence of large haciendas, socioeconomic exploitation, and political authoritarianism. Over the years, it has triggered occasional peasant challenges to governmental authority and, in response, repression of the local peasantry.

As the oil boom matured in the area during the 1970s, it complicated matters as hundreds of thousands of Mexicans flooded the area in search of jobs. The interlopers imposed stresses and strains on the sociopolitical fabric of the region. To make matters worse, the exploitation of the area's petroleum riches also brought land condemnations, soaring inflation, increases in crime, environmental damage, water pollution, and unmanageable demands on the local infrastructure. All of that, in turn, catalyzed an angry response on the part of the southerners, in the form of petitions, protest marches, and roadblocks; they also occupied drilling rigs and construction sites. It is a familiar story: an economic boom sparking social dislocation leading to political protest.

Yet the dismal tale does not end there. Migrants from the Central American nations have added their destabilizing influences. The entire southern region, in short, is experiencing unparalleled sociopolitical change at the same time that the Central American nations are caught up in revolutionary turmoil. Managing such change is, assuredly, a challenge to domestic policy; but it is also tied to Mexico's security interests because of its potential link to the external threat of Central America's revolutionary contagion.

Psychological influences must also be taken into consideration for their effect on the foreign policy–national security policy equation. Both active foreign policy and incipient national security policy in Mexico derive from domestic changes that transcend the bricks and mortar of economic growth or the bittersweet agony of sociopolitical mobilization. Important psychological changes have also contributed to the matrix. Nor, to be sure, have the economic problems of the 1980s beclouded the significant impact of the economic successes of the "Mexican miracle," which transformed the nation from 1940 through 1981. The contemporary positive posture in foreign affairs evolves from those successes and, in the process, marks a significant threshold in Mexico's global political ambitions.

Indeed, the present posture may be interpreted as a kind of messianic ambition that winds its way through Mexican revolutionary history. In decrying the excesses of the commitment to internal industrialization, Frank Tannenbaum once said that "the idea of bigness is upon them." The Mexican elites were captivated by the grandeur of "big plans" and "great industries."[25] As a more positive foreign policy has evolved in Mexico, the nation's elites have increasingly extrapolated the "idea of bigness" to the global arena. The Mexican leadership is anxious for the country to exercise influence in international politics equal to its size, wealth, level of industrialization, petroleum holdings, and political sophistication. A sphere of influence in the Caribbean Basin combined with a voice in third-world politics is the point of departure.

Mexico's military modernization and the move to frame a national security policy form part of the same ambition. Upgraded military might and preparedness are the handmaiden of the nation's foreign policy in Central America and the Caribbean. Just as the nation's political leadership has contracted ambition, so too it appears that the same psychological inclinations have been carried over into the military establishment. The Mexican military is increasingly visible as it assumes a more vigorous posture than it has for more than a generation. New military hardware, coupled with an expansion of personnel, has contributed to rising expectations and growing ambition in the military sector.

In sum, protecting the nation's industrial infrastructure is not the only domestic determinant connecting Mexico's national security considerations to its foreign policy plans. In truth, this determinant probably also transcends the necessity to complement present foreign policy. In some part, the equation is conditioned by expanding political ambitions fed by expectations of greater political influence as Mexico assumes greater influence in the world arena and, more specifically, in Central America and the Caribbean.

The international environment. The international environment informing Mexico's embryonic national security policy may be even more compelling than the domestic determinants of that policy. At the outset, it features a Mexican military traditionally smaller and less sophisticated than putative opponents. Moreover, the scenario counts several aspiring regional powers engaged in an arms race linked to their desire to protect their interests or expand their influence in the Caribbean Basin. At the same time, U.S. sway in the region has diminished, thereby placing more responsibility on (and offering more opportunity to) the several regional power contenders.

As a point of departure, it is important to emphasize that the Mexican military has been (and continues to be) quite limited in comparison with other nations. Comparative analysis illustrates the point. Looking to the three "regional powers" who may logically be in competition in the Caribbean Basin (Cuba, Mexico, and Venezuela), Mexico has ranked lowest in all relative indexes of martial might. In only one area in absolute numbers has it surpassed Venezuela. Mexico is roughly six times more populous than Cuba and five times more populous than Venezuela. Yet in 1979 when Mexico had just initiated its military modernization program, data show Mexico spending less than half as much for its military as Cuba (U.S. $519 million versus $1,168 million) and considerably less than Venezuela ($706 million). In per capita terms, Mexico spent $7 per head on its military, dramatically below Cuba's $118 and Venezuela's $52. As a percentage of government spending, Mexico's expenditures were again far below those of Cuba and Venezuela, respectively 1.1 percent, 8.9 percent, and 6.5 percent. Only in absolute numbers in the armed forces did Mexico surpass Venezuela, though it was still far below Cuba. In 1980, Venezuela counted 40,500 men in arms; Mexico, 107,000; and Cuba, 206,000.[26]

Although Mexico is expanding and upgrading its military establishment, several other regional powers are doing the same. The militarization of the Caribbean Basin, in the first instance, features ongoing Cuban efforts to maintain military superiority in the region. In an address to the United Nations General Assembly in mid-1982, Cuban Vice President Carlos Rafael Rodríguez announced Cuban receipt of "huge quantities of modern and sophisticated weapons." The United States is particularly concerned with the Cuban naval buildup. An

American admiral charges that the Soviet Union is encouraging the effort "to modernize the Cuban navy's arms with the general thrust of turning it from a defensive organization to an organization with offensive interdiction capacity." Mexican officialdom is, of course, less vocal in its concern about the improvement of the Cuban navy, but good information indicates similar feelings in Mexico, particularly among the nation's naval leadership.[27]

The Venezuelan military buildup is no less impressive than Cuba's and also contributes to the increasing tensions in Central America and the Caribbean. The cutting edge of the Venezuelan military effort is the purchase from the United States of twenty-four advanced F-16 jet fighters along with an additional twenty-four Hawk fighters from Britain destined to be used as training vehicles. According to one source, the new equipment will make the Venezuelan air force the most powerful in Latin America, with the exception of Cuba. The Venezuelan navy is also being updated. In mid-1982, Venezuela received the fourth of six missile frigates being built in Italy. Two German submarines are also being constructed for the Venezuelan navy.[28]

Although perhaps less threatening to Mexico's regional political interests, other nations in the area are also engaged in military expansion. The Nicaraguan case is well known. With an army numbering 40,000, supplemented by a 200,000-person militia, Nicaragua surpasses the combined military strength of the rest of the Central American nations. El Salvador's military, of course, has been expanded, modernized, and better trained as the United States has taken a growing role in that nation. In much the same way, the United States has prompted the Honduran military to increase its capability. In Guatemala, the military continues to be the dominant force, eating up the lion's share of that troubled nation's financial and human resources. Before the Falklands/Malvinas crisis, indeed, it appeared that the Argentines were in the early stages of projecting their own military force into the area.[29]

In sum, the militarization of the Caribbean Basin has created an environment contributing to a Mexican response. To be sure, the modernization of the Mexican military and the formulation of a national security policy are propelled by factors beyond the arms buildup in the region, but the international context certainly plays a role. A logical hypothesis posits the connection in two ways. In the first place, the security of Mexico is better served if its military is prepared to counter the martial might of its neighbors. Traditionally, save Costa Rica, Mexico has been the most poorly defended nation in the entire area. Moreover, Mexico's evolving foreign policy interests in

Central America and the Caribbean are obviously better served if its military can project itself as a complement to the nation's regionalistic diplomatic, political, and economic strategies.

The gradual decline of U.S. influence, combined with the reverberations of the Falklands/Malvinas imbroglio, defines the final factor informing Mexico's integration of national security concerns into its regionalistic foreign policy. Over the longer term, U.S. influence has been eroded, facilitating a relative expansion of other powers' presence in the Caribbean Basin. Referring in passing to some of the domestic determinants discussed previously, one analysis crystallizes the significance of the international context for Mexican foreign policy in the region:

> Mexico has changed internally over the last decade, and so has the international environment. Most fundamental, the decline of United States economic, political-ideological and military hegemony throughout Latin America and the Caribbean over the 1970s in comparison with the decades of the 1950s and 1960s has enabled Mexico to assume an independent role in hemispheric affairs. . . .Today Mexico faces an increasingly "Gaullist" or "balkanized" international system in which it is not only possible but imperative for Mexico to assume a more assertive role to protect and foster its national interests. The dissolution of the Pax Americana is nowhere more in evidence nor more threatening to Mexico than in Central America and the Caribbean.[30]

In a more speculative vein, finally, the post–Falklands/Malvinas syndrome in Latin America may well intensify the initiatives in Mexico (and elsewhere) to assume increasing responsibility for its own security. Although most of the early analyses of the imbroglio tended to exaggerate the damages wrought in U.S.–Latin American relations, it does not take a doomsayer to recognize that suspicions have intensified concerning the commitment of the United States to its southern neighbors. One commentator makes this point in saying that the crisis taught the Latin American nations that the United States is less than a completely reliable ally. Therefore, he says, they must tend to their own security. A Latin American social scientist declares more cynically (but equally cogently) that the Latin American armed forces "are reading the Malvinas lesson as making it necessary to buy many, many new toys."[31]

In sum, the evidence from time and place buttresses the argument from elementary logic that Mexico has linked its national security policy to its foreign policy. If the logic of the relationship has military presence as an intrinsic part of statecraft, then the present situation in Mexico gives additional salience to the Mexican case study. Economic changes on the domestic scene have produced strategically significant installations that want defending. Sociopolitical modernization on the domestic scene has produced a dynamic situation that wants watching. Psychologically, the train of events has produced novel foreign policy ambitions that many in Mexico want nurturing. At the same time, the international environment has been changing. A mini-arms race confronts Mexico on the one hand, and a relative power void on the other hand, as U.S. influence diminishes. All of that, to press the point, quite clearly suggests the wedding of military might and national security policy to Mexico's foreign policy; it also compels the conclusion that the Central American caldron has been a significant catalyst of the meld.

Mexico's Military Modernization and Central America. The final level of analysis connecting foreign and national security policies lends further support to the argument, but it is not so clearly crystallized. In the best of all analytical worlds, the evolving force structure and other components of the military's modernization program ought to be integrated into an overall strategy designed to support Mexico's foreign policy posture in Central America and the Caribbean. In some instances, national security measures seem to fit the model, but in others the purpose of the military buildup and other initiatives is clouded.

The probable explanation for the confusion is twofold. First, the evolution of national security policy is still unsettled in Mexico. No coherent design has emerged; the component parts, therefore, are bound to be uncoordinated. Second, as in all nations, the well-laid plans of decision makers must always contend with competing political factions and military services informed by different ambitions and motivations ranging from vested economic interests, to pride and prestige, to rational planning. As the tentative nature of the new national security policy combines with the vagaries of Mexican domestic politics, the rational model is buffeted and deformed.

Despite this, several propositions can be confidently proposed. The military buildup clearly encompasses more and different equipment than is necessary for maintaining internal order, the traditional role of the Mexican military. In the same vein, the debates on a national security doctrine focus more on foreign aggression than in the past, and the source of the potential threat is increasingly depicted as emanating from the south. In a somewhat different way, finally, both military force structure and other security initiatives suggest a pre-dominantly defensive mentality, but there may be some potential for offensive projections into Central America and the Caribbean.

The Mexican military's modernization, other security initiatives, and the predominantly defensive tone of present strategic thinking regarding national security policy are best illustrated by a series of initiatives in Mexico's troubled south. Activities in the area bordering upon Central America provide the link between security policy and foreign policy considerations. The image is captured by a newspaper analysis of the turmoil in the state of Chiapas that "is increasingly approaching a social explosion that is accelerated by the influence of the conflicts in Central America."[32] Mexico City's decision makers recognize the vulnerability of the area, and they have launched programs and policies calculated to ensure domestic stability and ward off the revolutionary contagion from Central America.

Looking first to the modernization program, several measures are clearly designed to equip and prepare the Mexican military to counter potential national security challenges in the area. The Pilatus aircraft purchased in Europe are to be armed for anti-insurgency warfare. The military's intention to purchase additional helicopters is also part of an evolving anti-insurgency capability. The 1982 announcement of the organization of a quick reaction force pertains to the same strategy and to the same regional focus in the nation's south. One report quoted "official sources" as explaining that the "4,000-man quick reaction force is designed to defend the country's southern border and lucrative oil fields against a possible spillover of Central America's turbulent guerrilla wars."[33] The Mexican navy's program to build up its capability for coastal and river patrol is also part of the larger picture. The patrol boats can be used to guard the coastlines against contraband and infiltration and to transport troops in the southern region.

Other military and politico-military initiatives in Mexico's south imply further evidence of national security concerns. Additional troops have been sent to the region; military maneuvers have been conducted in the area; military governors have been selected to head two southern states; and socioeconomic programs for the south have been upgraded.

According to one analysis, the nation's south "is in some ways almost a war zone" and "civilian officials are now given military rank before they can work in the area."[34] Without necessarily ascribing to the "war zone" image, it is clear that strategic and national security initiatives pervade the environment. Exact figures are difficult to obtain (and contradictory), but all agree that military garrisons in the region have been reinforced with additional troops. In the south, in 1980, the Mexican armed forces conducted the largest military maneuvers ever undertaken in Mexico.[35]

The foci of the military's activities, moreover, highlight the nature of the perceived security threat in the south. Both foreign and domestic challenges preoccupy the Mexican military. The foreign threats emanate from Guatemala and include incursions by both the guerrilla forces and the Guatemalan army. General Galván, referring to the spillover of Guatemalan guerrilla activity, noted that the troops in the area were exercising "a strict vigilance, particularly concerning the problems which confront the country [Guatemala]: the guerrillas. That is, Mexican troops take care that Guatemalan guerrillas do not pass into our country, in which case they have orders to apprehend, subdue, and deliver them up to the proper [Mexican] authorities." Beyond guerrilla infiltration, the Mexican government is increasingly concerned with the incursions by the Guatemalan army troops in "hot pursuit" of refugees (guerrillas?) fleeing to Mexico. The Mexican government has issued two official protests to Guatemala, and the situation is tense.[36]

Other signs of the government's concern with security in the south are reflected in domestic military, socioeconomic, and political activities, and in governmental programs in the region. Troops have been called in to put down peasant challenges to the local governments and landlords. A commentary on the 1980 war games in the south charged the military with designing the maneuvers to "intimidate the popular movements that are evolving in the rural zones." In the area of socioeconomic responses, Mexico City has launched a series of developmental programs calculated to win the support of the local peasantry. The several initiatives include road construction, medical clinics, new government stores, and agricultural extension programs to distribute new seed and provide tractors at nominal fees. The military and political linkage is exemplified by the selection of two military governors in the south. In 1981, retired General Gracialano Alpuche Pinzón assumed the gubernatorial mantle in Yucatán, and in the following year another military man, General Absalon Castellanos Domínguez, won the governor's post in the troubled state of Chiapas.[37]

Defense considerations certainly predominate in the strategic planning component of Mexico's foreign policy as regards the nation's south and Central America. There is no question that the southern strategy is the keystone of Mexico's evolving national security doctrine. This definition of the strategy, however, ought not becloud the fact that offensive potential is implied in some elements of the military's modernization in tandem with other government programs. This proposition does not for a moment suggest aggressive intentions among the nation's decision-making elites, but it does recognize that several initiatives under way in Mexico imply the possibility of projecting military power beyond the borders into the Caribbean Basin.

There is some potential offensive capability already. As a step toward realizing its ambitions for increasing its sea power, Mexico is committed to policing its patrimonial waters and to solidifying its control of offshore territories. One part of that commitment is illustrated by a policy statement proclaiming that "no matter what the cost," Mexico will ensure the sovereignty of its territorial seas. A second nuance of the growing concern is exemplified by a recent inventory of the nation's islands, keys, and reefs. Within the same context, the nation's shipbuilding industry is being upgraded to produce larger vessels, and a comprehensive program is under way to improve Mexico's port facilities. To be sure, the shipbuilding industry is scheduled to produce merchant vessels and the port facilities are designed to handle Mexico's growing foreign commerce, but both initiatives also imply the possibility of enhanced military capability.[38]

More directly, recent additions to the fleet begin to sketch out an embryonic blue water capability with the potential to prepare the Mexican navy in developing a force presence in the Caribbean Basin. From the United States, Mexico has purchased two Gearing-class destroyers, an LST, and an oceanographic research vessel. All can be interpreted as adding to the Mexican navy's blue water capability. From Spain, Mexico is purchasing six frigates. Although the frigates are designed for coastal patrol, they have the ability to operate in the Caribbean. These initial steps, moreover, should be understood within the context of a blue water tradition in Mexico's past that many are eager to revive and expand.

The Mexican air force buildup is the second area ripe with potential for the military to project its power into the Central American and Caribbean region. The Pilatus aircraft are part of the calculation, but the F-5s, with their offensive capabilities, are probably the more salient aerial component. Twelve came on line in mid-1982, and indications point to the purchase of twelve more.

In combination with the two other levels of analysis presented here, in sum, the military modernization suggests a significant link between evolving foreign and national security policies in Mexico. The relationship is manifest in the nation's south, where additional troops and military hardware, together with other strategic, socioeconomic, and politico-military programs and policies, highlight Mexico's sensitivity to the threat of Central American revolutionary contagion. As Mexico's foreign policy nurtures the friendship and support of its Central American neighbors, national security policy makes its contribution by guarding the nation's southern flank. Finally, the modernization program in Mexico—though predominantly defensive in character—also implies the germ of a more dynamic element, with the potential for projecting Mexican military presence in the region in support of its larger foreign policy in Central America and the Caribbean.

Conclusion

The Central American revolutionary caldron has led to national security considerations being increasingly integrated into the formulation and implementation of Mexico's Central American policy. The new vibrancy in Mexico's foreign policy is particularly germane to the Central American region, where Mexico has taken a leading role. With the exception of the United States, Mexico is the most important exogenous political actor intimately involved in the day-to-day drama of that troubled region. The modernization of Mexico's military establishment has also been discussed. All of those enterprises are still in progress, and all promise a significantly more potent military force for Mexico in the future.

Most significantly, the new course in military modernization has combined with Mexico's foreign policy ambitions in Central America and revolutionary ferment in that area to contribute to a full-scale review of Mexico's national security policy. In the process, the foreign policy and security policy nexus has crystallized as the nation's decision makers begin to envisage the relationship between the two elements of a larger foreign policy posture anent the Central American region. To be sure, the scenario is still tentative and incomplete, but it is sufficiently adumbrated to invite investigation and significant enough to demand discussion and analysis.

The crux of the foreign and national security policy nexus is revealed in three levels of analysis. At the level of elementary logic, Mexico's increasing martial might is bound to contribute to its foreign policy presence. In the imperfect, atomistic environment of international politics, military power adds a special nuance to any nation's diplomatic skill, political sophistication, or economic prowess, no matter what the conscious intentions of the policy makers may be. As Mexico's former secretary of defense has aptly noted, the nation's military modernization will elicit growing "respect" from other nations in the Caribbean Basin.

This scenario, however, is really more complicated than implicit saber rattling. It emanates from the very marrow of changes wrought in Mexico's domestic and external environment over the last thirty years or so. Fundamental and permanent changes have taken place, calling up a completely new scenario demanding new departures in security policy. A sophisticated industrial network has been put into place, and an enormously lucrative hydrocarbons complex has been constructed. Both may invite the envy of potential enemies, and both want security. Flowing from the same process, different social forces have been mobilized and politicized, and national security demands their management. In a rather different vein, finally, the successful modernization program also suggests rising ambitions for this middle-level power which envisions an enhanced role in global politics and which, in turn, demands a national security apparatus commensurate with its other goals.

As luck would have it, finally, significant elements of Mexico's developing economic wealth and important numbers of its newly mobilized peoples are found in the nation's south, bordering on the Central America caldron. Challenging sociopolitical mobilization has reverberated throughout that troubled region. Many fear the revolution will intensify and that the contagion will spread northward from Central America. In response, Mexico City has launched programs upgrading its security in the region. Just as Mexico's southern states border on Central America, Mexican policies in these states clearly show the link between the nation's foreign and national security policies regarding Central America. Activities in the region, furthermore, illustrate the overriding defensive tone of Mexico's embryonic national security policy. Some other elements of the nation's military modernization program hint at a more dynamic projection of power beyond the frontier in the future, but they are possibilities rather than realities.

Notes

1. Edward Mead Earle, "Notes on the Term Strategy," *U.S. Naval War College Information Service for Officers*, excerpted in *Advanced Military Strategy* (Carlisle, Pa.: U.S. Army War College, 1982), p. 60.

2. See George W. Grayson, "Mexican Foreign Policy," *Current History* (March 1977), pp. 97 ff; William H. Hamilton, "Mexico's New Foreign Policy: A Reexamination," *Inter-American Economic Affairs*, vol. 29 (Winter 1975), pp. 51–58; Errol O. Jones and David La France, "Mexico's Foreign Affairs under President Echeverría: The Special Case of Chile," *Inter-American Economic Af-*

fairs, vol. 30 (Summer 1976), pp. 45–78; Olga Pellicer de Brody, "Pragmatismo y tradición revolucionario en la política exterior de México," *Proceso*, August 28, 1980, pp. 13–14; and Guy E. Poitras, "Mexico's 'New' Foreign Policy," *Inter-American Economic Affairs*, vol. 28 (Winter 1974), pp. 59–77.

3. Jorge Castañeda, in Carlos A. Astiz, *Latin American International Politics* (Notre Dame, Ind.: University of Notre Dame Press, 1969), pp. 155–56.

4. See Anthony T. Bryan, "Mexico and the Caribbean: New Ventures into the Region," *Caribbean Review* (Summer 1981), pp. 4 ff; René Herrera Zúñiga, "De cara al sur: México ante Centroamérica," *Nexos*, vol. 3 (April 1980), pp. 3–10; John F. McShane, "Emerging Regional Power: Mexico's Role in the Caribbean Basin," in Elisabeth G. Ferris and Jennie K. Lincoln, eds., *Latin American Foreign Policies: Global and Regional Dimensions* (Boulder, Colo.: Westview Publishers, 1981), pp. 191–209; Edward J. Williams, "Mexico's Central American Policy: Apologies, Motivations and Principles," *Bulletin of Latin American Research*, vol. 2 (October 1982); and Williams, "Mexico's Central American Policy: Revolutionary and Prudential Dimensions," in H. Michael Erisman and John D. Martz, eds., *Colossus Challenged: The Struggle for Caribbean Influence* (Boulder, Colo.: Westview Press, 1982), pp. 149–70.

5. For the discussion and analysis, see Ramón Medina Luna, "Proyección de México sobre Centroamérica," in Centro de Estudios Internacionales, *México y América Latina: La Nueva Política Exterior* (México, D.F.: El Colegio de México, 1974), especially pp. 15–20.

6. Olga Pellicer de Brody, "El Acercamiento de México a América Latina," in James W. Wilkie et al., eds., *Contemporary Mexico* (Los Angeles: University of California Press, 1976), p. 449.

7. Herrera Zúñiga, "De cara al sur," pp. 3–10.

8. See Aurora Berdejo, "Nuestro Destino," *Excelsior*, January 8, 1982, p. 1; Herrera Zúñiga, "De cara al sur," pp. 4, 9; Alan Riding, "Oil and Salvador Issues Upset Mexico," *New York Times*, September 13, 1981; and "Foreign Relations: Something More Than Oil on the Presidential Tour," *Comercio Exterior*, June 1980, p. 202.

9. It is clear, of course, that the Mexican military's modernization also has profound implications for the nation's domestic policies. Those implications want analysis, but they are beyond the ken of this effort.

10. The relative puniness of Mexico's military is explained by more than the absence of external threats. On the domestic scene, Presidents Calles and Cárdenas worked for more than a decade to neutralize the large and politically influential military that existed after the revolution. The standard work is Edwin Lieuwen, *Mexican Militarism: The Political Rise and Fall of the Revolutionary Army* (Albuquerque: University of New Mexico Press, 1968).

11. Steve Wager, *The Mexican Military 1968–1978: A Decade of Change*, master's thesis (Stanford University, Latin American Studies Program, 1979), p. 8. See also Franklin D. Margiotta, "Civilian Control and the Mexican Military: Changing Patterns of Political Influence," in Claude E. Welsh, Jr., ed., *Civilian Control of the Military* (Albany: State University of New York Press, 1976), p. 222.

12. See Olga Pellicer de Brody, "La Seguridad Nacional en México: Preocupaciones Nuevas y Nociones Tradicionales" (Presented in seminar of the Program on U.S.-Mexican Studies, University of California, San Diego, September 1980), p. 1.

13. The data are from Coronel Ricardo Maldonado Baca (Lecture at the U.S. Army War College, Carlisle, Pa., November 17, 1981); "Military Eye on Central America," *Financial Times*, March 22, 1982, Information Service on Latin America (ISLA) 1060; and Wager, *The Mexican Military*, p. 9.

14. See "Mexico/Arms," *Latin America Weekly Report*, January 30, 1981, p. 11; "Mexico Modernizes Army as Revolution Spreads," *Miami Herald*, October 17, 1980, ISLA 1370; Alan Riding, "Mexican Army, Parading Pride, Raises Concern," *New York Times*, October 5, 1980, ISLA 1371; Marlise Simons, "U.S. Said to Approve Jet Sale for Mexico's Military Buildup Plan," *Washington Post*, February 24, 1981, ISLA 531; and Roberto Vizcaino, "La seguridad del país: fin primordial del Estado," *Proceso*, September 22, 1980, pp. 6–8.

15. See "Mexico/Arms," p. 11; Sam Moriarity, "Spain, Mexico Ratify Joint Industrial Projects," *Journal of Commerce*, October 30, 1980, ISLA 1402; and Simons, "U.S. Said to Approve Jet Sale."

16. See José López Portillo, "Análisis de los Artículos 1/o. y 3/o. Constitucionales: Conferencia Sustentada por el C. Presidente de los Estados Unidos Mexicanos" (México, D.F.: September 3, 1981); and Steve Wager, "The Modernization of the Mexican Military and Its Significance for Mexico's Central American Policy" (Paper presented at the Military Policy Symposium, U.S. Army War College, Carlisle, Pa., November 1982), pp. 7–8.

17. John Child, *Unequal Alliance: The Inter-American Military System, 1938–1978* (Boulder, Colo.: Westview Press, 1980), p. 190.

18. Vizcaino, "La seguridad del país," pp. 6–8.

19. For the quotation, see Roberto González, "Modernizar al Ejército, Garantía de Seguridad: JLP," *Excelsior*, January 5, 1982, p. 1.

20. André Beaufre, *An Introduction to Strategy* (New York: Praeger, 1965), p. 124; and Vizcaino, "La seguridad del país," p. 7.

21. For the analysis, see Samuel P. Huntington, *The Common Defense: Strategic Programs in International Politics* (New York: Columbia University Press, 1961), pp. 7–8, 11.

22. Howard F. Cline, *The United States and Mexico* (New York: Atheneum, 1965), p. 54; and Vizcaino, "La seguridad del país," p. 7

23. See Herrera Zúñiga, "De cara al sur," p. 3; and William Chislett, "Mexico's Bid to Bridge the Oceans," *Financial Times*, May 15, 1981, ISLA 1948. The following analysis is extrapolated from Edward J. Williams, "Mexico's Modern Military: Implications for the Region," *Caribbean Review*, vol. 10 (1981), pp. 12 ff.

24. Guy Gugliotta, "Mexico Is Flexing Its New Muscle," *Miami Herald*, August 31, 1980, ISLA 538.

25. See Frank Tannenbaum, in Charles C. Cumberland, ed., *The Meaning of the Mexican Revolution* (Lexington, Mass.: D. C. Heath, 1967), p. 82; Cumberland, *Mexico: The Struggle for Modernity* (New York: Oxford University

Press, 1968), p. 258; and Manuel Germán Parra, in Cumberland, *The Meaning of the Mexican Revolution*, p. 85.

26. "Balancing the Military Books," *Latin America Weekly Report*, September 19, 1980, p. 9.

27. The quotations are from "Cuba Reports Getting 'Huge' Supply of Arms," *New York Times*, June 17, 1982; and "Latin America/Navies," *Latin America Weekly Report*, August 14, 1981, p. 12. For a more comprehensive discussion and analysis of the Cuban military buildup, see Edward H. Kolcum, "Cuban Military Forces Being Updated," *Aviation Week and Space Technology*, May 3, 1982, pp. 62–63; and David C. Isby, "The Cuban Army," *Jane's Defense Review*, vol. 3 (1982), pp. 145–53.

28. See "Venezuela Comprará 'Hawks' Para Entrenar a Pilotos de los F-15," *Excelsior*, April 6, 1982, p. 27A; and "Venezuela Upgrading Weaponry," *Harrisburg [PA] Patriot*, May 31, 1982, p. 20.

29. See "Argentina Hovers on the Brink of Central American Adventure," *Latin America Weekly Report*, February 12, 1982, pp. 1–2; and "Nicaragua Is Now the Gun in Central America," *Business Week*, February 1, 1982, p. 40.

30. Bruce Bagley, "Mexico in the 1980s: A New Regional Power," *Current History* (November 1981), p. 354.

31. Warren Hoge, "Latins Weigh War's Effort," *New York Times*, June 8, 1982. The quotation is from Guillermo O'Donnell.

32. Mario R. Redondo, "Chiapas se Acerca al Estallido Social," *Excelsior*, January 4, 1982, p. 1.

33. Marlise Simons, "Mexico Trains Quick-Reaction Force," *Washington Post*, February 2, 1982.

34. George Philip, "Mexico and Its Neighbors," *World Today* (September 1981), p. 360.

35. Again, the numbers of troops engaged in the maneuvers tend to imprecision. Two published sources quote 43,000 and 45,000. A private source thinks that the number did not exceed 20,000. For the public quotations, see "Mexico/Army," *Latin America Weekly Report*, December 12, 1980, p. 12; and Marlise Simons, "Mexico Fights Unrest," *Washington Post*, April 18, 1981, p. 1.

36. For the Galván quotation, see Oscar Hinojosa, "Cualquier regime de gobierno, con apoyo popular, será respetado por el Ejército," *Proceso*, March 29, 1982, p. 6. For the tensions between Guatemala and Mexico, see "Guatemala nunca ha incursionado en México: Mejía," *El Informador* (Guadalajara) August 11, 1983, p. 1.; and Alan Riding, "Mexico Tense as Guatemala's Strife Continues to Spill across Border," *Arizona Daily Star* (Tucson), October 9, 1982.

37. For the facts, figures, and analysis of the several activities and programs, see "Después de 30 Años, un Militar Gobernará a Chiapas," *Proceso*, March 29, 1982, p. 22; "Los Intocables," *Excelsior*, January 7, 1982, p.1; "Mexico/Accident," *Latin America Weekly Report*, November 20, 1981, p. 12; Redondo, "Chiapas se Acerca al," p. 1; Simons, "Mexico Fights Unrest," p. 29.

38. For the several initiatives, see "Inventario de Islas, Cayos y Arrecifes," in "Frentes Politicos," *Excelsior*, April 28, 1981, p. 10A; Ignacio Herrera, "Cuesta lo que Cuesta, se Hará Respetar la Soberanía del Mar Mexicano,"

Excelsior, December 24, 1981, p. 4A; Stanley Mantrop, "Mexico Bolstering Ship Fleet," *Journal of Commerce,* March 17, 1981, ISLA 1050; and Federico Ortiz, Jr., "Inauguran el Centro de la Industria Naval Pesada," *Excelsior,* January 17, 1982, p. 4A.

11

U.S. Security and Latin America

JEANE J. KIRKPATRICK

While American attention in the past few years has been focused on other matters, developments of great potential importance in Central America and the Caribbean have passed almost unnoticed. The deterioration of the U.S. position in the hemisphere has already created serious vulnerabilities where none previously existed and threatens now to confront this country with the unprecedented need to defend itself against a ring of Soviet bases on its southern flanks from Cuba to Central America.

In the past four years, the Soviet Union has become a major military power within the Western Hemisphere. In Cuba, the Soviets have full access to the naval facilities at Cienfuegos, nuclear submarines, airstrips that can accommodate Backfire bombers. From these, Soviet naval reconnaissance planes have on several occasions flown missions off the east coast of North America. Cuba also has electronic surveillance facilities that monitor American telephone and cable traffic and a network of intelligence activities under direct Soviet control. And, of course, a Soviet combat brigade.

During the same four-year period the Soviets have continued to finance, train, and staff a Cuban military establishment which has by now become a significant instrument of Soviet expansion in Africa, the Middle East, and South Asia as well as throughout the Caribbean and Central and South America. Today Cuba possesses a small navy; a sizable number of supersonic aircraft—including Il-14s and MiG-21s and -23s—that can be quickly armed with nuclear weapons; modern transport planes capable of airlifting Cuban troops anywhere in the area; a huge army; and an estimated 144 SAM-2 antiaircraft missile

Originally published, in a somewhat different version, in the January 1981 issue of *Commentary*.

sites. The presence of more than 50,000 Cuban troops and military advisers in Africa and the Middle East provides one measure of the size and utility of Cuba's armed forces. The Cuban role in training, supplying, and advising revolutionary groups throughout the Caribbean and Central America illustrates the hemispheric implications of this buildup.

The first fruits of these efforts are the new governments of Grenada and Nicaragua, whose commitments to Marxist-Leninist principles and solidarity with Soviet/Cuban policies led Castro to brag on returning from Managua, "Now there are three of us." There may soon be four. El Salvador, having arrived now at the edge of anarchy, is threatened by progressively well armed guerrillas whose fanaticism and violence remind some observers of Pol Pot. Meanwhile, the terrorism relied on by contemporary Leninists (and Castroites) to create a "revolutionary situation" has reappeared in Guatemala.

Slower but no less serious transformations are under way in Guyana, where ties to Castro have become extensive, tight, and complex, and in Martinique and Guadeloupe, where Castroite groups threaten existing governments. (In Dominica and Jamaica, the recent electoral victories of Eugenia Charles and Edward Seaga have for the moment reversed the Castroite tides there.) Fidel Castro is much clearer than we have been about his interests and intentions in the area, and frequently declares, as at last year's meeting of the nonaligned nations in Havana, "I will pursue to the end the anti-imperialist struggles of the Caribbean peoples and especially those of Puerto Rico, Belize, Guadeloupe, Martinique and Guyana."

American policies have not only proved incapable of dealing with the problems of Soviet/Cuban expansion in the area, they have positively contributed to them and to the alienation of major nations, the growth of neutralism, the destabilization of friendly governments, the spread of Cuban influence, and the decline of U.S. power in the region. Hence one of our most urgent tasks is to review and revise the U.S. approach to Latin America and the Caribbean.

Such a review should begin not just with the previous administration's policy in the hemisphere, but with the quiet process by which new theories of hemispheric relations came to preempt discussion within that somewhat amorphous but very real group known as the foreign-policy establishment. For to an extent unusual in government, Carter administration policies toward Latin America and the Caribbean (as in the world more broadly) were derived from an ideology rather than from tradition, habit, or improvisation.

Indeed, nothing is as important as understanding the relationship between the recent failures of American policy—in Latin America and elsewhere—and the philosophy of foreign affairs that inspired and informed that policy. Such an effort of understanding requires, first, that we disregard the notion that the failure of the Carter policy was the personal failure of a man unskilled in the ways of diplomacy; and, second, that we look beyond superficial day-to-day policy changes to the stable orientations that reasserted themselves after each discrete crisis in world affairs.

Those orientations had their roots in the Vietnam experience, less as it was fought in Southeast Asia than as it was interpreted in Washington and New York. President Carter, after all, was not the only political leader in America to have lost his "inordinate" fear of Communism, lost his appetite for East-West competition, grown embarrassed by the uses of American power, become ashamed of past U.S. policies, and grown determined to make a fresh start. By the time Richard Nixon had left office, a large portion of the political elite in America, including a majority of the Congress, had withdrawn not only from Vietnam but from what was more and more frequently called the cold war—the revisionists' preferred term for U.S. determination to resist the expansion of Soviet power.

From these feelings were inferred the famous "lessons" of Vietnam: that the cold war was over, that concern with Communism should no longer "overwhelm" other issues, that forceful intervention in the affairs of another nation is impractical and immoral, that we must never again put ourselves on the "wrong side of history" by supporting a foreign autocrat against a "popular movement," and that we must try to make amends for our deeply flawed national character by modesty and restraint in the arenas of power and the councils of the world. Underpinning these "lessons" was a new optimistic theory of historical development which came in the decade of the seventies to focus the discussion of the future within the dominant foreign-policy elite.

No one expressed the new spirit better than Zbigniew Brzezinski, whose book *Between Two Ages*[1] (sponsored by the Council on Foreign Relations) spelled out the implications of the new spirit for Latin American policy. Brzezinski argued that our Latin American policies were inappropriate to the new realities of declining ideological competition, declining nationalism, increased global interdependence, and rising Third World expectations. The United States should therefore give up its historic hemispheric posture, which had postulated a "special relationship" with Latin America and emphasized hemispheric security and, since World War II, anti-Communism. We should, instead, make an explicit move to abandon the Monroe Doctrine, "concede that in the new global age, geographic or hemispheric continuity

331

no longer need be politically decisive,"[2] adopt a "more detached attitude toward revolutionary processes,"[3] demonstrate more "patience,"
and take an "increasingly depoliticized" approach to aid and trade.[4]

The views of hemispheric policy expressed in *Between Two Ages*
were further elaborated in two other documents born in the bosom of
the foreign-policy establishment: the reports issued in the name of the
Commission on United States–Latin American Relations headed by
Sol Linowitz and composed of "an independent, bipartisan group of
private citizens from different sectors of U.S. society" funded by the
Ford, Rockefeller, and Clark foundations. The intellectual framework
and most of the specific recommendations of the two Linowitz reports
were identical. Both affirmed that economic and technological developments had created new international problems, and that interdependence had generated a pressing need for a new global approach to
those problems. U.S. policy toward Latin America, "from the Monroe
Doctrine through the Good Neighbor Policy to the Alliance for Progress and its successor, the Mature Partnership," was outmoded because it was based on assumptions which had been overtaken by
history. Earmarked for the dustbin were the beliefs that the United
States should have a special policy for Latin America; that Latin America constituted a "sphere of interest" in which the United States could
or should intervene (overtly or covertly) to prevent the establishment
of unpalatable governments; and that national security should be an
important determinant of U.S. policy toward that area. Now, the first
Linowitz report counseled: "It [U.S. policy] should be less concerned
with security in the narrowly military sense than with shared interests
and values that would be advanced by mutually satisfactory political
relations."[5] The new approach was to be free of paternalism, "respect-
ful of sovereignty," tolerant of political and economic diversity. Above
all, it was to be set in a consistent global framework.

Most of the specific recommendations of the two Linowitz reports—negotiating the Panama Canal Treaties, "normalizing" relations with Cuba, "liberalizing" trade and "internationalizing" aid,
promoting human rights, and never, ever, intervening militarily—
flowed from these new assumptions. Given detente, the United States
should "keep local and regional conflicts outside the context of the
superpower relationship" and no longer "automatically see revolutions in other countries and intraregional conflicts . . . as battlefields
of the cold war." And given interdependence (manifested in global
phenomena like inflation and multinational corporations), the United
States should no longer hope for or seek "complete economic and
political security" but instead participate in the new international
agenda.

Despite the commission's determined globalism, it recognized that Cuba constituted a special case. Both reports recommended U.S. initiatives toward "normalization" of relations with Cuba and some acts (removing restrictions on travel, increasing scientific and cultural exchanges) regardless of overall progress on normalization. But the second report also noted Cuba's military involvement in Africa and its support for "militant" and violence-prone Puerto Rican *independistas* and concluded that full normalization of relations, however desirable, could take place only if Cuba gave assurances that its troops were being withdrawn frm Angola and that it had no intention of intervening elsewhere.[6]

The most striking characteristic of the Linowitz recommendations was their disinterested internationalist spirit. U.S. policy, it was assumed, should be based on an understanding of "changed realities" and guided by an enlightened confidence that what was good for the world was good for the United States. Power was to be used to advance moral goals, not strategic or economic ones. Thus sanctions could be employed to punish human rights violations, but not to aid American business; power could be used "to the full extent permitted by law" to prevent terrorist actions against Cuba, but not to protect U.S. corporations against expropriation. Nor was power to be a factor in designing or implementing economic aid or trade programs *except* where these were intended to promote human rights, disarmament, and nuclear nonproliferation.

Like Brzezinski's *Between Two Ages*, the Linowitz reports were, in the most fundamental sense, utopian. They assumed that technological change had so transformed human consciousness and behavior that it was no longer necessary for the United States to screen policies for their impact on national security. To be sure, neither argued that self-interest, conflict, or aggression had been entirely purged from the world. But Brzezinski asserted (and the Linowitz commission apparently believed) that only the Soviet Union was still engaged in truly "anachronistic" political behavior against which it was necessary to defend ourselves. Since no Latin American nation directly threatened the position of the United States, relations with them could be safely conducted without regard for national security.

Adopting the Linowitz commission's recommendations thus required abandoning the strategic perspective which had shaped U.S. policy from the Monroe Doctrine down to the eve of the Carter administration, at the center of which was a conception of the national interest and a belief in the moral legitimacy of its defense. In the Brzezinski-Linowitz approach, morality was decoupled from the national interest, much as the future was divorced from the past. The goals recommended for U.S. policy were all abstract and supranational: "human rights," "development," "fairness."

Still, if the Linowitz reports redefined the national interest, they did not explicitly reject it as a guide to policy or name the United States as the enemy. This was left to the report of yet another self-appointed group whose recommendations bore an even closer resemblance to the actual policies of the Carter administration. This report, *The Southern Connection*, was issued by the Institute for Policy Studies Ad Hoc Working Group on Latin America. The group included key personnel of the Linowitz commission, and it endorsed most of the specific recommendations of the second Linowitz report: divestment of the Panama Canal, normalization of relations with Cuba, strict control of anti-Castro activists, aid through multilateral institutions, nuclear nonproliferation, and systematic linkage of human rights concerns to all other aspects of policy. But the IPS report went beyond these in various respects.

First, it not only proposed a break with the past, but contained a more sweeping indictment of past U.S. policy as reflecting an "unquestioned presumption of U.S. superiority" and an "official presumption of hegemony" which was not only outdated but also "morally unacceptable."[7]

Second, it went beyond the call for normalization of relations with Cuba to a demand that the United States *"support* the ideologically diverse and experimental approaches to development"[8] (emphasis added), recognizing that "both the need for change and the forces propelling such change in the developing areas are powerful and urgent."[9] Latin America's "most challenging development experiments" were identified as Cuba, Jamaica, and Guyana.

Third, the IPS report located the ground of human rights violations and "institutionalized repression" throughout Latin America in U.S. interests, "virulent anti-Communism," and "national development based on free play of market forces."[10] The remedy: "practical steps to reduce [socioeconomic] inequities are . . . steps toward the mitigation of the broader human rights crisis of our times."[11] That is, fight for human rights with socialism.

The ease with which the Linowitz recommendations were incorporated into the IPS analysis and report demonstrated how strong had become the affinity between the views of the foreign-policy establishment and the New Left, how readily the categories of the new liberalism could be translated into those of revolutionary "socialism," and how short a step it was from utopian globalism and the expectation of change to anti-American perspectives and revolutionary activism. And the impact of these ideas on the Carter administration was enhanced by the appointment of members and associates of the IPS group (such as Robert Pastor, Mark Schneider, and Guy Erb) to key Latin American policy positions. In the administration these officials joined others with like-minded approaches to the Third World, including U.S. Ambassador Andrew Young and his deputy Brady Tyson.

This whole cluster of ideas—of facing painful truths, making a fresh start, forswearing force, and pursuing universal moral goals—was enormously attractive to Jimmy Carter. No sooner was he elected than he set out to translate them into a new policy for dealing with the nations of the hemisphere.

The repudiation of our hegemonic past was symbolized by the Panama Canal Treaties, to which the Carter administration—from the President on down—attached great importance and of which it was inordinately proud. As Vice President Mondale put it in Panama City, the treaties symbolized "the commitment of the U.S. to the belief that fairness and not force should lie at the heart of our dealings with the nations of the world." [12]

Anastasio Somoza's Nicaragua had the bad luck to become the second demonstration area for the "fresh start" in Latin America. Just because the regime had been so close and so loyal to the United States, its elimination would, in exactly the same fashion as the Panama Canal Treaties, dramatize the passing of the old era of "hegemony" in Central America and the arrival of a new era of equity and justice. As the editor of Foreign Affairs, William Bundy, noted, "Somoza [was] as good a symbol as could have been found of past U.S. policies in Latin America." [13]

The "global" approach adopted by the Carter administration constituted another sharp break with past U.S. practice. The "special relationship" with Latin America was gone. In speech after speech, the President, the Vice President, Secretary of State Vance, and Assistant Secretaries for Inter-American Affairs Terrance Todman and Viron Vaky explained that henceforth there would not be a U.S. policy toward Latin America. Instead, hemispheric policy would be incorporated into a global framework and Latin America would be treated in the context of the "North-South" dialogue. "What we do in Latin America," Vaky asserted, "must be a consistent part of our global policies." [14]

Incorporating the nations of Latin America into a "global framework" meant deemphasizing U.S. relations with them. Especially, it meant reducing U.S. assistance to the area, since from the perspective of North-South relations, Latin America's claim to assistance was not nearly as impressive as that of most other nations of the so-called

Third World. And, once the strategic perspective was abandoned, there was no reason at all for military assistance.

Not surprisingly, therefore, U.S. assistance to the countries of Latin America declined steadily during the Carter years. By 1980 the administration was requesting only half as much economic aid for Latin America as a decade earlier. Military assistance declined even more drastically—both quantitatively and qualitatively. Fewer countries were slated to receive military assistance, and more strings were attached to how they could use the amounts received. No new weapons systems could be purchased; instead, everyone was to be encouraged to acquire nonlethal weapons. Assistance in military training (which had produced many personal and professional ties between U.S. and Latin American officers) was cut sharply.

The "global" approach also encouraged the imposition of unprecedented curbs on the sale of arms. By 1978 the United States, long the most important supplier to Latin America, accounted for only 10 percent of arms sales. President Carter bragged to the OAS, "We have a better record in this hemisphere than is generally recognized. Four other nations of the world sell more weapons to Latin America than does the United States."[15]

The impact of the global approach was felt beyond arms sales. Although the nations of Latin America are major trading partners of the United States, and in 1979 accounted for one-sixth of total U.S. exports and 80 percent of U.S. private investment in the developing world, the Carter administration's manifest unconcern for hemispheric economic ties (as recommended in the Linowitz and IPS reports) resulted in a steady loss of ground to European and Asian competitors, all of whom enjoyed heavy support from their governments.

The global approach involved deemphasizing Latin American relations, not destabilizing governments. But other aspects of the Carter doctrine committed the administration to promoting "change." "Change," indeed, was the favorite word of administration policymakers. In speeches with titles like "Currents of Change in Latin America," Carter, Vance, and their associates voiced their conviction that the world was in the grip of an extraordinary process of transformation which was deep, irresistible, systematic, and desirable. Administration spokesmen reiterated in the fashion of a credo that our national interests align us naturally and inescapably with the forces of change, of democracy, of human rights, and of equitable development. And the belief that the whole world was caught up in a process of modernization moving it toward greater democracy and equality subtly transformed itself into an imperative: the United States should throw its power behind the "progressive" forces seeking change, even if they "seemed" anti-American or pro-Soviet.

If commitment to "change" was the rock on which Carter's Latin American policy was built, his human rights policy was the lever to implement change. Two aspects of the Carter approach to human rights are noteworthy. First, concern was limited to violations of human rights by governments. By definition, activities of terrorists and guerrillas could not qualify as violations of human rights, whereas a government's efforts to repress terrorism would quickly run afoul of Carter's human rights standards.

Secondly, human rights were defined not in terms of personal and legal rights—freedom from torture, arbitrary imprisonment, and arrest, as in the usage of Amnesty International and the U.S. Foreign Assistance Acts of 1961 and 1975—but in accordance with a much broader conception which included the political "rights" available only in democracies and the economic "rights" promised by socialism (shelter, food, health, education). It may be that no country in the world meets these standards; certainly no country in the Third World does. The very broadness of the definition invited an arbitrary and capricious policy of implementation. Panama, for instance, was rather mysteriously exempt from meeting the expansive criteria of the State Department's human rights office, while at the same time the other major nations of Central America were being censured (and undermined) for violations.

Why Panama, a dictatorship with a higher per capita income than Nicaragua, El Salvador, or Guatemala, did not qualify as a gross violator of human rights while the latter countries did; why and how an administration committed to nonintervention in the internal affairs of nations could try to replace an unacceptable government in Nicaragua with one more palatable to it; why such an administration should attempt not only to "normalize" relations with Cuba but also to destabilize the governments of El Salvador and Guatemala—to answer these questions required on the part of policymakers an intuitive understanding of which governments were outmoded and which reflected the wave of the future. What was *not* required was an ability to distinguish between which were Communist and which non-Communist. The President and other members of his administration apparently believed with Brzezinski that in most of the world ideological thinking had already given way to pragmatism and problem-solving, and that a concern with Communist ideology was therefore just another artifact of a past epoch, "the era of the cold war."

Ignoring the role of ideology had powerful effects on the administration's perception of conflicts and on its ability to make accurate

predictions. Although Fidel Castro has loudly and repeatedly proclaimed his revolutionary mission, and backed his stated intentions by
training insurgents and providing weapons and advisers, Carter's Assistant Secretary for Inter-American Affairs, William Bowdler, described Cuba as "an inefficient and shabby dictatorship" [16]—a description more appropriate to, say, Paraguay, than to an expansionist Soviet
client state with troops scattered throughout the world. The refusal to
take seriously, or even to take into account, the commitment of Fidel
Castro or Nicaragua's Sandinista leadership to Marxist-Leninist goals
and expansionist policies made it impossible to distinguish them either from traditional authoritarians or from democratic reformers, impossible to predict their likely attitudes toward the United States and
the Soviet Union, impossible to understand why in their view Costa
Rica and Mexico as well as Guatemala and Honduras constituted
inviting targets. Ignoring the force of ideology—and its powerful contemporary embodiments—fatally distorted the Carter administration's
view of politics in Central America and elsewhere.

The policies which grew out of these expectations have had a large
impact on U.S. relations with most nations of South America. In
Central America in particular, the direction of administration policy
interacted with the presence there of weak regimes and Cuban-sup-
ported insurgents to transform the region into a battleground in an
ideological war that the administration did not understand and could
not acknowledge.

Except for Mexico, the nations of Central America are quite small
and, by North American standards, quite poor. There are significant
social and economic differences among them. Guatemala's large traditionalist Indian population and multiple linguistic groups are unique
in the region, and bring with them special problems of economic,
social, and political integration. El Salvador's overcrowding places
especially heavy strains on its institutions. Revenues from the Canal
and the Canal Zone give Panama a higher per capita income than any
of its neighbors except Costa Rica and about twice that of the sparse,
scattered people of Honduras.

Despite their differences, these countries also share a good many
social and economic characteristics. All are "modernizing" nations in
the sense that in each of them urban, industrial, mobile, "modern"
sectors coexist with traditional patterns of life. In each, a large portion
of the population is still engaged in agriculture—most often employed
as landless laborers on large estates and plantations that have long
since made the transition to commercial agriculture. Economic growth
rates in Central America have been above the Latin American average,
and per capita income is high enough to rank these nations among the

"middle income" countries of the world. But in all of them, wealth is heavily concentrated in a small upper class and a thin but growing middle class, and large numbers live as they have always lived—in deep poverty, ill-nourished, ill-housed, illiterate.

Things have been getting better for the people of Central America—infant mortality rates have dropped, years in school have increased—but they have been getting better slowly. It has been easier to break down the myths justifying the old distribution of wealth in society than to improve access to education, medical care, decent housing, good food, respect, and political power.

There are also political differences among the small nations of Central America. Costa Rica has managed to develop and maintain (since 1948) a genuine democracy. Honduran politics has been especially violent, while Nicaragua (under the Somozas) was the most stable political regime. But again, despite differences, Guatemala, Honduras, El Salvador, Nicaragua, and Panama (like Costa Rica before 1948) share several characteristics with one another and with most of the nations of Latin America. These include a continuing disagreement about the legitimate ends and means of government, a pervasive distrust of authority, a broad ideological spectrum, a low level of participation in voluntary associations, a preference for hierarchical modes of association (church, bureaucracy, army), a history of military participation in politics, and a tradition of *personalismo*.

The boundaries between the political system, the economy, the military establishment, and the Church are often unclear and unreliable. Weak governments confront strong social groups, and no institution is able to establish its authority over the whole. Economic, ecclesiastical, and social groups influence but do not control the government; the government influences but does not control the economy, the military, the Church, and so on.

A democratic façade—elections, political parties, and fairly broad participation—is a feature of these systems. But the impact of democratic forms is modified by varying degrees of fraud, intimidation, and restrictions on who may participate. Corruption (the appropriation of public resources for private use) is endemic. Political institutions are not strong enough to channel and contain the claims of various groups to use public power to enforce preferred policies. No procedure is recognized as *the* legitimate route to power. Competition for influence proceeds by whatever means are at hand: the Church manipulates symbols of rectitude; workers resort to strikes; businessmen use bribery; political parties use campaigns and votes; politicians employ persuasion, organization, and demagoguery; military officers use force. Lack of consensus permits political competition of various kinds in various arenas and gives the last word to those who have at their disposal the greatest force. That usually turns out to be the leaders of the armed forces; most rulers in the area are generals.

Violence or the threat of violence is an integral, regular, predictable part of these political systems—a fact which is obscured by our way of describing military "interventions" in Latin American political systems as if the systems were normally peaceable. Coups, demonstrations, political strikes, plots, and counterplots are, in fact, the norm.

Traditionally, however, actual violence has been limited by the need to draw support from diverse sectors of the society and by the fact that politics has not been viewed as involving ultimate stakes. The various competitors for power have sought control of government to increase their wealth and prestige, not to achieve the "higher" and more dangerous purpose of restructuring society. In traditional Latin American politics, competitors do not normally destroy each other. They suffer limited defeats and win limited victories. The habit of permitting opponents to survive to fight another day is reflected in the tendency of the regimes to instability. In such a system a government normally lasts as long as it is able to prevent a coalition from forming among its opponents. Because there is no consensus on what makes government itself legitimate, successive regimes remain vulnerable to attacks on their legitimacy. They are also especially vulnerable to attacks on public order, which tends to be tenuous and to lack a firm base in tradition, habit, and affection.

To these patterns of political interaction there has been added in recent years the unfamiliar guerrilla violence of revolutionaries linked to Cuba by ideology, training, and the need for support, and through Cuba to the Soviet Union. Such groups rely on terrorism to destroy public order, to disrupt the economy and make normal life impossible, to demoralize the police, and to mortally wound the government by demonstrating its inability to protect personal security and maintain public authority. As Robert Chapman has emphasized, with the advent of terrorism as a *form* of revolution, a revolutionary situation can be created in any country whose government is weak or whose economy is vulnerable or dependent, with or without the participation of the masses.

Other new participants in the traditional pattern of political competition include the Socialist International and the Catholic Left. A number of socialist leaders (Willy Brandt, Olf Palme, Michael Manley), unable to win popular support for peaceful revolution in their own countries, have grown progressively enthusiastic about revolution elsewhere and less fastidious about the company they keep and the methods utilized. As for the Catholic Left, its interest in revolution on this earth has waxed as its concern with salvation in heaven has waned.

Traditionally, the ideological content of Latin American politics has been low, but since both the Socialist International and the radical Catholics conceive of themselves as specialists in rectitude, their participation has enhanced its moral intensity at the same time that Cubans have increased their violence.

The United States is by no means a new participant in Central America's politics, having played an important if intermittent role in its political struggles throughout much of the century. The United States has been important as a source of aid and has also exercised a veto power over governments in the area and reinforced with its tacit approval acceptable governments. Therefore, the objective economic and political dependency of nations in the area has been reinforced by a widespread sense of psychological dependency. Under the Carter administration the character of U.S. participation changed. Formerly, American representatives had been content to press the cause of U.S. economic or strategic interest. They now ask for something more problematic: internal reform, democracy, social justice—goods which even strong governments find it difficult to produce.

The nations of Central America (including Mexico) and the Caribbean all suffer from some form of institutional weakness because significant portions of the population have not been incorporated into the political system, and/or because political action is not fully institutionalized, and/or because the legitimacy of the government is in doubt, and/or because there is no consensus concerning legitimacy within the political elite, and/or because the economy is vulnerable to shifts in the international market, and/or because regular infusions of aid are required, and/or because rising expectations have outstripped capacities. All are vulnerable to disruption, and must rely on force to put down challenges to authority.

It is at this point that the roles of Cuba on the one hand, and the United States on the other hand, become crucial. Cuba stands ready to succor, bolster, train, equip, and advise revolutionaries produced within these societies and to supply weapons for a general insurgency when that is created. If customary aid and comfort from the United States in the form of money, arms, logistical support, and the services of counterinsurgency experts are no longer available, governments like those of Nicaragua, El Salvador, and Guatemala are weakened. And when it finally sinks in that the United States desires their elimination and prefers insurgents to incumbents, the blow to the morale and confidence of such weak traditional regimes is devastating.

341

The case of Nicaragua illustrates to perfection what happens when "affirmative pressures for change" on the part of the United States interact with Cuban-backed insurgency and a government especially vulnerable to shifts in U.S. policy.

The Nicaraguan political tradition combined participatory and autocratic elements in a characteristic Latin American mix. *Personalismo,* popular sovereignty, and brute force were present in the politics of Nicaragua from its founding as a separate nation in 1938 to the Sandinista triumph in July 1979. Throughout the nineteenth century and the first three decades of the twentieth, geographically based political factions representing a single, small ruling class competed under a symbolic two-party system in elections in which neither contender was willing to accept an unfavorable outcome. Frequently victory was obtained by enlisting the help of foreign governments and/or financial interests.

The United States was repeatedly called on by incumbent governments for assistance in maintaining peace. In 1910 it was the Conservatives who requested financial assistance and advice, and in 1912, again at their request, the United States posted a 100-man legation guard to Nicaragua. From then until 1933 an American military presence was a regular feature of the Nicaraguan political system. These U.S. troops (who at their height numbered about 2,700) supervised presidential elections and organized the National Guard, which was conceived as a professional national police force that would remain aloof from politics. In 1936, less than three years after American military forces had withdrawn, the leader of this "nonpolitical army," Colonel Anastasio Somoza García, ousted the Liberal president, Juan B. Sacasa. In this manner began the more than four decades of Nicaraguan politics dominated by the Somoza family.

Somocismo was based in the first instance on the military power of the National Guard. Its durability, however, also owed much to the political skills of the successive Somozas who ruled the country and headed its armed forces. These skills were reflected in the construction of an organizational base to support their personal power, longstanding success in exploiting divisions among their opponents, and the ability to retain U.S. support. The organizational basis of the Somozas' power is the most interesting factor because, like that of Juan Perón, it was largely created rather than captured.

The Somoza organization rested on four pillars: a hierarchically structured national party forged on the base of the traditional Liberal party; an expanded bureaucracy whose members also served as party workers; a national federation of trade unions created by the Somozas; and the National Guard. The whole operated rather like an efficient urban political machine, oiled by jobs, pensions, profits, status, and perquisites of various kinds. Most urban machines, however, do not have a private army. The loyalty of the National Guard was the most powerful testimony to the Somozas' political skill, for in Latin America armed forces are more easily won than retained. Nicaragua's National Guard remained loyal until after the last Somoza had fled.

Nicaraguan politics in the Somoza period featured limited repression and limited opposition. Criticism was permitted and, in fact, carried on day after day in the pages of *La Prensa* (whose editor was an opposition leader). Although the Somozas had large landholdings, the government enjoyed no monopoly of economic power, and made no serious effort to absorb or control the Church, education, or the culture. The government was moderately competent in encouraging economic development, moderately oppressive, and moderately corrupt. It was also an utter failure at delivering those social services that Americans and Europeans have come since the Depression to regard as the responsibility of government.

Anastasio Somoza Debayle, a West Point graduate with an American wife and an expansive appetite for women and alcohol, had accommodated successive American administrations and received aid from successive Congresses. He had every reason to suppose that his regime would continue to enjoy U.S. favor, and no reason to suppose that his power could be brought down by the small group of Cuban-backed terrorists who periodically disturbed the peace with their violence.

Three things seem to have upset these calculations. One was the progressive alienation of certain members of the country's *oligarquía* and business class when after the earthquake of 1972 Somozistas raked off too large a share of the international relief; a second factor was Somoza's heart attack; the third and most important factor was the election of Jimmy Carter and the adoption of an all-new Latin American policy.

At the time the Carter administration was inaugurated in January 1977, three groups of unequal strength competed for power in Nicaragua: the President and his loyal lieutenants, who enjoyed the advantages of incumbency, a degree of legitimacy, a nationwide organization, and the unwavering support of the National Guard; the legal opposition parties, which had been gathered into a loose coalition headed by Joaquin Chamorro, editor of *La Prensa*; and several small revolutionary groups, whose Cuban-trained leaders had finally forged a loose alliance, the FSLN (Sandinist National Liberation Front).

From the moment the FSLN adopted the tactics of a broad alliance, the offensive against Somoza was carried out on a variety of fronts. There was violence in the form of assassinations and assaults on army barracks. When the government reacted, the United States condemned it for violations of human rights. The legal opposition put forward demands for greater democracy which had the endorsement of the FSLN, thus making it appear that democracy was the goal of the insurgency.

Violence and counterviolence weakened the regime by demonstrating that it could not maintain order. The combination of impotence and repression in turn emboldened opponents in and out of the country, provoking more reprisals and more hostility in a vicious circle that culminated finally in the departure of Somoza and the collapse of the National Guard.

What did the Carter administration do in Nicaragua? *It brought down the Somoza regime.* The Carter administration did not "lose" Nicaragua in the sense in which it was once charged Harry Truman had "lost" China, or Eisenhower Cuba, by failing to prevent a given outcome. In the case of Nicaragua, the State Department *acted* repeatedly and at critical junctures to weaken the government of Anastasio Somoza and to strengthen his opponents.

First, it declared "open season" on the Somoza regime. When in the spring of 1977 the State Department announced that shipments of U.S. arms would be halted because of human rights violations, and followed this with announcements in June and October that economic aid would be withheld, it not only deprived the Somoza regime of needed economic and military support but served notice that the regime no longer enjoyed the approval of the United States and could no longer count on its protection. This impression was strongly reinforced when after February 1978 Jimmy Carter treated the two sides in the conflict as more or less equally legitimate contenders—offering repeatedly to help "both sides" find a "peaceful solution."

Second, the Carter administration's policies inhibited the Somoza regime in dealing with its opponents while they were weak enough to be dealt with. Fearful of U.S. reproaches and reprisals, Somoza fluctuated between repression and indulgence in his response to FSLN violence. The rules of the Carter human rights policy made it impossible for Somoza to resist his opponents effectively. As Viron Vaky remarked about the breakdown in negotiations between Somoza and the armed opposition: " . . . when the mediation was suspended we announced that the failure of the mediation had created a situation in which it was clear violence was going to continue, that it would result in repressive measures and therefore our relationships could not continue on the same basis as in the past."[17] When the National Palace was attacked and hostages were taken, Somoza's capitulation to FSLN demands enhanced the impression that he could not control the situation and almost certainly stimulated the spread of resistance.

Third, by its "mediation" efforts and its initiatives in the Organization of American States (OAS), the Carter administration encouraged the internationalization of the opposition. Further, it demoralized Somoza and his supporters by insisting that Somoza's continuation in power was the principal obstacle to a viable, centrist, democratic government. Finally, the State Department deprived the Somoza regime of legitimacy not only by repeated condemnations for human rights violations but also by publishing a demand for Somoza's resignation and by negotiating with the opposition.

Without these "affirmative pressures," William Bundy concluded in *Foreign Affairs:* "It seems a safe bet that Tacho Somoza would still be in charge in Nicaragua and his amiable brother-in-law still extending abrazos to all and sundry in Washington as dean of the diplomatic corps."[18]

Why did the Carter administration do these things? Because it thought the fall of Somoza would bring progress to Nicaragua. Viron Vaky put it this way: "Nicaragua's tragedy stems from dynastic rule. Times have changed. Nicaragua has changed, but the government of Nicaragua has not."[19]

History was against Somoza. He was an obstacle to progress. He should relinquish power to make room for "change." When he declined to do so, the Carter administration accused him of "polarizing" the situation. When the National Guard responded to FSLN violence with violence, the State Department said that the National Guard had "radicalized the opposition."

On the other hand, the fact that Cubans were supplying arms to the FSLN was not regarded as being of much importance. Brandon Grove, Jr., Deputy Assistant Secretary for Inter-American Affairs, explained to the Foreign Affairs Committee of the House (June 7, 1979):

The flow of such supplies is a symptom of the deeper problem in Nicaragua: polarization and its attendant violence that day by day are contributing to the growing alienation of the Nicaraguan government from its people. . . . The real cause for concern today should be the breakdown . . . of trust between government and people essential for the democratic process to function.[20]

Since the "real" problem was not Cuban arms but Somoza, obviously the United States should not act to reinforce a regime that had proved its political and moral failure by becoming the object of attack. Because the State Department desired not to "add to the partisan factionalism," it declined to supply arms to the regime. "The supplying of arms in a war situation we feel only adds to the suffering. We have urged others not to do that."

In the event, the Carter administration did a good deal more than "urge." In June 1979, after the United States and the OAS had called for Somoza's resignation, and U.S. representatives William Bowdler and Lawrence Pezzullo had met with the FSLN, the State Department undertook to apply the final squeeze to the Somoza regime—putting pressure on Israel to end arms sales, and working out an oil embargo to speed the capitulation of Somoza's forces. They were so successful that for the second time in a decade an American ally ran out of gas and ammunition while confronting an opponent well armed by the Soviet bloc.

The FSLN was not the State Department's preferred replacement for Somoza. Nevertheless, from the spring of 1977, when the State Department announced that it was halting a promised arms shipment to Somoza's government, through the summer of 1980, when the administration secured congressional approval of a $75 million aid package for Nicaragua, U.S. policy under Jimmy Carter was vastly more supportive of the Sandinistas than it was of the Somoza regime, despite the fact that Somoza and his government were as doggedly friendly and responsive to U.S. interests and desires as the Sandinistas were hostile and nonresponsive.

The Carter administration expected that democracy would emerge in Nicaragua. Their scenario prescribed that the winds of change would blow the outmoded dictator out of office and replace him with a popular government. Even after it had become clear that the FSLN, which was known to harbor powerful antidemocratic tendencies, was the dominant force in the new regime, U.S. spokesmen continued to speak of the events in Nicaragua as a democratic revolution. In December 1979, for example, Deputy Secretary of State Warren Christopher attempted to reassure doubting members of the Senate Foreign Relations Committee that "the driving consensus among Nicaraguans" was "to build a new Nicaragua through popular participation that is capable of meeting basic human needs."[21]

The expectation that change would produce progress and that socialism would mean social justice made it difficult for Carter policymakers to assess Nicaragua's new rulers realistically, even though grounds for concern about their intentions, already numerous before their triumph, continued to multiply in its aftermath.

Revolution begins with destruction. The first fruit of the destabilization of Somoza's government and the reinforcement of his opponents was a civil war in which some 40,000 Nicaraguans lost their most basic human right (life), another 100,000 were left homeless, and some $2 billion worth of destruction was wrought. Nicaragua was left in a shambles.

Where did the expectations, the hopes, the intentions of the Carter administration then lead us, and the Nicaraguans who took the consequences? Although the FSLN had solemnly committed itself to hold free elections, its leaders have shown no disposition to share the power they seized in July 1979. To the contrary, the consolidation and centralization of power have moved steadily forward. Despite the strenuous opposition of the two non-FSLN junta members, the Sandinista directorate which has effectively ruled Nicaragua since the fall of Somoza moved in the spring of 1980 to institutionalize its control of Nicaragua's Council of State by expanding and "restructuring" it to ensure the Sandinistas a permanent majority. (Under the reform they would be assured of twenty-four of forty-seven seats where previously they had been entitled to only thirteen of thirty-three.)

Meanwhile, the election to which the FSLN had committed itself has been pushed further and further into a receding future, even though the new rulers, who need all the help they can get, have been under heavy pressure from the governments of Venezuela, Costa Rica, and the United States to set a date. Sandinista leaders have made no secret of their opinion that competitive elections are an unsatisfactory and unnecessary mechanism for choosing rulers. Junta members have asserted that the people spoke through the revolution—"with their blood and with the guns in their hands the people have cast their votes"[22] (as a junta member told *The Economist*)—and that anyway, having been brainwashed by forty years of Somoza rule, they are not capable of choosing among candidates—at least not until they have been "reeducated."

In the last days of August 1980, the restructured Council of State announced that elections will not be held before 1985. And those elections, declared Humberto Ortega Saavedra (Minister of Defense), "will serve to reinforce and improve the revolution and not to give just anyone more power, which belongs to the people." Meanwhile, no "proselytizing activities" on behalf of any candidate will be permitted before candidates are officially designated by an electoral agency which itself will be created in 1984 (and violations will be punished by terms of three months to three years in jail).

Decrees accompanying these decisions have underscored the junta's distaste for criticism. Henceforth, dissemination of news concerning scarcities of food and other consumer goods is prohibited on pain of imprisonment (from two months to two years), as is "unconfirmed" information concerning armed encounters or attacks on government personnel.

These restrictions constitute one more significant step in the Sandinistas' gradual campaign to control the climate of opinion. Television and radio have already been brought under control. Among opposition newspapers, only *La Prensa* remains; it has already come under pressures more harsh than those applied to the media during the Somoza era, and its continuation as an independent critical voice is at best uncertain. The requirement that all professional journalists join a new government-sponsored union as a condition of employment represents yet another move to bring the press under control. The literacy campaign has extended the junta's reach further into the minds of Nicaragua's people as well as into the countryside. Every lesson in the literacy textbooks instructs students (and teachers) in the prescribed interpretation of Nicaragua's past, present, and future.

Parallel efforts to organize and coordinate other traditionally nongovernmental entities reflect the characteristic totalitarian desire to absorb the society into the state, to transform social groups into agencies and instruments of the government. This has required taking over some existing institutions (banking, industries, television and radio, trade unions), co-opting and/or intimidating others (the private sector, trade unions, the educational establishment, portions of the press), and forcibly eliminating still others (such as the National Guard, whose members have either fled into exile or remain in prison with little prospect of ever being tried, much less released).

When, in early November 1980, representatives of the private sector (COSEP) and the labor federation (CUS) withdrew from the State Council to protest the Sandinistas' ever-tightening grip on all aspects of the economy, no concessions were forthcoming. Instead, the offices of the leading opposition party, the social-democratic MND, were sacked, and an unarmed leader of the private sector, Jorge Salazar, was gunned down by Sandinista police.

Among the traditional pillars of Nicaraguan society only the Church remains relatively intact. While the presence of priests in prominent roles in the Sandinista directorate has facilitated communications between the two groups, this has not been translated into political domination of the Church hierarchy.

But the Sandinistas do not rely on control of these agencies or rules to preserve their power. To accomplish that task new institutions have been forged, the most important of which are an enormous, all-new revolutionary army whose training (military and political) and equipment have been provided by Cubans, and a new internal police force which is already more extensive and effective than Somoza's.

Other institutions developed to support the new government include the "block" committees, which were found to be so useful in Cuba (and in Nazi Germany), and the revolutionary brigades, initially assigned to the literacy campaign.

The most telling indicator of the Sandinistas' intentions and commitments is their unambiguous identification of Nicaragua with the foreign policy and perspectives of the Soviet Union. The first step was somewhat tentative: Nicaragua merely abstained on the U.S. resolution condemning the Soviet invasion of Afghanistan. Subsequent moves have left less room for doubt. At the Havana conference of the nonaligned nations, Nicaragua became one of the few countries in the world to recognize Kampuchea (the regime imposed by North Vietnam on Cambodia), an act which Foreign Minister Miguel d'Escoto explained as "a consequence of our revolutionary responsibility as Sandinistas to recognize the right of the peoples of Kampuchea to be free." In Pyongyang, another Sandinista leader, Tomás Borge, assured the North Koreans of Nicaraguan solidarity and promised, "The Nicaraguan revolution will not be content until the imperialists have been overthrown in all parts of the world."

In March 1980 the Sandinista directorate offered a public demonstration that its ties extended beyond Cuba to the Socialist Fatherland itself when four top leaders—Moisés Hassán Morales, Tomás Borge, Henry Hernández Ruiz, and Humberto Ortega Saavedra—paid an official visit to the Soviet Union. A joint communiqué formalized the attachment of Nicaragua to Soviet global policy. In addition to signing multiple agreements concerning trade and cooperation, condemning South Africa and Chile, and applauding Zimbabwe, Khomeini's Iran, and the "legitimate national rights of the Arab people of Palestine," the "two sides" strongly attacked the NATO decision to deploy medium-range nuclear missile weapons and condemned the "mounting international tension in connection with the events in Afghanistan, which has been launched by the imperialist and reactionary forces aimed at subverting the inalienable rights of the people of the Democratic Republic of Afghanistan and of other peoples . . . to follow a path of progressive transformation."

Since "Zionism's loss of a bastion in Nicaragua" (Moisés Hassán), the ties with the "Palestinian people" have become not closer, but more public. The PLO and the Sandinistas had long enjoyed a relationship of mutual support, we are now told. Sandinistas trained in Palestinian camps and participated in PLO raids; the PLO reciprocated by ferrying arms to the Sandinistas in their hour of need. Yasir

Arafat received high honors when in July 1980 he opened a PLO embassy in Managua, where he assured the "workers" that "the triumph of the Nicaraguans is the PLO's triumph."

"We have emerged from one dictatorship and entered another," asserted MND leader Alfonso Robelo recently. "Nicaragua has become a satellite of a satellite of the Soviet Union."

Nothing that happened in Nicaragua seemed able to dampen the Carter people's enthusiasm for "change" in Central America. In El Salvador, Guatemala, Bolivia, and wherever else the opportunity presented itself, the administration aligned the United States with the "forces of change." "The fundamental problem we share with our neighbors," Warren Christopher explained, "is not that of defending stability in the face of revolution. Rather, it is to build a more stable, equitable, and pluralistic order. That is the challenge of Nicaragua in the present day and that is the challenge of the whole region."

To meet the challenge, the administration welcomed with enthusiasm a military coup in El Salvador which, in October 1979, overthrew President Carlos Humberto Romero, an event the State Department described as a "watershed date" on which "young officers broke with the old repressive order" and along with "progressive civilians" formed a government committed to "profound social and economic reforms, respect for human rights and democracy." Carter policymakers, had they taken more account of El Salvador's political culture and traditions, would have been less sanguine.

El Salvador is a prototype, almost a caricature, of a Central American republic. Its political history since it was established as an independent republic in 1838 has featured oligarchy, violence, revolution, militarism, and the slow evolution of the institutions of a modern polity.

To an extent unusual even in Latin America, El Salvador had been dominated by a relatively small, homogeneous economic and social aristocracy which controlled a large share of the arable land, much of the country's commerce, and a significant portion of its wealth. As elsewhere in the region, however, the social homogeneity of the elite did not lead to political harmony or stability. Factionalism, schism, low consensus prevailed. Elite factions operating under the symbolism of a two-party system competed for power by legal and nonlegal means. There were periods of peaceful alternation in power and periods when coups and countercoups, uprisings and revolts, were common. At the beginning of the century there occurred a period of unusual stability. Gradually participation in El Salvador's political process was expanded, and after 1931 large numbers of Salvadorans participated in decision processes—now by legal means, such as the intermittent elections, now through strikes, demonstrations, and other forms of direct action. Through most of the last fifty years, politics in El Salvador was carried on through conventional political parties, occasional elections, military coups, student strikes, trade union actions—that is, by the multiple means and in the multiple arenas common in Latin American politics.

The fifteen-odd constitutions in El Salvador are perhaps the best indicator of its regime instability, and the periodic coups, the last of which occurred in October 1979, are perhaps the best indicator of the chronic institutional weakness that has made it impossible for any government to endure long. The important role of the military, the frequent recourse to force, the multiple constitutions, provide all the evidence required that El Salvador is a polity in which there is little agreement on who should rule, or on the means by which the question should be decided. This is, of course, another way of saying that El Salvador's governments and processes have a low level of legitimacy and authority. The absence of agreement about what makes government legitimate leaves all holders of power vulnerable to the charge that their power is *not* legitimate, gives a certain plausibility to *any* claim for power presented in the name of any conception of the public good, and ensures that there will be no generally accepted means for settling the dispute about who among the rival claimants for power should hold it. Moreover, the ubiquity of violence in the political tradition guarantees that resorting to violence will not be viewed as a disqualification for governing.

The fact of regime instability means that generalized loyalty to the "system" has no opportunity to develop. Under these circumstances, distinctions common in political science between "system" parties and "anti-system" parties become meaningless. There are only incumbents and their policies, and all those who are not with them are against them. Thus, to be anti-incumbent usually means to be anti-system. There is no constitutional means for resolving any dispute about the composition of a government or its policies, because there is, effectively speaking, no constitution, no generally accepted "arrangement of offices" (Aristotle's term). There are only those *persons* who hold power.

Yet serious students of politics agree that legitimacy is an irreducible element of a stable political regime. Max Weber emphasized this principle when he said: "Custom, personal advantage, pure affectual or ideal motives of solidarity do not form a sufficiently reliable basis for a given domination. In addition, there is normally a further element, the belief in *legitimacy*." [23] And Rousseau put it more succinctly at the beginning of Chapter III of his *Social Contract*: "The strongest is never strong enough to be always master, unless he transforms strength into right, and obedience into duty."[24]

Any government whose claim to obedience depends on the fact that it possesses power is vulnerable because any competitor who is able to seize power will then possess an identical claim to obedience. "Obey the powers that be," Rousseau commanded. "If this means yield to force, it is a good precept, but superfluous."[25]

El Salvador's political culture compounds the problem of legitimacy. Like the broader culture, its political culture emphasizes strength and *machismo* and all that implies about the nature of the world and the human traits necessary for survival and success. Competition, courage, honor, shrewdness, assertiveness, a capacity for risk and recklessness, and a certain "manly" disregard for safety are valued. There is a predictable congruity between the cultural traits and political patterns in El Salvador, a congruity expressed in the persistent tendency to schism and violence within the political class. Intermittent disruption and violence make order the highest value in such political systems.

Order, as John Stuart Mill emphasized, is the "preservation of all existing goods." It is also the precondition for all other public goods, as Mill understood better than is generally realized. And, as always, heroes are people who make a special contribution to highly valued goods.

In El Salvador, Hernández Martínez is viewed as such a hero by many. General Maximiliano Hernández Martínez, who governed El Salvador from 1931 to 1944, had been Minister of War in the cabinet of President Arturo Araujo when there occurred widespread uprisings said to be the work of Communist agitators. General Hernández Martínez then staged a coup and ruthlessly suppressed the disorders—wiping out all those who participated, hunting down their leaders. It is sometimes said that 30,000 persons lost their lives in the process. To many Salvadorans the violence of this repression seems less important than the fact of restored order and the thirteen years of civil peace that ensued. The traditionalist death squads that pursue revolutionary activists and leaders in contemporary El Salvador call themselves Hernández Martínez Brigades, seeking thereby to place themselves in El Salvador's political tradition and communicate their purposes.

There is, inevitably, an arbitrary quality about governments which can reform themselves only by force or intrigue. And there is an inevitable brittleness about a polity in which political loyalty means loyalty to particular individuals—not to individuals who have been institutionalized in the fashion that kings and presidents are institutionalized, but to individuals whose claim to power rests ultimately on the fact that they *have* it.

Where there is no legitimacy, there is also no authority. There is only power and the habit of obedience to whoever successfully claims the power of government. *Under these circumstances, a government's status depends, even more than usually, on its capacity to govern, to secure obedience, to punish those who disobey—in sum, to maintain order.* Such a government can command obedience only insofar as it can secure acquiescence in its policies, can rely on habits of obedience, or can impose its commands by force and fear. Such a government is, then, especially vulnerable to terrorist subversion, and for three reasons.

First, not having been chosen by the people, it has no persuasive claim to a popular mandate for its programs. Neither are there institutionalized means for securing such a mandate. Moreover, men who have gained power by force are rarely content to submit their programs for popular approval.

Second, the principal function of terrorism is to disrupt the ordinary life of the society, disturb the normal expectations of ordinary people, and destroy habit and order, which is the central value of a system that has no unique claim to a popular, legal, or moral mandate.

Third, where neither habit nor duty can be relied on to compel obedience, force will be necessary to maintain order. But force also disrupts order and feeds the impression that there is no important difference between rulers who govern by force and challengers who compete with force. *The ultimate weakness of a government that arrives in power by force and must govern by force is its defenselessness against the use of force by others.*

To secure order in El Salvador would either require that all participants (military, guerrillas) agree that they *should* obey the policies of the junta—agree, that is, that the government has a *legitimate* claim on their obedience—or require that the government be able to compel their obedience. But the traditional lack of consensus on the ends and means of government and the broad ideological differences among the parties make agreement on legitimacy unlikely. Like most of its predecessors, the present government probably lacks the necessary force, and moreover, has been inhibited in using the force at its disposal by our policymakers' powerful proclivity for believing that a government's using force is the equivalent of violating human rights.

Until the violent events of November–December 1980, which also saw the suspension of U.S. aid, the Carter administration backed the new Salvadoran junta in the only way it knew how: by helping it to bring about "profound social and economic reforms." In the effort to preempt the revolution and expedite the achievement of "social justice," the administration supplied experts who have planned the most thoroughgoing land reform in the Western Hemisphere. To encourage and finance these and related reforms, the U.S. embassy provided nearly $20 million in long-term loans at very low interest. Under the direction of the American Institute for Free Labor Development, and sponsored by the AFL-CIO, a plan was drafted to transfer to some 250,000 of El Salvador's 300,000 peasants ownership of the land they work.

So far, not all the land has been transferred, and titles have not been delivered for much of what has been transferred. Few of the former owners have yet received any significant compensation. In theory, the reforms will vaccinate the masses against Communism by giving them a stake in the society. In practice, as was made dramatically clear by the murder of three American nuns and a social worker in early December 1980, continuing violence from Communists, anti-Communists, and simple criminals has brought death and destruction to El Salvador. Under the pressure of that violence, the society has begun to come apart. "There is no name for what exists in my country," commented a Salvadoran, describing the random murder, intimidation, and looting. But there is a name; it is "anarchy."

The United States under Carter was more eager to impose land reform than elections in El Salvador. Although claims and counterclaims have been exchanged, there is no way of knowing whether the junta (in any of its manifestations) has enjoyed much popular support. It combines Christian Democrats committed to finding a middle way of "true democracy" between capitalism and Communism with representatives of various tendencies within the armed forces. It is chronically threatened with schism from within and coup from without. Though its civilian members and their State Department supporters have consistently emphasized the danger from the Right—that is, from authoritarian, intensely anti-Communist defenders of the status quo—El Salvador is more likely in the long run to fall to a coalition of revolutionaries trained, armed, and advised by Cuba and others. The cycle of escalating terror and repression is already far advanced. By failing to offer the junta the arms and advice required to turn back the well-equipped insurgency, the Carter administration undermined the junta's ability to survive and encouraged the insurgents in their conviction of ultimate victory.

More than nine thousand persons were slaughtered in El Salvador during the year since the new day dawned. The reforms that were counted on to provide social justice have been stalled by administrative inefficiency and sabotaged by both communitarians and defenders of the *status quo ante.* The harvests counted on to help El Salvador's acute balance-of-payments problems are being menaced and destroyed by revolutionaries for whose cause worse *is* better. Meanwhile, violence perpetrated by Communists, anti-Communists, and simple criminals continues.

What is to be done? It is not a problem to which the American temper is well suited. The problem confronting El Salvador is Thomas Hobbes's problem: How to establish order and authority in a society where there is none.

There are few grounds for thinking that Americans who have shaped U.S. policy toward El Salvador have been aware of the distinctive characteristics and problems of such political systems. Had they understood them, then some aspects of our policy would surely have been different. The administration would have been inclined to greet the coup of October 1979 which toppled President Carlos Humberto Romero with mixed feelings, instead of greeting it as Assistant Secretary of State William C. Bowdler did, as the dawn of a new era, a "watershed date," in which "young officers broke with the old repressive order" and along with "progressive civilians" formed a government committed to "profound social and economic reforms, respect for human rights and democracy."

A more prudent appraisal of politics in Central America would have left policymakers a little less enthusiastic about the destruction of any even semi-constitutional ruler, not because they approved the ruler but because they understood that authority in such systems is weak, stability fragile, and order much easier to destroy than reconstruct.

Second, a fuller understanding of the political system of El Salvador would have left U.S. policymakers a bit less sanguine about the short-range contributions of reform to political stability, not because reforms are not desirable but because political traditions and cultures change slowly, not rapidly.* Third, clear comprehension of the problem of order in El Salvador would have made U.S. policymakers more sympathetic to the inability of the government to control the situation, and less anxious to inhibit the use of force against violent challengers.

Armed with an optimistic, deterministic theory of social change, a profound distaste for existing governments in the area, a predilection for confusing revolution with progress, and a doctrine of human rights that makes illegitimate the use of force by governments, U.S. policymakers participated actively in the creation and control of a

---

* There are, of course, other good reasons for undertaking reform, such as promoting well-being, alleviating poverty, and enhancing the quality of community.

government and policies with which they are now profoundly unhappy.

One of the fictions widespread in our times is that a successful
society can do without force, and that the resort to it is evidence of
failure. We like to think that the "force" that decides political contests
is *moral force* that derives from the loyalty and allegiance of the people.
This was of course the premise of the U.S. campaign for the "hearts
and minds" in Vietnam. It was (and is) also the grounds for the
argument that land reform would reinforce the junta in El Salvador:
Government would give land to landless peasants; peasants would
give loyalty to the government. Revolution would wither away because peasants would be immune to its appeals.

The problem with this theory of course is that revolutions are not
born out of the resentments of landless peasants but (as Plato understood) in the bosom of the ruling elite.[26] As Lasswell, Lerner, and
associates showed[27] (and dozens of subsequent empirical studies confirmed), revolutions in our times are born in the middle class and
carried out by sons of the middle class who have become skilled in the
use of propaganda, organization, and violence. Modern tacticians of
revolution seem to have understood as well as American policymakers have misunderstood the vulnerability of societies like El Salvador
to challenges based on and pressed by force. They seem also to understand the special vulnerability of Western liberals to appeals that feature murder and morality.

Central America was not the only target of the Carter administration's restless search for "constructive change" in the hemisphere.
Pressures were applied, and resisted, in Argentina, Brazil, Uruguay,
and Bolivia. In Bolivia, the State Department withdrew our ambassador, "drew down" the embassy staff to approximately half its normal
size, canceled U.S. aid, terminated the Drug Enforcement Agency's
program that aimed at reducing the production of cocoa (and cocaine), and indicated in a dozen other ways its determination not to
accept the military junta whose seizure of power prevented the inauguration of Hernán Siles Zuazo as President.

Why did the United States work so hard to undo a coup which
had prevented the accession to power of a man whose Vice President
had strong Castroite leanings and ties, whose coalition included the
Communist party of Bolivia and the Castroite MIR, and whose eleva-
tion had been strongly supported by the Soviet Union? When Siles
Zuazo polled 38 percent of the vote in a race against moderate socialist
Victor Paz Estensorro and the more conservative Hugo Banzer Suarez,
the selection of the President was left to the Congress. No legal or
conventional niceties required that U.S. influence be exerted in behalf

of the selection of Siles Zuazo rather than one of the other candidates. Yet Siles Zuazo became the "American candidate" even though the military had made clear that his selection would not be tolerated. After conversations with the U.S. ambassador that included both threats and promises of aid, Paz Estensorro withdrew and Siles's selection was ensured. The predictable coup occurred.

Even five years ago, the United States would have welcomed a coup that blocked a government with a significant Communist/Castroite component. Ten years ago the United States would have sponsored it, fifteen years ago we would have conducted it. This time, however, the U.S. ambassador to Bolivia and the State Department lobbied hard in Washington and with the press against the new military rulers, insisting that what had occurred was not a coup like the two hundred previous ones, but a singularly objectionable coup marked by unique violence, engineered by foreigners, and led by drug traffickers. The State Department's campaign coincided with a Soviet press offensive, resulting in a sustained international campaign bent on bringing Siles to power.

One understands the desire to see constitutional democracy replace authoritarian governments in Bolivia. Despite a good deal of recent mythmaking to the contrary, Americans have always believed that democracy is the best government for everyone. What was unusual about the Carter policy was the *intensity* of the expressed disapproval and of the administration's preference for a government that included in its leadership persons effectively attached to Soviet policies and hostile to the United States. The decision to throw its weight behind Siles reflected the characteristic predilections of the Carter administration in Latin America, including its indifference to strategic concerns and its tendency to believe that leftists were more likely than any other group to bring democracy and social justice to the area. Supporting Siles seemed to offer the Carter administration an opportunity to assume its preferred role: trying to "moderate," by its goodwill and friendship, the "extreme" elements in a governing coalition committed to "basic" social change.

Because it failed to take account of basic characteristics of Latin American political systems, the Carter administration underestimated the fragility of order in these societies and overestimated the ease with which authority, once undermined, can be restored. Because it regarded revolutionaries as beneficent agents of change, it mistook their goals and motives and could not grasp the problem of governments which become the object of revolutionary violence. Because it misunderstood the relations between economics and politics, it wrongly assumed (as in El Salvador) that economic reforms would necessarily

357

and promptly produce positive political results. Because it misunderstood the relations between "social justice" and authority, it assumed that only "just" governments can survive. Finally, because it misunderstood the relations between justice and violence, the Carter administration fell (and pushed its allies) into an effort to fight howitzers with land reform and urban guerrillas with improved fertilizers.

Above all, the Carter administration failed to understand *politics*. Politics is conducted by persons who by various means, including propaganda and violence, seek to realize some vision of the public good. Those visions may be beneficent or diabolic. But they constitute the real motives of real political actors. When men are treated like "forces" (or the agents of forces), their intentions, values, and world view tend to be ignored. But in Nicaragua the intentions and ideology of the Sandinistas have *already* shaped the outcome of the revolution, as in El Salvador the intentions and ideology of the leading revolutionaries create intransigence where there might have been willingness to cooperate and compromise, nihilism where there might have been reform.

The first step in the reconstruction of U.S. policy for Latin America is intellectual. It requires thinking more realistically about the politics of Latin America, about the alternatives to existing governments, and about the amounts and kinds of aid and time that would be required to improve the lives and expand the liberties of the people of the area. The choices are frequently unattractive.

The second step toward a more adequate policy is to assess realistically the impact of various alternatives on the security of the United States and on the safety and autonomy of the other nations of the hemisphere.

The third step is to abandon the globalist approach which denies the realities of culture, character, geography, economics, and history in favor of a vague, abstract universalism "stripped," in Edmund Burke's words, "of every relation," standing "in all the nakedness and solitude of metaphysical abstraction." What must replace it is a foreign policy that builds (again Burke) on the "concrete circumstances" which "give . . . to every political principle its distinguishing color and discriminating effect."

Once the intellectual debris has been cleared away, it should become possible to construct a Latin American policy that will protect U.S. security interests and make the actual lives of actual people in Latin America somewhat better and somewhat freer.

Notes

1. Zbigniew Brzezinski, *Between Two Ages: America's Role in the Technetronic Era* (New York: The Viking Press, 1970).

2. Ibid., p. 288.

3. Ibid., p. 289.

4. Ibid., p. 288.

5. *The Americas in a Changing World*, report by the Commission on United States–Latin American Relations, Center for Inter-American Relations, October 1974, p. 2.

6. *The United States and Latin America: Next Steps*, Center for Inter-American Relations, December 20, 1976.

7. *The Southern Connection: Recommendations for a New Approach to Inter-American Relations*, Ad-Hoc Working Group on Latin America, Transnational Institute, a program of the Institute for Policy Studies, Washington, D.C., February 1977.

8. Ibid., p. 3.

9. Ibid., p. 4.

10. Ibid., p. 5.

11. Ibid., p. 6.

12. *Department of State Bulletin*, November 1979, pp. 54–55.

13. William P. Bundy, "Who Lost Patagonia? Foreign Policy in the 1980 Campaign," *Foreign Affairs*, vol. 58, no. 1 (Fall 1979), p. 10.

14. *Department of State Bulletin*, April 1979, p. 61.

15. Ibid., September 1978, p. 55.

16. Statement to House Subcommittee on Inter-American Affairs, May 20, 1980.

17. *U.S. Policy toward Nicaragua*, Hearings of Subcommittee on Inter-American Affairs, June 21–26, 1979, p. 40.

18. Bundy, "Who Lost Patagonia?" p. 9.

19. *Department of State Bulletin*, April 1979, p. 58.

20. Ibid., p. 62.

21. Ibid., March 1980, p. 69.

22. *The Economist*, May 10, 1980, p. 22.

23. Max Weber, in *Economy and Society*, Gunther, Roth, and Wittich, eds. (New York: Bedminister Press, 1968), p. 213.

24. Jean Jacques Rousseau, *The Social Contract and Discourses*, translated with introduction by G. D. H. Cole (London: J. M. Dent & Sons, 1913), p. 188.

25. Ibid.

26. Plato, *The Republic* (Oxford, England: Clarendon Press, 1941).

27. Harold D. Lasswell and Daniel Lerner, eds., *World Revolutionary Elites: Studies in Coercive Ideological Movements* (Cambridge, Mass.: MIT Press, 1965).

12

The Apple of Discord:
Central America in
U.S. Domestic Politics

MARK FALCOFF

On July 19, 1979, a revolution in Nicaragua brought an end to the
thirty-five year rule of the Somoza dynasty, and just under four
months later a coup in neighboring El Salvador deposed a military
dictator and installed in his place a joint military-civilian junta, including the reformist Christian Democratic party. By mid-1980 Salvadoran
society was plainly coming apart, as elements of the new government
fell to quarreling among themselves. Meanwhile, armed formations of
the revolutionary left—representing themselves as the "authentic" expression of the Salvadoran people—sought to overthrow the new government. A general strike called for this purpose on August 13–15
failed of its purpose, and in December, José Napoleón Duarte, a
Christian Democrat with a record of liberal political commitment, was
installed as president of the junta. While Duarte, with the support of
the U.S. government, began preparations for elections, scheduled for
March 1982, the rebels stepped up their activities, plunging the nation
into a protracted civil war.

These were momentous, one might even say epochal events for
Central America. But they were far less so for the United States,
whose attentions at the time were absorbed by a round of presidential
primaries. Insofar as it took note of foreign policy issues at all, U.S.
opinion was wholly absorbed by the invasion of Afghanistan and the
hostage crisis in Iran.

This was no coincidence: in the best of times Central America has
never occupied a very important place in the foreign policy conscious-

The author expresses appreciation to Andrew Hoehn and Janine Perfit for research
assistance.

360

ness of Americans. In this, 1980 was wholly typical. A survey conducted in the first days of 1981 found that respondents ranked the conflict in El Salvador as the fourteenth most important news story of the previous year, just above the marriage of Prince Charles to Lady Diana Spencer but, strikingly, also less compelling than the air controller's strike, the passage of the income tax cut, and approval of the sale of AWACS to Saudi Arabia.[1] A year later the state of public knowledge was not appreciably greater—three-fifths of the American public, including two-fifths of college graduates, still did not know which side the United States was supporting in El Salvador.[2] But by then feelings about that country were running exceptionally high. As Bill Moyers remarked at the close of a television documentary, "We're not only poorly informed but confused and divided. . . . Unfortunately, the debate over Central America has become polarized."[3]

How had Central America become—in a brief twelve or thirteen months—the most divisive foreign policy issue in the United States since the Vietnam War? Without doubt, the immediate precipitant was a deliberate decision by the Reagan administration itself to raise the visibility of the issue during its first days in office. "We consider what is happening [in El Salvador] is part of the global Communist campaign coordinated by Havana and Moscow," Secretary of State Alexander M. Haig, Jr., declared at one of his first press conferences, and he repeatedly spoke of "drawing the line" against Soviet expansionism there, partly by "going to the source of the problem," which he plainly identified as Cuba.[4] With respect to actual developments in El Salvador, the secretary was quite unequivocal. As he told a television news conference,

> What is clearly evident to us is that the leftist movement, the rebel activity, its command, control, and direction, now is essentially in the hands of external forces. . . . We have very sophisticated, detailed, hard evidence to confirm it.[5]

On February 23, 1981, the State Department released a collection of captured rebel documents, a portion of which were eventually published as *Communist Interference in El Salvador* (hereinafter referred to as the White Paper), with an accompanying *Special Report*, which summarized its content. Therein was demonstrated, the secretary explained, that the Salvadoran guerrillas were receiving several hundred tons of arms and other military equipment from "the Soviet bloc, Vietnam, Ethiopia, and radical Arabs," with "most of the equipment, but not all, entering via Nicaragua."[6] To meet this challenge, the Reagan administration proposed to send $26 million in new military assistance and $87.7 million in economic aid to the beleaguered Salvadoran government.

Almost immediately the president and his secretary of state faced a roar of domestic opposition which caught them utterly off balance. Congress was flooded with letters, visits, and phone calls protesting the administration's proposals. Of this campaign much more will be said in due course: for the moment it is sufficient to note that it was spearheaded by human rights organizations already in place from the Carter years, and—in what one seasoned Latin Americanist called "a foreign policy first"—by the Washington lobbies of the Catholic and mainline Protestant churches.[7]

Eventually the aid bill went forward, but over Secretary Haig's objections both House and Senate committees voted

> to place conditions on U.S. aid requiring that the President certify every six months that the Salvadoran government was making "a concerted and significant" effort to control human rights violations, including those by its own armed forces, and was committed to holding free elections and [to implementing] agrarian reform, and to negotiation with opposition groups for a peaceful settlement.[8]

Within weeks the administration was furiously backpedaling from its original rhetoric. For example, in a television interview with Walter Cronkite on March 3, 1981, President Reagan redefined Haig's comment about "going to the source" as using "diplomacy, trade, a number of things" to persuade the Soviets to alter their role in the area. "I don't think in any way," the president assured his listeners, "that he was suggesting an assault on Cuba."[9] A few days earlier, somewhat shellshocked from sustained barrages of hostile questions, Secretary Haig exclaimed to journalists,

> I wouldn't want anyone here to think that we are not very concerned about, if you will, the improvements that are necessary in the Salvadoran regime. That means that we expect to see progress towards pluralization, toward the achievement and preservation of human rights, toward the rejection of excesses by the right as well as the left.[10]

Thus, from defining El Salvador largely as a theater of the cold war, the Reagan administration had been brought back to a position not very different from that of its predecessor.[11] It too now acknowledged that—whatever the role of Cubans, Nicaraguans, or others—there were domestic causes of disorder in El Salvador. It too called for an improvement in the human rights performance of the Salvadoran government and armed forces, and—to the dismay and even disgust of its more conservative supporters at home—it supported the land reform program, which in El Salvador had expropriated the 350 largest holdings, destined for conversion into cooperatives.

Moreover, in order to obtain the military and economic aid it needed in the short run, the Reagan administration was compelled to mortgage its own policy to elements largely beyond its control. That is, every six months the White House would have to make a case for continued progress in human rights and social reform in El Salvador in order to assure a continued flow of aid. Meanwhile, some of the forces which—through their pressures on Congress—had brought about this change of policy, heady with victory and in any case guarding more ambitious agendas of their own, moved the boundaries of the debate further to the left—insisting upon a coalition government with the armed left, or "power sharing." This assured that the Reagan administration, even by compromising one of its major foreign policy goals, could not buy domestic peace.

What Had Happened?

It would be comforting to think that the American public, after decades of neglect, had finally begun to take a serious interest in the affairs of Central America. But—as the previously mentioned survey indicates—this was very far from the case. Rather, the events just described trace the parameters not of an informed debate on the merits of a specific issue, but of a virtual revolution in the U.S. foreign policy-making process, in which El Salvador figures purely by accident. Indeed, however events in that country are finally resolved, the same kind of debate inadvertently unleashed by the Reagan administration in early 1981 is bound to ensue in the future any time any American administration chooses to oppose any leftist insurgency in Latin America, and possibly also in other areas of the third world. The purpose of this essay is to explain why and how that is so.

The U.S. Foreign Policy Environment

It is surely no secret that the greatest single casualty of the Vietnam War was the consensus which had underpinned the foreign policies of every American administration since at least 1947. The main lines of that consensus were, of course, the centrality of the East-West struggle and the need to subordinate all other foreign policy goals to the containment of communism. Since the late 1960s that world view has been increasingly challenged by a new form of liberal internationalism, which emphasizes "north-south" issues (development, global interdependence, mutual cooperation, and, latterly, disarmament) and downplays (sometimes quite disingenuously) the Soviet threat. Advocates of the latter approach are also unalterably opposed to U.S. military and covert intervention in the affairs of other nations (though they do favor other forms of intervention, such as trade and arms embargoes, against anti-Communist authoritarian regimes such as those of South Africa or Chile).

What is often overlooked, as public opinion expert William Schneider has pointed out, is that this great schism has been restricted to foreign policy elites—what he calls the "attentive public." In contrast, the "inattentive public"—which he estimates at two out of every three American adults—"is neither consistently liberal nor consistently conservative in its foreign policy beliefs." Rather, that vast, unformed majority is generally "predisposed against U.S. involvement in other countries' affairs, unless a clear and compelling issue of national interest and national security is at stake."[12]

Thus, in any policy conflict, each wing of a divided foreign policy establishment must reach outside its own precincts and appeal to an indifferent (and largely undifferentiated) public. In this contest, no outcome is foregone. Whether considerations of national security prevail over the traditional distaste for involvement in the affairs of other nations—or vice versa—depends wholly on the circumstances and also on the way in which the issue is presented to the public. In the case of El Salvador, for example, most surveys conducted in 1982 showed that a decisive majority of the American public is opposed to military or even major economic and diplomatic involvement in that country.[13] It was also apparent, however, that more than residual apprehension existed about the possibilities of a Communist victory there and its consequences for the national security of the United States.[14] One survey showed, for example, that "though . . . Americans are leery of getting drawn into the conflict in El Salvador, they decisively believe we should sometimes support nondemocratic governments in Latin America to keep them from Communist takeover (66 percent)."[15]

Perhaps the most critical consideration of all in determining the way in which the public tilts on the balance of national security versus intervention is just how long and how costly intervention is likely to be. As Schneider points out, the largely "non-internationalist" American public likes strength and toughness in foreign policy, but it likes this precisely "because that prevents us from becoming involved in the business of other countries." To the degree to which that policy does not prevent involvement, the same constituency switches its support to the liberal elite.[16]

These considerations had much to do with the way both the Reagan administration and its critics approached the subject of El Salvador in early 1981. The former recurred to the tried-and-true considerations of national security and the global balance of power, often with compelling evidence to support its argument. But the latter had a more powerful weapon still—the most extreme metaphor of intervention, the specter of "another Vietnam." * This it brandished uninhibitedly (and often, quite unscrupulously), passing over all considerations of historical context or strategic reality. Thus, in the certification hearings before the Foreign Affairs Committee of the House of Representatives in March 1982, Representative Gerry Studds (Democrat, Massachusetts) lectured Assistant Secretary of State Thomas Enders:

> We have given El Salvador more military aid than we have ever bestowed upon any Latin American country, and it hasn't worked. And in response you—and you have some experience in this area [making reference to Enders's previous experience in Cambodia]—have resurrected the State Department approach to Vietnam: If it doesn't work, do more of it . . . . I suggest to you that this is just one more step, one more poke into that tar baby. How in the world are we going to get out of this one? [Applause].[17]

At the same hearings, former U.S. Ambassador Robert White, dismissed from his post in El Salvador by the Reagan administration, shaped similar arguments, but in a "Catch-22" fashion:

> In my view . . . the most responsible thing we can do . . . is to cut off military assistance [to El Salvador] immediately. . . . I am not in favor of sending in more American advisors. But I tell you, gentlemen, it would be a thousand times more responsible to send in thousands of American military people rather than to send deadly weapons to those Genghis Khans down there.[18]

In other words, whatever the United States finally chose to do in El Salvador, it was in for "another Vietnam," the only choice being Vietnam, 1965, or Vietnam, 1974. Such hyperbole led the normally liberal *New Republic* to comment editorially that "the decision facing us now in El Salvador is a post-Vietnam decision about economic and military aid, not a pre-Vietnam decision about sending troops." But, it

---

* Arguably, the administration had invited this line of attack, since during its first days Secretary Haig had spoken endlessly of the need to emancipate the American people from what he called the "Vietnam syndrome." Many people assumed, not unnaturally, that this meant emancipation from a fear of foreign intervention or the consequences of foreign war.

added, "we won't even get to . . . the complicated moral and strategic calculus" an aid cutoff involved, "as long as the focus continues to be on keeping the United States out of another hopeless and unwinnable ground war." [19]

The facts of the case notwithstanding, the specter of Vietnam survived to haunt dozens of "teach-ins" and protest rallies held on university campuses across the United States in the early months of 1981.[20] At one, held at Wayne State University in Detroit to coincide with a meeting of the Organization of American Historians, a journalist noted that "many of the participants were the same people who had organized the opposition to the Vietnam War." One speaker, Kenneth Boulding of the University of Colorado, quipped, "I feel like the ghost of teach-ins past."[21]

By mid-1982 the "war" at home was as stalemated as the one abroad. A particularly welcome tonic for the Reagan administration were the March elections for a constituent assembly in El Salvador, which, in spite of dire predictions of fraud by administration critics,[22] went off without difficulty and with the massive participation of the Salvadoran electorate. But it was obvious that the balance could be tipped at any time, since the forces opposed to U.S. policy were at least as well organized and, in their own way, as well positioned to appeal to public sentiment as the administration itself. This phenomenon deserves closer inspection.

Elements of a Foreign Policy Revolution

New Foreign Policy Publics. The Vietnam War marks not only a division within America's foreign policy elites but also the widening and diversification of the foreign policy public. By now the role of the academic community—both faculty and students at American colleges and universities—has been the topic of much informed comment. Less well known is the fact that international agendas now figure in the desiderata of such organizations at the National Education Association, the American Association of University Women, even the Screen Actors Guild. Although it is not always possible to know precisely what foreign policy views (if any) the membership of such groups hold, their leadership, and particularly their nonelected staff, almost without exception are dissenters from the pre-Vietnam foreign policy consensus, and they exploit their organizational base in support of their views.

The NEA is a particularly egregious but by no means atypical case. Although approximately 70 percent of American classroom teachers describe their political philosophy as "conservative" or "tending" that way, the NEA advocates, among other things, "cessation of aid to the current administrations of Guatemala and El Salvador" and publishes materials frankly favorable to the governments of Nicaragua and Cuba.[23]

The most significant addition to this wider public have been the secretariats and social justice commissions of the Roman Catholic and mainstream Protestant churches. The case of the Roman church is particularly interesting in the light of the conservative tradition of the American hierarchy, as well as its historic reluctance to become involved (in the United States, at least) in controversies outside the area of personal morality (divorce, pornography, abortion). As explained by the Reverend J. Bryan Hehir, director of the Office of Foreign Affairs, U.S. Catholic Conference, "what the Church is doing in El Salvador, through congressional testimony, constituency education, and the use of the press, is part of a larger pattern of activity that . . . has its roots in Vatican II." One aspect of that movement was increased interaction between dioceses in the United States and the third world ("mission in reverse") which Father Hehir noted, "emphasizes not simply the need for funds or support, but also the need to address those dimensions of foreign policy and private practice—e.g., corporate activities—that adversely affect the people missionaries serve."[24]

In the particular case of El Salvador, Catholic concern in the United States at all levels was notably heightened by the assassination of San Salvador's Archbishop Oscar Romero in March 1980, but even more by the brutal murder of four American Maryknoll missionaries—three nuns and one lay worker, that December, presumably by elements of the Salvadoran armed forces. But it should be emphasized that the Church's opposition to military aid to the Salvadoran government and in favor of a "negotiated solution" to the conflict there predates both those episodes.

The Protestant churches have pursued similar foreign policy goals through both the National Council of Churches and their individual denominations. The Methodist Church has become, according to one report, "the busiest center of El Salvador lobbying" in the nation's capital."[25] In addition to housing the social offices of a half-dozen denominations, the Methodists offer shelter to the Washington Office on Latin America (WOLA), a human rights lobby of decidedly leftist hue, and the Coalition for a New Military and Foreign Policy.

The Protestant churches have also sent representatives to testify on Central American issues before appropriate congressional committees; they too have lobbied intensively on Capitol Hill for a cutoff of U.S. military aid to El Salvador and in many cases have arranged contacts for lawmakers and aides visiting El Salvador, Guatemala, and elsewhere in the region. They have kept up a steady stream of anti-administration arguments in church publications and sermons.

On Central American policy, perhaps the most important activity of the churches has been sponsorship of a letter-writing campaign to members of Congress. One parishioner of a Unitarian congregation in the suburbs of Washington, D.C., explained to the present writer that in his experience the letters were already written—one merely needed to recopy them in one's own hand, sign them, and send them off. A weary recipient of this sort of correspondence, Representative Peter Kostmayer (Democrat, Pennsylvania), noted, perhaps not remarkably, that his mail was running "100 percent against aid." And, he added, "I find that, with all due respect to my constituents, that their opinions are somewhat uninformed on this matter and that they are quite intolerant of what is happening" in El Salvador.[26]

The emergence of what for lack of a better term must be called a clerico-leftist foreign policy lobby in Washington has generated a fair amount of controversy within the sponsoring churches themselves, though to date the dissenting voices are barely audible. Efforts in favor of administration policy are few, poorly organized, and generally underfunded: one exception is the Institute for Religion and Democracy, founded in 1980 by Michael Novak, Paul Ramsey, and Richard Neuhaus, to champion democratic values in church councils and before the general public. The institute has been particularly active in documenting abuses of religious and political freedom in Nicaragua and other "progressive" third-world countries. In 1982 it sponsored a visit to the United States of Archbishop Miguel Obando y Bravo of Managua, a staunch critic of both Somoza and the Sandinistas.

Although the American Jewish community has been traditionally liberal in its foreign policy views, on Central America it is somewhat divided. The Union of American Hebrew Congregations, an umbrella organization of Reform groups, opposes the Reagan policy, but the B'nai B'rith and the American-Israel Public Affairs Committee are both apprehensive of ties between Central American revolutionaries and the Palestine Liberation Organization (PLO).

In their new role, the churches have found themselves thrown into new and unaccustomed political company. As Penn Kemble of the Institute for Religion and Democracy complained, "So many left activists are linked with church groups that it's hard to know what a church group is."[27] Meanwhile, liberal members of Congress have found the Central American imbroglio an unexpected political harvest. "I've never seen anything like it," exulted Bruce Cameron, aide to Representative Thomas Harkin (Democrat, Iowa) and former foreign affairs lobbyist for Americans for Democratic Action. "Members of Congress who have had trouble with the Catholic hierarchy in their districts because of abortion, have suddenly found re-entry on this issue."[28]

Overlapping the work of church lobbies and to some degree an extension of them are the human rights organizations. Some, like WOLA or the Council on Hemispheric Affairs, receive significant financial subsidies from the National Council of Churches and major denominations. Others, like Amnesty International or the Americas Watch Committee, do not. During the Carter years, the era in which most such organizations burst upon the scene, there was much comment about their "double standard" of judgment,[29] and to some degree they remain rather defensive about their methodologies.[30] With the honorable exception of Amnesty International, for example, human rights violations in Cuba or Nicaragua do not normally fall within their purview. They do, however, act as important clearinghouses of information; as centers of reception and orientation for exiles, expatriates, and visiting Latin American leftists; and as liaisons between them and members of Congress, their staff, and the media.

During 1981 the El Salvador controversy also generated a host of what one report called "short-lived alliances of like-minded people, with no staff, track record, or firm future plans."[31] These included the Committee to End U.S. Intervention in El Salvador, the Citizens Committee on El Salvador, and the Committee in Solidarity with the People of El Salvador (CISPES). The latter, formed in October 1980, is frankly pro-insurgent, and although it is avoided even by staunch administration critics like Representative Studds, it achieved a major propaganda triumph by organizing a protest march in Washington on March 27, 1982—the day before elections in El Salvador. Since an estimated 10,000 persons from all parts of the country participated, it would appear that even "short-lived alliances with . . . no firm future plans" are capable of effective mobilization.

Churches, universities, and human rights groups, as well as single-issue "solidarity" organizations, have thus come to form an alternative foreign policy establishment in the United States, and what is even more interesting, Central American revolutionaries have discovered as much and are actively working within it. For the latter this constitutes a major step forward in political sophistication, since Latins of all political persuasions have generally underestimated (or ignored) the pluralistic nature of the American political system. One remarkable sample of how things have changed is a trip report and diary kept by Farid Handal, brother of Salvadoran Communist party chief Shafik Handal, on a tour of the United States in early 1980. This exhibit turned up in the cache of documents which formed the basis of the State Department White Paper.[32]

The diary reports visits to Washington, D.C., New York City, Chicago, San Francisco, and Los Angeles. In Washington Handal met with CISPES leaders, Isabel Letelier of the Institute for Policy Studies, "three priests [sic] from the National Council of Churches, [who] completely supported our plans," Uruguayan leftist expatriate Juan Ferreira ("I contacted him through WOLA"), Representative Ronald Dellums (Democrat, California) ("Black, but very progressive"), who in turn arranged for him to present his case before the Black Caucus in the House of Representatives ("the liver of the monster itself"). In New York, he met with members of the Cuban Mission to the United Nations, the Central Committee of the Communist Party USA, the World Peace Council, and a representative of the PLO ("who spoke about help in scholarships [training] for use of arms").

Among other things, the document reveals the remarkable porousness of U.S. boundaries and the large number of Salvadoran (and other) revolutionaries resident in this country. It also reveals a mordant sense of humor on the part of its author, who had few illusions about some of the individuals he met (people with "a lot of personal problems . . . a mix of political ignorance with calculated roguery and with a lot of personal vanity in all of them"). It also demonstrates that, in spite of persistent ideological tensions within the El Salvador solidarity network, it has been able to sustain itself as a very broad political front.

Congressional Assertiveness on Foreign Policy Issues. Since the early 1970s Congress has been moving to constrain the executive power in the area of foreign affairs, particularly with regard to the use of military or paramilitary force abroad. It has also elevated to a central place certain policy goals the president was thought to neglect, such as human rights. The result has been, in the words of a sympathetic critic, that Congress has "made positive foreign policy enormously difficult to carry out under any administration."[33]

This state of affairs is not likely to be reversed, for its main features have since been institutionalized. Perhaps the most important change as applies to the present situation is the War Powers Act (PL 93-148), enacted in November 1973 over President Richard Nixon's veto. This law specifically provides that before American troops are introduced "into hostilities or situations where imminent involvement in hostilities is clearly indicated by the circumstances," the president must consult with the Congress "in every possible instance." After troops are so introduced, in the absence of a declaration of war, the president is required to submit a report to Congress within forty-eight hours. And then, sixty days—or in special circumstances, ninety days thereafter, the involvement of the troops is *automatically* terminated, unless Congress has taken positive action in the meanwhile to give specific approval.

Under this law Congress can also terminate the involvement before the sixty days have elapsed, by passing a concurrent resolution, which does not require the president's signature and therefore is not subject to a veto.[34] In effect, the War Powers Act "is designed to force Congress to act either to approve or to end any long-term U.S. military involvement abroad."[35] It is still difficult to say just how effectively this law inhibits the executive, since Congress has not chosen to invoke it in the situations which have arisen since its passage—the Mayaguez incident in 1975, the attempted rescue of Iranian hostages in 1981, and the stationing of U.S. Marines in Lebanon in 1982. These lines were written prior to September 1983 when Democrats in the Senate finally raised the issue in connection with Lebanon. A Supreme Court decision in June 1983 redefining the boundaries of executive and congressional power might eventually undermine (or even nullify) the War Powers Act, but—as the *Washington Post* put it—until the law itself is brought before the court, or until Congress asserts itself, "the role of each of the two branches in sending Americans into conflict will remain unclear."[36]

Certain changes internal to the organization of Congress itself have also enlarged the legislative effect on foreign policy. These changes have been described as part of

> a broad reform movement [which has] opened up legislative procedures and decentralized congressional power. Staffs [have grown] in size and foreign policy experience. Legislators who were not on the responsible committees sponsored several major actions . . . by adding amendments to legislation on the House or Senate floor. Committed, activist staff aides were the driving force behind many such initiatives, particularly in the Senate.[37]

As the 1970s drew to a close,

> there existed a complex system of congressional foreign policy restraints—specific prohibitions, legislative vetos, reporting requirements, and miscellaneous procedural hurdles. Only a few of these were absolutely binding, but most offered vehicles for those in Congress motivated to challenge a particular action or proposal . . . . Cumulatively, the system was quite restrictive, particularly on second-

order issues dealt with below White House or Cabinet level. But the administration could usually win on any single issue, if it expended enough energy and political capital.[38]

In spite of their familiar ring, these passages were actually written before President Reagan assumed office. They foreshadow to perfection, however, what took place in Congress when Central American issues surfaced in early 1981. The clerico-leftist foreign policy lobby could not reverse or nullify the new administration's policy, but it could restrict it greatly and force the White House to expend far more "energy and political capital" than it had originally anticipated. Again, though Congress had no authority to certify or decertify El Salvador (or, for that matter, any other country) in the area of human rights, it could hold as many hearings as it wished, parading an army of hostile witnesses (produced especially for the occasion by the human rights network), forcing the administration to meet it on distinctively disadvantageous political and media terrain.

These agendas meshed with a legislative jealousy of the foreign policy prerogatives of the executive going back to the earliest days of the republic. This sentiment, vastly exacerbated by the Vietnam War, was further nourished by the Reagan administration's own maladroit actions. In the early months of 1981, for example, an exasperated Secretary Haig threatened at one point to recur to already appropriated "emergency funds" if Congress failed to authorize the requested amount of military aid for El Salvador or, worse still, to go over the heads of Congress and appeal directly to the American people. This sort of thing was bound to alienate even administration supporters in the Senate and House.

The New Foreign Policy Role of the Media. One of the most hotly debated issues since the El Salvador controversy began has been whether newspapers and television—and, in particular, the people who write for them—are purposely distorting events there, with the effect (if not the intent) of undercutting support for the administration's policy. Because the issues concern new methodology as much as matters of substance, the controversy cannot be resolved here. But several points are beyond dispute.

First, the media has grown in influence since Vietnam and Watergate precisely by emphasizing its independent, even adversary, role vis-à-vis any administration. Logically, it sees no reason to reverse this process and abdicate its new importance. This has implications for foreign policy but does not of itself suggest any particular orientation—merely the need, much like that of Congress, to reaffirm and strengthen further its institutional importance.[39] Thus, it can be argued that the media's treatment of the Iranian hostage situation in 1979–1980 did as much to discredit the Carter administration's "liberal" foreign policies (particularly in the matter of human rights) as its coverage of events in Central America called into question the Reagan administration's more "conservative" approaches.

Second, since some of the great media careers of the past decade and a half were made in Southeast Asia, there is, as a former Carter administration official observes, "a Vietnam generation ready to replicate the biggest story of the 1960s." To which he adds, there is also

> a new generation ready to cut its teeth on a new war. This partly explains why coverage of the conflict [in El Salvador] has been so extensive, even though there are less than 50 U.S. military advisers [there]; either the media are anticipating or they are trying to recapture the war of the past on a new battlefield.[40]

Third, the Salvadoran rebels themselves recognize the importance of the media. "We have to win the war inside the United States," one leader based in Mexico City frankly admitted to a *New York Times* correspondent. To which another added, "the American media, especially television, turned [your] public against the [Vietnam] war." "We have tried to change our public image," he added, by inviting reporters into rebel strongholds and contacting editorial writers at major American newspapers. At the time of the interview the rebels were reportedly considering using a computer "to store and organize the names of reporters in the United States with whom they have regular dealings."[41]

Fourth, there have inevitably been abuses of reportorial integrity; the real issue is how many there have been and how significantly they figure in the overall pattern of journalistic coverage. One particular cause célèbre arose out of a dispatch by Raymond Bonner in the *New York Times* (January 27, 1982). Taking advantage of the opportunity to visit rebel territory, Bonner quoted various residents to the effect that hundreds of civilians were killed in the village of Mozote, department of Morazán, in a sweep of that area by the Salvadoran army in December 1981.[42] It later appeared that although there had been a military operation there, no systematic killing of civilians had occurred, and in any case the population of Mozote was only 300 "before the attack in which 926 people supposedly died."[43] The journalistic fraternity later defended Bonner on the grounds that he was merely reporting what he was told, not commenting on its veracity,[44] but to some this

373

seemed—given the context—a rather tortured response. Significantly, shortly thereafter Bonner was quietly taken off the Central American story by his paper.

How typical is this case? An unpublished study by Daniel James, based on a sample of 3,000 pieces of data taken from the *New York Times, Washington Post, Time,* and *Newsweek,* asserts that "the press has been guilty of errors of commission and omission"—advocacy journalism at its worst. When his conclusions were presented at a forum of leading media personalities in Washington, they were hotly disputed.

Has television coverage been balanced and objective? In the particular case of El Salvador, an unpublished study by Montague Kern, based on content analysis of ABC and CBS Evening News in 1981 and 1982, reached mixed conclusions. On one hand, she found that U.S. official statements were generally reported without comment; there was no negative "commentary" on CBS and very little on ABC. Also, the administration had the advantage in the area of total numbers of story themes which it purposely and intentionally raised. But there were other problems.

First, the Reagan administration was shown to be at odds with itself and with its allies—"clarification of positions or discrepancies in administration statements—or there were stories which in some way or other put the administration on the defensive." Of course, one could argue that the electronic media were merely reporting things as they were, rather than making up problems out of whole cloth. Nonetheless, even without wishing to, merely reporting these things could not help undermining the credibility of official policy and therefore playing a policy-specific role.

Second, coverage from El Salvador itself tended to convey impressions unfavorable to the administration and indeed to the government of that country. Official declarations were tellingly juxtaposed against visuals of fighting or the human cost of war. The graphic contrast between relatively well-equipped government troops and the (apparently) less well armed guerrillas—who were shown to be "on foot, as adolescents, and with children"—also tended to humanize the latter (and dehumanize their pursuers). Kern found as well that ABC coverage of El Salvador tended to present "the situation as less simple than the administration would have one believe, together with stories about the Vietnam parallel."

Third, while the guerrillas received little coverage on ABC during this time, whenever they did manage to appear, it was "in a way which . . . cast them in a favorable light." This she contrasted with

Yasir Arafat and the PLO, who received no such benevolent media treatment during this period.

> The major difference [she speculates] was in the domestic politics of the situation. In early 1981 there were major critics of the administration's El Salvador policies within the former administration, Congress, the Catholic church, and liberal interest groups—all main-line authoritative sources for journalists. . . . Thus depiction of the guerrillas as human and as more successful than the [U.S.] government claimed reinforced the view of the Congressional critics—already expressed in 4–6 minute stories—that the El Salvador situation indeed contained the seeds of another Vietnam quagmire.

Fourth, Kern found decisive evidence that on Central American issues Congress was covered "according to a double standard which worked to its advantage at the expense of the administration." Congressmen were most frequently quoted running opposite an administration spokesman, such as Secretary Haig, at a hearing. More anti-administration congressional figures were quoted than pro-administration ones. Conservative and moderate Democrats, who supported the administration, were "almost invisible." [45]

Fifth, on issues of this sort there appears to be a peculiar synergism between the media, Congress, and the public. The fact that Congress mandated a semiannual certification for El Salvador determines in advance that twice a year that country will be a "big story." The media naturally go to cover it, encouraging new floods of constituent mail, suddenly reawakening congressional interest, and "therefore driving the policy process." [46]

Finally, in the controversy over Central America, television has played a qualitatively different role from the print medium. Unlike the reader of newspapers, the television viewer does not "select" the topics that interest him—they are shoved on his plate, as it were, and his only escape is to change channels (and not always then), or turn the set off. When it comes to foreign affairs, for instance, most American newspaper readers pass right over the column heads to sports, fashion, gossip, or the advertisements. Television, however, forces them to consider issues they would prefer to avoid. It has therefore "created opinions where formerly there were none." [47]

In the specific case of Central America, television inevitably magnifies the horrors of poverty and war, presenting an unappetizing tableau which cannot but release the wellsprings of isolationism which always lurk just beneath the surface of the American political landscape. Also, by presenting a vision of Central American society which—given time constraints—must necessarily be somewhat caricatured, it reinforces feelings of repulsion and even loathing for Hispanic culture and civilization which run very deep in all "Anglo-Saxon" countries.[48] Again, whatever the intentions (or lack thereof) of media people, the effect is to strengthen the hand of those at home who, whatever their ultimate purposes, wish the United States to withdraw from the area.

Has Central America Become a Partisan Issue?

Of course, the answer is yes, in the sense that almost all foreign policy questions capable of eliciting sustained public attention and debate become, perforce, domestic issues. But the reverse is also true, and increasingly so: foreign policy controversies can be "driven" by purely parochial political considerations. The nuclear freeze debate is a case in point: the concrete realities of the U.S.-Soviet arms balance did not suddenly change after the 1980 elections; what changed was the position of the Democratic party, suddenly liberated from the burdens (and restraints) of incumbency and in sore need of an issue to win back the ideological terrain lost over the hostage crisis in Iran and the Soviet invasion of Afghanistan.

Domestic political considerations have weighed even more heavily in determining the posture of both parties on Central America. As already noted, the Republicans came into office in early 1981 determined to pursue a "hard-line" policy there, from which stance they were forced to retreat to the center by political realities at home. The Democrats, too, have moved back and forth according to their own perceptions of political advantage or liability. During its first three years in office, the Carter administration pursued a policy of human rights within the region so single-mindedly as to undermine friendly governments. In its final year, however, when the undesirable results of this approach could no longer be ignored, the administration shifted to a position not far distant from that of its critics.

This much was evident by the 1980 elections, in which the differences between the party platforms on Central America had become ones of tone rather than substance. Both, for example, pointedly condemned Cuban adventurism in the region, as well as in the Horn of Africa and elsewhere. Predictably, the Republicans took the Democrats to task for having dispensed aid to the Sandinistas, but in reality a few weeks before—confronted with irrefutable evidence of Nicaraguan arms shipments to the Salvadoran rebels—President Carter had suspended such assistance. Shortly before leaving office, he also lifted a four-year arms and training embargo on El Salvador and increased military assistance to Honduras. In spite of brave claims in the Democratic platform to support "those who [in Central America] are trying to build a better future out of the aftermath of tyranny, corruption, and civil war," the outgoing administration had in effect drastically reined in its commitment to radical change in the region.[49]

Then in early 1981, with the shoe on the other foot, the Democrats once again rediscovered that poverty, inequality, and injustice were the sole and unique causes of all Central American ills. This did not lead—as one might then logically expect—to a sudden outpouring of congressional largess or even a groundswell of support for the modest aid package put forward by President Reagan in his Caribbean Basin Initiative. Rather, the Democratic approach was purely negative: to make the Central American issue a permanent embarrassment for the administration. This it did by documenting human rights abuses—some real, some alleged; by imposing a series of conditions for continued military aid to El Salvador; and finally, by specifically prohibiting the use of U.S. money to pursue covert action against the Nicaraguan government. As of mid-1983 the administration had managed to forestall a complete cutoff of military assistance, as well as congressionally mandated "negotiations" with the rebels in El Salvador but only by mobilizing the full powers of the presidency behind the policy—including an unprecedented (for Central America) address to a joint session of Congress.

The real significance of President Reagan's speech was that it placed under harsh examination all of the unspoken assumptions of Democratic policy. The first of these was that the position of the Central American governments—particularly that of El Salvador—was strong enough to stand some rough handling from U.S. officials. The second was that the Soviet and Cuban threat to the region was negligible, if not nonexistent. The third was that most Americans did not care what happened to the countries of the area in any case. And the fourth—in some ways the most operative of them all—was that Central America was an issue from which the opposition could reap unlimited benefit at virtually no cost or risk.

In his address the president broadly hinted that the situation was far more serious than the public had been led to believe; that a collapse of the government in El Salvador would have multiplier effects throughout the region whose costs to U.S. security would not be slow in manifesting themselves; that if the Democrats persisted in their opposition, he would not hesitate to blame them for the consequences in the 1984 elections. In effect, also, he was reminding his critics of something they instinctively knew—that the same undifferentiated electorate which did not want "another Vietnam" did not want "another Cuba" or "another Iran" either.[50] In effect, it appeared that the Central American issue had vast potential to damage either party, but—at least in the longer term—it could benefit neither.

Final Observations

As the first serious debate over foreign affairs since the Vietnam War, the controversy over Central America affords us some opportunity to evaluate how U.S. policy is likely to be made or influenced in the future, at least with regard to countries whose sole importance is strategic or geopolitical.

First, the internal organization of such societies will come under sharp critical scrutiny, far more so, at any rate, than in the past. Put another way, if countries such as Turkey or South Korea were not already in the U.S. security net, given the nature of their political regimes, they would probably find it impossible to enter it today. Second, the mere fact of a guerrilla movement (whether purely indigenous or not, whether widely supported or not) is for many Americans prima facie evidence that the government of that country either "deserves" to be overthrown or at any rate is unworthy of U.S. assistance. Third, the general public remains traumatized by the Vietnam experience, and all of the features of the "Vietnam syndrome" (Haig) can be readily summoned up, by accident or by design, by the press and electronic media. Fourth, there now exist constituencies throughout the United States roughly linked together by university, church, and other organizations capable of mobilizing large numbers of people in opposition to U.S. foreign policy agendas—and not just in the third world. Such constituencies may represent a minority of the electorate, but they are active citizens whose voices are clearly heard by politicians. Since most countries do not have an organized public working in their favor within the United States, this makes those forces opposed to them all the more powerful.

Fifth and finally, although Congress cannot make foreign policy, it can in effect veto whatever course the executive branch chooses to pursue. All of these characteristics point not to new directions in U.S. foreign policy, but to immobility—no direction at all, in fact. Central America threatens to become the first example: a vast apple of discord, split apart by ideology, partisan interest, the changed circumstances of the political process, and once again, a traditional ambivalence on the part of Americans about foreign affairs generally and about their country's proper role in particular.

Notes

1. *Roper Reports*, January 1981.
2. CBS News–*New York Times* Poll, March 11–15, 1982.
3. "Central America in Revolt," CBS-TV, March 20, 1982.
4. *Baltimore Sun*, February 20, 1981.
5. Interview on "Meet the Press," March 29, 1981, U.S. Department of State, *Current Policy No. 271*, p. 2.
6. *New York Times*, February 21, 1981.
7. Paul Sigmund, "Latin America: Change or Continuity?" *Foreign Affairs* (Winter 1981), p. 635.
8. Ibid., p. 634.
9. *Department of State Bulletin*, April 1981, p. 8.
10. "Secretary Haig: News Conference with the British Press," February 27, 1981, ibid., p. 18.
11. Sigmund, "Latin America," p. 637.
12. William Schneider, "Bang-Bang Television: The New Superpower," *Public Opinion*, vol. 5, no. 2 (April–May 1982), p. 14.
13. CBS News–*New York Times* Poll, March 20, 1982; *Los Angeles Times* Study No. 51, March 14–17, 1982; ABC News–*Washington Post* Poll, March 1982.
14. ABC News–*Washington Post* Poll.
15. *Roper Reports*, April 1982.
16. Schneider, "Bang-Bang Television," p. 15.
17. U.S. Congress, House, *Presidential Certification of El Salvador*, vol. 1, *Hearings before the Subcommittee on Inter-American Affairs of the Committee on Foreign Affairs*, 97th Cong. 2nd sess., February 2, 23, 25, and March 2, 1982, p. 17.
18. Ibid., p. 238.
19. "The Vietnam Analogy," *New Republic*, March 17, 1982.
20. Malcolm G. Scully, "Amidst Protests over U.S. Involvement in El Salvador, Academe Stages Reprise on the 'Lessons' of Vietnam," *Chronicle of Higher Education*, February 23, 1981.
21. Karen J. Winkler, "Organizers of El Salvador 'Teach-In' Hope It Will Be Catalyst for Protestors," ibid., April 13, 1981.
22. See particularly U.S. Congress, House, *Presidential Certification of El Salvador*, pp. 276, 360, 377. One witness even suggested that "hard-line support for immediate elections" (whatever that might be) would be "counterproductive."
23. Chester E. Finn, "Teacher Politics," *Commentary* (February 1983).
24. "A View from the Church," *Foreign Policy*, no. 43 (Summer 1981), pp. 85–86.
25. "Interest Groups Focus on El Salvador Policy," *Congressional Quarterly Weekly*, April 24, 1982, p. 897.
26. Margot Hornblower, "Frustration Builds in Congress over El Salvador," *Washington Post*, February 10, 1983.

27. "Interest Groups Focus on El Salvador Policy," p. 896.

28. Ibid., p. 898.

29. The classic statement remains in Jeane J. Kirkpatrick, "Dictatorships and Double Standards," *Commentary* (November 1979).

30. For example, Thomas E. Quigley, Latin American specialist of the U.S. Catholic Congress, responding to charges that the U.S. bishops have paid "scant attention to the military aid supplied by Cuba and the Soviet Union" to Central American revolutionaries, countered that "while the church deplores the military aid from all sides . . . that the U.S. bishops consider U.S policy their immediate responsibility. 'We speak to Washington. We don't speak to Moscow or Havana,' " Quigley said. "Interest Groups Focus on El Salvador Policy," p. 899.

31. Ibid., p. 896.

32. This particular exhibit did not appear in the document book but was one of nearly five hundred items made fully available to the press at the time of the White Paper's publication.

33. I. M. Destler, "Dateline Washington: Congress as Boss?" *Foreign Policy*, no. 42 (Spring 1981), p. 167.

34. Pat M. Holt, *The War Powers Resolution: The Role of Congress in U.S. Armed Intervention* (Washington, D.C., 1978), p. 3.

35. Ibid., p. 35.

36. Editorial, "Who Has War Powers Now?" June 29, 1983.

37. Destler, "Dateline Washington," p. 169.

38. Ibid., pp. 171–72.

39. That media people have foreign policy views different from (that is, to the left of) the rest of us seems clear. On this see Linda Lichter, S. Robert Lichter, and Stanley Rothman, "The Once and Future Journalists," *Washington Journalism Review* (December 1982). The controversy begins when one tries to determine to what degree this has been carried over into actual reporting. For views different from Lichter et al., see Michael Jay Robinson, "Just How Liberal Is the News? 1980 Revisited," *Public Opinion*, vol. 6, no. 1 (February/March 1983).

40. Robert A. Pastor, "Our Real Interests in Central America," *Atlantic Monthly* (July 1982), p. 34.

41. Philip Taubman, "Salvadoran's U.S. Campaign: Selling of Revolution," *New York Times*, February 26, 1982. Unlike the situation which existed during the Vietnam War, some members of the revolutionary camp in El Salvador (those affiliated with the Federación Democrática Revolucionaria) can move freely within the United States, working and broadening their contacts. One staff member of the House Subcommittee on Inter-American Affairs remarked to me in February 1983 that FDR leader Rubén Zamora was "on a first-name basis with most members of the Subcommittee."

42. A similar story by Alma Guillermo Prieto appeared in the *Washington Post* the same day.

43. Editorial, "The Media's War," *Wall Street Journal*, February 10, 1982.

44. This was the point of view advanced by leading figures of the prestige press at a round-table luncheon in Washington, D.C., in February 1983 organ-

ized by the Institute for the Study of Diplomacy, Georgetown University, to consider the role of the media in the El Salvador controversy.

45. At the certification hearing on March 2, 1982, Representative Robert Lagomarsino (Republican, California) could not help observing out loud that in the afternoon session, when witnesses friendly to the administration session were being heard, there was only one television camera present. That morning, to hear witnesses hostile to it, there were "six or seven." "I think that almost all people, if they were honest about it," he observed, "would have to admit that the press coverage has been one-sided on this issue, if not more than that." U.S. Congress, House, *Presidential Certification of El Salvador,* p. 464.

46. "Television, the Reagan Administration, and El Salvador: Was There a Policy Role for the Media?" Unpublished manuscript cited by permission of the author, Montague Kern.

47. Schneider, "Bang-Bang Television," p. 13.

48. On this topic, see Philip Wayne Powell, *Tree of Hate: Propaganda and Prejudices Affecting United States Relations with the Hispanic World* (New York: Basic Books, 1971), esp. pp. 145–58.

49. For a particularly interesting view on the shift in Carter administration policy during the administration's final year, see the account of a former member of the State Department's Policy Planning Staff, Susan Kaufmann Purcell, "Carter, Reagan, et l'Amerique Centrale," *Politique Etrangère* (June 1982).

50. President Reagan, "Central America: Defending Our Vital Interests," U.S. Department of State, *Current Policy No. 482,* April 27, 1983.

Index

383

A NOTE ON THE BOOK

This book was edited by Dana Lane
and Claire Theune of the
Publications Staff of the American Enterprise Institute.
The staff also designed the cover and format, with Pat Taylor.
The figure was drawn by Hördur Karlsson.
The typeface used for the text of this book is
Palatino, designed by Hermann Zapf.
The type was set by
Hendricks-Miller Typographic Company, of Washington, D.C.
R. R. Donnelley & Sons Company of Harrisonburg, Virginia,
printed and bound the book, using Warren's Sebago paper.

SELECTED AEI PUBLICATIONS

AEI Foreign Policy and Defense Review (six issues $18; single copy, $3.50)

Interaction: Foreign Policy and Public Policy, Don C. Piper and Ronald J. Terchek, eds. (235 pp., paper $8.95, cloth $16.95)

Terrorism: What Should Be Our Response? John Charles Daly, mod. (25 pp., $3.75)

A Conversation with Dr. Saddoun Hammadi: Iraq's Foreign Policy (14 pp., $2.25)

Conversations with Harold H. Saunders: U.S. Policy for the Middle East in the 1980s (101 pp., $5.25)

Human Rights and U.S. Human Rights Policy, Howard J. Wiarda (96 pp., $4.25)

Prospects for a New Lebanon, Elie Salem (14 pp., $3.75)

Southern Africa in Conflict: Implications for U.S. Policies in the 1980s, Robert S. Jaster (48 pp., $4.75)

U.S. Interests and Policies in the Caribbean and Central America, Jorge I. Dominguez (55 pp., $4.75)

• *Mail orders for publications to:* AMERICAN ENTERPRISE INSTITUTE, 1150 Seventeenth Street, N.W., Washington, D.C. 20036 • *For postage and handling, add 10 percent of total; minimum charge $2, maximum $10 • For information on orders, or to expedite service, call toll free 800-424-2873 • When ordering by International Standard Book Number, please use the AEI prefix—0-8447 • Prices subject to change without notice • Payable in U.S. currency only*

AEI ASSOCIATES PROGRAM

The American Enterprise Institute invites your participation in the competition of ideas through its AEI Associates Program. This program has two objectives: (1) to extend public familiarity with contemporary issues; and (2) to increase research on these issues and disseminate the results to policy makers, the academic community, journalists, and others who help shape public attitudes. The areas studied by AEI include Economic Policy, Education Policy, Energy Policy, Fiscal Policy, Government Regulation, Health Policy, International Programs, Legal Policy, National Defense Studies, Political and Social Processes, and Religion, Philosophy, and Public Policy. For the $39 annual fee, Associates receive
  • a subscription to *Memorandum*, the newsletter on all AEI activities
  • the AEI publications catalog and all supplements
  • a 30 percent discount on all AEI books
  • a 40 percent discount for certain seminars on key issues
  • subscriptions to two of the following publications: *Public Opinion*, a bimonthly magazine exploring trends and implications of public opinion on social and public policy questions; *Regulation*, a bimonthly journal examining all aspects of government regulation of society; and *AEI Economist*, a monthly newsletter analyzing current economic issues and evaluating future trends (or for all three publications, send an additional $12).

Call 202/862-6446 or write: AMERICAN ENTERPRISE INSTITUTE
1150 Seventeenth Street, N.W., Suite 301, Washington, D.C. 20036

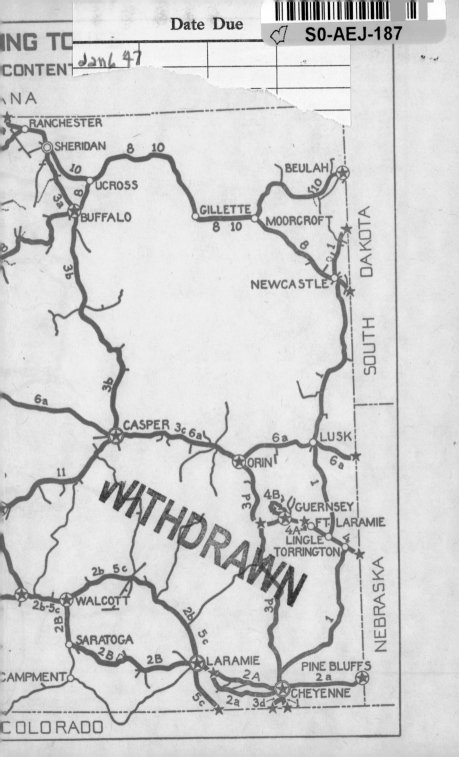

WYOMING

A Guide to Its History, Highways, a